THOUGHT, RETHOUGHT

Consciousness, Causality, and the Philosophy Of Reason

By T. Max Devlin

Library of Congress Cataloging-in-Publication Data
Devlin, Max 1963–
/ Max Devlin.
Includes index.
1. Philosophy. 2. Religions/rationalism

Copyright © 2018 by T. Max Devlin.
All rights reserved. No portion of this book may be reproduced, by any process or technique, without the express written consent of the publisher.

ISBN 13: 978-1-61305-017-0
ISBN 10: 1-61305-017-8

Published in 2018
HPL Publications, PO Box 564, Douglassville, PA 19518
www.HPLConsortium.com
Printed in the United States of America
The paper used in this book complies with the
Permanent Paper Standard issued by the National
Information Standards Organization (Z39.48–1984).
10 9 8 7 6 5 4 3 2 1

All trademarks, service marks, registered trademarks, and registered service marks are the property of their respective owners and are used herein for identification purposes only.
Library of Congress Catalog Card Number:

www.HPLConsortium.com

THOUGHT, RETHOUGHT

Consciousness, Causality, and the Philosophy Of Reason

By T. Max Devlin

Table of Contents

Introduction 1
Prologue 3
Ontology 17
Experiments 21
Reality 51
Epistemology 73
Selection 97
Paradigm 115
Schematic 149
Jellybeans 187
Language 203
Evolution 213
Morality 251
Argument 263
Society 293
Rituals 309
Ending 323
INDEX 329

Introduction

This book is not well written. I'm running out of time, and no longer have the luxury of waiting until I can organize this material concisely, package it effectively, and present it in an entertaining format. So what you're about to read (or should I say "slog through") will most probably seem, at first, like nothing but a sequence of arbitrary unsubstantiated claims and personal declarations with little rhyme or reason. But as I said, I'm running out of time, both in terms of my lifespan and the endurance of the free and lawful society I've been privileged to be a part of. Age and the forces of oppression and dishonesty are catching up with us, so I must risk sounding like a madman to get these truths written down, in the vain hope that it might someday help humanity rise above our stupid and ignorant habits. I will simply warn you not to take it for granted that you understand any of what I am saying simply because you recognize the words I am using. Most importantly, if you feel the need to disagree with it. I may very well (and will most definitely) be using those words to say something so unfamiliar to you, so contrary to what you've been taught to assume must be true, that it is going to take a lot more than a casual perusal to grasp the ideas I'm trying to convey. Consider it a challenge, then. This is not a work for the faint (or feint) of heart or the intellectually timid, nor for the pedantic and certain.

If you have been educated at all in philosophy, neurology, or linguistics, you're going to be quite sure I don't know what I'm talking about, saying things that simply aren't true, using words the wrong way, in complete ignorance and contradiction to their well-established definitions. This is inevitable, because almost everything you have been taught is erroneous. Not because it is not based on facts, but because it is based on incorrect interpretation of those facts. I'm going to have to disagree with what you have learned, with what your college professors knew with certainty to be true. If what you think about thought were right, there would be no need to rethink thought, no existential angst driving the world to ruin and destruction, no increasingly powerful justification for extremism in religion and politics, no anger and hatred in our social discourse.

I'm going to be trying to re-wire your brain, essentially, and there are going to be times when you are certain that I've gone crazy. Bear with me, and give it some effort, and in the end, I believe you will thank me, regardless of whether you are convinced to agree with me. It's going to be unevenly written, strangely composed, and as bizarre as it is baffling, but it is the truth, as I have witnessed it.

I believe that the universe began, once, about fourteen billion years ago from our perspective, and that everything that has occurred since then is the uncontrolled result of the interaction of physical forces.

On this statement of faith, I wished to build a coherent, complete, and comprehensive philosophy; one which can unite science, religion, life, and all human behavior. My goal was no less than an intellectual and spiritual Theory Of Everything; materialist without being materialistic, providing judgment without being judgmental, and satisfying but not smug. I needed a worldview, and way of thinking, that includes logical positivism as well as emotional truth, that both explains and guides my reasoning and actions. Most of all, this philosophy of all philosophies should be identifiable because it provides the secret of happiness, without requiring secrecy, and without simple-minded circular explanations that would make comfort only available through complacency. A philosophy of life that says, pessimistically, "Be happy with what you have, because whatever will be, will be," would be unsatisfying; a pretense of cheerfulness that lacks the energizing joy that I demanded.

It took many years, my whole life up to this point, but believe it or not, I think I've achieved my goal, and I want to share it with you. It requires re-assessing a lot of what we think we know, what we've been taught that experts know, about the experience of experience. It is, in a sense, reactionary, and recursive. Every idea we have about human reasoning; what we've been told to call, and fallen into the habit of calling, human logic, needs to be reexamined, reassessed, and possibly revised. It is more than thought, it is rethought.

This is the Philosophy Of Reason.

Here goes.

Prologue

I could take any two words, and give you a book on them. Looking at any two words, my mind, my brain, is going to unavoidably put another word between them, one that is the same as both, but different, maybe opposite to both too. I can build a word between those two words, that dichotomy, name it as the dialectic, and write whole chapters on them. What happens before they happen, what purpose they might serve as both words and ideas. This is the only, most primitive, true philosophy. All the fancy theories and hypothetical conjectures called ideas that anyone has said before don't matter. Two people, here restricted to author and reader, wondering about things, contemplating words, and whatever problems might be barring us from turning what is happening, or what will happen, into happiness. It sounds foolish, 'happiness', when placed in that context, like a word that suddenly feels more unfamiliar on the tongue the more you repeat it. Happiness is the necessary dialectic for what separates what is happening from what will happen.

Even if you believe that we have free will, we really only have a fraction of a second to make any difference between what has already happened and what might happen next. We can try to philosophize, but that just spoils the moment. The whole reason we're here, however you think we got wherever we are, is to try to find a reasonable amount of happiness. And we have a split second to decide what to do, to make a choice about how to deal with our problems. And we do have problems. If you don't have any problems, then I've got plenty to spare. *Those people*, and what they're doing, could be a problem for us both, even if we don't have any other problems already. If you have problems, I have problems, because I am you. If the thing that is me were in your brain, I'd be thinking your thoughts, feeling your feelings, and making the exact same decisions you are. There is no "I" without "you". There is no "you" without "I". If your me-ness, your consciousness, your soul, were in my body, you would think the same thoughts, have the same dreams, and want the same thing as I do. Which is to help you with your problems, especially the problem posed by *those people* and what they're doing.

A fraction of a second, before our implicit biases kick in, while the moment we're thinking about becomes the past instead of the present, or the present instead of the future. And then the future becomes the past, and you and I are just hapless souls being swept along by time and other people. We should both want to choose happiness, be able to decide that things are going well and will get better if we do more. Hopefully, at least. Is happiness a choice, is it a state of being, is it a thrill or is it a comfort? Now we're back to philosophizing. Times a-wasting. That's not why we're here, to philosophize pointlessly, we're here to hope to find happiness, real happiness, the kind that makes you want to make other people happy, too. Even *those people*. Perhaps, if we find it, we can help *them* find it, and maybe they'd stop doing that thing they're doing that threatens to be a problem for *us*, you and me.

It doesn't matter what we do, though, ultimately we can only hope for the best, because irregardless of what we do, something can still go wrong. It all comes down to knowing what to do, doing it, and hoping it works. So what shall we do? Well, that kind of depends on who it is that was "*those people*" in your mind, and why whatever it is they are doing could be a problem for me or you. Now who those people are would suggest what you hope for; I know it does for me. So maybe we need to figure out what hope is, to find happiness, is all.

Hope is an irrational expectation. We have a word for a rational expectation: "expectation". Hope is irrational expectation. To hope is to expect something that is not expected. You can anticipate, you can desire, you can want, without hoping, but you can't hope without those things happening, no matter how irrational the expectation, how fantastical the anticipation, how fruitless the desire, how desperate the want, which can be pretty extreme. Hope is better than wishing, but not by much, or it cheapens the word to reduce it to a rationality.

Hope is not rational.
Hope is good.
Therefore, being irrational can be good.
QED

I spent most of my life being miserable. At times I was so despondent that I felt I had no hope at all. No hope for the future, because society seemed insane, and the powerful rewarded themselves by fixing the system to make themselves still more powerful. No hope for myself, because I felt alone and dysfunctional, powerless and without any control over my life. I had no hope that I would ever be anything but anonymous and powerless. Yet somehow, even when I felt that I had no hope at all, I still couldn't help but hope that someday I would have hope. And so, in the most important way, I always had hope. Not because I wanted to, not because I thought I should, not even because I had to. Just because I did. Even when you have no hope, you can still have hope that you will someday have hope. No matter how hopeless you are, you might still hope to hope.

Hope is like a lighthouse keeper's beam. Hope, the master cobbler of our dreams. For hope believes in desert streams.

Most, maybe even all, of the problems in your life, and in the world, today, are simply the lack of hope. We know that hope is irrational, and we are taught that being irrational is bad because being rational is good. Suicide, depression, drug abuse, even war and violence, oppression and terrorism, tyranny and crime, are all caused, not by any inherent or innate flaw or failure in human beings, but by the hopelessness and forced, and false, irrationality enforced by society. When we see power rewarding itself for having no virtue but lust for power, when we see abuse of authority and tolerance of abusive authority, when we can't avoid wanting to visit harsh retribution on those who persecute others and enjoy unjustified luxury, it is the lack of hope, the inability to expect, however irrationally, that compassion and good can overcome these evils.

My intention in writing this book is to completely and entirely revise how you think about how you think. You have been taught to praise and revere rationality above all things. And, perhaps, if you have lived a very fortunate and privileged life, you have been able to maintain your faith in that fiction, that thinking logically results in success and wisdom. Based on this erroneous idea, people believe and insist that to be irrational is, by definition, to be insane, to be wrong. The very word 'rational' has come to be a synonym for 'sane'. And of course, being insane has to be the opposite of being sane, because language is a matter of logical application of etymology and prefixes, right? (In case you can't recognize it, that is called 'being facetious': language is definitely not a matter of logical application of etymology and prefixes, no matter how hard we might try to do that or even how often it appears to work.) It isn't going to be easy to overcome this delusion, this insistence that hope is improper because it is irrational. But at the heart of the Philosophy Of Reason, this is the ultimate truth. I cannot convince you of this truth. You will have to convince yourself. And to do that, you'll have to want to be convinced.

Do you hope to be happy? Do you hope to be successful? Do you hope to live in a world filled with peace and prosperity instead of war and conflict? It might seem like I am promising an awful lot, to suggest that the Philosophy Of Reason can not only provide personal happiness, but world peace. Surely it should be enough for any philosophy, scientific or religious, to do one or the other, and ludicrous to believe anything could do both, and not just make it possible but to accomplish it effortlessly. The Philosophy Of Reason (POR) can provide both, social and personal hope, peace, and happiness, once it is understood and embraced. It wouldn't even be difficult to understand, and then embrace it, if only people had not been so badly misinformed to begin with. We must surmount these problems, but it will take time and intention.

The only thing that anyone can know with absolute certainty is that from birth to death, they are alive. Of course there are people who deny even that, but they can only be doubting other people's existence, not their own, because they have to have one to doubt it. Cogito Ergo Sum. Given that, I think it makes the most sense to live my life as if there is a purpose to mercy and justice. I don't think it's <u>in order to</u> earn a blissful afterlife. I think any afterlife would be a nightmare beyond comprehension, regardless of everything else, no matter what kind of afterlife it is. I don't want to live forever. I used to want to live as short as possible; now I want to live as long as I can. But any "surprise! you're not really dead" kind of existence just makes everything that is me scream in terror. So I don't believe in being a good person because of any Pascalean wager; I know there is no God providing immortality, even if there is a God providing justice and mercy. I don't expect any reward once I'm dead other than the infinite peace of dreamless unconsciousness. I can't believe in any pretense of cosmic karma to balance fairness in the past but not the future. If there was any real mechanism like an afterlife behind ethics or morality, it would rob ethics and morality of their legitimacy.

It is not Pascal's wager concerning the enticement of an afterlife that demands my morality, my desire and intention to be a good person, it is my entirely self-referential desire for honesty and integrity during the only life, the only consciousness, the only existence that I can or will ever know. I want to do good in the world, regardless of whether I do well, because I want there to be good in the world. It is unfortunate that people doing good is the only way there can ever be any good, and it is unfortunate how difficult it is sometimes to know what good is and what good can be done. But if you think that doing good can be assessed or dismissed as a mathematical calculation, you aren't doing any good at all. The only possible just God that could exist would be more than a mathematical solution, and provide only the nothingness of unconscious non-existence both before and after the life of any person, or else real life simply can't have meaning at all. If there were an after-life, our only purpose would be as puppets of a diabolical cosmic torturer, regardless of whatever purported morality It deigns to impose on us, or magical free will It provides, that somehow doesn't extend to escaping the torture except by obeisant obedience.

The attraction to afterlife metaphysics that most people have is usually accepted, and denounced, as both wishful thinking and self-centered delusion, presuming it is not embraced as intuition and truth. The assumption is that people want to deny the reality of their mortality, and they invent heaven to justify believing they will live forever, and invent the need to follow God's commandments to be good in order to explain the existence of this mechanism of everlasting life. I think this might be backwards, that people actually are trying to explain their compassion and altruism, and invent God to excuse it, and immortality to justify it. This chain of reasoning, which is cause and which is the result, will become important later. Right now, I just want to point out it's significance, regardless of whether the afterlife is invented to justify morality, or morality is invented to justify the afterlife.

The perspective of the Philosophy Of Reason is that <u>people always act reasonably whenever they have the opportunity</u>, and the mechanics of reward and punishment are simply reasonable approximations of why we feel an urge to be virtuous and help people, *but only sometimes*. This is the real fly in the ointment of any philosophy, religious or scientific, that seeks to explain human morality; the inconsistency of whatever effect causes humans to behave well. These moral theories of an afterlife as reward have not yet been entirely (or even substantially) replaced by more scientific ones, but that is not the fault of the religious theories. It is the fault of their suggested alternatives. Again, through cultural osmosis if not scholastic lessons, people assume that scientists know that ethics are an evolved trait, that a biological advantage of helping others and being compassionate can explain human's inconsistent desire for goodness and God, but there is no part of this idea that is actually true. These supposedly scientific explanations of ethics or kindness aren't even scientific, let alone true, as I will explain later. More importantly now, the point is that abandoning theistic religions, or all religions, does not result in abandoning the uncivilized behavior that people blame on their religion. Humans are perfectly capable of inventing new justifications for their evil if religion didn't exist, getting rid of religion won't get rid of the evil.

The alternatives to religious explanations for morality, justice, and honesty are supposedly scientific ones, which would have to reduce those things to logical algorithms in order to be successful science. But real truth and justice is not a logical algorithm, it is based on emotional reasoning, not mathematical calculation. For thousands of years, philosophers, scientists, and even many priests based their thinking on the presumption that reasoning is some sort of logic, that being careful with words can create a mathematical precision that automatically provides accuracy. The root of this problem will be explained later, but the truth of it can be established now. Reasoning through language is neither the product or the substance of mathematical operations of any level of sophistication. Words aren't symbols in a calculus of neural interactions. Truth does not come from dictionary definitions. The *ideas*, not any quasi-physical 'concepts' which equate your word to mine with any mathematical integrity, are what we agree bind our acceptance of a common vocabulary and grammar. This is a very difficult truth to accept, even though it is a fact, because through indoctrination or assimilation you have learned to accept the false idea, the postmodernist lie, that words are just symbols, meaningless without a dictionary to define them for you. The truth, evident but rejected, is that there is no method other than a human's perception of identifying the truth, integrity, or righteousness of any linguistic statement. Well-rehearsed but false philosophies insist that there is no method for identifying truth or righteousness, that the only integrity is a mindless consistency, that human perception is not algebraic enough to determine the truth, but should try anyway. This leads people to put faith in their own flawed logic on the assumption it must be good reasoning, and dismiss even the most rigorous attempts at logic from others as bad reasoning. Thus, we are taught to remain stupid and ignorant if at all possible. The assumption that we are thinking logically becomes a tar pit from which we cannot escape.

The truth is that our faith in math as the best, perhaps only, mechanism for determining truth is as misplaced as any faith in a biblical God. Which is to say it isn't misplaced unless it is misapplied, and it is misapplied all the time. Language, words, knowing the truth of any 'symbol separated by spaces', is not a mathematical process. It is not simple arithmetic, nor is it a query into a database of facts. Identifying, not to mention understanding, truth, integrity, and righteousness is not an algebraic computation. At best, we can program grammar checkers, but knowing what righteousness is can't be reduced to grammatical rules. And distinguishing righteousness from self-righteousness is even harder. Not even grammar, let alone proper grammar, is logically consistent. Thousands of rules, even hundreds of whole systems, of generative, stochastic, semantic, and other grammars have been developed by very sober and serious researchers of linguistics and language. This is generally thought to demonstrate how mathematical language is, how logical parsing reveals the information being transmitted through sentence structure and vocabulary. But the opposite is the truth: the variety of such systems, the need for thousands of rules with thousands of exceptions requiring thousands more rules to be hypothesized, proves that language is not a computational scheme. Philosophy is much more than grammar, and for centuries and longer, philosophers have been unsuccessful at overcoming the illogical inconsistencies, the logical inconsistencies, the lack of logical consistencies, in language or reasoning. What is more, they have been unsuccessful at overcoming philosophy's logical consistencies, leading to two 'blind spots' in existential philosophy that should be addressed.

These two blindspots have been given popular names through fiction, but have ancient analogs. The first one is the Matrix, or 'brain in a jar' problem. This covers all manner of similar philosophical demonstrations of hope or terror. In theory we can't know anything for sure except what we experience ourselves, the sense data we feel and the thoughts we have. Therefore, it is possible that you aren't experiencing a 'true reality', but a false reality presented by falsified sense data transmitted through your nerves to your brain and, somehow, your consciousness. In practice it is an unfalsifiable claim: if you suppose that a perfect simulation of a universe is possible, there's no way to way to know if you're experiencing one. And if you think an imperfect simulation of the universe is possible, you're either right that you're a brain in a jar or else you're insane and think there is something inconsistent about the universe you're experiencing. The second blindspot is the same but in the other direction; you can't know for sure if you're asleep and dreaming, or insane and deluded, or awake and going crazy. Or even dead and in hell. You can't know what is right, either in a physical or in a moral sense. This is the

Inception blind spot. It permanently prevents us from even guessing at what we could do to find true happiness rather than mere pleasurable sensations, which in the real world as in fiction is accomplished by figuring out what is real. But if our senses can be fooled or we might be crazy, we might not know what is good or bad. Even if 'good' just means hoping we can figure things out, how can we know what that means, how can we figure out the right thing to do? What should you do, not knowing for sure what the right thing to do is? This is usually thought to be the same as the 'brain in the jar' problem, but is subtly, yet importantly, more than that. Without stepping through all intermediate ideas that connects the problem in existential philosophy identified by 'Inception' and the problem in moral philosophy known as 'the problem of evil', both of which are far more complex than the average amateur philosopher bothers to know, I will simply note that they are essentially the same.

These two blind spots in our consciousness, the 'brain in a jar' problem of only knowing of our own existence directly, which Descartes identified, and what amounts to the problem of knowing what 'good' means, the potentially arbitrary nature of morality in an arbitrary existence, have been drilled into people so well they have a hole clean through their heads. "We cannot know." People are taught that only logic can be a reliable guide to the appropriateness of their behavior, and they are left in a universe in which every person's actions are not logically predictable, including their own. To say it is hellish is something of an understatement. We have to recognize that for most if not all of the people who commit suicide, and there are ever-growing numbers of them, they found such a life unbearable, and supposedly chose to take the one action that seemed reasonable to them, however illogical anyone else thinks it might have been. Morality can't only be useful in hindsight, to know that we shouldn't have taken some action, because once any action is taken, it cannot be undone. This is startling and undeniable in the case of suicide, but is really just as true for every other choice we make. That non-mathematical interaction we call thinking, feeling, and speaking, in order to make moral decisions as well as do other things, has to have a meaning and purpose beyond computation. A non-conscious brain mass is more than capable of executing mathematical calculations of any possible complexity we might imagine, *other than being conscious*. We live behind an existential wall that makes the brain in the jar theory and the conundrum of morality unavoidable. Knowing only the universe that our senses and memories provide, knowing that either is subject to failures, temporary or not, we cannot know with any absolute certainty that we are not dreaming or insane. We can believe we are in control of ourselves, correctly perceiving the actual world beyond your own consciousness, we can hope it at least. But we could still be dreaming, insane, or even dead if you still believe that thinking is possible without a brain. You can't be in control of yourself if you're asleep or crazy, and everyone has been asleep or crazy at some time. So you aren't always in control, and you aren't in control of when you are in control. If you can't control when you are in control of yourself, you aren't ever really in control of yourself; whatever determines when you are in control of yourself is in control of you. The entire idea of 'controlling yourself' is a rhetorical reference to not requiring any such control, because your current behavior is already appropriate, or at least reasonable.

Both the brain in the jar problem and the conundrum of morality are ephemeral nonsense when you dispense with the inaccurate theory that language and human thoughts, and therefore the resulting behavior, are manifestations of an algorithmically reducible hidden calculus. You don't exist to perform logic, you aren't a computer. The fact that humans have trouble being logical is not a flaw, it is our purpose; it is what makes us reasoning creatures, human beings rather than just another sort of primate. Logic is mathematics, perhaps using words as if they are symbols but not as words. We can do math, when we try, but that is different from knowing what math to do, which formulas to use, and making the right measurements, and double-checking the results if not second-guessing the whole point of the exercise. And we still only have our own experiences, a fraction of a second at a time, while life goes on with or without us.

The brain in the jar is a shorthand for the physical nature of our neural equipment that apparently is the entirety of the necessary and sufficient biological processes that generate our thoughts and behavior; the existential wall eternally and perfectly separating our intellectual experiences from the entire rest of the universe. The conundrum of morality is the inability to reduce morality to mathematics, to logical selections from among predefined alternatives. In the Philosophy Of Reason, that method I propose to replace standard thinking on the human condition, both blindspots go the way of Last Tuesdayism, we can say. Last Tuesdayism is the philosophical postulation that the universe didn't exist until some prior moment, iconically last Tuesday at 2:17 pm. At the moment the universe began, it was in a state that is exactly what it would have been if the universe had been around for about 14 billion years of time. Since there is no logical way to distinguish a universe that started 14 billion years ago and changed state constantly until last Tuesday, and a universe that started last Tuesday and only looks like it is billions of years old, then logically the universe could have started Last Tuesday at 2:17 pm. It is an unresolvable postulate, logically, but in any reasonable analysis it remains preposterous. The most obvious flaw is the arbitrary nature of the accuracy or precision of the duration of reality, and the lack of any other moment to support any improvement in selection. It might not be last Tuesday, it could have been six thousand years ago, or it could be four seconds ago. Or in twenty minutes: the universe hasn't happened yet, you're just what will have happened once it does. Since any other moment would serve just as well as last Tuesday at about quarter after two in the afternoon, why not the moment 14 billion years ago when the universe actually started? Logically Last Tuesdayism could be countered with a plea for infinite possibilities to produce even the most unlikely circumstance, but piling preposterous logic on top of preposterous logic does not make it more reliable.

A more current and common philosophical perspective, essentially similar to Last Tuesdayism, is the infamous Flat Earth hypothesis. Flat earthers are denounced and mocked, but stick to their position as not 'anti-science', but 'anti-scienceism'. The issue seems simple, like knowing the universe didn't start last week, because we remember last month. But what if the universe started not just last week, but four seconds ago, yet started with your brain in a state that included memories of things that didn't happen, last week? Flat earthers can be defeated logically, supposedly, but not easily. You can say that they simply are ignoring that we have flown rockets into space and so we know the earth is not flat. But Flat Earthers aren't looking for empirical evidence, they want first-hand experience, supposedly because they are willing to trust their own senses, but not reports from other people. I have seen many very reasonable, supposedly logically-minded people, insist they have defeated Flat Earth theory, but never achieve their goal, or even be logical about doing so. They want a lot of inductive claims to be taken as a deductive proof, and that simply isn't the way deduction and induction work. Logic isn't that easy, that you can say "close enough", ever. You might call that logic, but it doesn't make it so. (Epistemological, Humpty Dumpty reasoning, we call that, but the explanation of those terms will, again, be left for later.) The only personal method of proving to yourself, really proving to yourself, if you want logical, mathematical proof, that the earth is round requires a level of precision that you can't achieve without extraordinary effort. Go to a flat plain next to a high mountain, the plain being wide enough and the mountain being high enough, and then move away from the mountain. The bottom of the mountain will become difficult to distinguish from the plain at the horizon, whether the earth is flat or not, and this is why tremendous precision, nearly impossible precision, is necessary. The difference between a flat earth and a round earth is that the bottom of the mountain will recede down over the horizon while the top of the mountain is still visible. But to dismiss this as 'job done' is not logical, because the whole mountain will be shrinking in size, visually, and becoming harder to see, through atmospheric effects, and the 'base' of the mountain isn't a geometrically precise line. This is why simply standing on a plain and noticing that the ground appears to curve up in a bowl around you, or extend out to the edge at the horizon, or curve down away from you a long way away, does not make Flat Eartherism as easily refuted as earnest scientists insist it should be. And so with creationism, and so with global warming. Honest people insist that Flat Earthers are being illogical, but really they are just taking logic more seriously than the honest people do. Of course, neither the honest (reasonable) people nor the Flat Earther (unreasonable) people are being logical; logic is math, and reasoning is not logic, though people have been taught it is, or at least should be. The cognitive dissonance involved in confronting a world where people are always irrational, but only sometimes unreasonable, while being told that only being rational is reasonable, is what is driving the world insane, while we watch, helpless and almost hopeless to do anything about it. If taken seriously, this Philosophy Of Reason can fix that.

In general I'm an incredibly lazy and useless guy. But I have exhaustively and with dedication been grappling with these 'cosmic realities', as we called them, since I was a young boy. In fact I had always believed that it was something of a mental defect that I was so obsessed with them, rarely able to put them out of my thoughts for long. I suppose, in the end, it's still true. As a student, I had never been able to believe in anything that isn't true, and I saw many flaws in the explanations people gave about what is true. I saw a lot of squirming around, literarily and literally, whenever I examined how people dealt with the holes in their logical pretense of our understanding of ourselves or the society around us. The conundrums of the brain in the jar, or Last Tuesdayism, or Flat Earthers, are iconic and illustrative, but only the obvious and simple cases. Every time I thought I wanted something, until I got it and realized it didn't satisfy me, and every time I saw social injustice or government corruption, I wondered, like many other people do, why it happened. Eventually, in order to understand the flaws in myself or society, and both, I had to essentially reconstruct all of religion, science, and philosophy. A retcon. A retcognstruction. I had to rethink thought itself. It all had to be struck, as Descartes did, except for the most rigorous and essential framework. Progress was slow, the decades turned, and the world around me started falling apart at an ever faster pace. And then one day, after my own life had nearly entirely disintegrated, it all came together and I understood. I'll tell you what I discovered on that day; you're not going to believe it has to do with jellybeans. Once I explain how it does have to do with jellybeans, you'll probably think it hardly seems groundbreaking. But it changed my life, and with any luck it will change yours, or someone else's, and my entire life will be worth every bit of angst and depression that I suffered through.

Think of the people who pose the greatest threat to your life and well-being. Whoever they are, they are motivated by the same problematic delusion that I have described, this pretense of logic: the assumption that being illogical always makes words and thought inaccurate and useless. Think about the social ills those people cause or represent, whatever or whoever they are. <u>Those social ills aren't the problem, they are just symptoms of the problem.</u> The real problem is this core motivation they all share. This delusion in thinking is what I'm going to call '*postmodernism*', for very specific and particular reasons I'm going to explain in detail later. It results in a depression, anger, existential angst, and self-righteousness, for them and for us, regardless of how you define 'them', or 'us'. It is becoming more damaging and more problematic, because it has become a quasi-scientific theory I'll call the *Information Processing Theory of Mind*, that hides behind all study of humans by humans in both academic research and conventional wisdom. Postmodernism derives from a still modern philosophical delusion I will identify and describe as *Socrates' Error*. Explaining all of these things is going to take some time, but the essence of the **Philosophy Of Reason** is this basic theory: that adoption of Socrates' Error by philosophers and thinkers led to postmodernism, which results in the Information Processing Theory of Mind, and these things allow, encourage and cause most if not all of our personal and social problems. Founded on both a materialist cosmology and a moral theology, this Philosophy Of Reason (POR) describes human existence and human behavior in a new, reliable, confirmable, realistic way that fulfills the entire field of requirements for all philosophies: moral, analytical, and existential. That should sound like a tall order, but if you keep an open mind and a quick wit, it can be done.

The Philosophy Of Reason is based on three fundamental theories. These are scientific theories, or at least are as scientific as theories about people by people can be. The first is that self-determination is not free will. The second is that reason is not logic. The third is that altruism is not genetic. These might seem simple, because so far they are presented in simple terms. If you'd like, you can simply agree, accept, and adopt these ideas and ignore the rest of this book. Most of what's written here is simply an extended explanation of these three theories, for those who might be skeptical of or opposed to them. These are all theories about minds, theories of mind, but there is a difference between being 'a' theory of mind, and being 'the theory of mind', or being "theories of mind", though the differences are obviously subtle. In some cases, it makes no difference, as with the Information Processing Theory of Mind, which could be all of them, but isn't any of them.

The real difficulty in understanding these theories isn't accepting them, but understanding them. It is easy to think for example, "I know we don't have free will, because our thoughts and feelings are controlled by hormones and neurotransmitters, so whatever is meant by 'self-determination' is irrelevant, because it is a fiction." But without knowing precisely what self-determination is, and recognizing it is real, actually rejecting 'free will' is impossible, because it would be evidence of your free will for you to decide whether or not you believe in free will. (A kind of reverse Cogito Ergo Sum.) Likewise, many a postmodernist that I have tried to explain 'reason is not logic' to, do accept it immediately, while harboring a sometimes silent reservation, "...but it should be." This is, again, to misrepresent the statement. Reason does not fail to be logic, it is simply inappropriate and delusional to believe it should be logic. If you disagree, that means you understand what I mean, and hope to convince you, through reasoning, is mistaken. I cannot use logic, of course, because I can only use words and words, like reason, are not logic. If you are unwilling to believe the truth is true, then you are not going to accept that it is true, no matter how true it is. Similarly, the third theory, that altruism is not genetic, is often accepted without being understood correctly, and so that isn't the same as agreeing with it. Kindness is not a biological imperative; that is often embraced as a principle. But the further truth, that kindness is not a biological trait, is more frequently rejected. The converse is also part of the claim; altruism is not supernatural, it is not divinely inspired; altruism does exist, but not because it is a commandment from God, or as a commandment from God. Indeed, the idea of God is invented to explain the existence of altruism, but it is no more accurate a theory than the idea that altruism is a biological adaptation.

The three fundamental principles embodied by these theories are generally separate and independent, but they also work together to provide a complete and coherent philosophy of life and consciousness, the Philosophy Of Reason. I'm going to explain them each separately as if they are unrelated, but in truth they are three aspects of a single discovery concerning consciousness, language, and humanity. If the explanations I'm going to provide seem too esoteric or arcane, consider that you may need to understand one of the other theories better before fully comprehending the one I'm explaining at that moment. The real reason why these are all going to be rather difficult to comprehend or accept is that they are each contrary to existing theories. This is inevitable, part of what is meant by the word 'theory', that new theories are not just novel ideas, they are novel ideas that replace previous, less accurate ideas. The existing, less accurate ideas are theories so familiar and popular that they aren't considered theories, but simply facts.

There once was a preacher (the story goes), that was reading to his congregation from their scripture, and mispronounced the word *sumpsimus* as *mumpsimus*. When his mistake was pointed out to him, he refused to accept that he had erred, and so from then on he always used the word 'mumpsimus' to refer to 'sumpsimus'. Of course, there isn't any such things as mumpsimus, but there isn't really any such thing as sumpsimus, either. These are gibberish words used to tell the story of the preacher, which is fiction, but instructive about facts, nevertheless. To this day, the word "mumpsimus" means something that almost everyone agrees is true, but isn't. And the word "sumpsimus" means something that nobody, or only one person, or a few people, realize is true, but is. Notice the ironic inversion in the usage, though; the story had the congregation knowing the 'reality' was "sumpsimus", and the preacher was the only one who thought it was "mumpsimus", but the definition of these terms today is that the reality is the inverse; the error is called mumpsimus, but is accepted by almost everyone, while the truth is sumpsimus, but denied by almost everyone. This provides an important lesson about authority versus popularity, but without coming down decisively on which is the truth. Unlike the story, where the omniscient author can omnipotently declare that the word was written 'sumpsimus', but read 'mumpsimus'. It is also worth noting that the story was apparently written soon after the Protestant Reformation, when the question of whether the congregation could be trusted to interpret the Bible with sufficient authority to be accurate. These days (the postmodern times we live in) people believe the matter is settled, but in truth it is both recurring and recursive. Some believe the matter is settled because science is the only guide to what is truth, some because religion is the path to truth, and the rest believe it depends on the subject matter. Regardless, postmodernism is the mumpsimus. Even the definition of what 'postmodernism' is, along with what 'reason' is, is mumpsimus; almost everyone agrees that what I mean when I use those terms is incorrect. But POR is sumpsimus, it is true regardless of whether you believe or understand it. In fact, it is true regardless of whether I believe or understand it, though I do, because it fits all the facts I have ever been able to sincerely and seriously consider. Free will is a mumpsimus, and self-determination is a sumpsimus. Logical reasoning is mumpsimus; irrational language is sumpsimus. Adaptive altruism and God are mumpsimus, while POR science and theology are the sumpsimus. The old theories must be replaced, because they are less true than the replacement. The old theologies can be abandoned, because they are more false than the Philosophy Of Reason.

Rather than continue with general statements about POR and its three (better) theories as a whole, making grand pronouncements, grandiose assertions, that you may or may not be able to agree with, I'm going to go straight to the explanations of the theories themselves. After each is detailed more completely, we can resume thinking about what POR means in its broader aspects, and how it can change not just our personal psychology, but our society and civilization in its entirety, simply by rethinking what we think about thought.

Ontology

The first theory in the Philosophy Of Reason is self-determination. As you would expect, 'self-determination' can be understood to mean the ability for our thought processes to direct our behavior. It seems simple enough, I dare say uncontroversial and irrefutable, but it gets very complicated very quickly. The existing theory that the POR theory of self-determination replaces is "free will". Now, it has to be said that many philosophical or supposedly scientific theories about human consciousness and behavior already claim to reject the idea of free will, but it isn't clear that any theory is truly successful at doing so. To understand this point, we will have to consider free will and how it fits in the standard philosophies that POR replaces.

Simply put, the hypothesis of free will is the belief that we consciously control our actions. It has been a bedrock part of philosophy for millennia, although it has been controversial that entire time, as well. Some accept it as self-evident, some consider it self-refuting. The POR philosophy of self-determination entirely replaces it, but also replaces its opposite. The opposite theory to free will is generally considered to be 'predeterminism' and its inherent 'determinism'. Stated another way, we could call it 'fate' or 'fatalism'. The hypothesis of determinism/fate is the belief that self-determination cannot exist; that what you will decide is as inevitable as any other future event, like a rock falling from a cliff, it just hasn't happened yet. So how can our POR theory replace both the theories of free will and the theory of determinism, which is the opposite of free will? What is the POR theory of self-determinism; how does it explain human behavior any better than free will? Well, I'm going to have to save the big reveal on that question for after we get further into what exactly self-determination is and what causes it to occur.

As I've already mentioned, the theory of free will has been controversial pretty much as long as there has been a theory of free will. Thousands of years ago, a great sage named Epicurus hypothesized that if we exist in a universe that is controlled by laws of physics, then free will isn't really possible. Whatever we rationally do is as inevitable as apples growing or rain falling; the rational result of physical processes, unable to change themselves. Our actions and behavior are the result of the physical interaction of chemical substances in our brains. (Epicurus was of course ignorant of the role of brains and neurochemicals, precisely, but his reasoning was accurate nevertheless.) To Epicurus, if our existence is the result of physical forces, than our behavior is the result of physical forces, as well. This does seem certain, even unquestionable. In principle, this is the accepted scientific and medical premise, without any doubt. And yet, even those who most rigorously try to adopt this seemingly fatalistic approach to the mechanism of volition find themselves almost routinely forced to fall back to 'free will' as a way of describing the results, if not the cause, of human behavior. In many cases, free will becomes a flaw, an explanation for people failing to behave as we hoped. This can most directly be observed in terms of medical theories of addiction and related psychological issues and frameworks. It is all about operant conditioning, in these frameworks. An addict ingests a substance that causes a psychoactive neurological effect, and becomes addicted to that substance if the effect results in pleasure. The person is helpless to prevent this, because it is this neurochemical action that causes them to desire the substance and, scientifically, there is no mechanism of free will, just the chemical activity in the brain. And yet, the only remedy for this addiction is to suppose that the person has free will, and can <u>choose</u> to not ingest the substance they desire, in order to achieve the sobriety they also desire. In this way, the only remedy for a problem caused by the failure of free will to exist is to invent the existence of free will. And so the theory of addiction becomes conflicted. There is no purpose to purity in this regard, I am not suggesting that we should deny the neurochemical mechanisms of addiction when trying to deal with its psychological and sociological ramifications. I am simply pointing out that there is some inconsistency there, certainly necessary and possibly even productive. Scientifically, free will is an illusion, everything in the universe, including us and our thoughts, can only be the result of previous occurrences, the only true 'cause' of any of it happening being the cause of all causes, with everything else being inevitable effects of physics, chemistry, and biology.

Another way of thinking about this is to try to dissect that word "desire", itself. Or perhaps a more simplistic term, "want". When we claim that we want something, we are expressing a desire for it, I think we can agree. I don't mean to make this a semantic issue, but when dealing with words it becomes almost inevitable. (This hints at the importance and value of the second theory of POR, that language is not mathematical, but that will be dealt with later. The purpose of mentioning it now is to point out that words become more communicative when they aren't parsed out mathematically than when they are.) An addict <u>wants</u> the substance they are addicted to, we must agree on that. But the very nature of addiction, the entire reason we use the word 'addiction', is because the addict supposedly does not *want to want* that substance. You see the conflict, the self-referential contradiction, being imposed by our language? This issue is taken to extremes and becomes quite evident in the case of addiction, but it is present in a lesser way whenever we speak of desire or even intent. It seems like it should be a simple thing, whether you want something or not. Whether your preference is determined by your free will or by the physical results of the processing of data in a neural network made up of your brain's synapses, the issue remains the same: what it is to desire or want something is not as simple as we might like to think, as we wish or want it to be.

We might also consider what mechanism produces this effect of free will, if we presume that such a thing exists and determines our preferences. Is it simply the unpredictability of the results of our neural network, whether circumstantial or mathematical? Is it some non-physical spirit or soul that infuses or inhabits our bodies and brains? This, too, is a topic of much debate in classical (modern) and standard (postmodern) philosophy. But it is all for naught, because such theories run into the same self-contradiction that we saw with the idea of 'desire'. Is it the metaphysical or supernatural spirit that 'wants', or is it that spirit that 'wants to want'? Trying to sort out human motivations and intentions honestly would require us to go even further, and consider whether a person wants to want to want something, or even wants to want to want to want it. A rabbit hole of wondrous but pointless thoughts opens up with such endless regression, though each moment along the way is still comprehensible; to want to want, and so to want to want to want to want to want, remains comprehensible, if only with varying degrees of ease.

The idea of free will has always been fraught, but it is maintained or revived constantly because the supposedly sole alternative is even worse. Previously, abandoning the theory of free will leaves only one determinism, the hypothesis that the mechanistic nature of neurobiology makes self-determination itself impossible. In this standard approach, 'free will' and 'self-determination' are linguistically interchangeable and physically identical; any distinction is illusory and dismissed as *semantic*, which is to say it is mere sophistry. It is this 'either/or' presumption, that if we do not have some mystical 'mind over matter' power of control over our physical actions, then we have no self-determination, which makes both free will and fatalism equally problematic. Lacking self-determination, the reasoning goes, we have no responsibility, ethical, legal, or philosophical, for our actions. The hypothesis of free will itself is invented for this moral theory, in order to provide some mechanism to hold people responsible for their behavior. If we have no control over our conduct, then we have no responsibility for our conduct, according to standard theories of ethics. This is such an integral part of common philosophy that it supposedly cannot even be coherently questioned. Whether religious or scientific, any theory that we should behave any particular one way has an inherent justification, indicated by the word 'should', that undesired consequences will or might occur if we don't behave that way. Whether the mechanism providing this link between bad action and bad consequence is moderated by metaphysical justice, simple cause and effect physics, or legal liability, the *assumption* is that our control over our own behavior is an essential part of moral responsibility for our actions.

But it is simply an *assumption*, and we should ask ourselves whether this assumption is true. Is it possible that ethical or moral responsibility for our actions derives from something other than having conscious control over our actions? It would seem unfair, certainly, that we can be held legally culpable for something that is beyond our ability to change. This reasoning relies on a further assumption, also false, that life, the universe, or physics is "fair" to begin with. Certainly people should be fair, but there's that "should", again. By what right can anyone dare to proclaim true 'fairness'? POR can and does replace the existing theory of responsibility with an improved one. Improved in comparison to the existing understanding of what responsibility is and why and how it occurs. It would cause an improvement in our actual applications of ethics, justice, and law, as well, this POR theory of responsibility, if we were to implement it consciously and conscientiously, instead of maintaining and reinforcing the false theories of free will or determinism, which we tend to flip between as necessary to both defend our own actions and indict the actions of others. To really understand the POR idea of responsibility, you need to get the second theory of epistemology and language as well as the first theory of ontology and self-determination, so we'll leave off worrying about it right now. Let's get back to the ways self-determination isn't free will, and how free will doesn't explain human consciousness or behavior.

Experiments

So far, I've just meandered around fancy ideas and imaginary arguments to show how free will doesn't make sense. The theory of self-determination in POR does not rest entirely on these intellectual arguments. I am going to present three empirical studies that demonstrate the inaccuracy of free will, its inadequacy as an explanation of human behavior. Standard philosophy would call them 'scientific', and for the most part they largely are, but for reasons that will be explained later, POR avoids calling them that explicitly. If you understand and accept these unrefuted and repeatable empirical studies then you should begin to get quite uncomfortable. Coming to grips with the fact that we really don't have free will, that we really are helplessly stuck in a physical universe in which our actions are caused by physics, not by our desires or intentions, is disconcerting and difficult, to say the least. Our desires and intentions are themselves caused by physical neurochemical activity, not the self-generator of desires and intentions you've been taught to refer to as your free will. Inevitably, though temporarily, recognizing that free will doesn't exist while learning how self-determination does can lead to a 'trapped' feeling. Because we are indeed trapped in that way; your conscious thoughts aren't what controls your movements. Your movements are themselves results, of the same neurobiological choices your brain executes that also result in your conscious thoughts. Your thoughts are generally independent of your movements; that, anyone sane is capable of agreeing with. You can pay attention to what you are doing, but you can also do things without paying attention to them. Even when you most believe your conscious thoughts are what are causing your movements, your conscious thoughts occur a few fractions of a second after your movements have already started as choices in your brain. You can slow down your actions as much as you want, in order to think about them, but when your brain chooses to take any action, it does so slightly before you decide to do so. We can't ever get ahead of this time gap, this existential wall, and so free will is relied on to fill in the magic necessary to keep moving.

Keep in mind when this trapped feeling happens that it is not the entirety of the narrative, that POR provides a very reliable and explicit mechanism to salvage self-determination, without the fallacious baggage of classical free will. We never regain volitional control over our actions, in POR, we simply dispense with the intellectual or emotional need to have that volitional control. We still take actions based on our intentions, we still take responsibility for those actions, we just have a clearer understanding of what connects the two things, and what those things themselves are and why and how they are connected. Life with self-determination is a better life than a life trying to exert free will, because we don't have free will. Our conscious thoughts do not control our bodies.

This is hard to accept, at first, I know. But it is absolutely true: you do not have conscious control over your body. You never have. Not for a moment, ever. So you should not imagine that if you didn't have control over your body, you would have acted any differently than you have, because you never have had that control. It doesn't matter how often or frequently you have been told otherwise, or how much sense it seems to make that you should, you cannot have conscious control over your physical movements, or your thoughts, or your feelings. To be "in control of yourself" is simply not having any need to be in control of yourself, because you're already behaving the way you would want to if you did have control of yourself. Most people insist that if they didn't consciously control their actions, they would act irrationally, insanely, angrily; they would attack, perhaps even murder, people who upset them a great deal, and so they consider the lack of wounds or casualties to be proof positive that they have free will. Such an argument is comforting, empowering, and simply egotistical. Whether it is fear of justice or an embrace of morality that actually inhibits them from acting unreasonably, the self-righteous and narcissistic insistence that without the willpower they believe is generated by free will, they would act on every criminal impulse or fantasy is simply self-aggrandizing bravado.

There are a variety of ways to consider and determine this issue of free will. The least convincing is simply intellectual. What is the "you" that you wish to control? If you were insane or unconscious, you would not have control over yourself. And you cannot consciously decide not to be insane, because if you are insane, you wouldn't be able to make that decision. You probably wouldn't even believe you *should* make that decision. Not needing to change the way you behave is not being 'in control' of your behavior, it is not needing to be in control of your behavior. And if you cannot consciously control when you can consciously control your behavior, then you aren't ever actually in control of your behavior.

All that sounds like psychobabble, self-referential nonsense, semantic games, I know. So let us move on from the intellectual to the more empirical demonstrations.

A few years ago, psychological researchers at Harvard University started a project to try to measure what is known as implicit bias. Prejudice. Specifically, racism. They wanted to measure bigotry, turn it into quantifiable data, and they figured out how to do it. They found that, using computer technology, they can detect a reliably measurable difference between the time it takes a person to associate ideas related to 'good' (happiness, pleasure, comfort, joy, rainbows, warmth, soft, etc.) with people that someone is comfortable with, and the time it takes to associate those same 'good' ideas with people they don't trust or like based on visual cues to their ancestry, which is to say 'race'. You can test this out yourself, and participate in their experiment, by searching online for the Harvard Implicit Bias Test. Conversely, of course, it takes a bigot longer to associate bad things (pain, sadness, danger, etc.) with people they aren't prejudiced against than people they are prejudiced against. This is a matter of statistical processing, involving milliseconds, so it is not all that profound or extreme. The same person might test within a relatively broad range depending on the specific examples and other factors, but overall the results are repeatable and accurate. They replicated the same results with features other than race: gender, age, even religion or nationality (based on garb or other ornamentation). As long as there are visual clues to the face's identity, it can take more or less time to hit a button marked 'bad' than it does to hit a button marked 'good' while viewing it, a reliable indicator of implicit bias.

Of course, there are plenty of people (even some other psychologists and sociologists) that dismiss the entire project. But the truth is, if there weren't something valid being measured, the results would be far more random and imprecise than they are. That doesn't stop the detractors, though, because this presents a very uncomfortable but necessary re-appraisal of how our conscious thoughts relate to our physical actions and even our feelings.

In the classic model of human behavior, our actions result from our conscious thoughts, at least some times. We consider the circumstance, we make a decision, and we act on it, usually implementing that decision as a choice. In the case of racial implicit bias, for example, we like to think that we are capable of being fair and just, even somewhat objective. In the most extreme case, a police officer examines the appearance and behavior of a person, decides how to react, and then does so. Is that person holding a gun? This is an objective truth or not, and though there might be uncertainty in whether we can visually determine whether it is true, it is either true or it is false. Based on the visual appearance and other information, training, memory, and other explicit facts, a police officer consciously decides whether to draw and fire their weapon in self-defense. It may happen in a split second, we might even consider it 'instinct', but we still want to believe that it is a choice that they can control and therefore (in the classic scenario of morality) can be considered responsible for their actions.

The implicit bias test indicates that this is not how things actually happen. The repeatability and reliability of this quantitative measurement of prejudice makes it clear that expectations, rather than observations, are the primary factor in the choice of whether to draw and fire the weapon, or indeed whether the cop sees the person (now "suspect") holding a gun. The small but important number of instances where a police officer firmly believes that a cell phone is a gun or a man reaching for his wallet is going for a weapon or just a person leaning forward is lunging towards the police officer's own firearm, these become more comprehensible when we accept that what we see is not an objective matter of photons striking our cornea, but our brain interpreting that visual stimuli. The implicit bias test shows that the 'observation -> choice -> action' model of human behavior isn't as accurate as we'd like.

It is not at all my intention to suggest that police officers are unique, this is merely the extreme case that makes the issues involved obvious enough to discuss. Whether or not someone is raising their hands to attack, or surrender, is not something that can be easily determined even if we did have conscious control over our every action. Robbed of the luxury of time for evaluating alternative possibilities, the split-second decisions that a police officer makes are more high pressure, but otherwise no different than whether we want to befriend a certain person or hire a particular employee. There are many people that firmly believe that there really isn't much racism in our society, and the implicit bias test is measuring something that is irrelevant apart from neurological studies, since even in the case of the cop deciding to use their gun to defend themself, the milliseconds involved in the computerized test is much shorter than the time it takes to perform any action, leaving more than enough duration to reconsider and re-evaluate what is true or not before committing the irrevocable act of pulling the trigger.

Let's consider another psychological experiment that seems to demonstrate that the classic 'consider -> choose -> act' model isn't as reliable as we believe. Instead of focusing on the control issue, this one deals with the body issue. Do we have conscious control over our body? We would have to know what is or is not our body in order to determine that, wouldn't we? And again, judging from typical daily life, it seems preposterous to suggest that we don't know what is or isn't our own body. Outside of things like nails and hair that have no sensation at all, it shouldn't be hard to tell where our flesh is and what position it is in. Generally, this is called the kinesthetic sense, usually grouped with the sense of touch in terms of neurology. But it turns out that it is easier to fool than we might think.

In this second experiment, a special apparatus is used that allows a test subject to look down at their hands on a keyboard and play a musical melody. Except in reality, the subject isn't viewing their own hands. Using mirrors or other mechanisms, the experiment is set up so that the subject is actually looking at somebody else's fingers on a different keyboard than the one the subject is touching. As the subject learns the tune, this stand-in mimics the movements of the subject as perfectly as they can, until the subject becomes convinced that it is their own hands they are viewing. Then, as the experiment continues, the stand-in hands purposefully make mistakes in picking out the tune on the keyboard, mistakes the subject didn't actually make. If the subject has already been convinced it is their own hands, a very curious thing happens. Rather than realize that the hands they are looking at aren't their own once those fingers make a mistake their own hands haven't, the kinesthetic sense gets fooled, and the subject continues to believe that they are the ones that made the mistake. Often, they will even provide some invented reason for the error, instead of recognizing what is actually happening. "Oops" they say, or "this is a tricky part", or some such, even though their fingers hit the correct key. The sounds of the wrong note combined with the sight of the finger doing so convinces them that they made an error, when they didn't.

You may not agree, but I believe that this keyboard experiment demonstrates that our assumption that we must have conscious control over our physical actions is incorrect. If we cannot even tell what our actions are, whether they are our actions or simply look like they are our actions, how can we possibly know that we caused those actions with our decision to activate our muscles and move our extremities?

The implicit bias test brings into question whether we control our bodies by indicating that control is imaginary: our behavior may be the result of our implicit bias rather than explicit consideration. The keyboard experiment brings into question whether we control our bodies by indicating that our awareness of our bodies and whether we are controlling our actions is far less reliable than we expect. These investigations might dispute whether the classic 'think -> decide -> execute' model of human behavior works as well as we want, but I will admit they don't quite make clear what is actually going on. Perhaps we might have some bias, but we can still overcome our prejudice. Maybe we don't know automatically whether it is our body or a nearly identical one when we watch things happen, but we still have nerves that connect our brains to our fingers that cannot be so easily fooled.

The last psychological experiment I'm going to describe is the clincher. It doesn't really matter if the first two managed to make you question the certainty of free will, that we consciously control our actions, this one should still be disturbing, if not convincing. I refer to it as the thumbswitch experiment. It is actually the oldest one of the three I'm presenting, first performed back in the 1980s. Since the results are quite disturbing, or simply incomprehensible, depending on your opinion, it has never received a great deal of attention, but it has been repeated often enough to know that it demonstrates something factual.

A subject sits in front of a computer screen, watching a slideshow. They have a button they can press with their thumb to change the picture. Simple enough.

The neurological component of the experiment is this; the researchers are measuring a variety of electrical signals in the subject's brain. What they are is unimportant, what they measure in particular is arbitrary. The important thing is that there are a number of them, all changing in different ways for different neurochemical reasons, and the researchers are measuring them all constantly. Then they use computer algorithms to determine what pattern among and between the 'brainwave' metrics precisely and reliably predicts when the subject will push the thumbswitch. What pattern never occurs unless the thumbswitch is about to be pushed, and always occurs just before the button is pressed. The neurological pattern that is both sufficient and necessary for the thumb to move is, for every intent and purpose we can imagine, the moment the subject has chosen to change the picture. This moment will be very shortly before the thumb actually moves, because the impulse first has to propagate through the brain, then down the arm along the nerves, and then activate muscles in the forearm that physically move the thumb. This 'propagation delay' may take a few hundred milliseconds, but it should be roughly the same duration every time the button is pushed.

It may be surprising or even disturbing that identifying this pattern is even possible. Again, it isn't any particular measurement that is being looked for, the researchers aren't actually reading the subjects' minds. But if the mathematical processing they use to decipher the moment of choice is accurate, they should be able to test it. And that is what they did. Without informing the test subject, they changed from using the thumbswitch to control the slide show, to using the neurological pattern. If they had correctly identified the 'moment of choice', when they thought that the subject had decided to switch the picture and then consciously moved their thumb to press the button, then the subject should not even notice that anything changed. When the thumbswitch was used, they made the choice, then it propagated through their brain and down their arm and they pressed the button. When the neural readings were used, they made the choice, the experimenters delay the picture change for the appropriate amount of time to mimic the propagation delay, and then the picture changed just as if they had controlled it by pressing the button. If free will exists, (or self-determination doesn't,) the subject is still controlling the slide show either way, and there really shouldn't be any noticeable effect from the change.

Of course, if the researchers had not accurately and precisely identified the moment of choice, the decision to change the picture, then there certainly would be a noticeable effect. The most likely outcome would be that the apparatus started switching the picture independently of the subject's conscious choice. When using the prediction from the brainwaves, the equipment determines the slideshow will be changed before the thumb moves, and since the prediction, not the switch, controls the picture, this disconnect between the two should be obvious very quickly. Sometimes when they just thought about switching, the picture would change. Sometimes they would press the thumbswitch over and over and the picture still wouldn't change. This would indicate that the researchers weren't really measuring what they thought they were measuring when their calculations indicated the necessary and sufficient neural pattern to indicate the decision to look at a new picture. Or perhaps there would simply be a delay, as reported by the subject, indicating that the neurological measurements being used by the researchers were the result of the decision to press the button, instead of the decision itself. This was probably the consequence most expected. If the theory of mind and the apparatus were accurate, but they weren't measuring the actual decision, just the neurological results of the decision, the choice and the picture would still be connected, but not as obviously, and a lag would appear. A few milliseconds delay between the moment when the thumbswitch should have switched the picture, noticeable only to the subject, when they would have anticipated it happening, and when the neural signals the researchers thought were the choosing but were themselves the result of the choosing, seems like the most probable effect, if any change were to occur when the prediction rather than the button controlled the slides.

So the possible results should be no change, or there would be no correlation between the switching and the switch, or there would be a delay between the switch and the switching. With any of these anticipated results, the 'free will theory of mind' can remain intact. Except none of those things happened. What actually happened seems at first like it would literally be impossible. Because every test subject, every single one, reported the same results, the exact same results. But that isn't even the spooky part. The consistency of the reports would be startling all by itself; when an experiment goes wrong, the results become unpredictable. But what the subjects all consistently reported is such a bizarre claim that simply trying to describe it with normal language becomes quite difficult. What the test subjects all reported is that the slide show *anticipated* their decision. Perfectly, and exactly. *Every single time* they were *about* to *decide* to change the picture, the picture immediately switched. Not when they decided, not after they decided. Not even *before they decided*, as if they were merely thinking about changing the picture, or thinking about deciding to change the picture, or randomly. But <u>just before</u> they actually did decide to change the picture, yet only when they ended up deciding. Not once when they saw that the picture had changed could a single subject sincerely say they had changed their mind about going to the next slide after merely considering it. Somewhere in the many dozens of milliseconds between the neurological choice to move the thumb and the movement, their free will was playing hide and seek. A more calming image of what would be happening in their brain is that they have 'higher thought processes', some 'executive function', that is beyond the measurements the experimenters were calculating, and that this 'ego' of cognitive volition commands the selection of changing the picture. The equipment should only be measuring the impetus and process of moving the thumb, so if anything the apparatus should cause the slide show to be delayed, not advanced. It can't be advanced, with this rational theory of mind, because until the choice happens, it hasn't happened, so how can the equipment be perfectly anticipating it happening?

There isn't really any way to check this. Only the subjects know whether they were about to decide, or just thinking about deciding. Only after the fact, after the picture had already changed, could they have thought back on the moment and realized that they actually would have changed the picture had it not already changed. Never once did the picture change because they merely planned to decide, and after the switch they thought that they might not have made that decision. The slideshow never advanced without them hitting the thumbswitch, *even though the thumbswitch was not controlling the slideshow*. Every subject all reported that the computer had, well, read their mind. Never once did they consider pushing the button and change their mind, but then the picture changed anyway. Never once did the picture change without the subject wanting it to at all. It didn't matter how long they considered hitting the button before deciding, or how quickly they made the choice after a new picture came up. Even if they tried to, they couldn't 'fool' the apparatus into doing anything other than perfectly anticipating their decision <u>by just a fraction of a second</u>. Their decision to push the button always preceded the actual pushing of the button, obviously. And the changing of the picture always followed that, though we don't know if it was by microseconds or centiseconds. There was a tiny slice of time, just a few fractions of a second, between the time that the decision had been made but the slide show had not advanced. Any person could simply say the change had happened more quickly than they expected. But instead they told the truth; that no matter how they tried, the machine always switched it **just before** they had decided, but reliably enough before that they could only explain it as *anticipating their choice*, and immediately enough so that they could never stop themselves from pushing the button anyway. Whether that was even possible, to see the picture change before the thumb moved, or the neurological delay was swamped by waiting time between switch activation and picture change, I do not know. I'm sure variations have been tried. It wasn't any lag in the choice, decision, button, or switch that controlled the results, it was simply that, while the subject couldn't fool the apparatus, they had to admit that it had somehow fooled them.

By increasing the delay between the necessary and sufficient pattern being detected and the picture being changed, the researchers determined that there was a period of <u>several dozen milliseconds</u> after the choice to switch the picture had already been made and before the subjects consciously decided to move their thumb. Once that extra delay was included, the apparatus behaved the way the experimenters expected, with the subject being unaware of any change between using the thumbswitch and using the neurological patterns. If they inserted too long of an extra delay, then the slide show seemed to lag. But as long as the total delay was only as long as it took for the propagation of the nerve impulse through the brain and to the muscles, the subjects insisted that the switch occurred before they did decide, but only when they would have decided.

Instead of 'consider -> decide -> act', the thumbswitch experiment demonstrates that the actual process is 'choose -> act -> decide'. Let me explain this more explicitly, since I know it becomes quite difficult to follow. The thumbswitch experiment relies on precisely identifying the moment of choice. This is done by finding a particular pattern of neural activity that always and only occurs when a choice to take a particular action occurs. In this case the action is activating a thumbswitch. We don't have to worry about why that happens or what it does, all we have to do is admit that it did happen: the button got pushed. Using hindsight, enabled by numerical measurements with no ambiguity, we can determine what readings only happen just before the thumb moves, and always happen just before the thumb moves. If we change what advances the slide show, the button or the pattern of measurements, there really shouldn't be any change evident to the subject. But there is, and it is always the same change, and it is described in impossible terms, that somehow the equipment knew that the subject had made a choice to push the button before they knew they had, as well as before the button was pushed. This proves, unquestionably, that it is the actual choice in the brain that we are measuring, because there are no times when the equipment changes the picture because the subject was merely considering changing the picture, or not considering it at all, but only *just before* they made that decision. This is a situation that can only be reported by the subject themselves. Only they know for sure whether the switch happened before or after they decided. It would be trivial for them to say that the equipment didn't anticipate their choice, but simply followed it. Since the the researchers could verify whether the button was pushed, they couldn't claim the equipment had simply 'gone rogue'. But they could have said that slideshow had changed after they chose but more quickly than they expected (from their previous experience when the button was actually used), and still that isn't what they report.

The situation can only be understood one way. That is, that the subject's *brains* had made the **choice** to change the picture *before* the subject's conscious mind became aware of that choice. Then, when the neural impulses caught up with whatever neural process results in their conscious awareness, their *minds* made a **decision** to change the picture. As long as the decision always follows the choice, and there was no way for the person's mind to become aware of what their brain is doing other than thoughts and actions, they would never know there was any possibility of distinguishing their choice from their decision. This would be like the keyboard 'phantom hands' experiment I described previously, with the subject remaining unaware that they weren't playing the notes they were hearing. But with the apparatus of the thumbswitch experiment making the result of their choice (the changing of the picture) independent of their physical action (pushing the button), it became not simply possible, but unavoidable, to notice that their conscious awareness of their choice follows several dozen milliseconds after the actual choice was made, and everything after that choice was just neurological processing and retransmission of that impulse. That includes their conscious decision, which only occurred after their unconscious choice.

So this is the new language we must use to describe thought, consciousness, and self-determination: our brains make **choices** before our minds consciously make **decisions**. Our brains choose, our minds decide only afterwards. In fact, what we call a 'decision' is not a selection among possible alternatives, but simply our brain inventing an explanation for the selection that our brain has already made. Sometimes, that is simple, like whether to push a button. Far more often, by astronomical orders of magnitude, are the times when it isn't so simple, and we need to deal with more complicated issues. The operation of our intellects is not as **executive functions**, but **narrators**. Every single choice we make, most without any conscious pre-consideration, has already occurred when our minds subsequently become aware of that choice and consequently develop explanations for that choice, and that, not the act of choosing, is called making a decision. The terminology has to be made formal, although it was just synonymous, if not over-synonymous, before. They are both concrete terms, both refer to a process of choice selection by human beings, or analogs or metaphors. But they are also opposite and separate. **Choosing** is what our brains do whether we are conscious of it or not, **deciding** happens after the fact, in the period of time between when we've chosen and when the nerve impulses resulting from the choice (not the decision) cause noticeable effects in our movements. Your choices are still your own, your decisions are still meaningful and purposeful, but the two aren't the same thing, and they occur in the reverse chronological order than what you've always been told.

Many people, including highly trained and experienced psychologists and neurobiologists, believe that the thumbswitch experiment doesn't actually negate the idea of free will. They say that there could easily be some 'executive veto' power that over-rides the choice our brain has already made when our conscious mind decides to do so. They might say that the thumbswitch experiment isn't important because whether to push a button or change a picture in a slideshow is too trivial. Or they might say the opposite, that in typical mundane actions, our conscious mind controls our actions, and only when intentionally tested or when we are consciously thinking about a decision we must make is it possible for our choice to precede the decision. There are plenty of ways to try to skirt the issue, but these are sophistry, these are semantics, these are ad hoc inventions used to try to deny reality. The reality is that our conscious thoughts do not cause our actions, our unconscious neural processing does, and our conscious thoughts are simply one of the resulting effects, explanations we construct to justify our actions, not to cause them to occur. No matter how important or trivial the test case or real life circumstance may be, only one theory fits all cases. Our brains make choices, those choices control our actions, and our conscious minds decide only how to explain those actions. The choices our brains make are often, if not always, based on pre-existing attitudes, as in the implicit bias test, and assumptions about conditions that aren't consciously evaluated, as in the keyboard test. No matter how much we might want to be able to believe that our conscious minds can over-ride the choices our brains have already made before we even find out about them, any such 'over-ride/veto' must, itself, <u>have already been a choice made by our brains several dozen milliseconds before</u> we 'decided' what that choice would be.

A decision is simply our minds coming up with an explanation for the choices our brains have already made. If that sounds incredible, even impossible, then that means you understand it correctly. Because it is true, and that is what 'true' means: it doesn't matter how impossible you think it is, it is still true.

This isn't the POR theory of self-determination, it is merely the proof that such a theory is necessary. It is the refutation of the theory of free will, which is the assumption that our actions are controlled by our conscious decisions. This proof is consistent with all of the issues and tests presented so far, and all the possible other issues and tests still unexamined. The fact that our binding choices are made in and by our brains several dozen milliseconds before we even find out about them is consistent with the theory of implicit bias, and the evidence of prejudice that prompts the theory of implicit bias. It is consistent with the keyboard test, which demonstrates that our conscious awareness of even our own actions is unreliable. It is consistent with the thumbswitch test that proves it is undeniable, because a decision to change our minds is a choice our brains make before we are consciously aware of it. In fact, even having a desire to change our minds is a choice our brains make several dozen milliseconds before we know it occurs. This refutation of free will is also compatible with and explains a lot about human behavior, wherever our desires do not apparently match our behavior. Finally, it is consistent with our language and our reasoning, concerning when and how we assign responsibility and can observe free will only in absence, when our actions don't match our desires. Even if we could control our actions, we couldn't control when we control our actions, so we don't ever really control our actions. We are our actions, and when we are 'in control', that's rhetoric for not acting unreasonably. Yet we consciously determine what we are doing, even without controlling it. We have the best seats in the house, more intimate familiarity with our past behavior than any other person could, and we become aware of our choices before they have any noticeable effect on anything but our own selves, usually. If you consider yourself a reasonable human being, conscious and self-aware, then you know what you're doing, and probably know better than anyone else why you are really doing it, even if you aren't used to expressing it in words, and have been taught not to because it sounds irrational. The mechanics of self-determination keep us a fraction of a second behind our impulses, if not our behavior, and only we can determine for ourselves which is which, ultimately. But we are self-aware and conscious specifically so that we can engage in self-determination as an internal witness of what our brains, our minds, are choosing, as we decide how it should be described.

If we take this seriously, and we must, we are left with two obvious and important questions. First, how can we be considered responsible for our actions? Second, what is self-determination? It is debatable, of course, whether these are even two different questions. We could say that they are simply the same question phrased two different ways. But there is a reason I've presented them distinctly. It might still be possible that we don't have any moral (or ethical, legal, physical, et.al,) responsibility for our behavior even if we do experience self-determination. And it might still be possible that our belief in or desire for self-determination is as inaccurate or false as our belief in or desire for free will, but that we still bear moral responsibility for our actions.

In POR, the answer to the two questions are inter-related, but not identical. Let's look at the second one first: What is self-determination. Epistemologically, self-determination is defined as the thing that causes us to be responsible for our actions regardless of whether we have conscious control of them. Ontologically, self-determination is what causes responsibility to begin with and what purpose it serves. (Don't worry for now what is meant by 'epistemology' or 'ontology', this is an instructive example but that's not otherwise relevant to self-determination. There are several possible official definitions, at least some of which might be conflicting, in interpretation if not in terminology. The educated postmodernist will balk at any definition I might provide, anyway, as an excuse to relieve them of the responsibility of reconsidering their assumptions. This is a misapplication of 'critical thinking skills', a bad example of the Socratic Method that I will address directly later.)

At first blush, 'self-determination' is simply what you've been taught to call 'free will'. It is the capacity for autonomy in human behavior. But that's kind of a backwards explanation, identifying a thing by its results, rather than its cause. Where does self-determination "come from"? How does it occur, and why? Are we just inventing it to salvage the idea of responsibility, when it turns out that free will is physically impossible? Or is it a naturally occurring ontological phenomenon, not simply an epistemological explanation?

In the end, self-determination is the reason for the inclusion of 'causality' in the subtitle of this book. It is a feature of the universe that results from our awareness of teleology.

Oh, my. Another big word. Is that all you're trying to do, T. Max, confuse enough people with confabulated vocabulary that you can declare anything you want to be true and pretend that contradiction is impossible? 'Epistemology' and 'ontology' weren't enough, now you're going to demand that the word 'teleology' has to be used in a way unsupported by any evidence but assertion, in order to truly understand human thought and behavior? Forgive my aside. It is self-indulgent, but hopefully at least slightly endearing. Let us proceed.

Teleology is one of the two possible uses of language. The other is 'tautology', and is the more familiar and easily accepted. In fact, an inappropriate familiarity with 'tautology', in meaning if not in terminology, is at the root of the postmodernism that POR is an attempt to reject. Let me start over, from the beginning, and see if I can do a better job of explaining myself.

There are two ways to use language. Two different 'modes', if you will, categories of ideas that can be expressed with words. The first and most common is *tautology*. A tautology is a simple equivalency: this thing is that thing, possibly with the two things being literally identical: a linguistic tautology. If you look it up in the dictionary (a compendium of literary tautologies) you will find that the word is mostly used to identify circular definitions using repetition of a single term; "Socrates is Socrates" and "words are words" are a tautologies. In non-linguistic terms, "1+1=2" is a logical tautology, and so is "Socrates is a man". A tautology in this sense is something that must be true because it is either circular logic or just a declaration of truth, but regardless of which. In POR, the word tautology is used more broadly for any description of anything: "Socrates walked down the street," or any other semantic perception of syntactic mechanics. That last bit, semantics and syntax, refers to the standard linguistic theory that words are tautological symbols for objective occurrences. The details of those terms can be ignored for now. "He walked" is not considered a tautology in classical theory, but it is in the Philosophy Of Reason. To say anything "is" or "does", or any other simple description, regardless of the terms used, is a tautology. Assignment of that kind of factual/linguistic equivalency is assumed to be the basic mechanism of language, in standard theories about language. A way of pointing at things in the real world and labeling them with symbols. This is the essence of postmodernist philosophy, according to POR. It can be and is also referred to as the classical theory of language, that words are symbols used as labels for objects or abstract ideas. This tautological assignment of vocabulary, the act of defining a term "as" the thing you're going to use that term to refer to, is described in postmodernist philosophy as a semiotic action. POR dispenses with the need for such inventions, but they remain somewhat helpful in trying to explain how language works, using only language as a tool for doing so, which can be intensely problematic and enormously difficult and is why this is not a well written book and you're having trouble understanding, or believing, what you're reading right now. Although POR doesn't dismiss all technical linguistics out-of-hand, it generally reduces all semiotic relationships and processes to the word 'metaphor', and considers metaphor a figurative tautology.

In the classical theory of language, tautology is all there is. Assignment of labels for semiotic "concepts". And we know that the concepts exist because we assign labels to them, and how can we do that if there are none? (I'm being facetious again. That was an example of a philosophical tautology, the idea that something must exist if you have labels for it, an error in reasoning as well as a classical logical fallacy.) This ancient yet most postmodern perspective, tautology as a solitary mechanism of language, should make language impossible, if we think about it logically. But we don't, because that is more effort than simply accepting what we are told must be true, and we are told that it must be true that words are symbols used to label concepts. We are told that it is logical, and so we insist that it is logical. We are also told that if words are not just labels for concepts, then language wouldn't work reliably. And this, I believe, proves my case, because it is undeniable that language does not in fact work reliably, if by 'reliable' we mean all or almost all of the time. The real question is whether it ever works at all. And more importantly, whether we can tell when it is working from when it isn't, and judge why that is, and can have any ideas better about what would happen if it worked all the time.

To answer that question, obviously, we have to define, at least for this context if not inclusion in a dictionary, what 'works' means in terms of language. What is it language is supposed to do, what is its cause, or its mechanism, or its purpose? We would like for language to be reliable, but the existence of such a desire is proof that language fails to be reliable, at least some times. If language automatically worked without fail, we could scarcely even imagine it not working ever. It would be like trying to envision how the universe would be if two plus two sometimes equaled seven instead of always equaling four. Like our perception of self-control, if we can't tell when language is being reliable, we can't really be sure it is ever being reliable. If it were always reliable, we could never even imagine it being anything else, and so wouldn't need to hope that it could be anything other than what it always is. Language isn't always reliable, and again we must backtrack and wonder whether it ever is. It certainly isn't being reliable, or at least useful, or at least working, now. Or is it?

The truth is that tautology, whether it is simply repetition of a word or the assignment of a symbol to refer to an abstract idea, or some more complicated statement of what exists or is occurring, is not all there is to language. It isn't even, as we are taught, the primary basis of language. There is another mechanism, that we can now return to, which is teleology. Teleology is assignment of cause and effect. When we use tautologies, we create definitions: "this is that". When we use teleologies, we create meaning: "this causes that". Teleologies are descriptions of **why** something happened, not just a declaration that it is, or happened, or will happen. Whenever we use the words "because" or "in order to" or "so that" or even "therefore", we are inventing or describing a teleology. If classical (modern/postmodern) philosophy were actually sufficient to truly explain all human behavior and experiences, we wouldn't need any teleologies, we'd be able to get along fine with just tautologies, with using words as otherwise meaningless symbols for physical objects or forces. If we were merely animals, or only biological robots programmed by natural selection, tautologies would suffice, and even the idea of teleologies, explanations of "why", would be superfluous and unimportant, or simply non-existent. Teleologies are where the hard parts of language come from, and thus they are the reason language exists at all to begin with. Most use of language tends to be tautologies, but codes are also tautologies. This has the tendency of encouraging the idea that words are symbols and language is codes, because, again, the standard (postmodern) theory of language is that it is based on tautologies, and teleologies are just a special case of tautologies, and mostly fictional. However, it is the need for teleologies, indeed the creation of teleologies, both real and fictional, that distinguish language from any code, and thought from any code system.

Standard grammar, syntax, semantics, philosophy, semiotics, physics, and linguistics consider teleologies to be nothing other than just another tautology; assigning a reason, justification, excuse, explanation, intention, or some other symbol as a label to a hypothetical abstract idea ("concept") of whatever occurrence is being expressed as a matter of causality. Causality is like heat; it may be really hard, could be even impossible, to define precisely, but saying 'heat is hot' is clearly a tautological assignment. Saying "heat causes heat" would seem to be an even more obvious tautology. POR identifies it as a teleology, and all teleologies as distinct from tautologies. "Heat is heat" is a tautology in the classical grammar and logic sense as well as the more broad and the POR sense. But "hot causes hot" is teleological, though simple and otherwise meaningless. "Why does heat cause hotness" is just as much a teleology; one that makes the individual metaphorical tautologies in each word more exquisite. "Socrates is a man so he is mortal" is also a teleology. We can make endless hay out of whether particular tautologies, alone or as part of a teleology, are categorical knowledge or empirical; we can try to deconstruct philosophy the same way thousands of philosophers have before. Such exercises are meaningless, though. They are less than ephemera, because they contained an unfortunate Error. The difference between tautological and teleological modes of language isn't in the words, it is in how we use them. This is the general rule (the 'first rule', it is called) of language, in POR: it doesn't matter what you call something, what matters is why you are calling it that.

No imprint of the rules of grammar, the dictates of semantics, or the laws of semiotics even has to occur in language for it to be communicative. Poetry is more meaningful than prose, though postmodernists find this consternating, and don't know quite why it is true. Teleologies are dismissed as opinion rather than fact, unless it is one the postmodernist likes, and then it becomes fact and all alternative explanations are reduced to opinion. Even identifying the existence of teleologies, categorically or individually, becomes difficult, if we presume that words are only symbols and language is a logical code. We can consider it fortunate that teleologies almost always announce themselves with the words 'cause', 'because', 'so that', 'in order to', or 'therefore'. There are others, and sometimes no obvious 'teleological operator' at all, and the very idea of teleologies may slip away at the borders into Socratic Ignorance. But teleologies are vitally important, and how they work is preternaturally consistent, more so than all of the other guidelines and standard constructions of language. They are critical and usually obvious for the same reason, they go beyond language to the root of consciousness itself. They are descriptions of the relationship of causes to effects, descriptions of causes and effects but mostly causes. The effects become a new tautology instead of an old one, once the cause exists and somehow changes the universe with time to become the result. And so teleologies can be seen has how one tautology is transformed into another.

Teleologies are all about time and causality. Time, we know (or do we?) only goes in one direction, from past to future. It is relative, measurements of duration being effected by the velocity of objects within a fixed framework, but it is also absolute, undeniable, inexorable, and strictly sequential. Time changes space, to maintain that sequentiality, that chronology of existences, by changing simultaneity if necessary. What distinguishes cause from effect, in the strictest sense of physics, is simply that the cause precedes the effect and the effect occurs after the cause. On the quantum level, that idea is quite literal: there isn't really any point to asking 'why' or even 'how' the circumstances we identify as a cause and the events we identify as their effect came into being, only that it happened. It just happens that way, every time, "because it does". We can ask "why is there gravity?" and the answer could be that mass warps space time. But like a child vexing their parents, we could then ask "why?" again. Why does mass warp space time? Once again, we could generate a factual answer, that the Higgs Field inhibits changes in momentum or some such, but really we're just rewording the 'because that's how the universe works' answer that was first paraphrased as 'mass warps space time'. But WHY does the Higgs Field inhibit changes in momentum? Well, we could write out some symbols to represent the need for the theory of a Higgs field or space/time, but of course it becomes obvious eventually that we're always just pushing off the fact that there isn't any answer to 'why' other than an otherwise unexplained 'because'. Because that's the way the universe is. But why? If we take this as long as can be reasonable, we'd end up with the ultimate question, "Why is there anything?" The 'cogito ergo sum' answer is because there must be something in order to ask the question. The theistic answer is because God made it so. The quantum theory answer is because something is more stable than nothing. And in each case we are left with, "But, why?"

As that illustration explains, teleologies are often kind of worthless. We like tautologies, we like believing that our facts and our words and our ideas and our beliefs and our opinions and our knowledge are based on logic and physical truth. We like having conclusive answers, that only symbolic math can provide. Teleologies seem pointless a lot of the time because of that child's pestering, "Why?... Why?...Why?..." Because people don't understand teleologies, and postmodernism teaches us to ignore teleologies as subjective because there can be no logical operator in an axiomatic system for 'why', so people don't trust teleologies. Since the chain seems endless, an endless regression like turtles all the way down, we avoid them, and train the wonder out of children, instead. There are still teleologies, though, as much as we might try to shield our children from them because a lot of them can be very embarrassing. Teleologies might seem useless because of the endless chain of them, tautologies more comforting because at least they are final. All teleologies are matters of opinion, but that doesn't stop some of them from being closer to the truth than the average. Later I will give some advice for wrestling with teleologies, but the relevance here is the simple matter of cause and effect. This supposedly unbreakable teleology appears built into the universe, action/reaction, dominoes fall, billiard balls ricochet. Forward teleology, this is called, supposedly the only kind there is. Mostly. In physics, it is the only kind there is. Mostly. There are hints in quantum mechanics, and then when you learn to notice them throughout science, that forward teleology cause and effect isn't as simple or unquestionable as we're used to assuming. Like Newton's theories being enough for routine masses, but Einstein's relativity for light and time and space being preeminent, though unnoticeable in routine conditions. A->time->B, we could symbolize this with, the standard forward teleology that the cause occurs, and inevitably and sequentially, consequentially, the result occurs. "A->time->B" is identical to "A->B". But what is that 'volition' of the universe that really 'causes' results to follow from the effects that precede them? It is different in every single interaction of objects, but it has the same character of being somehow inexplicable, that a universe of forces of energy as particles would hold together in evolving clumps well enough to keep these complex objects we surround ourselves in and the beautiful landscapes and worlds beyond them in a simple enough harmony that life as we experience it is possible, and not so brief and chaotic that nothing more than bacteria could possibly ever survive. Why does anything happen, why isn't the universe just quantum foam randomness?

Causation is not as simple to figure out as we initially think. If you think it is, you haven't thought hard enough about it, hard enough to regret it. One exercise, to make it less painful, is to try to imagine cause and effect without that assumed 'volition of the universe' making the world of mammals and people out of molecular forces, and molecular forces out of quantum wave functions. There is no cause and effect, just an unending sequence of occurrences. It is not the confluence of previous events that results in the effect following what we call a cause. Instead, it is simply the spontaneous occurrence of the effect that 'causes' it to occur, just as the emission of a radioactive particle from the decaying nucleus of an atom spontaneously occurs, 'caused' when a virtual particle occurs, caused by nothing other than being necessary to explain the decay. In this view, it is merely our observation afterwards that 'causes' what we think of as the events that result in that spontaneous occurrence which links them to it. Not causing their existence to be on a physical, ontological level, but causing their consideration as an observable occurrence that we can use to satisfy our need for a cause. On a sufficiently small subatomic scale, this is the only rational view, in fact, because of the extremely mysterious actions that make quantum chromodynamics necessary. If the smallest subatomic forces and particles (which aren't really two different things on that scale) behaved the same as the deterministic "billiard ball" interactions of objects on the larger scales where we can more directly observe them, then cause and effect would be a lot simpler. But then, the universe wouldn't be working the way we can prove it actually does, and there is no real way we can even guess what any such universe, if it could actually exist, would look like or how it would behave. If particles actually behaved like billiard balls subject to simple thermodynamic 'action/reaction' principles, they wouldn't result in the mega-quantum qualitative world of billiard balls and human beings that actually exists. Quantum physics isn't Newtonian objects; it is spooky action at a distance or God playing dice with the universe which characterizes the science of subatomic particles and their freedom from simple cause and effect. Quantum physics doesn't explain it, it merely observes it. Quantum mechanics doesn't exist because we want it to, it exists because we need it to, in order to mathematically predict the physical events we can observe at incredibly small scales. Physics cannot describe *why* a particular radioactive atom emits a neutron, only that it does. Science mathematically models *how* the atom and the particle behave, without providing any justification for doing so, apart from, perhaps, even more primitive mathematical models. There is no 'why' in science in general, not just quantum physics. Science describe what is, it only guesses at why it is that way. Tautologies without teleologies.

Since references keep popping up to quantum effects, I think I should give a more direct description of quantum mechanisms, and why (how) they don't work like Newtonian mechanisms. It all comes down to that much abused word, "quantum". What is it, why am I using it? More than a century ago, it was discovered that subatomic particles don't behave in what was considered rational ways. Rather than being continuous measures, the energy states of electrons came in only discrete quantities, quantums (quanta; the singular is 'quantum', the plural is 'quanta', 'quantums' is a made up bit of gibberish that you aren't supposed to be able to understand, supposedly.) There were no decimal values, only the simplest of fractions, and no amount of smaller measures than a full quantum had any effect on the interactions of particles. The way I saw it explained was as if an electron needed a quarter's worth of energy to move from one state to another, but it didn't matter how many pennies, nickels, or dimes worth of energy you poured into it, it wouldn't be enough; it needed a quarter. What happens to all the spare change, you may wonder, all the energy sub-quanta that disappeared? This is Newtonian thinking: the dimes and nickels can't exist, the only currency is quarters. If you ask 'why' things are like this, the only comprehensible answer is 'because that's how to make the math work out with the experimental results'. We know that the quantum foam of virtual particles and vectors of momentum continually resolves itself into rational substances, objects, and forces, but there doesn't seem to be any teleologies that are necessary or applicable.

So teleologies aren't part of the nuts and bolts part of the universe. We don't know yet exactly how to link up the quantum world with what we think of as the real world of billiard ball interactions and cause and effect. But despite that, we can physically prove that deterministic behavior is predictable at human scales, even though it doesn't occur at subatomic scales. And that only probabilistic behavior, without the Newtonian kind of cause and effect we are used to, occurs at subatomic scales. Even if a vending machine only takes quarters, twenty five pennies is still worth a quarter of a dollar. Once the necessary and sufficient causes exist, at human scales, then the resulting effect occurs, with 100% probability. (Of course, this is tautological, it is circular reasoning: that certainty of results is why the causes are described as "necessary and sufficient".) But the 'why' of causality isn't as simple as we're used to, because it is the same universe at both scales. We could go back and forth about how useful deterministic or probabilistic predictions are in any particular circumstance. We could even consider ejecting the whole idea of deterministic behavior at every scale, saying instead that all 'cause and effect' relationships are always probabilistic, but sometimes the probability is 100%. From this perspective, the seemingly perfectly predictable interactions of billiard balls or 'enough heat makes water boil' determinism are simply special cases of probabilistic behavior that end up merely appearing as if they are non-probabilistic, but are instead deterministic, because of their canny amount of repeatability. The uncanny behavior of quantum dynamics are simply the same probabilistic behavior as the more easily predictable effects at larger scales, but without some averaging of huge numbers of individual interactions that evens things out so that the uncanny behavior appears more canny.

It seems unavoidable to believe that this is in fact the case. Our universe doesn't actually have any 'cause and effect', we simply impose that assumption on our view of the universe because, for reasons we cannot yet explain exactly, it predictably averages out that way. Why would the universe appear as if there is cause and effect at large scales, when there is no real cause and effect, just effects following other effects probabilistically without any known mechanism forcing that to occur? The answer to this 'why' question is just like the answer to the question of "why is the behavior of subatomic particles predictable even in a probabilistic way?" Do you see what I'm saying? Why is the quantum world either as predictable as it is OR as unpredictable as it is? Are these two different questions?

Returning to the actual matter at hand, which is the nature of self-determination, I want to point out that I'm not in any way suggesting that it is quantum effects, chromodynamic, electrodynamic, or probabilistic, that produces the effect we have historically identified as free will, human consciousness. My point in bringing up the uncanny and spooky lack of teleologies at subatomic scales was simply to illustrate that teleologies aren't, apparently, as necessary for an explanation of physics or the objective universe as we assume or insist that they are. I'm certainly not saying we should abandon the idea of cause and effect simply because quantum physics has to, because quantum effects break down at larger scales when the coherence of quantum particles we call 'entanglement' breaks down. I'm sure that real physicists would contradict my very premise, that there is no 'cause and effect' at subatomic scales. When sufficient energy (one full quantum) is added, through whatever means, to an electron, it will, non-randomly, move to a higher state: hence, cause and effect. Subatomic particles do interact predictably, they just don't do so in keeping with our intuitions, our expectations of a deterministic rational universe. But that intuitive perspective of the universe is simply not as accurate or precise as most people think. In fact, most of the time when scientists describe things behaving in keeping with simplistic causality, forward teleologies of physical 'dominoes falling' sequences, that is still a shorthand for much more complicated relationships between initial tautological conditions, causes, and subsequent tautological conditions, effects. This can be easily illustrated by considering medicine rather than science (the distinction will be explained later.) We say that 'smoking causes cancer'. But that isn't true. The truth is that smoking causes cancer to be more likely. There are a lot of people who get lung cancer that never smoked cigarettes. There are a lot of people who smoke cigarettes that never get cancer. So using 'cause' to denote 'results in a greater likelihood of' makes the simplistic teleology appear tautological. Certainly there are some libertarian extremists, and plenty of tobacco company executives, that refuse to accept that smoking causes cancer. But they cannot factually deny or disprove that smoking cigarettes makes developing lung tumors far more common than not smoking does. This same rather straight-forward situation can obviously also be applied to people, not coincidentally often oil company employees, that reject the scientific consensus that CO_2 accumulation in the air results in atmospheric warming through the greenhouse effect and an increased rate of changes in climate. On an even larger yet more personal level, when psychologists and sociologists, or those they talk to, convert "tend to be" into "do" or "are" when describing human behavior, they are substituting a dubious deterministic teleological relationship for a more concrete probabilistic teleology. These situations illustrate the point, but even more subtle instances are more profound examples, from the orbiting of celestial objects (as if chaotic cycles were uniform elliptical paths) to the chemical interactions of atoms and molecules. Our reality is not as simplistic or "binary" is/is not as we envision for the sake of school lessons or emotional comfort.

As I mentioned earlier, this makes (tends to make) teleologies seem pretty pointless, oftentimes or even in their entirety. The postmodern approach to reality is that only tautologies exist, that all teleologies are fictional, or shorthand, that they are metaphorical. In more concrete science, backing away from the problematic areas of medicine or psychology or climatology, the situation doesn't improve, it just becomes less obvious. This is why the more basic 'cause' is replaced by the more nuanced and intricate 'necessary and sufficient conditions' to begin with. This method utilizes hindsight to make what was only probable before it happened into what is described as inevitable after it occurs. The familiar trope "correlation is not causation" is often used to attempt to dismiss relationships between conditions and results that are merely probabilistic or even coincidental. The greater the chances that something will happen after something else happens, the more comfortable we are using the language of causality, and saying that the first thing causes the second. But even if there is only a 1% chance that condition A precedes result B, it is possible to say that A caused B, once B occurs after A. And even if there is a 99% chance that result B follows circumstance A, it is possible, and perhaps even accurate, to say that A didn't cause B. In fact, scientifically speaking (because science is about math and there are no teleologies in mathematics, just tautologies) correlation is the only causation. Causation is merely a sufficiently reliable correlation.

We should accept that the chronological nature of cause and effect in our macro world is the only thing that associates cause and effect, not any other physical principle known to science. Because the effect always occurs once the necessary and sufficient cause exists, and because the necessary and sufficient causes have to exist before the resulting effect occurs, we assume there is a physical force of some kind that must be connecting the two. But it isn't a physical force, it is a mental image. We generate the idea of cause and effect, in our minds. And because of that, we can use it more flexibly than scientific formulas can express.

The primitive mechanism underlying self-determination is this teleological principle, related to the arrow of time, the cause and the effect of chronology. It is possible for us to reverse this arrow in our imaginations, if not in the physical world, making the resulting situation the *cause* of whatever events or occurrences previously happened to *effect* that situation. Cause becomes effect, effect becomes cause. We haven't changed the universe at all, or what objectively happened. We have merely changed how we perceive it and how we understand it and how we describe it. We have flipped the teleology with which we explain what happened. And we do this all the time, literally, whenever we use words or ideas like 'intention' or phrases like 'in order to'. Teleological ideas, which we flip back and forth, making the result the reason something happened, instead of the cause being the reason it occurred.

Our view of science has been a progression of proofs that remove these 'backwards teleologies' from our explanations of what happens in real life, or at least in a scientific laboratory or mathematical model simulating real life. The harder and, frankly, more successfully we do this, the more the scientifically inclined insist that there cannot be any God in the universe, least of all the 'old man in the sky' version of God that our ancient scriptures describe. And yet despite the undeniable and perhaps even startling success at removing backwards teleologies from the larger deterministic scales of the universe, there are two ways this effort or effect of removing God as a reason why things happen has consistently if not universally failed. The first is the undeniable if disconcerting (to the more science minded at least) fact that the more science dismisses backward teleologies as acceptable answers to questions of 'why?', the more people maintain (or, more dismissively, 'cling to') the explanation that there is a God that causes things to happen in some inexplicable and perhaps miraculous way. Aristotle developed the principles of symbolic logic which we have ultimately used as the bedrock foundation of science, thousands of years ago, even before Christ is said to have walked the earth. And yet scientific theory can reject the notion of God all it wants, people refuse (more dismissively, 'stubbornly refuse') to accept that exclusion of divine teleologies as answers to the questions of why things happen as they do and are as they are, at least outside of the scientific laboratories where they can be most rigidly tested.

The second place that the rejection of backwards teleologies has been unsuccessful is, ironically, within those same scientific laboratories. Rather than simply reject backwards teleologies, by reducing them to tautologies of cause and effect, the way literally anybody expected, science was eventually forced to admit that it could only reject all teleologies entirely. Both forward and backward, whether 'cause and effect' or 'intention and therefore'. "God does not play dice with the universe", one of the smartest humans who has ever lived famously said. And despite being one of the smartest humans who has ever lived, Albert Einstein was proven incorrect. We can't know if it is God doing it, but chance, mere probability, the opposite of any deterministic behavior, is what happens in the universe, always, and as far as we can tell, that is the entirety of what makes it a universe. In real science, there is no cause and effect, there are only necessary and sufficient circumstances and observable affects. 'This happens and then that happens' more than 'this happens because that happened'. Science explains why things happen categorically, by providing mathematical models that predict that they happen, statistically. Not really why, so much as what. Why things are the way they are, science leaves for philosophy and history to determine. Only the empirical parts are science, however much philosophy or history might be needed to describe the empirical science. Science itself learned to deal with reverse teleologies, a kind of teleology that starts with a result and works backward to the cause; whatever preceded an effect caused it, whether the link between the two is simple but fictional, rhetorical but unknown, or outrageously complex but only probabilistic. Reverse teleologies work when you have a lot of potential examples, and so to explain the ones that work out the way you want you invent a cause. In science, of course, you then test that cause against empirical data, to determine if it is necessary enough and sufficient enough to be probabilistically predictable, which substitutes for deterministic causality. The probabilistic consistency, no matter how large the data set you need to evidence it, leads to the appearance of a cause and effect that is more narrative, instead of a hypothesis about forward teleologies that deterministically link cause and effect. Effect<-cause<-effects would symbolize reverse teleologies, one of the two kinds of backward teleologies.

Inverse teleologies, the other kind of backward teleology, are still basically forbidden in science. The 'soft sciences' of psychology and sociology necessarily accept and even necessitate them, but that is part of what makes them soft sciences. (In POR, they're considered 'humanology', a serious and empirical research discipline, at least some times, but something apart from objective science.) Inverse teleologies are the impossible ones, the effect and cause being simply inverted, with force of will being the magic that converts intention to thermodynamics. Inverse teleologies only make sense as statements of intention, application of what we used to call free will and now know is self-determination. Perhaps the only thing we can determine is whether these teleologies apply to ourselves, but if so, that is more than any other creature, to our knowledge. The only other entity in the universe that we can unquestionably apply inverse teleologies for is God. God is the idea that an omniscient or omnipotent self-aware entity <u>intentionally</u> caused a result. This self-aware conscious intent is not simply observation of a backwards teleology, but enactment of it. Human inverse teleologies are involved whenever we express consciousness, desires, wants, or intentions. Not just for ourselves, or each other, but for anything, as a literary anthropomorphization. Infusing a self-aware perspective on objects, animals, or even abstract things such as communities, companies, states, projecting thoughts into an imagined head and goals as the cause for the actions taken to effect/affect those goals, these are all inverse teleologies. Only humans actually generate inverse teleologies, but then, only humans can observe or be aware of any teleologies. When a beaver builds a dam <u>in order to</u> dam a stream, it is not consciously associating the goal of damming the stream with the actions of building the dam. In whole, and in each subtask for the greater action, from the beaver's perspective it is merely performing actions that coincidentally result in the circumstance of a river being dammed because all of the beavers that don't perform the actions that result in the building of dams have died out, leaving it a genetic robot simply following its instincts. It isn't even building a dam, it is just taking whatever actions it's neurochemistry cause it to, which end up damming the stream. No conscious awareness, no planning or intention to achieve a goal, is needed. The result of having the river dammed is, from the animal's unconscious perspective, a fortunate contingency, albeit one the beaver's survival unknowingly relies on. What makes human cognition different from animal cunning is not simply to describe teleologies of intent, but to formulate and implement them.

So it shouldn't seem as incredible or shocking as it might when I tell you that the reason why people have always believed we have free will is because we have the otherwise-miraculous power that no other system, creature, or thing in the known universe has: The ability to flip teleologies, willy nilly, without any regard at all for any scientific or physical principles or theories. We can say that we did something *because we wanted it to happen*, rather than because the neurochemical interactions inside the cells of our brain tissue caused us to do so, or made us want it to happen. We can make the expectation of an a/effect the cause, the purpose and origin, of our actions. This replaces the inevitability of physical cause and effect with a purely intellectual (perhaps imaginary, but purposefully imagined) force that cannot be physically measured. We used to call it 'free will', and believe it was a magical power granted by a divine deity, or simply an unpredictability because of the complexity of neurochemistry. It is neither, and it isn't free will. It is self-determination: the ability to decide and <u>determine</u> for ourselves whether our actions are the result of the neurochemical interactions in our bodies or the cause that resulted in those neurochemical interactions. Our expectation of what those actions will cause in the external physical world becomes the impetus for causing those events to occur. We do things *in order to* achieve a result, not *because* we are helpless but to enact what our hormones or neurotransmitters or other molecules and subatomic forces make unavoidable due to the laws of physics.

That is not just the root of the theory of self-determination, but the reason for the theory of self-determination, after all. The common, postmodern, supposedly scientific, view of human behavior is that we are really just biological robots, programmed by natural selection and operant conditioning through genetic instinct and pavlovian responses. This fatalistic determinism seems unavoidable, and causes a great deal of anxiety and depression, along with academic philosophical pessimism. It isn't even all that successful in helping addicts cope with their dependencies. Many people might expect that once you explain to a drug addict that their craving for their psychoactive substance of choice is nothing more than their brain causing them, helplessly, to repeat whatever behavior previously gave their neural equipment a dose of dopamine, that their addiction should be cured. After all, there are reasons they want to stop using to begin with, the chaos or calamity they have 'caused' in their lives through drug-seeking behavior or as the 'result' of intoxication. If you believe in free will, they should simply be able to decide not to experience those results or seek those causes. If you don't believe in free will or any other ability of self-determination, having the knowledge that they are merely biological robots programmed by genetics and pavlovian conditioning should likewise enable them to choose to no longer steal money to get high, or ruin their relationships with lies so they can get high, or simply enjoy getting high when they know it will only lead to disease and death rather than anything but very short-term pleasure. Or perhaps you would think, whether or not you believe that free will exists or self-determination of any sort doesn't, that all addicts will simply always be in thrall to their dopamine spikes, or whatever other chemical interactions of neurotransmitters is responsible for their supposedly inevitable behavior, no matter how fatalistic. But then how and why should they ever want to stop being addicts? And how is it that sometimes they do stop getting high, despite wanting to get high? Do they want to stop, or do they merely want to want to stop?

People don't usually stop their addictive behavior when they are informed it is due to operant conditioning, but they do still sometimes stop, both when they are told about their genetic slavery but also when they are not so informed. Some people dismiss the results of the thumbswitch experiment with an explanation that our minds have veto power over the choice our brains make before we can possibly be consciously aware of them. But pressing the button isn't a special case, and our brains make all of our choices before we can be consciously aware of our decisions. Addiction, whether to drugs or anything else dismissed as simply a cause of serotonin or dopamine or some other chemical flooding or leaving our synapses or not, isn't a special case. With the thumbswitch experiment, some philosophers or psychologists insist that only a trivial or limited examination like a slideshow would be affected by the choice->action->decision teleological chain. In more complicated or less limited cases found in real life, they claim, it is the decision->choice->action teleology that provides either free will, if they believe in that, or volition despite a lack of free will, if they don't. Likewise, the matter of addiction, whether to drugs or anything else, is a special case where we either prove we have free will negatively, by failing to change our behavior despite a confessed desire and being physically capable of doing so, or a special case where we fail to prove we have free will positively, by doing the same thing. There are enough successes, where a confessed desire appears to result in avoidance of the bad behavior, that the mirage of free will is maintained, despite being illusory. And just as the connection or turn-over point where quantum unpredictability of forces somehow results in non-quantum deterministic behavior of physical objects has not, and perhaps cannot, be explained by science, the point or method that links the helplessness of operant conditioning and Darwinistic/genetic inevitability to our conscious experiences and volitional intentions has not, and perhaps cannot, be explained with empirical experiments and mathematical formulas.

Are you helpless but to embody whatever your neurotransmitter levels force you to think and feel? Or are you a metaphysical soul, inhabiting a mere physical shell that responds to your every command? This is not a once and done either/or choice, it is a decision that you make in real time, every time you contemplate behavior you have already started taking but the world has not yet recognized, or think about past behavior you have taken, but don't understand why you took it despite being helpless but to admit that you did. Most of the time, admittedly, we can simply dismiss the issue as foresight or hindsight. If our bodies are already going to push a switch because our brains chose to change the picture we're viewing, but we haven't moved our thumb yet, it is foresight, and we wish that we could have a veto power to circumvent the nerve impulses from continuing to travel through our tissues. If it is past behavior we regret, it is hindsight, and we can insist that we simply didn't know for certain what the results of our action would be, or don't know why we took an action even though we were the ones who took it. Either way, we would be relying on our own imperfect knowledge of the past, present, or future, to explain how we have free will, or how we don't. We're accepting not just ignorance, but the impossibility of complete knowledge, as an excuse for our bad selection from among better alternatives.

What good is a mental system that can't cope with uncertainty or lack of knowledge? The truth is the universe is always going to be pretty uncertain, whether because of quantum or chaotic unpredictability, or a lack of data, or a lack of certainty about the right method of analyzing what data we do have. And it is even more true that our mental system must be capable of coping with a lack of knowledge, since that is unavoidably the way it begins. We are born with an absence of experience, rather than an encyclopedic amount of data concerning the universe we are inexplicably born into. Certainly we could substitute the genetic palimpsest of our chromosomes for this imagined encyclopedia of data we would like to have about the world we're trying to deal with, but that is begging the question. It returns us to the actual conundrum, that is: why do we have a mental system that almost unerringly results in conscious awareness? We could propose the theory that all creatures have the 'accumulated effective knowledge' of genetic inheritance, and the neurological memory is a more dynamic addition, but this still leaves us wondering why our mentality is in any way distinct from other mammals, as evidenced by our development of both technological civilization and art. Should we not presume, until every possible explanation is entirely exhausted, that we have self-awareness for a reason? Doesn't it make sense to hypothesis that the reason we have self-awareness is so that we can determine our behavior? Lack of free will seems to thwart this, and so free will has been accepted as real even by those scientists, doctors, and lawyers that are most intimately familiar with its nonexistence. The ultimate result is philosophical pessimism, wherein progress is impossible; we can take actions, but we have no justification for calling the results an improvement over the previous circumstances. Most scientists, doctors, lawyers, and other philosophers give in to sentiment before reaching that extreme, and satisfy themselves with a vague shrug of the shoulders, accepting either a soft spirituality or a hard agnosticism in place of any clear moral or intellectual conviction.

The theory of self-determination in POR is the unavoidable truth, based on both our personal experiences and empirical demonstrations like the thumbswitch experiment. We do have the ability to determine our behavior, as our intuitive sentiments consistently suggest. But we do not have the ability to control our behavior, as the theory of free will insists. Still, we do not entirely lack any ability to direct our behavior, as the theory of fatalism requires; we can be apart from the time stream, as observers rather than part of the mechanism, without a metaphysical consciousness. By using self-determination to control our attitude rather than our movements, we motivate our behavior. Self-determination isn't a direct method for controlling or commanding our actions. But it is vital, irreplaceable, and both necessary and sufficient, for enabling us to direct our actions, regardless of whether the metaphor 'direct' you envision is simply pointing a light or a finger, or the more complex orchestration of an auteur instructing actors. Self-determination isn't the magical or mysterious yet physical power to cause our movements, feelings, or desires. It is merely the ability to determine whether we interpret those things using a standard (forward) teleology that goes cause-->effect or a backwards teleology that goes effect-->cause. The former is the one that unquestionably and absolutely models everything that happens in physics, chemistry, and biology. The latter, backwards teleologies, are what describes intention, design, and conscious decision-making. It is all too easy to dismiss backwards teleologies as simply fiction, but to do so requires us to dismiss the desires and dignity of human beings entirely *and leaves us with no comprehensible reason for the existence of consciousness or self-awareness.* The theory of self-determination doesn't just provide an adequate and important explanation for the existence of conscious experiences, a reason for self-awareness, but it supplies a mechanism that links the existence of the ability to consciously experience things and the awareness we have of both self and the principles of cause and effect. The connection of consciousness to causality is not that either one simply results in the other, the simple teleology of physical inevitability. Instead, the connection between causality and consciousness is both the dependence and the independence of these two things. They are dependent because consciousness results from causality and causality results from consciousness. They are independent because of the complexity of backwards teleologies, which are inherent in our ability to imagine if things had been different than they were, or will be different than they are, or may be different than we expect or even know, or at least believe, that they are. Causality results in consciousness, through some indefinite neurobiological mechanism. And consciousness results in causality, by inventing teleologies to explain why things are as they are or aren't as we imagine they could have been. Causality causes self-determination, self-determination causes causality.

The standard theory of free will is presented by postmodernist philosophers, scientists, and even doctors as if it were compatible with the standard teleology of physical cause and effect: our conscious thoughts are the cause, and our actions are the effect. Our conscious thoughts are themselves caused, by synaptic chemistry and preference, bias, or logic. But unlike everything else in existence, all of which are both the effect of a previous cause and the cause of subsequent events, we innately think of our thoughts as breaking the teleological chain; they are not caused, they are cause. Not causes that result in effects, but effects that result in causes. The philosophers and doctors can't avoid the theoretical, practical and empirical evidence that free will has to be considered a broad and unexplained exception to, an exemption from, the universal absolute of physical teleologies, the immutable logical chain of cause and effect. Teleologies of intention are simply wishful thinking, delusions, or perhaps just a misapprehension of cause and effect, to the postmodern conception. This last, 'misapprehension' explanation, is similar to the way evolutionary biology is described as 'why' things occur, when in actuality it is simply a recognition of 'how' things have occurred through the actions of random chance and natural selection. Fish species living in dark caves do not lose their eyes over generations *in order to* spare themselves the expense of developing organs that will not benefit them. In reality, they lose their eyes over time *because* there is no longer the force of competition ensuring that those fish who do maintain their sight can have more offspring than those that don't maintain that sense. But the 'reverse teleology' explanation is more convenient and comprehensible, and even the most dedicated evolutionary biologists will rely on it to communicate the mechanism of natural selection. That is not the 'inverse teleology' of intention that we are inventing when we describe our actions as being the result of our desires and expectations, or imagine God doing the same by employing Its even more awesome omnipotence. However, it is so similar that it can become almost hopelessly difficult to distinguish the two, since they are both contrary to the physical, or 'forward' teleologies of mechanical deterministic results we refer to as cause and effect. It would even be possible, philosophically, to construct a theory that describes every act of reasoning involving intention or planning in this way: every possible thought occurs in our brains, but only those that most closely correlate to the behavior that follows survive while all the others evaporate without evidence, leaving us with the appearance that our thoughts cause our behavior. It would be incredibly difficult to maintain this theory across an incomprehensibly large number of human thoughts and human actions, but it has the benefit of not needing to distinguish human actions from all other actions of all other things in existence. That is a benefit that some would find attractive, since in the postmodern age, the denial that there is anything 'special' or important and unique about the human species has become so fashionable it is considered mandatory, despite being contrary to the evidence. I don't mean the evidence of the existence of our civilization or technology or aspirations, though these are each convincing alone as far as I can tell. Instead I mean the evidence that we are able to wonder whether or not we are special; conclusive proof that we are indeed special, since no mechanism or confirmation that any other objects or entities, biological or not, have or can engage in that speculation exists. This is the same reasoning used for Descartes' notorious declaration Cogito Ergo Sum. His thinking was that the ability to question whether he exists is both a necessary predicate and unavoidable confirmation of that existence. The importance of his philosophical tenet is not a 'cry in the wilderness' kind of thing, "I exist because I wish I existed." But nevertheless, his existential position was that "I think therefore I am" is the only possible direct confirmation of his existence; "Wishing to exist is proof of my existence." He knew that anything else that demonstrates his real objective actuality must be derived at least partially from outside his brain, and that requires assuming the validity of the sense data that he was well aware could be mistaken, unreliable, even fraudulent.

Reality

Let's consider the ramifications of this new awareness of the relationship between consciousness and causality. Careful exploration of the scientific teleology, physical cause and effect we think of as being more aligned with the arrow of chronological time, unerringly if not inevitably results in the recognition that the objective universe we subjectively presume we exist within is a 'bottom up' affair. Physics does not explain why or even how our physical reality, which seems to behave deterministically at least some times, manifests consistently as a result of the non-deterministic lower level quantum interactions of physical forces. Nevertheless, it happens so consistently that we can and do assume that it requires no 'top down' influence: each particle in an object behaves in principle, in every way, exactly as it would if that particle were part of some other object. The interaction of particles, atoms, even molecules are with other particles, atoms, and molecules, respectively, not the objects those components result in. There aren't special behaviors of electrons that are part of a bacterium that are any different from the behaviors of electrons that aren't. This 'particle/atom' boundary is the most startling and counter-intuitive, but it isn't actually any different than all the others that our scientific perspective of reality produces. It is simply the most noticeable, because of the unintuitive behavior of subatomic forces. When ancient philosophers envisioned breaking a bit of something in half, and then in half again, and on and on, they imagined they'd get to the smallest piece of something, and it would be solid. But it isn't, it is this weird quasi-mechanistic almost conglomerate particle, made up in turn of other even weirder conglomerate particles, none of which are solid but are just wave functions. How the behavior of atomic forces results in the statistical averaging of results of those forces we call 'material science', how material science produces the fascinating intricacy of chemistry, and when and how that chemistry turns into the nearly miraculous mystery of biology, these are the same kind of boundaries. In each case, if we are being adequately rigorous in our logic, we have to accept that the behavior we see on the 'higher' level is an inevitable consequence of the behavior that occurs on the 'lower' plane, but that we are unable to exactly explain why. We can only demonstrate that it invariably occurs.

The accepted philosophical term for this side-stepping of the absence of noticeably important teleological explanations concerning why higher level behavior is related to but not easily predictable from lower level behavior in complex systems is "emergent properties". As is the postmodern habit, giving it a name is used as an excuse for dismissing the conundrum of its existence, for assuming the high priests of science have thereby explained both how it exists and why it exists. Only those particular scientists who specifically study any one particular variety of 'emergent property' then need to consider that it is not just unexplained but inexplicable; all other scientists, as well as amateur hyper-rationalists, can then enthusiastically pretend that it is both explicable and explained, in relatively blissful ignorance.

On the matter of the critically emergent property of consciousness, even when it comes to the biochemical activities in the neural equipment of other apes, our closest genetic relatives, or impressively vocal and sociable cetaceans that many people think of as possibly or at least potentially superior to our own intellect, we can and should recognize that it is the 'blind actions' of physical forces that produce and embody all the various chains of 'cause and effect' that we could describe or observe. The entire universe is based on 'bottom up' causality. But not all of reality, because once you get to us, that approach simply fails. Regardless of whether the 'forward teleologies' of cause and effect or the 'reverse teleologies' of the more complex selection and affect approach are taken, neither fatalism or free will can entirely and adequately explain what is going on. Only the 'inverse teleology' of intention, or 'effect and cause' in opposition to 'cause and effect' matches the behavior we observe, and only that can justify the meaning or purpose of its existence. Nowhere else in the universe, so far, but in ourselves; because we have theory of mind, we know that we have intentions, inverse teleological motivations, we can want to not want what we want, and not want to want what we want to want.

I would be willing to accept that we are nothing more than genetic robots programmed by natural selection and operant conditioning, if it could be demonstrated to me why consciousness exists in human beings, but not any other creatures, since they are all genetic robots programmed by natural selection and operant conditioning, too. There are a number of ways to approach this argument in contradiction to my position. For one, it could be theorized that consciousness isn't necessary in human beings, or that it doesn't provide any ability to transcend our existence as genetic biological robots. Our brains might or might not be computers, programmed by either DNA or conditioning or both, but consciousness could just be a side-effect or an unrelated occurrence. There isn't any logical way to refute those ideas, other than to point out that they both seem unlikely and leave unexplained both the reason consciousness exists at all, and the mechanism that causes it to occur. Philosophers can posit that no humans actually have consciousness, that instead we are all simply what they call "p-zombies", simulating creatures with consciousness, pretending for each other that we are self-aware, *acting as if* self-determination were possible but without actually experiencing consciousness, self-awareness, or self-determination. In this view, 'free will' is simply a measure of unpredictability, partially or possibly shared by not just all creatures, but all objects and even every molecule, atom, and particle that exists, and even perhaps virtual or imaginary ones that don't, really. This obviously makes the whole mass of theory pointless, but it is true that, captive in the grip of philosophical pessimism, some philosophers feel certain that existence itself is pointless, so being pointless would be a mark in a theory's favor rather than against it. Any theory that has a point, is considered to have purpose, is expounded with some intention, is by nature a self-serving delusion from their perspective.

I have to dismiss all that kind of musing both completely and even forcefully. If every person (except, according to Descartes, the "I" that is each of us in turn and therefore all of us) is not conscious but simply behaves as if they were, I must insist on asking "why?" Not simply 'to what purpose' but also 'through what mechanism'? The distinction between 'why' and 'how' and 'what' melts away when we examine each or any, as importantly but inexplicably as the entanglement of quantum particles when observed too directly. I do insist that consciousness exists, and is the self-awareness and self-determination we think it is, and I do insist that it is necessary to explain human behavior, and most explosively of all, I must and will insist that the mechanism of teleological flipping, arbitrary inversion of cause and effect into purpose and intent to suit our whims, our desires, and our goals, is both the cause and the e/affect, physically, of that consciousness. I mean this literally, scientifically, and conclusively: the mechanism of consciousness is language, specifically the capacity of language to represent inverse teleologies. The ability to not simply have intentions, but to hypothesis that other creatures have intentions, is the theory of mind: the thing that both generates and results from consciousness. Earlier I tried (perhaps successfully, perhaps not, for reasons you may be only beginning to understand now) to make a distinction between "a theory of mind" and "theory of mind". But really the difference is that there is only one true theory of mind, and all others aren't actually theory of mind, but simply proposed mechanisms of consciousness that aren't actually true: hypotheses of cognition. 'Theory of mind' is 'the theory of mind'; to imagine it is possible that others have minds is the only existence of our own minds. It is both cause and effect. It is the proof there is no ontological distinction that can be made between cause and effect, no categorical connection between them other than chronology. Forward teleologies are often (or always) just as fictional as reverse teleologies are. We imagine that a possible circumstance somehow 'causes' the resulting conditions, even when we have to invent a mechanism. No other creature or animal can do this, that is why we are so much smarter than all the others, and why we can develop mathematical science and other forms of empirical research, and civilization and society and morality and rights. Not because we can do mathematical calculations to prove things, but because we can use language to describe things, and can perceive things like time and causality that non-conscious creatures cannot.

You are not a computer, your mind is not the result or embodiment of a mathematical process. Yes, the forces of physics cause chemical interactions, and chemical interactions cause biological processes, and biological processes cause mental behavior. But mental behavior is much more complicated than simply 'that which results from biological processes', because it can be and is influenced from the 'top down', whether supernatural or self-determining, and biological and chemical and physical processes can't be and aren't. Physical processes are purely and always "bottom up", because they can neither perceive nor imagine. But we can. And it is worth noting that it doesn't matter, in general or even sometimes in any particular instance, whether our 'top down' belief is a perception of something real or just the imagining of something that isn't real. What "real" even means melts into epistemological and ontological uncertainty, leaving us with the same existential uncertainty that left Descartes stuck at 'cogito ergo sum' unless a benevolent deity granted him a rational universe to exist in.

Let's go back over this again, and consider some of the more difficult points of this reasoning. It is the contention and conviction of the Philosophy Of Reason that our brain makes choices using what may indeed amount to calculations, mathematical processes, but that our consciousness, our conscious minds, are not limited by any mathematical processes, and don't cause those calculations to be executed. How can this be, we might wonder, if those minds are themselves the result of those same brains? How can we be in conscious control of our decisions, even if those decisions are simply a choice between using forward or inverse teleologies, if those decisions occur within our brains, and the choices our brains make are the unavoidable if not inevitable product of unconscious (not 'subconscious' but unconscious) biological neural networks of physical (if unspecified) impulses? Another, hopefully less convoluted, way of addressing this is, "How can we be in control of our words if we are not in control of our brains?"

All we can do, given this paradoxical conundrum, is contemplate the validity of a 'top down' notion. Not that we <u>must</u> invent God and an immortal soul to justify or explain our existence, our "free will", our self-determination, but simply that we <u>can</u> do so. Or use some other excuse, mental image, or hypothesis. It remains possible, however incredible or heretical it might be as a scientific thesis, that the seemingly random, unpredictable, non-teleological behavior of individual sub-atomic particles, however statistically predictable, isn't really random and non-teleological. Instead, it could be that the 'predictably unpredictable' nature of quantum behavior is evidence that the physical universe isn't so entirely 'bottom up' in construction. It is possible, although it isn't necessary in a POR worldview, that the quantum world somehow does what is required to maintain the consistency of larger scale objects and events, and that explains the counter-intuitive results when we try to isolate that quantum behavior from the rest of the universe of macroscopic objects in a scientific experiment. Perhaps the incomprehensibility of Bell's Inequality is a result of experiments that explore this behavior, just as light somehow 'knows' if we are measuring it as particles or waves in demonstrations such as the 'split slit' experiment. Again, there is no connection between subatomic quantum physics and the POR theory of self-determination, but these are fascinating issues nevertheless, as dual and potentially parallel revelations about human perceptions. The real issue is not whether there could be any macro-world 'essence' that can change micro-world quantum behavior, but simply the question of why the seeming regularity of material substance and the seeming regularity of the standard model of physics has the demonstrably irregular construction of atoms in between. Science, as always, makes do with merely stating that it is so, rejecting the very notion that there can be any teleology, any reason why it is so. Just more precise and supposedly more reliable statements about what is, and a declaration that it is so; at most, a reverse teleology, that it is so because all of the alternatives fail to manifest.

Another illustration of the consternation inherent in expecting the world around us to behave in a way that is mathematically consistent and 'bottom up' is meteorology. Not as a science, but as a scientific principle. We are led to believe that the imprecision of weather predictions is an artifact of our lack of information. Supposedly, if we could model both the position and the velocity of every particle in the atmosphere, we can perfectly predict the weather, if we had sufficient computer power. But this perspective ignores the very real and important limit on such knowledge known as Heisenberg's Uncertainty Principle. It is a fact that it is simply not possible, and can't ever become possible, to know both the position and the velocity of any single particle [to an arbitrary level of precision] to begin with. Does this make weather prediction impossible? No, but it does make perfect weather predictions impossible. Despite our scientific assumption that physical forces and substances must always behave in accordance with mathematical principles, those physical forces and substances don't comply with our expectations. This imprecision is compounded by chaotic affects, the sensitivity to initial conditions and non-linear effects driving the magnitude of the computer power necessary to predict behavior towards infinity. We once thought of the world as all matter and predictable determinism, then we learned that probabilistic behavior is predictable on average. But only on average. If we can be absolutely certain that something will happen 70% of the time, that isn't absolute knowledge, that's just a calculated probability. Absolute knowledge would be knowing which 70%, and why. The complexities of meteorology are iconic, but not isolated. Heisenberg's Uncertainty Principle doesn't imbue the atmosphere with the unpredictability of self-determination, but it is not perfectly predictable through direct mathematical modeling, nevertheless. The standard, postmodernist, interpretation of this issue is that it is simply a matter of complexity and chaos. The interactions between all the molecules that make up the air being too complex to calculate, and the sensitivity to initial conditions exceeds the precision of our measurements.

But another possibility, or perhaps simply another perspective, is that the atmosphere exhibits a 'top down' organization that cannot be explained by current physics, which rejects the possibility of top down behavior and substitutes a fait accompli argument that statistical probability has to be enough to 'cause' all meteorological phenomenon. Describing weather as top down would be contrary to scientific principles, but that alone wouldn't make it incoherent. And, indeed, both amateurs and experts alike talk about the weather using backwards teleologies all the time. The difference between forwards cause and effect teleologies, reverse teleologies of selection, and inverse teleologies of intention, becomes academic in complex systems like atmospheric conditions because even the forward ones most acceptable to science are approximations and probabilistic rather than mechanical and deterministic. Does heat cause an increase in atmospheric pressure, or does an increase in atmospheric pressure cause heat? The difference is moot, one is a function of the other, which is a function of the other. Science simply described what is, not why it is.

The ontological theory of POR, self-determination, isn't dependent on, and doesn't condone, a hypothesis that quantum forces are complying with 'top down' teleologies, nor that the atmosphere could, either. This discussion is meant simply to illustrate the difficulty of envisioning how our brains can produce both our choices and our decisions, but the former can be explained as the unavoidable result of a neural network while the latter cannot be so simply dismissed. In the end, this affect is in keeping with our intuition and empirical results. It can be demonstrated that a very large majority of people's actions can be accomplished without conscious control. Athletes experiencing 'flow' and somnambulant behavior like 'sleep eating' are extreme if not stark examples of our brains producing movements without our conscious minds directing it. Most of our actions, and the belief we have that they only occur because we consciously will them to, can be explained as simply our mind's awareness of what our brain has chosen to do slightly before any external verification or ramifications are evident. When you raise your arm 'because you want to', that isn't because your conscious mind ordered it to, but because your brain caused it to and your conscious mind decided to take credit for it. If your arm raised when you didn't intend it, or did not move when you wanted it to, there is no doubt you could explain why. But we know you can be fooled, like watching yourself play a keyboard with someone else's fingers.

Learning to accept, understand, and embrace self-determination is revelatory. Abandoning the false belief in free will can be daunting, admittedly. It took me years, even decades, to even dare to believe that not ever bothering to even try to consciously direct my actions doesn't actually result in any change in what those actions are. It didn't take quite as long to notice that it wasn't just that it is possible, but that it is beneficial. Like every other human being on this planet right now, I was raised, steeped, entirely indoctrinated, even brainwashed into being a postmodernist. Giving up free will will result in bad behavior, both moral failures and simple mistakes, this is a given in postmodernist philosophies, all of them. It seems insane to think otherwise. We could practically define failures and mistakes as those times we aren't exerting conscious executive authority over our every movement, if we were more interested in definitions than in meaning. The general rule is that the delusion of free will is universal and impenetrable, but there are counter-examples. Accepting the POR theory of self-determination is quite like when "Born Again Christians" describe themselves as 'giving their life to Jesus'. In fact, spiritually accepting God into your life, putting yourself in the arms of the Lord, or acknowledging a "higher power" in a 12-step program, are, in essence and in reality, simply rejecting the false notion that free will is of any value at all. And this is a truth, *even if the theistic beliefs these experiences or convictions are wrapped in are as delusional as the theory of free will is* to begin with. Free will is a fiction that is only ever used to evade our responsibility or to justify insulting other people. POR doesn't just dismiss free will for ethical reasons, but for more practical ones as well. We could even argue that this strengthens the value and validity of the POR morality and the theology it is based on, that our ethics themselves are not a goal but a side-effect, and all the more constant and consistent for being that, because it is not about wanting to want, but simply knowing and accepting what is true. To know the truth about human behavior and our own life experience is both calming and invigorating, it brings both peace and motivation. When POR describes the cause of all the problems in the world as a single issue, postmodernism; all anger, all depression, all anxiety, anxiousness, and angst; when our philosophy attributes every argument to Socrates' Error, every attack, every fight, every war and insult and degradation; when we say that the Information Processing Theory of Mind (IPTM) dismissal of human reasoning is anathema, a petty taunt, an all-consuming self-righteous fiction, it is because of this: unhappiness comes from our efforts to insist we have free will when we don't. The frustration and desperation that comes from being confronted with this seemingly awful truth, our lack of free will, is not because it isn't true, but because you've been misled by other peoples' insistence that it must be true: that if you do not have conscious control over your behavior, than you cannot have self-determination of any sort. In reality, neither you, nor any other human being, has ever managed to be in conscious control of your body, ever even once for a moment. It is all too easy to assume and insist that this means you are helpless, and that failure to try to be in control leads to bad behavior or moral failure. In reality, it is trying to second-guess our feelings and actions, rather than simply double-check that they are sincere and moral, that leads to all of the ills that postmodernists blame on irrationality or human weakness. Failure to be in control leads to anxiety, existential angst, and depression. But it is not the failing to be in control that causes this, it is the trying to be in control that does so, because it is impossible to succeed.

Recognizing the proper relationship between our actions and the contemplation of those actions we call our decisions doesn't just free us from the oppression of false morality, it empowers our ability to correct our mistakes, avoid future errors, and feel gratitude and hope in a personally and socially productive way. We reject all false moralities, and find the true morality by doing so. Knowing how self-determination works means you aren't helpless just because you can't change the past, including whether your brain chose to do something you later wish you hadn't. It is only your conscious reasoning and intentions that can cause a different result in the future. Being good doesn't mean having been good, it means wanting to do good. And even if you're going to describe that in words relating to ancient mythology or atheist biological imperative, instead of the more accurate framework of self-determination and reasoning, it is still better than the alternative. Whether it adopts fatalism or free will, that alternative philosophy of postmodernism is counter-productive and corrosive. Both endless self-recrimination and lack of self-awareness ensue when postmodernist philosophy is internalized, the former being more damaging to the self and the latter more damaging to society.

That returns us to the thorny question of how to distinguish between the biochemical unavoidability of choices and the reasonable control of attitudes. How can we even think anything in contradiction to our choices if our thoughts are the result of that same biochemically unavoidable process? It is one thing to tell someone that whether you raise your hand is an act of volition, but it is another to claim that we control our thoughts. And if we can't control our thoughts, how is it that we can take responsibility for our reasoning? How can we have 'responsibility' at all, if our actions aren't ever the result of our conscious decisions, but begin to occur before those decisions are made, and might well be completed even before we are aware a selection from possible choices has been executed in our brains? That is what happens in the thumbswitch experiment that makes it so illuminating and confusing at the same time. Because the delay of the 'choice' impulse in propagating through our cerebrum and also down our arm when the subject 'chose' to hit the switch, but the 'decision' to want to change the slide always, **always** happened just after that choice, but never truly before it, not even the subjects could describe what happened in any way other than that the machine *anticipated*, perfectly and without error *predicted* the subject's decision, rather than merely detecting a desire that hadn't yet gone beyond contemplation or tardily following from a choice that caused their thumb's movement.

We have the impression of conscious control, the illusion of free will, the fantasy of mind over matter, because we've been taught to misinterpret our consciousness as being compatible with such a process. We learn to interpret every moment when we have no need for free will or conscious control, because our behavior already meets our desires, as a successful use of free will and 'executive functions'. We are taught to misinterpret every proof that free will and conscious control don't exist, that they are an illusory fantasy that is neither necessary or productive, as mental weakness or some other character flaw. We are told that without this fiction, our activities and even our desires will devolve and inevitably lead to ethical failures and moral hazards. This is done, by ourselves and by others, because there is a continuous and intentional desire for there to be a physical force to morality in the material world that it lacks. One can invent God to provide that moral force, or invent a moral imperative to biological evolution that is just as fictional. Or, now, with POR, one can accept that it is the lack of any moral power in the physical universe that causes us to wish there were one, and it is providing whatever limited and imperfect moral power of our own, in our deeds and in our words, that is the meaning and purpose of the very existence of human consciousness. Indeed, wanting and trying to do good in the world, not by exerting conscious control over our bodies but by making reasonable decisions about our lives, is not simply the cause and the effect of consciousness, it is the content and very being of consciousness and the self-awareness and self-determination that it makes possible, but not inevitable.

Ultimately, this issue of how to differentiate our biological form beyond our conscious control and our intellectual form that directs our behavior, ultimately without controlling it in direct and proximate ways, comes down to the same difference as between our words and our [other] actions. Nowhere is the 'split horizon' of whether we only do what we intend or ever intend to do something without realizing it more stark and visceral than in our use of language. We consider it a far more deliberate act, more intimately tied to intentional volition, to speak our thoughts, our minds, and our opinions, whether sincerely or not, whether honestly or not, whether truthfully or not. The remove between the gross muscle movements of raising a hand and the fine orchestration of generating words seems trivial when considered either existentially or in detail. If speaking or writing isn't really categorically exempt from our lack of conscious control, how can language provide any relent from our 'biological robot' existence as expressed by the postmodern Information Processing Theory of Mind? Can simply making certain sounds or marks really be anything different than any other actions? The answer to that question requires us to consider whether words are just sounds or marks used to symbolically label terms in a mathematical code, or something more than that. It is not in the uttering or publishing of words that their transcendence above squeaks and shapes can be proven, but only in the hearing and reading. The act of communication is not simply a more capable or nuanced method of signaling, it is an exchange of ideas that only occur in a reasoning person's mind, and can only be recognized by a likewise reasoning person's mind. Even if it is merely a statistical coincidence when the speaker and a listener understand the same meaning in the words the speaker transmits and the listener receives, that substantiates that meaning isn't a matter of codes, but of intentions, and cannot be mathematically translated, only comprehendingly interpreted. To confront the difference between math and language, axiomatic systems versus vocalized thoughts, we must first consider the standard approach, the Information Processing Theory of Mind.

The Information Processing Theory of Mind is everything it sounds like. It is a theory of mind, but a false one. It is premised on the assumption that our brains are computers, performing data processing as an unconscious calculating device can. It is not simply a hypothesis that our thoughts can be modeled as a mathematical process of calculations, but that our thoughts are themselves a mathematical process of calculations. The difference is very important. Anything can be modeled as a mathematical process; that is definitive of mathematics. Not that every particular thing can be modeled by every mathematical process, but mathematics models physics, it does not cause physics. As with chemistry, as with neurobiology, all the way to consciousness, which happens without our physical volition causing it to occur, and then it stops. Our ability to use mathematics to model physics and chemistry and even biology does not give rise to an ability to model thought. We cannot use mathematics to model even a single human mind, yet or ever. We can assume we could, and act as if we have, and that is the primitive foundation of postmodernism, and the Information Processing Theory of Mind, and Socrates' Error. But it is an unsubstantiated assumption, and a posed act, at best. Our thoughts aren't the execution of a program on computer hardware, calculating how best to survive and copulate, though that is the essence of the postmodern perspective, and the entirety of the scientific perspective. Even when thoughts appear that way, seem to be algorithmic, or are described as arithmetic, they are not a calculus of any kind. Our reasoning and imagination and language and ideas are obviously not prevented by our biological meatware. But thoughts are not caused by biology alone. The cause of our reasoning and imagination and language and ideas is our reasoning and imagination and language and ideas. They are self-determined; each with enough I to be mine, and enough You to be something more than just the flickering of switches inside my head. Our desire for and capacity to do good, to help others, find happiness, enjoy life and be productive and of benefit to the people around us, our community and society and civilization; these aren't programmed into us, they are an intellectual choice as much as they are any instinct.

Stated completely, the Information Processing Theory of Mind (IPTM) is the assertion that our brains are organic computers programmed by natural selection and simple conditioning, our memories are recordings, our thoughts the execution of symbolic logic. The premise of IPTM is that thinking and behaving logically, or mimicking what we think a robot thinking logically would do, results in evolutionarily successful reproductive behavior. Because that's what natural selection requires, and operant conditioning is supposed to be capable of doing so as well. There is no part of the Information Processing Theory of Mind (IPTM) that is true. Our minds are not the execution of any sort of programming, naturally selected or otherwise; humans are not Turing Machines. This can be known through three considerations. The fact that we are notoriously bad at calculating the very mathematical probabilities that IPTM demands we specialize in. The fact that our memories are only very rarely reliable recording mechanisms. And the fact that when people are given facts that contradict their opinions, they use those facts to reinforce rather than revise their opinions. There doesn't seem to be much correlation between human thought and the ways we would expect human reasoning to work if it were logical data processing. What is more, when it appears to fail it doesn't fail as we would expect if it were configured as, or supposed to be, logical data processing. The reality is that what we call information processing is nothing more than data processing: calculating numbers. Yes, we've learned to program computers, actual Turing Machines, to appear to process information, things that look more sophisticated than numbers, like letters, text, pictures, sounds, and contacts, groups, and messages and more. But under it all is just silicon chips and binary digits, not a theory of mind or consciousness. Computers only compute, they perform mathematical operations, they do not process information as human brains or human minds do. This fact is acknowledged by postmodernism and IPTM, but dismissed as a flaw in human brains or mind, rather than a flaw in the theory of IPTM itself

The seed of IPTM was planted by Socrates, germinated by Plato, but it was and is fiction. It is a mistake, it is Socrates' Error. The assumption that ideas and language are logical, or should be logical, or can be logical, or are ever successfully logical, or would be improved by being more logical, is erroneous. The theory that words could benefit from being treated as logical and deductive, that we benefit by doing so, is not simply contrary to the truth, it is counterproductive to our well-being most of the time. It is a convenient fiction that does enable us to establish an axiomatic system in an existential universe, and is productive in the strictest applications of **science** and **law**. But real life isn't an axiomatic system, so use of Socratic Ignorance, the necessary basis of the Socratic Method, is counter-productive, even toxic, in **every other context**. Socrates' Error thrived for thousands of years, while both technology and society progressed. But when the modern age of philosophy ended and the postmodern age began, following the scientific discovery that humans are descended from animals, Socrates' Error gave bloom to IPTM as a social faith if not a religious one. The critical moment came when a mathematician named Alan Turing, fantastically accomplished in code theory and encryption, contemplated what it would mean if one of his Turing Machines was programmed to mimic a reasoning intelligence. All calculators and programmable computers are Turing Machines, systems composed of arbitrary symbols being algorithmically processed. The Information Processing Theory of Mind was well summarized by his response to this contemplation, which was the claim that any computer that can convince a person that the computer is intelligent would be intelligent. Given postmodern affects on words, which I'll describe later as POS, the terms 'intelligence', 'consciousness', and 'free will' become at least somewhat, and possibly entirely, interchangeable; so I will take the liberty of considering them identical when discussing this Turing Test. The idea that a computer would be conscious if it could demonstrate consciousness by convincing human beings that it was conscious is accepted by many postmodernists because of the nature of logical positivism. (Logical positivism is the idea that only things that can be proven to be true should be considered to be true.) To many if not all postmodernists who believe in IPTM, humans are Turing Machines, and a computer that passes this Turing Test is intelligent, self-aware, in the same way that humans are.

Essentially, this computational theory of mind is the hypothesis that either consciousness would spontaneously occur in the execution of a mathematical program, or that it would only appear to occur, and that if there is a theory of mind that applies to humans and not computers it is, at least potentially, likewise only an appearance. No consideration needs to be given to who exactly needs to be convinced that the computer is acting intelligently instead of simply malfunctioning, or doing a poor performance of mimicking human intelligence and conscious reasoning. Whether it is a consensus, or democratic consideration, or just a subset of gullible people that need to think there would be a consciousness inside a computer, regardless of whether the computer was malfunctioning or properly executing its mathematical processes, is a moot point. Perhaps Turing was merely dismissing the idea that the word 'intelligence' has any meaning, or that it could only apply to conscious reasoning. Most postmodernists generally regard it as something vague in between, as if it could matter whether computers could be intelligent in any meaningful way, like in a movie where the heroes are the only people who believe a computer is "real". The unnamed soul in all the robot movies and characters is IPTM, and it fundamentally signifies that human consciousness isn't really a thing according to modern philosophy. The basic question of whether it is because self-awareness can spontaneously occur in any data processing system with enough complexity, or because humans can be easily fooled into anthropomorphizing any sufficiently sophisticated automated process, is left to the individual philosopher. If they are classically religious, they can choose either, though most go with a theistic or deistic agent creating another life, like It did or does with all humans. Without an organized religion to fall back on, the a-theistic postmodernists become anti-theistic. They are left with only the second option, the p-zombie route of philosophical pessimism, denying anything but their own existence, and sometimes even that. It is as if intelligence, self-aware thoughtful conscious reasoning, is not actually so real and unmistakable. As if it could be logically constructed with automatic programming of enough precision, and that it wouldn't swiftly become obvious, to people who are intelligently reasoning, that the computer simulation is algorithmic rather than organic. If intelligence is that all-too-easy, or all-too-difficult to spot, is it real to begin with?

People can project consciousness into all sorts of things that are far less complicated than computers; cars, toasters, even light switches. And computer programs have become far more intelligently designed, with automated software that easily passes as a real person in short brief topical interactions. On the other hand, our postmodern experience with cybertraffic and social media makes it all too obvious that there really isn't any simple way to discern whether information is coming from a human being of dubious honesty or a calculated result of automated processes. The distinction between "bots" and "trolls" continues to evaporate, in our cybernomenclature and the real world, both. It isn't at all coincidental that this issue resonates with current events, nor surprising, since it is erasing the validity of any such discrimination that makes postmodernism, IPTM, and Socrates' Error so problematic and critical.

I feel compelled to digress a bit here about Godwin's Law. The broader audience tends to represent Godwin's Law as an injunction: Thou Shalt Not Accuse Someone of Being a Nazi. But that isn't why it is called a law; the allusion isn't to statutes or commandments, but laws like the laws of physics: mathematically inescapable predictable results. Godwin's Law is that any online conversation that lasts long enough will eventually result in one party calling the other a Nazi, and the conversation ends. Anyone who has spent much time online has seen this happen. I saw a rather startling proof of Godwin's Law, which I think was something of a special case, in the relatively early years of the commercial Internet. Two engineers were coordinating their work over a mailing list, a group discussion involving dozens of computer experts that was entirely technical. These men were towering intellects in their industry, designing a new version of the simple network management protocol used on Internet equipment. The issue resolved to the contradicting desires for security and remote configuration. How to design the protocol, the mathematically unambiguous rules for transmitting and receiving data across both your network and possibly all the others, to balance these two opposite but equivalent requirements? The connection between computer programming and Nazis seems all too short in that context, after all, since the topic was security and control, and the two engineers ended up melting the mailing list into slag with their flamewar, which dragged on for days and weeks. Personal insults, supposedly dispassionately proclaimed with that combination of sincerity and insincerity we call passive aggressive. Not just adults, but well educated and highly intelligent adults, supposedly not lacking in self-awareness, ended up sounding like children bickering in the basest of manners.

Properly understood, Godwin's Law is instructive and real: people tend to lose their shizzle, if not their humanity, when their intellectual discourse becomes too far removed from their physical existence. In the hands of postmodernists, though, it becomes a bludgeon hidden inside a messy bundle of critical thinking skills, a dismissal of autocratic behavior that doesn't just defend autocratic behavior, it justifies, recommends, and applauds autocratic behavior because it exemplifies autocratic behavior. Words have meaning, metaphors have purpose, and sometimes you have to call a fascist a Nazi. To the accomplished postmodernist, every unflattering term, however accurate, can be dismissed as name-calling, and their Socratic Ignorance, hastily formed and controverted as convenient in order to make their opinions unfalsifiable, becomes impenetrable, no matter how inappropriate and fraudulent it becomes. So this experience watching two men, both convinced that they were not just Turing Machines but highly skilled in logic, reduced to the most patently illogical squabbling, rather than the technical development of computer programs, was a dramatic demonstration that reasoning is not logic. This experience cemented my conviction that nobody, not the most astute or the most casual person, can even approximate the Vulcan-like objectivity that standard philosophy, the Information Processing Theory of Mind, dictates as the goal for all human interactions and reasoning. Postmodernism has merely replaced the scriptural religious conviction that humans are flawed because we act sinfully with the secular religious conviction that we are flawed because we act irrationally. Though the details of what is designated sinful or illogical vary, the basic attitude of the two world views are the same: finding fault when humans do not behave as either God or mathematics commands us to. This incident involving Godwin's Law in a technical discussion between people who were most profoundly convinced they were, or should have been, acting algorithmically prompted me to consider the possibility that it was not <u>failing</u> to achieve this dispassionate objectivity of Socratic/Aristotelian logic, but <u>attempting</u> to do so, that was making people so angry and mean, as the Twentieth Century was ending and the Twenty First was beginning.

There is no shaking IPTM, of course: it is an unfalsifiable theory, a tar pit of assumed conclusion. So much so that some adherents insist it is possible that we already are just software running on some unseen unknowable hardware, that everything in our world is. Whether your consciousness is itself artificial, or everything else is as conscious as you, is an unfalsifiable side-note in this unfalsifiable fantasy/horror story. You can find adherents to this philosophy on the Internet with the key words "are we in a simulation". You might as well wonder if you're dreaming, or insane, or the world began Last Tuesday. The theory, however unfalsifiable in logical terms, doesn't match up with facts. So chances are, reality is real, you're awake right now and, as long as nobody thinks you're acting unreasonably, you're sane. But if you think life makes sense, especially these days, you're crazy. The postmodern IPTM is part of that, both why things are so crazy and why you can't make sense of them. IPTM gets in your way because you waste a lot of time and aggravation trying to act logically instead of just being reasonable. And it makes other people act crazy when they try to apply IPTM, and they convince themselves that crazy things are true. Because they're convinced that they became convinced of these crazy things by logic, it becomes impossible to convince them otherwise. And the more any of us tries to exert free will, to act logically or even reasonably, the more we find that we have no free will, not any more than computers do, or doornails do. This increases the frustration and existential angst, increasing the extremism a person is willing to go to in order to justify what they insist is logical, but is actually crazy. What began as a tar pit becomes a black hole, not just swallowing the victim but dragging others into its event horizon. POR explains this seemingly unavoidable drive towards extremism that we can observe in people in the [post]modern world. Not just religious extremism and violent terrorism, or political partisanship and division, but extremism in more mundane aspects of life and social interactions. Adopting POR methodically does not just relieve the adherent of the existential angst and intellectual uncertainty that causes us to respond to other people's dramatics and absolutism more calmly and reasonably, but avoid even nascent extremism in our own thoughts and actions that can otherwise seem unavoidable when we are driven by that same postmodern angst. When we abandon reasoning and believe that the only way to respond to violence is with violence, especially when we invent the idea that we can only prevent violence by using violence, we become postmodernists, and extremists, in a very real, not simply philosophical or intellectual, way.

Human beings don't act like information processing systems. We don't have the programming or the mathematical skills, by nature. This is considered a failure by postmodernists, but something more important in POR. Human beings' memories can't be trusted any more than our logic. Or at least we say that our memories can't be trusted, simply because it does not perform like a recording system would, and we are told to envision it as a recording system. In truth, it is extremely reliable, although not perfectly reliable. This includes being reliable about being extremely unreliable, if you're comparing it to an imaginary recording system of experienced sensations or occurrences. It isn't just unreliable when convenient, or when it doesn't matter, but at any time and in any way. Conscious recall does not behave like a recording system. It is a recreational system. Not an entertainment system, but one that recreates things: re-creational. It recreates past experiences, not by recording them with any fidelity and then replaying the record, but by reconstructing experiences after the fact from whatever clues are available, unplanned and undirected by any organized method. Every molecule in our brain cells is part of the system; our intellect uses reason to explain why the condition of all of our brain cells is not what would otherwise be expected, and imagines what must have happened to explain the difference, and that is the memory we consciously review.

This actual mechanism of our memory, reconstructive rather than transcriptive, is demonstrated by our experience of dreaming. Dreams are not conscious experiences that occur while we are asleep; we have no conscious experiences when we are asleep: sleep involves loss of consciousness. Rapid eye movements and other physiological occurrences notwithstanding, any medical indicator that a dream will be 'remembered' is not evidence that a dream is 'occurring'. This independence of neurological activity and psychological dreaming is evidenced when the dream that someone remembers after talking in their sleep does not coincide with their vocalization while asleep. Similarly, a dream that supposedly occurred hours before while in REM sleep is recalled as ending with a noise that happened at the conclusion of the dream; for instance, a firetruck's siren in the dream becomes the ringing of an alarm clock upon waking. I have experienced both of these situations personally, so although the mumpsimus of 'REM dreaming' is accepted, defended, and supposedly scientifically demonstrated by researchers for decades, the POR theory indicating this is a misinterpretation of the factual data seems more convincing, to me. Given the nature of consciousness, there never can be a way to determine when a dream "truly" happens, since by definition, a dream is a memory of something that cannot be remembered, since it never truly happened.

The experiences in the dream never happen, and the experiencing of the dream doesn't happen while we're unconscious and unaware. The dream actually occurs during the few dozen milliseconds when you regain consciousness, as your intellect attempts to reconstruct memories of things that never happened in order to explain why your brain's chemical state is not the same as it was the moment you lost consciousness, which was the previous moment from your conscious mind's perspective. The time gap is not directly observable. The chronological sequences of events while you were unconscious cannot be considered to have happened by your consciousness until it/you become aware of those events, and their character (whether they are the neuronal chemical changes or the imagined events that would have caused them had you been awake and actually experiencing them). This is why dreams feel like memories of things that happened while we were asleep, but don't really feel like the memories of things that happen when we aren't asleep feel like. Dreams are elusive to recall, and even more elusive to describe, often melting away or changing as we consider them, because they aren't real memories of imaginary events, they are imaginary memories to begin with. Our minds/brains cannot imagine the events, we can only imagine imagining them. Recalling dreams and experiencing dreams is the same single process, which is neither recall nor experience. Dreams are just our mind trying to interpret changes in our brains that weren't caused by actual experiences as if they were caused by actual experiences. This is also why sometimes, when life gets really crazy, that we can feel as if we are living in a dream, if what is actually causing our memories seems as fantastical and confusing, from our experiential perspective, as what we invent as explanations when we're dreaming, or rather when we 'remember' dreams that never happened as we're waking up.

The mechanism and sensation of dreaming is a clue to how memory works, and it does not indicate our memories are a recording function in our meatware. There are counter-examples of high fidelity memory, of course, but the wide variance of the accuracy of memory, between people and even at different times for the same person, makes these outliers not just explainable but predicted. Whatever organic memory is available to our consciousness, it works unbidden and <u>reconstructs</u> what we remember, rather than re-decodes it from any recorded data as part of a dedicated recall system.

Every rigorous psychological, psychiatric, or sociological experiment ever performed demonstrates that our thought processes are not logical. Every occurrence in real life, too, because it is the truth. But this isn't a bug, it's a feature, as the old hacker's gag goes. Every competent study into conscious human memory, or any other sort of human memory, confirms that as a recording function to store data for recall later in mathematical processing, it sucks. Our every reminiscence and testimony reconfirms that human memory is more ad hoc reconstruction than it is recording and decoding. The past is recorded on every atom and molecule in any physical system, if you can identify its initial state and figure out how it got in the state it is in. We don't <u>consciously</u> "detect" our way through our memories to deductively rebuild them every single time we want to 'recall' something from the past, but that is the better model of the process than even an analog, let alone digital, recording device. What really happens is that we <u>unconsciously</u> reconstruct every memory, every time we think about it. There aren't any dedicated recording subsystems in our brains. Our brains themselves are (can compared to in an analogy) a recording feature, more than they are an electronic calculator, whether programmable or not. But they are lousy at being a recording device, relatively speaking. Our memories generally function more than adequately, as our current civilization demonstrates, but the Philosophy Of Reason suggests that it is not their insufficiency as recording devices that causes problems for people. POR indicates that the problems come from trying to act as if they were a recording capability rather than a reconstructive ability. This is parallel to the problem of free will and existential angst; it is not failing that causes a problem, but trying. This seems odd, because we are so used to assuming that free will is volition, that if we don't try to exert free will, we will no longer have volition. Likewise, we are taught to believe that when conscious memory appears to 'edit' what happened after the fact, that is what makes our memories unreliable, but in reality our memories would be no more reliable if we did not recreate our experiences, and in fact we would not have any (conscious) memories if we did not do so, because there is no dedicated 'recording' mechanism in our neurobiology. Researchers study 'short term' and 'long term' memory in human beings, and become sincerely convinced that there are such things, simply because that is the way they intentionally interpret every bit of data they accumulate. But there are sufficient examples of these distinctions, and even the process of recorded memory, failing when deductively considered, that the theory I'm professing is not entirely novel. The idea that it is not a flaw in human memory that we reconstruct our experiences rather than recollect them but the mechanism itself, a bug rather than a feature, is not exclusive to POR, but it is a central feature of it's refutation of IPTM. Either way, in both dreaming specifically and memory in general, presuming that human intellect (recall and reasoning) is a logical data processing mechanism causes cognitive dissonance in researchers and laypersons alike, and the POR sumpsimus is the more accurate description of reality that relieves us of that psychiatric frisson.

Why does IPTM persist even in the face of routine and incontestable demonstrations that it is a false theory? IPTM is the contemporary model of aenthrocentric philosophy, all those arts and sciences that relate to humans dealing with humans, in no uncertain terms. How could it be false, just because I say so? Well, it's not because I say so, it's because it is untrue. Not just because it doesn't work well, as I hope I've demonstrated above. (No, not that way. You know what I mean.) IPTM isn't a true theory because it isn't a theory of mind, it is a theory of lack of mind. Logical mathematical processing does not require intention or consciousness, and the postmodern IPTM postulates that intellect is irrelevant, because simple mechanical cyphering of precise and deductive 'concepts' are sufficient for producing all human thought and action. Most people who use the Information Processing Theory of Mind as either an explicit or implicit presumption can accept that it is simply a narrative, an analogy, a metaphor for whatever electrochemical interactions are actually going on in our neurons. In centuries past, people talked about brains and thoughts in terms of mechanical contrivances, and we still talk about gears turning and screws being loose today. So what is so wrong with using words like 'circuits' and 'programs' to describe how and why people behave as they do? Even taking all of POR into account, we are still animals, and if animals can be described as organic robots with meatware brains programmed by genetics and classical or operant conditioning, why not humans? Well if you have to ask, you won't like the answers. Which one do you not want first?

It is scientifically inaccurate: it is the conscious mind, reasoning, and memory that we wish to explain, not animal behavior. This means that even if IPTM can justify or model our movements, that focuses on the wrong problem, which is the existence of our perceptions and subjective experience, and what we call human foibles. It is also scientifically imprecise, because it seeks to describe only the behaviors it judges favorably for being sufficiently robot-like, while simply dismissing without explanation all the other human behaviors, as failures of the system. IPTM is almost always used to be purposefully demeaning, denigrating some behavior to be chastised or lauding any behavior to be mandated; in this way it resembles a religious theology more than a scientific theory. Just as souls were invented to explain how we fail to obey God, IPTM is invented to explain how we fail to obey logic.

Finally, in addition to its scientific inaccuracy and imprecision, IPTM is categorically mistaken; our cerebral cortex is still a biological organ, but that does not make its working principles identical to the rest of our brain. The assumption that the electrochemical neural activity that produces consciousness is even similar to the electrochemical neural activity that our more primitive brain structures execute to control our movements, like any other animals brain does, may be a simpler assumption than the alternative, but it is still an assumption, and an unsubstantiated, possibly counter-intuitive one, at that. Occam's Razor precludes us from inventing unnecessary entities, but does not advise against accepting necessary ones. It may be necessary to assume that the inter- and intra-cellular chemistry behind conscious thoughts are not identical to the molecular principles that explain non-conscious neural activity.

So although IPTM is a comprehensible model, a mental image, more of a cartoon than a diagram, and could be of use as that alone, a metaphor rather than an analytical theory, we shouldn't even tolerate it for that. We can at least return to mechanical expressions, because everyone can know and tell that cogs and wheels are just imagery. When evolutionary psychologists and those who take them seriously speak of circuits and modules, they're being all too literal, not figurative, in their expectations that humans should be more like inanimate objects that calculate numbers, are malfunctioning if they don't have perfect memory, and can't be more than animals by using natural language or experiencing consciousness.

The basis of IPTM is Socrates' Error. I will finally explain that jargon more fully shortly, but for now, pretend you know what it means just by the words used to identify it. Socrates' Error is the assumption that language is a logical process, or should be. Once you assume that words and reasoning should be logical, you get stuck in the tar pit with that assumption, because words and reasoning become useless to disprove anything else, since they aren't actually a logical process, and so cannot prove or disprove anything, including the assumption you've made to the contrary. This leaves you with only a false assumption and no possibility of recognizing, let alone accepting, any alternative, so long as you insist on trying to use logic, whether to prove or disprove the hypothesis you've already assumed is true. Technophiles and bad philosophers have built this error in reasoning into an unfalsifiable scientific model, which is to say a false scientific model. But they keep the model anyway, not with nefarious intention but simply because they are unable to believe there is or even could be a better model. Socrates' Error is the belief that they already have the best model, and perhaps the only possible model; hence the tar pit. If we could presume that the model was an analogy, perhaps we could surmount its limitations, but since the nature of IPTM is, itself, the idea that only mathematical models are actually models, any non-mathematical models are simply fictions, to be rejected as subjective and uninformative, this is not a possibility.

IPTM is a failed scientific approach, it is a false theory of mind, in fact a false hypothesis of cognition, and what is more it is a confusing metaphor. I must admit it does not seem confusing, but that is only because it is so familiar and ubiquitous, and so the habit of skipping over its contradictions and inconsistencies usually goes without notice. So what to replace it with? What better imagery, hypothesis about consciousness, and testable theory should we use? As a first approximation, perhaps air. The atmosphere, the whole thing of it; weather, seasons, climate, all. Future conditions seem to be foreseeable, but accurate and precise predictions are frustratingly unattainable. The gaseous parts of our fluid atmosphere correspond to our self-aware conscious reasoning, while the liquid seas can be an analogy to our supposed subconscious. It is controlled entirely by thermodynamic principles, but can be thought of as self-guiding at the same time. Chaotic, yet regular, the atmosphere might be a very powerful model for our intellectual existence and behavior.

I can predict, as a scientific hypothesis, that whatever neurochemical events are involved in producing any single person's conscious thoughts, words, and actions, they are more complex in number and scope than the complete atmospheric conditions of our entire planet. We are no closer to actually knowing and understanding any one thought in any one person's mind and brain as a physical mathematical process than we are to predicting with 100% accuracy the exact time and amount it is going to be raining at any one spot. Both will always remain practically impossible, but in truth they are also theoretically impossible. Chaotic interactions between particles make it so, even if we could perfectly map the position and velocity of every individual particle, which we can't. The weather is not a perfect analogy, but it is better suited than the electronic or digital one that is IPTM.

Even if IPTM were valid in some way, it would not explain what free will is or how it could occur. Since it is not just the computational mechanism of consciousness but the conscious control it was supposed to provide that does not exist, how can this classical model of self-determination exist? We are taught to assume that our conscious thoughts, whether they are logical or not, are what controls our movements and actions, that we have free will. Intent->command->act, would be the teleological sequence, and it seems unbreakable. Without free will, we shouldn't have any reason for consciousness, or moral responsibility for our actions. Conscious control, cognizance, cognition, these are the source of our choices, according to IPTM. Even though the computational hypothesis of cognition doesn't actually explain free will, it is still considered compatible with it, somehow, in truth if not in name. To postmodernists, who embrace IPTM, free will (and self-determination, which they refer to and think of as free will) is assumed to arise spontaneously from a sufficiently complex or large set of logical processes, execution of mathematical calculations. There is no explanation for how or why this happens, and any particular postmodernist will either simply assume it does without further consideration, or accept that it only looks that way. Either any computer system with enough transistors or network connections will become self-aware, or else it will just appear to become self-aware due to the unpredictability of its results. Most IPTM adherents switch back and forth between these possibilities, whenever convenient, to keep their dual and perhaps hypocritical faith in the accuracy of IPTM and free will from being disproven.

A better theory than the Information Processing Theory of Mind must (not scientifically, but practically) deal with both issues. We must identify a process that can result in self-determination to replace free will as well as a process, hopefully the same one, that will result in reasoning. The first, I hope I have already done, with the POR theory of teleological flipping. But this returns us to the original conundrum, which is: how can I suggest that we aren't in conscious control over our bodies but can consciously choose our words?

So am I in conscious control of the words I'm writing at this very moment? **No more so than you are** in conscious control of them, although I experienced them first. But the responsibility to be capable and willing to understand these words remains, as does my responsibility to be consciously aware of writing them. This doesn't answer the question of where these responsibilities come from, if it is not a physical force in the universe or a metaphysical association with conscious control. So far, I've said that simply being able to flip teleologies in our mind is somehow supposed to cause responsibility for our actions, but that doesn't explain what responsibility itself is. What is responsibility? To answer that question, we need to learn to understand words better, finally moving on from the first POR theory of ontology, self-determination, to the second POR theory of epistemology, reason. But I can give you a hint now, because we are not quite yet ready to move on.

This is a trick used quite often, though not necessarily unerringly, in the Philosophy Of Reason. It relates to how we recognize the meaning of words without having read their dictionary entries or accumulate a statistically significant number of citations to allow us to calculate what concept they label, which are the two methods that IPTM would rely on exclusively. One of the quasi-logical ways that words gain their meaning is etymological construction, and we can use its reversal, dissection by deconstruction, here. The source of 'responsibility' is inherent in the word itself. Responsibility does not come from any physical process or deific commandment, it has no objective necessity or magical power of karmic balance. It is simply the ability, opportunity, and duty to **respond**, to answer questions of why we acted as we did. Whether those responses are sincere is something only we can judge for ourselves, whether those responses are honest is something that can only be verified against facts rather than our sentiments. Whether those responses are truthful is something history or God alone can know. But it is up to us to respond, and to do so reasonably, simply because we can. This is not just the theological and ethical imperative *of* language, it is the physical and biological reason and purpose *for* language. It does not lessen our aspiration to be moral and good when we accept that we do not have the conscious control over our choices that free will requires. It fuels and strengthens that aspiration by explaining it truthfully, honestly, and sincerely, without any need to rely on mystical or hypothetical forces greater than our own ability to reason.

Language is the root, the seat, and the heart of self-awareness, not free will or IPTM's computer-like deductive mechanics. The POR theory of our physical, empirical, ontological cerebral existence, self-determination through teleological flipping, does a better job of explaining all the facts we can observe about that activity, in congruity with all of the facts we can observe about everything else. I don't suppose that the thumbswitch experiment and all of my gibberish makes the conclusion unavoidable in your mind, but going over the details and implications further at this point certainly won't change the situation. So with that, now we are ready to move on.

Epistemology

Whether or not we believe, accept, or take for granted that we experience self-determination because of our ability to flip the chronology of cause and effect however we desire at any one moment, and do so authoritatively for our own selves individually, we must believe and accept that it has been scientifically proven that we are a particular species of apes. This is the only factual explanation for our existence, and what most people would consider the ontological theory, presuming they know what ontological means. There are many theories, some religious, some scientific, some neither, to explain or describe what it is that makes us different than all the other varieties of apes, animals, or creatures in the world. There is even the obvious but also obviously untrue theory that we aren't different from all the other varieties of ape. *But just because we are animals does not mean we are just animals.* As human beings, we have developed technology and a civilization that is unlike, or at least in excess of, anything that any other animal in the history of our planet has achieved, by leaps and bounds and any measurement you care to make. You could say that the very fact that our technology and civilization clearly or at least potentially threatens the existence of all animals on the planet, including ourselves, is empirical evidence that we are different from, or even superior to, any other creature or thing that we know of. Far too often, of course, people who are most concerned about "the planet" proclaim that we are inferior to all other animals, for the same reasons. But we are certainly different, if only in being able to describe how we believe we are different.

That isn't the argument I want to address now, though. In this chapter, we are not going to examine the effect of the difference between us and all other creatures, but the cause of that difference. What is it that makes us more than just animals? It would be simple but uninformative to rely on what I've already explained about the POR theory of self-determination. We are different because we can imagine the world being different from what it is, because we can envision 'what if' and question 'why?' But how is it that we can do that? Is it merely the mechanism of self-determination itself, this miraculous ability to reverse the arrow of time in our minds even when it is physically impossible in any other way? Without meandering too far back into musings about cause and effect, since we now know those are more malleable than we might have previously thought, we should still try to understand and comprehend some fundamental mechanism or method, some process or procedure, some principle or ability, that enables us to transcend the limits of standard teleologies or divine dictates, both. How is it that we can imagine anything, let alone reversing cause and effect, to provide wisdom relating to affects and intentions?

The POR explanation is direct, though it might seem insufficient or unsatisfying at first, just as the 'no free will' principle did in our ontological theory of self-determination. We can reverse teleologies, circumvent chronology at least in our imagination, and derive value of a very practical sort from that effort, merely by having the words to do so.

Children have difficulty, when they are extremely young, grasping the very nature of time. They develop an understanding of cause and effect, and learn the idea of chronology by being able to distinguish the one from the other, pretty quickly, but it can be shown through some crafty psychological experiments that they don't start out being able to do so. Even adults can be fooled, which can also be empirically demonstrated. Suggest to a person that time is running backwards or that effects result in causes using a physical rather than merely intellectual method, and they will accept it, at least to some extent, while still marveling at its impossibility. The possibility of either fooling our senses, using the illusions of sleight of hand or the technology of special effects, or defrauding our expectations, using those same tricks of stage magic or manipulation of expectations or vision, should be convincing evidence that we don't have any built-in biological or mental process that requires us to assume that time really can only run in one direction. The experience of dreaming, once again, also suggests that neither our conscious or unconscious perceptions have any inherent or innate chronographic mechanism or process. Recognizing that dreams illustrate this independence of sequence and chronology seems valid, if not convincing, regardless of whether you accept the standard or the POR hypothesis about dreams, whether they occur during sleep or only in hindsight while waking.

The nature of time is trickier than our intuition suggests, and whether this is a cause or effect of time, or our intuition, is paradoxical. Or perhaps it is simply unknowable, or unknown, and the uncertainty as to which is, itself, paradoxical. Further, whether those two paradoxes are the same or separate is either similarly or identically a paradox. And turtles all the way down, which leads us back to the nature of time. Our intuition is that it is universal and uniform; that every bit of space and matter 'travels' forward through the same moment of time at the, well, same time. While the true nature of time remains something of a mystery, we do know one thing about it with absolute certainty: this intuition is erroneous. Time is not absolute, with the entire cosmos ticking forward in lock step through each moment out of the past and into the future. Einstein figured out that this intuition must be mistaken by trying to sort out the nature of the speed of light, which is always the same velocity regardless of perspective. If you are traveling at half the speed of light, and measure the speed of light that is coming towards you, our intuition insists it should look like (be measured as) approaching faster than it would if you were standing still, just as an oncoming train approaches faster if you are on another train heading towards it. Likewise, if you were measuring the velocity of light particles/waves while racing away from their source at nearly the speed of light, it should, we imagine, take longer for those particles/waves to reach you than if you were sitting still waiting for them to arrive. But Einstein cemented his reputation as one of the greatest geniuses of all time by figuring out why the velocity of light doesn't work like that; it is always the same speed from your frame of reference (and every other), no matter how fast you are going towards or away from it. By imagining that he was 'surfing the wave' of light particles rushing towards some point in space, he realized that to get the measurements to all work out, time itself had to be relative to velocity. The faster you are moving, the more slowly time passes for you. But because time is passing more slowly for you, you can't notice the change. Instead, it looks to you like time is moving more quickly for everyone else. This 'time dilation affect' is real and can be measured, but is so miniscule at the mundane speeds we are able to achieve, it requires great effort and very precise equipment. But it is true, that time slows down the faster you are traveling; it can only be measured based on some particular frame of reference, and every point in space (and velocity of speed) is a distinct frame of reference. If it were possible to travel as fast as it is possible to travel (the speed of light), then time would effectively stop, from your perspective, while the rest of the universe goes on ticking away at a "normal" rate.

There are particles of radiation, photons, that have been traveling through empty space since just after the Big Bang itself, the first moments that the universe existed, when time began. Having never accidentally run into any matter particles, these photons have been racing at the speed of light for almost fourteen billion years. We can and do detect some of these particles, every moment, hear on Earth, and we call them the Cosmic Background Radiation (CBR). From the perspective of these photons/waves, since they have been traveling at the speed of light since the Big Bang, no time has passed since they started, since the beginning of the universe. It hasn't been fourteen billion years since time and space and matter and atoms and stars and galaxies and molecules began, you see; it only looks that way from our perspective. Given another, no less real, frame of reference, that of the CBR, it is still the same moment when it all began. Our intuitions about time aren't because of a limitation in our brains, but because of a limit in reality itself.

This lack of a built-in awareness of time may or may not be related to the fact that the science of physics likewise can't explain or guarantee that chronology is unidirectional. Back down on the quantum scale, again, it turns out that there doesn't seem to be any known physical force that prevents reverse time from occurring just as easily or frequently as the forward variety. No scientist will claim they can demonstrate that time can be run backwards, at least outside of a carefully selected and executed special case involving slivers of time so brief they can only be measured with the most powerful computers. That they may be able to do, showing the particle of photons arriving at a target before the wave front describing those particles could, or vice versa. But scientist's simply can't provide any mathematical formula or explanation why, in the real world, time always and only goes one way, they can only observe that it does or unerringly appears to. As I've stated already, of course, 'why' isn't really something Science can ever explain. Mathematical formulas calculate what happens, without either explaining or knowing why it happens. To science, 'why' doesn't really exist. When a scientific theory provides information described as, for example, "why human beings evolved", that is simply a system of demonstrating that human beings evolved the way they did, with the greater idea of any teleological 'why' being dismissed with a simple 'because that's the way it happened'. A fait accompli argument that, logically speaking, we shouldn't accept, but rationally speaking, we have no choice but to accept.

The issue of time and the nature of causality relates to the teleological mechanism in the theory of self-determination. I can't say for sure that the scientific consternation on the matter of time is directly related, either automatically or coincidentally, to our ability to envision or employ backwards teleologies. I will and do theorize, though, that a consideration of time as a physical reality beyond the observable occurrences we, or any other animals, use to identify or respond to the passage of time, is unique to humans.

So, why? Not just why, but how? Not just how, but when? What is it that makes human beings different than every other creature, which also evolved no less than we have? Our capacity to wonder why, why we are different, why we are the same, why you have consciousness and theory of mind and language and other creatures do not.

The ontological theory in the Philosophy Of Reason was that self-determination is not free will, and included an explanation and proof as to how and why self-determination works even though free will is impossible. The epistemological theory in POR is that reason is not logic, and likewise includes an explanation and proof as to how and why reason exists and isn't logic, despite the fact that every philosopher and scientist in modern times and every reference book you can find in the modern world insists that they are and/or should be. The standard theory of epistemology (be aware that I am aware that I might be using that term slightly differently than you are used to, on the rare chance that you are so used to that term at all that you could detect or wish to invent a distinction between how I use it and how someone else might) is that language is the result of consciousness and conscious decisions. We invent language because we can imagine how useful it will be, and learn language because we turned out to be right. In the standard theory, human beings start with self-awareness, and cannily develop a method of sending and receiving information with other human beings, and eventually come to realize that those other humans are self-aware, as well. This 'data transfer theory of language' is even more tightly held and ferociously defended than the theory of free will or the general IPTM. It is integral to IPTM, obviously, but is itself even more enduring and assumed, which bleeds into linguistics. 'Language as tool' is like free will, because it is a false theory. As with free will, we've also had to develop an alternative explanation concerning language, for those times when it becomes too obvious that language as a conscious construct is an untenable supposition.

To excuse ourselves when we fail to exhibit free will, we simply rely on the nihilistic theory of operant conditioning to explain human behavior. Likewise, when it becomes too apparent that language isn't something that humans have consciously developed as a data transfer mechanism, we invent the notion that all animals use equally powerful (if only in potential) mechanisms for transferring data to other organic robots, at least within their own species or to physically if not genealogically nearby creatures. In this standard theory of language, human language itself is essentially identical to the songs of birds or whales, the squeaks of rodents or insects, or the chemical alerts of plants or bacteria. In POR, we identify these non-human forms of biological messaging as "**signaling**", to distinguish them from the human facility of language that we use for "**communication**". I use these two terms, 'signaling' and 'communication', much, much more rigorously and strictly than standard science or philosophy does, and certainly more so than the common vernacular that relies on science to accept or reject what people call things. (That process, of desiring or accepting scientists [or, also, lawyers rather than scientists] to provide authority to regulate what something 'is' by disseminating and judging what we call things, is something POR rejects, as Socrates' Error.)

Signaling is data transfer between organisms or other entities. But speech, language, human communications, these are not simply a matter of signaling, and is independent of the forms of signaling we have evolved or implemented through strictly biological means. Linguistic communication, as the name (derived from the Latin for 'tongue') implies, seemed to be restricted to oral, phonetic signaling for tens of thousands of years, until eventually textual markings were accepted as an alternative, at first sufficient, later equivalent, and in some postmodern philosophies, independent mechanism of implementing the methods of signaling that communication can utilize. To [post]modern sensibilities, the idea that writing is not 'as much' language as speaking may seem incredible and incredulous, but it is generally taken for granted by those same sensibilities: that inscribed symbols, both grammatical and alphabetic (or hieroglyphic, ideographic, logosyllabic, etc.) are transcriptive. As is typical of the mumpsimus/sumpsimus nature of POR, the postmodern habit of assuming logical certainty outside a specialized subject (such as the relationship between written and spoken language) in order to deal with the ongoing and constant uncertainty within that subject, makes it possible for postmodernists to try to have their cake and eat it, too. While scoffing at my naïve approach to the dicey matter of whether ideogrammatical writing actually exists, they can ignore the fact that it is not at all a settled matter to begin with, only that they wish to act as if it were.

Regardless of how it is defined or categorized or analyzed, language, the ability to use signals such as sounds or gestures or marks on a stone tablet or piece of paper to evoke intellectual ideas rather than merely transfer data, is what really makes humans different from all other animals or creatures of any known type. Animal signals can be represented as symbols, but they aren't symbols to the animals, they're just patterns of sense data. POR theory is that words are not symbols, but I wouldn't argue that human communications doesn't use symbolism, and even symbols. Letters are symbols, perhaps, but it is only their memorized sequence that makes them logical, otherwise they are arbitrary and irregular shapes. They are symbols without any symbolism, not phonetic identifiers based on any more primitive symbology. The association of each letter in the alphabet with certain oral sounds leads most people to believe that there is some logical or even reasonable correspondence between the two, just as the sequence of letters is often thought, at least when we don't think about it too much, to have some significance. Of course, neither of these things are at all true. They don't even vaguely resemble the truth, as many if not every letter has more than one phonetic sound or diphthong assigned to it, many if not every phonetic sound has more than one letter or digraph assigned to it, and just about every letter can be silent, having no sound assigned to it, in some word or other. Likewise, the very fact that every child has to memorize, with painstaking repetition, almost always with a melodic mnemonic device, the sequence of letters in the alphabet proves that the order is arbitrary, and yet that very practice makes the pattern so familiar that people consider it natural and innate, as if letters couldn't exist without an alphabetic string to define them.

Accepting that letters are symbols that don't symbolize anything, that they, and the spelling we use them to form, are not logical transcriptions of sounds or the ideas that prompt us to make those sounds, is difficult, but not too. Accepting that words themselves aren't even that loose approximation of symbols, that they have no logical construction, arrangement, definition, or use, is much harder. But it is not impossible, nor is it untrue, and accepting this very true premise, this fact, that language is not a logical mechanism of data transfer, is one half of the epistemological theory of POR. The other half is its mirror image, made necessary and certain, while being independently yet equally as difficult to accept, at first: reasoning is not logic, either. Before tackling that profound but consternating principle, let us consider the question of just how fundamentally related, indeed interchangeable and identical, thoughts and words are. The POR theory is that language is the mechanism of consciousness, rather than only one possible result of it, as standard (postmodern) theory insists. Language is not a tool we invent and use because it is of practical value; language is the process that causes consciousness itself, by enabling perception and manipulation of teleologies. Not a data transfer method, but a source of meaning.

We can accept that it is genetic equipment that provides the capacity for speech, but it is conscious intentions that enables the purpose of speech. We aren't born knowing a language, we are born with the potential and instinct to learn language. But where do we learn it from if people weren't previously using it? Just as the POR perspective examines, perhaps even explains, the link between quantum uncertainty and deterministic certainty in the external world, it likewise explores the link between knowing words and using words. And likewise, it can be extremely complicated and easily dismissed for that reason, unless you accept that it isn't just wishful thinking but a necessity. It isn't sufficient to suppose that human language is like the sounds other apes make, just more precise or sophisticated. One reasonable analogy would be that apes making noises to signal to (nee 'communicate with') other apes is to human language as hitting a shellfish with a rock is to using a jackhammer. They may be accomplishing similar physical results, but one is innate and can occur accidentally, the other requires a great deal of equipment and orchestration. They may both be categorized as 'tool use', but only the human using the jackhammer, not the otter using the rock, is capable of categorizing things.

So what is it that makes the ability to use words something more complex and powerful than the ability to make sounds to transmit data? Although I will explain how to develop this mechanism more explicitly later, from rudimentary mental processes to advanced and enlightened decisions, for now I will simply cut to the chase and lay it out assertively. What makes human communication something more than simple signaling is a theory of mind. Or, rather 'theory of mind' rather than 'a theory of mind'. The difference is seemingly trivial, perhaps even pedantic or, as we dismissively say, semantic. But is it entirely linguistic or grammatical, or is there really a difference between what is meant by 'a theory of mind' and just 'theory of mind'?

A theory of mind is a hypothesis, putatively successful or at least successful enough to replace any previous hypothesis, that there is such a thing as 'mind' and hopefully but not necessarily to explain what that thing is, or how it occurs. Conversely, "theory of mind", without the participle, is either the need for or result of "a" theory of mind; perhaps even an application of any possible singular thesis of mind. When you are a neurobiologist or psychologist and you are trying to derive a scientifically testable mechanism that explains how or when people have self-determination, your hypothesis is 'a' theory of mind. When you are a scientist or philosopher or priest considering that humans aren't like other animals regardless of whether they can prove or you can describe how they aren't like other animals, your idea is 'theory of mind'. Whether there really is any actual distinction between these ideas, and indeed whether they are actually ideas, and further whether there can be any such thing as ideas, brings us back full circle to what language is and what makes us human and how self-determination occurs in our experience, regardless of whether you believe it occurs in the real world.

When entity 'A' signals the existence or quantity of external event or object 'z' to entity 'B', regardless of whether these entities are consciously aware of this transmission of data, no theory of mind needs to be or in fact can be invoked. Simple natural selection OR operant conditioning is sufficient for enabling such a signaling system to exist and to be effective. When entity 'B' cannot successfully receive and automatically recognize the signal or the data it supposedly conveys unless it interprets it based on a theory of mind, because entity 'B' has theory of mind and hypothesizes that entity 'A' would need to have that same theory of mind in order to generate the transmission, that is communication rather than signaling. What's more, this step, of interpreting signals supporting a theory of mind using theory of mind, is necessary for the process we rightly call communication. It is not merely an etymological or epistemological mechanism. It is what differentiates, both causing and recognizing, the difference between signaling and communicating. Signals are unidirectional, they are one way. Neither transmitting nor receiving and acting upon signals requires any theory of mind, whether a specific hypothesis ('a' theory of mind) or a general principle (theory of mind). Communication requires bidirectional signaling, not simply two unidirectional signals. The distinction between two separate unidirectional transmission events and one bidirectional communication is not merely semantic (epistemological), but is comprehensive (ontological). It is the difference between two one way roads and one road (or lane, in fact) that supports (and even requires) two way traffic. The latter is, hopefully obviously, much more complicated than the former. The analogy makes it seem as if one road is less efficient because it requires some laborious mechanism or methodology for regulating traffic, but only if it is presumed that the roads are real rather than analogical. The figurative nature of the analogy masks the fact that the road or roads must be built anew for every single exchange of intercourse between entities. If the existence of the road were miraculously persistent, with a separate path between any two entities, (agents or agencies,) then the postmodern method of socially negotiated definitions would be the only conceivable mechanism for communication, and the dictionary acts as a 'traffic cop' to control the two-way traffic on a one-lane road. But instead, in reality, only a protocol for sharing the road is necessary, since it is metaphorically the same road, not miraculously persistent but magically rebuilt, between every two individuals, or rather connecting every member of a community simultaneously. A "language" is this undefined protocol, establishing the very meaning of 'community' as a group that can 'communicate'.

Most signaling used by even the most sophisticated animals are clearly one way. A prairie dog emits a particular yelp when it senses a shape in the sky of a hawk, and the other prairie dogs react as if they "know" there is a hawk in the sky. An insect or a plant emits particular signals and other insects or plants change their behavior based on that signal. But none can question whether that transmitting insect or plant is right or accurate. Any object in the shape of a hawk causes the prairie dog to yelp, and the insect or plant can be equally fooled into emitting a signal regardless of the ontological reality. This enables us to experiment, quite readily, in order to examine how "animal communication" as it is wrongfully called, works. But animals cannot communicate. They can only signal. In the rare but possible case that one animal transmits a signal, and a second animal that receives that signal might signal 'back' to direct or influence the behavior of the first animal, this is still just a signaling mechanism. No communication occurs, and no theory of mind is necessary. Even a contingent response would be simply sequential signaling, rather than communication of sentience. Thus, animals can produce noises or other signals that appear as if they are a method of communicating, but they do so without the benefits of consciousness of any type. When people communicate, even with the most rudimentary method of alerts or orders, we cannot avoid applying our theory of mind, because we have theory of mind, by way of the direct knowledge that we are capable of and experiencing not just awareness, but self-awareness, and ultimately self-determination.

This isn't an issue of hopeful but potentially misguided semantic hair-splitting. The distinction between signaling and communication is at the center of what makes human language different from any other biological 'data transfer' systems we might euphemistically but erroneously identify as "animal language". It should go without saying that the same reasons apply to any non-biological data transfer systems involving 'computer language' or 'coding languages' or 'protocols'. These mathematical primitive instruction sets might sometimes conveniently model 'if/then' teleological statements, but not the teleologies themselves, or the tautologies we program them with to calculate. This similarity between conditional processing and teleologies, "if/then" suggesting "therefore", substantiates the false theory of IPTM, convincing engineers, programmers, and other hyper-rationalists that they are Turing Machines, and their thoughts are transient data states in a CPU, their memories persistent data states in RAM, and Mr. Spock was intellectually superior to Dr. Spock. It would be acceptable to say that computer consciousness is far less possible than animal consciousness, but they are both not simply hypothetical, they are fictitious. It should be noted, further, that there are different types of fictitious existence. It was once fictitious to send people to the Moon. It was once also fictitious to send people to the Moon with a huge gunpowder cannon. The one of these two things that is still fictitious will remain eternally fictitious, thermodynamics being what they are. The distinction between 'far less possible' and 'impossible' evaporates under the postmodern gaze of scientists and philosophers, but remains not just important but real. Consciousness cannot exist independently of the capacity to communicate its existence. If it could, the philosophical if not actual result would be that any pet spider and toaster experiences consciousness, but cannot signal it to us so that we could communicate. The possibility of inanimate (or animal) intelligence is not rejected because it is uncomfortable to think of all those trapped agencies in non-human entities, but absurd. Why stop at toasters, why not doornails? Why stop at spiders, why not amoeba? Why stop at all, and not make every quantum particle self-aware, but helpless to express itself? There is an ontological distinction, beyond any epistemological category or theological dictate, between animal cognition, if such a thing can even be imagined, and human cognizance. Between having senses and experiencing sentience. Between lack of consciousness and self-aware experience.

There is no way to empirically test this distinction, if we don't simply presume that there might and therefore must be such a distinction. This is itself the theory of mind. Biological signaling is, teleologically and tautologically, a mechanism that requires no consciousness or theory of mind: it occurs in microbes that no scientist and few philosophers would consider conscious. Signaling is a mechanism that requires no consciousness or theory of mind; it occurs in systems that nobody would consider conscious. Intellectual communication is more than a sequence of signals, as each transmission and reception of putative data relies on, enables, and in fact requires an intermediary supposition that each message is generated by and judged by a mind capable of being both inaccurate and imprecise. Not just fooled by a shape or circumstance mimicking some other, but incorrect in how it is assessing or how it is reporting that shape or circumstance and why. We don't just have neurobiological impulses running through our heads, but conscious thoughts. And even if those thoughts are not controlling the actions of the creatures involved, namely us, in keeping with our inability to achieve free will, those actions and the signals they cause are influenced by self-determination. Our theory of mind requires a theory of mind, and the embodiment of theory of mind isn't dependent on whether a particular theory of mind is accurate in terms of logically justifying self-awareness and the capacity for self-aware experience. It is only dependent on its consistency with itself, its own theory of mind, a universal premise of identity and consciousness.

This all might be difficult enough to understand and apply, but it is merely the beginning of understanding the POR theory of language. Just accepting that signaling is merely a component of, rather than the entirety of, communication isn't enough. We also have to consider how the method and mechanism of language enables self-determination. To be self-determined, as explained previously, we need to know (or imagine) that teleologies exist, and are helpful if not necessary in interpreting the world around us, including the sounds that other organisms of our species are generating. Further, we have to be able to reverse those teleologies, making intention a force of nature that physics cannot describe or justify. So the first step in understanding how language works is to accept that it isn't merely signaling to transfer arbitrary data from one organism to another. The next step is even more intricate and confusing. And yet it is even more undeniable. This second step is the reason for how the POR theory of language is embodied and expressed. Namely: "Words have meaning". This can seem deceptively self-evident, except what exactly is meant by 'words' and what exactly is meant by 'meaning' (and indeed what is meant by 'have') is not as apparently self-evident.

I mentioned earlier that it has been several thousand years since the great philosopher Aristotle formulated the rudiments of symbolic logic. When I did so, I referred to the thought that logical formulations do not seem to have successfully replaced the religious formulation of a deity. The existence of God doesn't seem as if it is physically necessary, to us, since matter and energy work according to mathematical rules, and these laws of physics could be either innate or arbitrary, but they are perfectly consistent and seem self-enforcing. Before Aristotle's time, before modern science advanced much beyond the most primitive idea of empirical experimentation, simply dismissing the existence of God as unnecessary was neither obvious nor even possible. Not even Socrates doubted the existence of gods, just the existence of any particular god. Infused by Platonic imagination, the Socratic Method, and Aristotle's symbolic logic, science has excluded all God from every corner of the universe besides human psychology. Over the millennia that followed in the shadow of Aristotelian logic, we should expect that more and more people adopted a worldview that dispensed with the notion of a deity, and adopted an atheistic perspective. Certainly, many people have done so. But empirically it does not appear as if the proportion of people that adopt an atheist attitude is growing substantially, if at all, despite a trend away from authoritarian 'organized' religions and towards a more 'personal spirituality'. Why do people still believe in God when it is not simply logically unnecessary, but reasonably refutable "magical thinking"? If we are engaging in good reasoning, as opposed to simply formulating correct logic, we should question whether the theistic theory is really as unnecessary as we might believe. Indeed, we should wonder whether it is even logically refutable, whether through a simple application of fundamental principles of logic, such as Occam's Razor, or more sophisticated or complex methods of reasoning or empirical discovery. Are the laws of physics either automatic or random? Why is something to be more stable than nothing on a quantum level? Are there turtles all the way down?

Occam's Razor baldly states that 'the entities used to explain the world with our philosophies should not multiply needlessly'. This is generally interpreted as meaning "the simplest explanation is the true explanation". It isn't a certainty, of course, because we aren't contemplating yet whether any particular explanation is simple, or merely simplistic. To be logically true a theory must be logically valid; it must apply in all cases, not just enough for convenience's sake. And in the case of the existence of a theistic hypothesis, this can't ever be the case. Not because it cannot apply in all cases, but because it cannot be logically applied in any case. This is because the notion of God is the idea of an entity that is not bound by either physics or logic. Even if every empirical experiment ever devised and performed demonstrates that God has no influence on the outcome and is therefore an entity which is unnecessary in order to explain the universe we exist in, that can't and doesn't disprove the existence of God, or prove the non-existence of God as an unnecessary entity. If it were possible for an experiment, or a whole host of experiments, even infinite in number, to prove that God does not exist, God could simply be causing those results through omnipotence and omnipresence. God can exist even if it is physically impossible for God to exist, because the notion of God presupposes an entity that transcends physicality. If God can fake the results of every test that It is ever put to, and does so, is it ever faking those results? A real God must be as impossible to prove as It is to disprove. Although an unfalsifiable theory is considered untrue in science, it is a necessity in theology.

In POR, we believe that the universe began, once, about fourteen billion years ago, from our perspective, and that everything that has ever or will ever occur since then is the result of the uncontrolled physical interaction of physical forces, substances, and objects. This excludes the necessity of any God to cause those interactions, or is able to change those interactions, and so POR is essentially and quite purposefully atheistic. But this only dismisses the necessity for the existence of God, it does not dismiss the necessity for the idea of God. This is why POR is an atheist philosophy, but not an anti-religious philosophy. Not just 'before there was a scientific theory explaining our existence', but after such a scientific theory has been demonstrated to be true, the notion of a force beyond any physics that dictates unilaterally what 'good' means, that acts as a source of not physical but moral knowledge or belief, is still not merely possible, not simply productive, but **necessary**. God doesn't have to exist for the need for God to exist, just as God doesn't have to physically exist in order to actually exist. This is not merely a feature of God, it is the definition of God, as a supernatural moral agency.

This idea of the need for an intellectual notion of God is, admittedly, something of a digression from the discussion of how words have meaning. It is really just an example of how words can, at least potentially, have a much more important role in reasoning than even logic itself. People continue to believe in God, and dismissing that as delusion or a philosophical blindspot doesn't change the fact that most people believe in God. They may dispute whether they all believe in the same God, but if there is any God or gods, there is still only one idea of what a god is. God remains an important word, when confined to the proper context, but It is not a logical construction. To understand the POR theory of language, we have to go beyond logic, something that postmodernism insists is not possible without becoming incomprehensible. But like the idea of God, it remains necessary, despite that philosophical cynicism. And so, like the idea of God, being conceivable as fiction makes it real as truth. The POR theory of language explains language better than the Socratic theory of language as 'flawed math', because logic can be encompassed by illogic, but illogic can only be rejected by logic. This choice or approach, of going beyond logic, might doom POR as a comprehensible philosophy, but only if we assume our conclusion, that language is a logical mechanism, or that only logical selections are possible. The answer to our question of why people still believe in God when Aristotle supposedly gave us the tools to dismiss and reject belief in God millennia ago is this: that language is not a logical mechanism. In fact, reason itself, the use of thoughts to contemplate and decide what is true and determine how we should behave, is not a logical process. This is, to put it bluntly, heresy, to standard philosophy. And yet, it isn't just possible, it is unavoidable and self-evident, if we examine the issues with sufficient honesty and integrity. Nihilists and absurdists, both, would disagree, perhaps, and embrace the idea that logic is the limit of what is true because all physical things, indeed everything in the physical universe aside from human beings, is limited to acting logically. For thousands of years, long before it was certain that everything else in the universe is driven by logic alone, the irrationality of humanity was accepted as a flaw in humanity. It is time to rethink that thought.

Aristotle didn't invent logic, of course. But he did develop and define the use of logic using symbols and syllogisms that most if not all philosophers, scientists, and even religious scholars have used faithfully, in both the modern age and the postmodern one. Most serious thinkers have found that applying the method of logic faithfully isn't sufficient to use it productively in every case. In fact, it only actually works in severely limited and particular cases. Explaining this is difficult, if you start with the presupposition, the assumption, that logic both can and must explain everything that is explainable. So to get us closer to understanding the epistemological theory of POR, that language, words, and reasoning are not logical processes or components or applications of any axiomatic system, I will now try to explain more explicitly what, in POR, we refer to as Socrates' Error.

The notion that words are logical derives pretty directly from the power of symbolic logic that Aristotle demonstrated through deductive syllogisms. But it is an error, in fact. Aristotelian logic works, without exception, when it utilizes symbols, because that is something inherent in the way we use symbols. In other words, symbols are logical because we use symbols logically. (A brief aside is necessary here to address the issue of 'deductive' versus 'inductive' logic. Throughout POR, the term 'logic' is used to refer to only deductive logic, and the presumption is that Aristotle, and all the analytic philosophers that followed him in Socrates' Error, considered 'inductive' logic to be 'bad logic', because it could not "prove" things. In POR nomenclature, deduction is math, and induction is not. The distinction between deductive and inductive logic, indeed the existence of induction as logic rather than irrational reasoning, devolves into epistemological quibbling, and will not be further addressed in this volume. If you wish to adopt the pretense that 'reasoning' is 'induction', that is acceptable, though not entirely accurate, but to use the term 'inductive logic' makes the vocabulary counter-productively ambiguous.) Aristotle demonstrated that words can be used <u>as if</u> they were symbols, and did so very productively, because it is easier to explain to other people what logic is, how it works, and why we use it, (when we manage to use it properly) using words. "Socrates is a man":"men are mortal"::"Socrates is mortal" is more comprehensible and instructive than simply "A=B:B=C::A=C". This is because we don't need to explain what 'Socrates' refers to; we already know it is a person's name. Nor do we need to explain what 'man' means, or how it relates to the similar term 'men'; we know they refer to singular human organisms and multiple human organisms, and they do so regardless of whether we comprehend or implement the idea of gender. Again, we don't need to define 'mortal' in logical terms, but can simply presume that any human capable of interpreting the statement "Socrats is a man" already is aware of the meaning of physical death and how it limits mortality.

But if we are to take the linguistic expression of "Socrates is a man":"men are mortal..." as a truly logical statement, those definitions cannot be assumed. We would have to define them in logical terms first, or accept that they are purely symbolic and otherwise meaningless. Symbols cannot work without definitions of those symbols, they are useless otherwise, arbitrary and uninformative. But words aren't like that, even when we observe that they, too, are supposedly arbitrary and often uninformative. The use of words as logical terms in a process of deduction (or induction, for that matter) can be very instructive; it enables us to learn what logic is and how to use it. The problem occurs, and has occurred, when we take that instructive value an illogical step further, and assume that because we can treat words *as if* they are symbols, they are *therefore* symbols.

This was not a big deal during the time between the age of ancient Greek philosophers and the more recent moment when Darwin discovered the physical explanation for our existence as biological creatures. This span of time is identified as the age of **modern** philosophy in POR. The time from Darwin's discovery of natural selection, as the primary if not exclusive mechanism of biological evolution, to today is called the age of **postmodern** philosophy. In the modern age of philosophy, it could be presumed that words can be used as symbols, but they are also somehow divinely described; that being able to talk was interchangeable with the ability to think, which God supposedly granted us as a species during the act of creation. The idea that words had to be logical primitives that supported the processing of symbolic logic could be accepted as an approximation or merely a convenience. A cartoon rather than a blueprint diagram. Assuming that language is a logical process, that reasoning is identical to (or even synonymous with) logic, and that words are symbols only became truly problematic in the postmodern age. Once any notion of a benign deity is ejected from our consideration, as it rightly should be once we discover that humanity can be produced by unguided biological occurrences alone, then the habit of assuming that words are symbols, or labels for supposedly logical yet undefined objects or entities such as 'concepts', becomes not simply problematic but erroneous. Prior to Darwin, "concepts" were Platonic forms, intellectual abstractions, because the physical nature of 'ideas' was not easily conceivable. After Darwin, these 'free floating abstractions' postmodernists now call "concepts" are merely subjective fictions, false because they are scientifically unfalsifiable.

The error underlying postmodernism dates back to the time of Aristotle. In fact, slightly before Aristotle and his mentor, Plato, to the time of Socrates himself, who was supposedly Plato's teacher, in turn. According to Plato, if we presume he was accurately if not precisely transcribing Socrates' actual lessons, Socrates was rather explicit about his desire to assume, if not take for granted, that words and language are matters of symbols and logic. Because the method that Socrates developed (or Plato imagined and assigned to Socrates, who may not have been a mortal man but a literary fiction) became and is so valuable in all human intellectual endeavors, we know it as "the Socratic Method". In this process, questions are asked of someone who claims to be certain about something. In particular (at least as far as the examples Plato used) certain about the meaning of words. Using reasonable analysis, Socrates demonstrated that, whatever definition his partner (or victim) came up with to describe the meaning of a word, there was always some hypothetical circumstance that indicated or required or proved that definition to be incorrect, and therefore supposedly false and useless. By using this Socratic Method, Socrates repeatedly arrived at a point of ignorance, professing that we, or at least he, 'does not know' what any particular word meant. In Plato's writing, the words used for this exercise were always relatively abstract, "strength" or "virtue" or "courage". But the same Method can almost as easily be used to deconstruct the definition, if not the meaning, of more concrete terms, such as 'horse' or 'table' or... well, anything. Words simply don't support the logical process. For logic to be used at all, to be successful, let alone to be useful, it has to be constrained to symbols or mathematical quantities. Socrates repeatedly proved by demonstration that any word he 'wasn't certain of' could be dismissed as meaningless. But neither he nor Plato (presuming they weren't one and the same through the act of authorship), nor Aristotle, nor an uncounted sequence of philosophers since that time, seem to have noticed that the same could be said of every word that they used to perform the demonstration.

What is "virtue"? What is "meaning"? What is "what"? What is "why"? What is "is"? What is a "horse"? I recall my own grade school introduction to the post/modern perspective on the ancient Greek philosophers, using the example of horse's teeth. The over-simplified didactic lesson was that before the development/discovery/invention of empiricism, these benighted thinkers would sit on rocks and debate how many teeth a horse had, without considering the idea of looking in a horse's mouth and counting them. A less over-simplified telling of the same mythology is that Aristotle claimed that women have fewer teeth than men because mares have fewer teeth than stallions. "Aristotle never consulted Mrs. Aristotle," the saw goes. Of course, the uncertainty of dentition in the age before medical dentistry makes this dismissive approach less wise than it might at first seem, but even still, we are applying our postmodern faith in logical absolutes too egregiously. The average of how many teeth any one, or any number, of horses might have is today assumed to be certain, because we average them, and because we know about the genetic definition and development of animals. We are used to ignoring the problem of induction, and assuming that when we say "a horse has 40 teeth", it does not mean that an animal stops being a horse if it somehow has 44 or 38 teeth. But this ignores the issue, recognized at the time, as now, but taken more seriously then, apparently, of the problem of induction: an infinite number of examples does not logically prove a categorical declaration. The ineffable nature of what a horse "is" gets set aside when we use the word 'horse', because we know how biological reproduction and evolution causes a horse to be. Likewise, the ancient Greek philosophers ignored the fact that when a definition of "virtue" was recognized as false using inconsistencies in how the term 'good' or 'best' were applied, the method only worked because these other words were assumed to have greater integrity than 'virtue', merely because they were not the ones being dissected.

Instructively, ironically, and in POR iconically, Socrates himself lamented the fact that he could not be certain what a word means. According to Plato, he seems to have *wanted* to be something other than ignorant. Whether he 'wanted to want' to be ignorant remains uncertain. Regardless, he maintained the hidden (?) assumption that the meaning of words can be captured in a singular definition. And when Aristotle used the lessons, that Socrates taught Plato and Plato taught Aristotle, to derive a method for distinguishing 'true statements' from 'false statements', he made the same error that Socrates did.

This mistake isn't simply the hidden assumption that meaning comes from definition(s). The full extent of Socrates' Error is the assumption that words would work better as a form of communication (or signaling) if they were (or were treated as) simply alternative labels for logical objects or quantities. Whether these great thinkers actually believed that words are symbols, or merely that they could and should be used as if they were symbols, we cannot know for sure. But Socrates did more than deconstruct words and remain disappointed that he could do so. He directly explained that he wanted language to be a mathematical process. To do so he used the illustration of a slave who he instructed to execute a series of instructions in order to calculate a particular geometric fact. He pointed out to those he was teaching (which wasn't the slave he was instructing, pointedly, but the slave's owner, Meno) that the slave could accomplish this process and accurately report the result of the calculation, as long as he precisely followed the steps Socrates ordered him to execute. What's more, the slave could provide this correct result even if he had no comprehension or knowledge of the purpose or justification for any of the steps he was performing. The slave only had to properly interpret and implement Socrates' instructions, provided in words, and the result of the mathematical formula was unerringly true.

In this way, Socrates presaged the method of algorithmic processing we use for an astounding number of procedures, today, with the slave substituting for a computer (specifically, a Turing Machine) and the instructions that Socrates gave the slave substituting for a computer program. Socrates' idea (assumption, in fact, and the root of the Error that plagues us to this day) was that if words could be used as consistently and precisely as labels or mathematical symbols, then any person, even one so uneducated as a slave, could easily tell, by simply executing a prescribed series of steps, whether any linguistic statement was true, or false. This was the ideal that Socrates strived for: the ability to calculate, without any judgment necessary, whether something, anything, not just an arithmetic fact, was true.

In POR, we refer to this idea as 'math envy', the thought that if words are used precisely enough, then whether they are accurate becomes obvious. Socrates wanted language to provide results as consistent and repeatable as mathematical calculations do. He wanted it so much, in fact, that he simply assumed that it was possible, and generations of philosophers and thinkers since then have adopted his belief and his reasoning. But it is an _error_, it turns out. It is a fantasy, this idea that if only we are precise enough, we can tell by simply examining someone's words whether what they are saying is true, without any need to compare those claims to any other statements or facts. This 'math envy' results in the problematic assumption we call "Socrates' Error", and define as the belief that words are logical, or can be logical, or should be logical, or would be improved by being logical. Of course, people don't really believe that using words precisely makes them more truthful. In fact, quite the opposite; most people realize that the more careful someone is in what they're saying, the more likely it is they're being dishonest about something. Words are not about being used precisely, but being used accurately, and although precise, that fact is more accurate than any less precise one. (More on the exact distinction between precision and accuracy will be provided later, and it isn't unexpected that you might be having difficulty with this issue right now.)

Judging accuracy requires judgment. Calculating precisely, even with false precision, is far simpler. If words could be logical, if they were improved by trying to make them logical, they'd only succeed in being mere signals, arbitrary sounds or marks without symbolism. Words cannot be improved by even wanting them to be, let alone trying to make them or believing you've made them, more logical.

Those last two words exemplify the issue, if you think about them hard enough. Because the fact is that it isn't possible for anything, whether a linguistic statement or a mathematical calculation, to be either more or less logical. That is an anathema to what the term 'logical' is supposed to mean, regardless of how it is defined. Something simply can't be 'more logical' or 'less logical'. That isn't how logic works, it is the opposite of what logic is. Something can only be either 'logical' or 'not logical'. There are no degrees, no amounts, no quantities of logic. There is only 'perfectly logical', and everything else which is not at all logical. This premise, that only absolute logic is logic, has been rejected more and more of late, by otherwise astute thinkers who are anxious to preserve the intellectual value of the Socratic Method, while confronting the fact of Socrates' Error, even while denying it's existence. We are told that there can be something like 'informal logic', that isn't quite as rigorous as 'formal logic' but is still logic. An alternative, and stricter but still erroneous, approach is to assume that 'inductive logic' is better than inexpert human reasoning, or that human thought is still mathematical but uses a more complex methodology such as probabilistic abduction or Bayesian statistics.

The Philosophy Of Reason refuses to get caught up in trying to find a mathematical process that can describe or replicate human reasoning. Instead, we simply dismiss the assumption that human reasoning is mathematical, because it is true that human reasoning is not mathematical. Those who believe in IPTM as a faith are willing enough to accept that fact, that human intellectual reasoning does not have the precision and consistency of mathematical processing, but they maintain Socrates' Erroneous math envy and proclaim that this is a failure or flaw in human reasoning. Rejecting Socrates' Error is more difficult than we might suppose because of Socrates' Error itself, and how it has been not simply continued and extended in the postmodern age, but essentially converted into a parallel religious dogma.

While atheistic, like POR, this postmodern doctrine, that human thought has to be somehow mathematical in essence if not in practice, generally becomes antitheistic, and anti-religious, as well, but sometimes as part of a self-loathing, even potentially violent, religion. Math envy, Socrates' Error, remains an essentially religious article of faith in secular society as well. It is an erroneous assumption that is encouraged and supported, but not actually substantiated, by the progress of algorithmic processing in conquering ever more complex and complicated problems. The mere existence of functional 'neural networks' that approximate some successes and limitations in human reasoning convinces most postmodernists of the very notion that it is impossible for reasoning to be anything but logic, good or bad, and it is therefore assumed that it is a foregone conclusion. But if we think about it properly, we can see, and ultimately learn to accept, that this is simply not the case. Words aren't logical symbols, and language is not a mathematical calculus. Sentences are not equations or formulas, no matter how proper or rigorous their syntax or grammar. Even more importantly, trying to use words as if they had deductive integrity does not increase their usefulness. Instead, as in the iconic example of the original demonstrations of the Socratic Method, trying to use words as if they had deductive integrity makes them useless, and can only leave us ignorant, not just of any particular word, but all words, and all ideas, and all things. Like the "Socrates is a man" syllogism, sentence structure is sometimes used to mimic a pretense of logic, and if we don't look too closely, we can be fooled into believing it therefore is logic. And this is how a mistake in reasoning like Socrates' Error leads real people, who believe their actions are entirely unrelated to academic philosophy but are instead motivated by political reality, to horrifying extremism under the guise of acting based on facts and logic.

This is the comprehensive substance of POR, when it comes down to it: learning to grasp the idea that we are not simply biological computers programmed by natural selection and operant conditioning. Animals can be described that way; all other biological creatures from the first single-celled replicators to the largest and most impressive mammals, and every insect and plant and fish in between, lack consciousness and are basically nothing but outrageously complicated chemical interactions between molecules in very large arrangements of very large groups. But humans transcend our physical form, and humans have always recognized this, whether we maintain belief in a supernatural soul or merely embrace the idea that our minds didn't evolve in order to calculate probabilities or execute mathematical strategies. These mathematical, logical things can be done without the need for conscious thought. And so conscious thought cannot be believably explained as merely a logical, calculating thing.

The root of human reasoning is judgment, not calculation; guessing, not estimating; imagining, not equating. Comparing without use of mathematical operations. In fact, it is the ability to do more than simply use mathematical calculations that separates the human experience from animal 'intelligence'. But so long as the problem of Socrates' Error is ignored, and we continue relying on the false assumption that the proper math can solve all of our problems, political, social, or personal, it is difficult if not impossible to convince anyone of that. And so self-centered cunning and a self-justifying lust for power becomes the norm. The 'math envy' that Socrates confessed to has become an epidemic of postmodern insistence that having feelings, compassion, and hope is simply a mistake, an aberration, a flaw, or a side-effect of imperfect knowledge. Or worse, a genetic trait that evolved as a biological adaptation but is somehow missing in anyone that disagree with us. Any motivation beyond self-interest is dismissed as mere sentimentality, subjective opinion and rationalizations. Or else self-interest itself is denigrated as selfishness, a lack of concern for an ill-defined "greater good" or a Darwinian imperative to serve the species. But no system, no matter how mathematically extensive and rigorous, can even represent 'knowledge' at all, or meaning, merely data. The human power of reasoning evolved, quite obviously from the POR perspective, to transcend and even benefit from the difficulty of making choices based on limited information, rather than to produce cold, calculating logic.

So what is 'meaning' at all, if not the simple tautological definition of words? How can we even presume, let alone insist, that there is any such thing as 'meaning', and is it merely a coincidence or representation of our initial state of ignorance that we have such a word at all? Humans have been using words for tens of thousands of years, at least, if not longer, before any dictionaries were ever written. How can it be that we developed civilization, at least enough to produce great minds like Socrates and Plato and Aristotle and Darwin and Turing and Einstein, if we cannot know what a word means without looking it up in a book?

According to postmodern theory, we merely get by, we never have been anything but animals. Language, in this view, provides meaning to words because of a calculation of probabilities of what sounds link to what thoughts based on logical terms that somehow exist independently of either words or ideas. And yet examining the reality of human language, we find that all the various grammars and vocabularies of all the humans in the world do not relate to any presumably objective 'concepts' that exist. If 'concepts' are independent of human reasoning, not merely figments we imagine in order to claim that the meaning of a word has some objective validity beyond our languages, then we could expect that statistical calculations can be used to equate nomenclature to external events or occurrences. "External" to our minds and thoughts, present in the physical universe beyond our senses. But the experience of the Rosetta Stone and the rather inconsistent results of automated translations systems indicate this isn't the case. Humans can rather easily, even unconsciously, translate between multiple languages, interpreting cognates and idioms with amazing facility, but turning that ability into algorithmic processing has proved far more difficult than we should expect if language and reasoning were themselves algorithmic processing.

The first rule of language in POR is, "It doesn't matter what you call something, what matters is why you're calling it that." Notice the important inclusion of the term 'why' in that sentence. 'Why', as I've already explained, is a thing which is beyond those equations that we can express with symbols. It may well be something we simply invent as an explanation, that has no significance at all in the physical world. But then why do we invent it, how could it possibly be of enough benefit that we continue to apply it, when any child can illustrate that it is a rabbit hole which becomes a bottomless pit? For every answer to 'why', the question 'why?' can still be asked, until we give up in frustration (or enlightenment) and accept the plain fact that teleologies are real, that cause and effect does explain the world of objects and occurrences that our brains have evolved to deal with. And when cause and effect are not enough, some greater (or lesser) moral purpose or intention is involved.

This is the most mind-bending part of comprehending (as opposed to understanding) POR, because we, as postmodernists educated by previous generations of postmodernists, have so internalized the assumption that the term 'meaning' as it applies to words is interchangeable with the term 'definition'. When asked, "What do you mean?" we almost instinctively want to point to an authoritative (authoritarian) dictionary definition, and wish to consider the matter resolved thereby, relying on that argument from authority to justify our supposed logic.

"Meaning" is not simply "definition". The meaning of a word isn't any one, or any group, of definitions. Definitions come from meaning; why a word is used is meaning, and how it is used defines it. Words are used, and reused, quite often, they are rethoughts; so dictionary entries can't and don't encapsulate or limit meaning, they simply observe and illustrate it. When we look up a word in the dictionary, we are not faced with any mathematical symbology. We aren't even provided a single entry which explains how to use a word. Instead, we are presented with a number of entries, sometimes similar, sometimes contradictory. It has become a postmodern habit for people, in trying to deal with difficult arguments about not just human activity but the reality of the physical (objective, external) world, to either present a single entry and insist that is "the" definition of a word, or to list a number of entries and ask "which one is it you are using?" The answer is always unspoken, unrecognized, and when the truth is explained, unbelieved or ignored: "All of them." When we use a word, we are not relying on any external definitions, whether from memory of other uses or calculated from them. We are, instead, defining the word anew with every utterance, while maintaining the same meaning the word has always had. *Definition in context* is not the source of meaning in the words we use, but it is the evidence of it, the mechanism that allows ill-defined phonemes or letters to become words.

Words have meaning. But what does the word "word" mean? And what does the word "meaning" mean? And what, ultimately, does the term 'have' mean? The answer is self-referential, seemingly tautological (and thus logically either false or pointless, if we accept that language is a mathematical process.) The word "word" in the statement "words have meaning" means "those things that have meaning". The word "meaning" can be and is defined thereby as "what words have". And the grammatical 'operator' "have" simply designates "the relationship between words and meaning". There are other definitions for 'have', there is one for each and every use of that sound or set of marks that anyone has ever used. And yet the meaning of all of them is not just related but identical, because it isn't what word you use that matters, it is why you are using that word, and not some other, or none at all, that has significance. "Meaning" as it applies to words isn't any different than "meaning" as it applies to our existence: What is the "meaning" of life? What is the "meaning of life"? "What is the meaning of life?" If you're keeping up with this vexingly difficult yet simplistic explanation, you now know the answer to that question and perhaps why I asked it three different times while shifting around the quotation marks. The meaning of life is what "life" is. And life is "what has meaning". And the grammatical operator "of" is that thing which relates life to meaning. Is it the meaning <u>for</u> life? The meaning <u>in</u> life? The meaning <u>to</u> life? All of these, now, are part of the context, and so all of <u>this,</u> each and together, and more, is what defines 'of', and thereby illustrates the meaning, and complexity, of life. The purpose of life is that life is complicated.

Again, I must commit the potentially fatal error of comparing the nature of words to quantum particles. We think of them as objects, existing in three dimensional space, but they are "point particles", they do not even exist in one dimension, which is a line, let alone two dimensions, a plane, or the three dimensions that all objects inhabit. Their actuality in four dimensional space-time, necessary to be real objects, is even more abstractly esoteric. The reality of a photon as a point particle is simply that the rest of the universe reacts as if the photon existed; it has no kinesis (energeia/entelecheia) of its own. Similarly (or identically, depending on whether we consider this a literary analogy or a literal comparison) the existence of a word, it's definition and meaning in context, is merely that all the other words around it force it to make sense, that the word stands for whatever truth it must in order for all the other words to mean anything. And likewise, every other word in that context has a definition that only exists because it must in order for the other words to mean anything. A word isolated from all context is simply a noise or a squiggle or a gesture, and so the postmodernist insists it has no meaning and is simply a symbol for something metaphysical, a *concept*. But it is the concept which has no meaning, is non-existent; the fact that the word becomes ineffable when removed from context is not an indication the word does not have meaning within the context, but the definition of what meaning is, itself. Each word, in any context, is defined by all the other words in that context, and the meaning of the word is, simultaneously, whatever it must be in order to make the whole statement comprising all the words true **and** identical to the meaning of that same word in every other context. With physical (but not three dimensional) particles, we have the advantage of quantitative measurements, and so we can conceive of them existing even though nobody can supposedly actually comprehend quantum mechanics. With words, no more but also no less physical, that mathematical logic is not available, because it is the very purpose and nature of words to be something different, whether greater (metaphoric) or lesser (fictional) than logical.

The larger issue of what it means that words are not, can not be, logically defined brings up several questions, of course. What do we mean by logic? How can words exist or have meaning if not in a way that can, should, or must be described as logic? How do words continue to exist, despite the incessant possibility of denial of that existence by denying the meaning of them, as in the original demonstrations of the Socratic Method? To introduce the lengthy and hopelessly esoteric answer to those and other questions about how and why and when the illogical nature of words displays its benefits, let's reexamine where Socratic/postmodern math envy came from, and how the Information Processing Theory of Mind goes astray.

But first, an interlude.

Truth is a hologram. Not one of those 3d videos, "Help me, Obi Wan, you're our only hope," holographs. The truth is a hologram, like the tiny sticker of an eagle on a credit card; a two dimensional surface with a three dimensional image printed on it. They're made with lasers, using the interference patterns produced when one laser hits the surface directly and the other, with the exact same wavelength, is reflected off an object before striking the surface, precisely aligned. That doesn't matter, how they're made, or why it works. The most interesting thing about holograms is something most people don't know. But it makes them like truth, in a way that most people also don't know. Truth and holograms both display the exact same, unintuitive behavior.

We are taught to believe that the truth is like a diagram; a blueprint. If you cut a blueprint in half, you end up with two halves of a blueprint. You cannot build a structure with only half the blueprint; if you tried it would probably collapse. But the truth isn't like a blueprint, it isn't a diagram. It is a hologram. When you cut a hologram in half, you don't end up with half a hologram. Instead, what you'll end up with is two whole holograms. This is literally true. Cut a hologram (or is it just the object the hologram is printed on?) in half, and each piece will still display the entire picture, but a bit fuzzier, and from two slightly different perspectives. It is part of the reason holograms work in the first place, a three dimensional picture on a two dimensional surface, the surface of a card usually made of plastic. Slice that card into a dozen pieces, and you end up with a dozen holograms showing the whole eagle, or whatever other image the lasers imprinted on/in the plastic. They become less focused, and you can't necessarily see the whole object without "looking around" as if the piece of plastic were a keyhole you were looking through. A piece of plastic from the right hand side of the original hologram card will show the image from a perspective to the right side of the imprinted object, one from the top will show a view from above looking down. So you can't see the whole picture all at once, but it is all still there. You couldn't see it all at once when the card was whole, either; that's why it appears as a 3D image. When you move your head, you see different parts; look from the right side and you see the right side of the object, move to the left and you can see it from the left side. Parallax, it's called. When you break the hologram into any number of pieces, though, each one still contains the entire three dimensional image of the object, not like the blueprint diagram. (I won't digress into why they're called blueprints, it has to do with a pre-industrial printing process that produced the iconic white lines on a blue background we have come to associate with construction plans. I call them blueprints to indicate their purpose, not their origin.)

Each part of the blueprint only shows one single part of the diagram. Without all of the pieces with any part of the diagram printed on them, you cannot reliably reconstruct the object or structure it represents. Postmodernists, those who are convinced that knowing the truth is possible by precise parsing of language as if it is logical data, believe that the truth is a blueprint, and if one tiny portion is missing, the rest can be dismissed as useless. This is a false impression, a descendant of Socrates' math envy, and actively prevents people from even recognizing, let alone comprehending, what the truth is.

Truth is a hologram. Every individual portion is the whole, or it isn't true to begin with. Half a truth is no truth, and because this is true, people think that truth is like a blueprint and having only half of it is like having none of it. But the reality is the opposite, even if people don't believe the truth. Half the truth is not truth, but if it is actually truth, then you can't have only half of it, even if you try. Like half a quantum, half a truth simply cannot exist, no matter how mind-boggling or unintuitive it might be. It can be hard to think about, when you try, but our language recognizes it instinctively. A half truth is the opposite of a truth. Parts of the truth can be obscured, difficult to see, even too vague to recognize or make out clearly. But if it is truth, it is always the whole truth. Because that's what truth means. The truth is a hologram, not a blueprint. If you cut it in half, you don't end up with two halves, you end up with two wholes, or else it isn't the truth at all.

Selection

Logic is really just math. Whether or not it is reduced to the symbolic notation of formulas, logic is supposed to, and must, have the same precise and consistent reliability as arithmetic, not just in the internal syntax and symbolism, but with an unerring correspondence to the ontological, measurable, objective world. Logic can derive intellectual entities more complex than direct measurement, but the validity of that derivation can only be assessed by comparing the non-physical result of a chain of logic to real events. Unverifiable math is simply strange glyphs or imagined quantities, not what any reasonable person must mean by 'math', if they are willing to admit that the word has a meaning beyond the example of a single arbitrary referent. "Whatever I call math is math because I called it that"; the epistemological rather than the ontological perspective.

Math works independently of simple physical measurements, and must be considered more reliable in its every actual execution (to be considered 'math' rather than 'error') than any one particular, or whole categories of, actual measurements. The difficulties of measurement are replete and existentially unavoidable, from the philosophical problem of measurement to practical complications in quantification, from Heisenberg's Uncertainty Principle to the Halting Problem, and a not-coincidentally unmeasurable number of other potential reasons why "2+2=4" is more reliable than your measurements of two and two and five, if that ever seems to be your results in the real world. Still, if nothing else we can say that math and metrics both have to mathematically trend towards an average, a mean, where they agree, and a mathematical formula can be used to predict the measured results whenever they can be empirically isolated from unknown influences.

However externally reliable logic is, though, despite both existential and analytical problems with measuring whatever it is the symbols are supposed to symbolize, it must be an unbroken chain of absolute states in between the inputs and assumptions, and the calculated answer. One single inaccurate quantification, one improperly selected formula, one incorrectly performed algorithmic step, or even one uncertain value or erroneous operator, and the entire chain from beginning to end is worthless, along with any further logic that depends on its conclusions as assumptions for deriving any additional solutions. This is both the strength and the weakness of logic as a method of selecting from among alternatives that we variously call choosing or deciding or figuring. It is absolutely precise (as absolutely precise as it is, precision being a mathematical feature) and perfectly repeatable (in the abstract, because no matter how many times you perform an activity, imperfections or unknown variables in the real world can overwhelm intellectual expectations) but it is only those things: precise and repeatable. It is not self-sufficient or self-correcting; Logic cannot really be used to verify the **accuracy** of either a logical process of calculation or a physical process of measurement, it can only be used to verify their **precision**. Logic cannot be used to verify the conclusions of an accurate logical process or objective measurement, either, because it can only replicate the same conclusion, or else either the first or second process is in error, and therefore not truly logical. Without at least a third logical process, or some non-logical method, for judging the first two, it is impossible to determine which of those first two was erroneous. To even wonder, let alone ascertain, why one is accurate and the other is not requires much more than just logic, it requires reasoning. But before we try to define reasoning in logical terms, a doomed effort from the start, let's dismantle logic even further, by asking not "how reliable is it?" but "what does it do?"

Logic and reason are both methods of determining a selection from among alternatives. If there are no alternatives, there is no possibility of error detectable by either method, because there is no selection. The meaning and purpose of logic is selection from among alternatives. From the simple 'what is the right answer to this arithmetic formula from among all the possible numbers?' to the more complex 'is Socrates mortal or immortal?' (I refer here to the logical syllogism used earlier, not any of the infinite list of other ways to interpret that question.) With logic, the process is both straight-forward and complicated. We must start with either quantities or things we think are quantities, or assumptions we think approximate quantities, as data. Whether purely symbolic or directly or indirectly metric, this data not only has to be accurate, it has to be accurately labeled. One or a series of logical operators, transformations, are applied to this data. Again, both the validity (the right formula out of all possible formulas) and the correctness (properly applying the transformation designated by each operator, independently of whether it would be judged 'the right' operator) have to be metaphysically if not supernaturally perfect for the result of the process to benefit in any way from the precision and consistency of the mechanical process of logic.

That last set of terms might be vexatious to those familiar enough with logic to understand what I'm on about. In using the words "metaphysical" and "supernatural", the postmodernist's instincts are triggered, and they might seize on the opportunity to dismiss my meaning without sufficiently rigorous examination of the grammar. If you read it too fast, or are not careful enough, it might have looked like I said that logic has to be impossibly perfect in order to be valid or correct. This is a common problem with postmodernism, that I'll mention again later, where words become synonyms too easily. If you aren't paying close enough attention, the terms 'metaphysical' and 'supernatural' mean the same thing as 'impossible', since most, perhaps all, things that are called metaphysical or supernatural are impossible. Without jumping too far ahead, I will simply try to re-describe what I was trying to say, so it can hopefully become clearer. Less fuzzy. The validity and the correctness of a logical chain of reasoning have to be more perfect than any one mathematical calculation can ever be. It cannot be assumed that every attempt at mathematical calculation is free of error. Mistakes can happen, both in the input and the processing, so any numeric or logical result has to be double-checked, at the very least, before it can be relied on blindly. So we have to have something to check our results against, and we also have to have a method of checking. The validity and correctness of these hypothetical 'right answers' and the process we use to compare them to the calculated results need to be more valid and correct, categorically, than the calculation and results we're checking. Our knowledge of a 'right' answer and our mechanism for comparison must have a certainty more absolute than a single physical measurement (metaphysical) or the nature of logic itself (supernatural) can guarantee, since it is the physical measurement and logical process we are trying to verify.

These things I've said about logic may seem overwhelmingly skeptical, but they are mere refinement, because logic must be capable of withstanding all skepticism to be considered true. The 'kick the chess board over' philosophical pessimism that has become all too normative in postmodern discourse does a far better job than I can ever do dismissing the validity and profound power of true logic, even the most symbolic sort. Socrates did not find knowledge through his Method; he found only Ignorance. Remaining ignorant might be considered true knowledge in a courtroom or science lab, but it isn't what we mean by knowledge in any other situation. As explained before, you aren't just changing symbols or symbol types when you go from "A=B" to "Socrates is a man". There is no logical disputation of what 'A' means, and I'm sure the great thinker wouldn't mind his name being used as a replacement for an arbitrary noun in a formulaic syllogism, but that's presuming that Socrates was once or was ever a man. Either way, using the name as a word for a symbol in a perfect logic where God has written a code book matching concepts to signifying patterns can be productive, rhetorically, without having any analytical or much metaphorical importance.

There is an inborn and unquenchable thirst in our minds, perhaps even a lust, for predictability in the universe. Part of this is born out of the postmodern insistence that we have free will and/or/so we don't have self-determination. Unconsciously recognizing the difficulty, the impossibility, of having free will's conscious control over ourselves, we subduct that into an almost terror-filled passion for trying to master the external universe, and the other people in it. Of course, there is obviously great benefit to making valid predictions. But also, our ego or conscience prods us to try to be right in our knowledge and our predictions, independent of any practical value. We would all like it if simple (or complicated, because all logic is simple or it isn't logic) answers could just be programmed and computed to tell us how to deal with complicated (no matter how simple, because life is always complicated) problems in our heads and in our communities, at least supposedly. We want there to be a simple answer to any problem, no matter how complex. But this idea, like free will and IPTM both, is a fiction. I say that because they are all the same fiction: Socrates' Error; math envy; postmodernism.

Any actual world where matters of right and wrong or hope and despair could be reduced to machine code or simplistic sequences of symbolic syllogism would be the nightmarish one where we actually were flies trapped in amber of fatalistic hopelessness or nihilistic pessimism. And yet, we do still want everything to be predictable, we believe that predictability gives us control. We thought we had this predictability, this logical rationality, that we long for, when Newton discovered how calculus can be used to describe the motion of all objects in the cosmos, from stars and planets to apples and oranges. We feared we'd discovered it when Darwin realized that biological evolution explains the existence of all species of creatures ever seen, including our own. We hoped we'd mastered it with Einstein's relativity, only to find that the physics of time and space dissolve into foam at the smallest measures of our objective concrete world.

The key idea in the Philosophy Of Reason is that reasoning isn't logic. Reason is what our species evolved, that put us beyond if not above all other creatures. Reason is what every human being needs in order to comprehend both their lives and what they want their lives to be. Logic is a useful tool, when you can use it. It is of astounding and profound, and astoundingly profound, and profoundly astounding power and usefulness. Its validity is demonstrated with every use of technology we engage in. Its irreplaceable consistency lies at the heart of our ability to use it for fantastic works of engineering and production. And, still, it is not simply entirely worthless, but deeply detrimental, when misused, and even worse when its mere pretense is used in its place. Your thoughts, your mind, your life and your words and your being, are not about logic. You weren't born to be logical, you can't succeed at being logical when you need to be logical the most. You don't base your choices or your decisions on logic, no matter how much you may believe you do and have, or how easy it is to pretend you have or should. People can do logic if they want to, in some cases quite accurately, but it isn't the Swiss army knife of intelligence that postmodernists are convinced it is, and have tried and succeeded in convincing us of. We can do better, and we will, because the fact is that humans have never used logic for decision-making. We don't need to, and we screw it up when we try, almost all of the time. (All the time.) We use reasoning, which is a better method of choice-selection or decision-making than logic or randomized, arbitrary, or patterned selection mechanisms. And to exemplify and explain these considerations of processes to select among alternatives, we have to consider not just the content but the lesson of Socrates' Error.

Words don't have logical, or randomized, arbitrary, or patterned meaning. None of those things are capable of sustaining anything that might rightfully be called "meaning", except in the most limited contexts. Meaning comes from not being any of those things, or any other selection mechanism. Meaning comes from reasoning, and causes reasoning, and causes all causes. Quite a tautology, eh? Causes all causes. If what you thought of next after reading that was "Does it cause itself?" then you are a true postmodernist in great need of rehabilitation, if you've gotten this far into this book. It causes the very existence of causes, so of course it causes itself. **Meaning means meaning**. Kind of an 'ultimate' tautology, where the more typical 'is' operator is completely replaced with a tautological reference. If what you thought of when you read "Causes all causes" was God, then you are theist, but probably still postmodernist, and could use some correction on both counts, but frankly not as much as an atheist postmodernist does. Getting back to "meaning means meaning", the ultimate tautology, the fact is that it is as useless as most other tautologies. What is meaning? Is "meaning is meaning" the same as "meaning means meaning"?

Meaning has to do with origins, it is the area of being where you are considering the predicates and only guessing at the purpose or expected results. So meaning is the beginning of things, and is associated in POR with epistemology, which is considered the study of meaning, including the meaning of what it means to 'study' or "know". Words have meaning. Meaning is the thing that words have, and it seems pretty important, however much any individual use of words may be deranged or denigrated. Math isn't what built civilization. Human reasoning built civilization, and maintains it if it is going to continue, or else it will logically degrade. Reason is what built civilization, math is only a tool we used while constructing it. We can define logic as a mechanism that uses assumptions as inputs, mathematical transformations as the process, and conclusions as output. Let's now turn to reason, and see if and how it differs from logic.

If you look in any non-POR reference book, you will find, of course, that the words are synonyms, if not simply used to define each other, but with more words added for affect. One of the effects on language of the postmodern quest for rationality is called 'postmodern over-synonimization', or POS for short. The previous example we've seen is 'metaphysical' and 'supernatural' becoming interchangeable (both with each other as well as) with 'impossible'. If language is logical and the meaning of words is only however they're defined in a dictionary [real or imagined], then two words that are synonyms in any context should become interchangeable in every context. This technique or habit of excessive synonymization isn't inherently wrong but it is inherently flawed. It is never acknowledged or recognized by postmodernists, either, but it is clearly identifiable no matter how strongly it is denied. POS isn't practiced for its own sake, but to support a Socratic Ignorance that allows a postmodernist to unshakably believe that a preferred fiction is truth and an inconvenient truth is fiction. With POS, any word must be interchangeable with some synonym, and in turn is identical to the unspoken 'concept' (idea) behind another synonym, which is in turn interchangeable with another synonym, until up is down and sideways is pistachio. The next thing you know, your hovercraft is full of eels; semantic quibbling and purposeful blindness to reasonable interpretations of idiom make all language incomprehensible. Eventually, using postmodern over-synonimization, all words just become codes for 'good' or 'bad', depending on whether the speaker wants to compliment themselves or insult others. This doesn't just go for all of the pedagogues and demagogues who constantly try to infuse society with hostile rhetoric, but the well-intentioned intelligent people who unknowingly practice postmodernism in their opinions and conversations. Always remember, it doesn't matter what word you use, what matters is why you're using it. The general rule of POR rhetoric, which will be expanded upon later on, is that it is generally wrong to use disparaging words about someone else that you can't tell describe you as well, and that it is always a good idea to use flattering words sparingly, most especially on yourself.

The difference between logic and reason isn't something you're going to find in a common dictionary or encyclopedia or thesaurus. Because of POS, simply acknowledging that there is a difference is beyond the pale. In postmodern intellectual discourse, it is only acceptable to suggest there might ever be any distinction between logic and reason, whether detectable or hypothetical, in order to denigrate human reasoning as something flawed compared to the pure sanity and perfection of logic. Most particularly, their own logic, whoever authors the discourse. No matter what it is, their reasoning will be deemed logic, informal if necessary but never illogical, never irrational, never acknowledged as anything less than mathematically consistent and precise. The point is that, at best, you're going to find that every modern intellectual you consult is going to tell you that logic and reason are overlapping circles on a Venn diagram, at best, or use postmodern over-synonimization to align them both as synonyms that mean 'good'. In POR epistemology (language), it is recognized that every word is perfectly synonymous only with itself, and rarely even then, and also can mean the opposite. Not 'can' in a way that it might or might not and we don't know and can't predict which, but 'can' in the way a photon 'can' be a wave. Meaning it is, even when all you're measuring is particle, and vice versa, too. It goes beyond whether we know which, or can determine which, or can even hope for one or the other. Light is both particles and waves, at the same time, until you open the box and the cat is dead. (Occasionally, in POR, we use the neologisms "warticle and rave", to refer to wave/particle or ray/wave duality, and this dubious distinction, or the relationship between quantum uncertainty and linguistic uncertainty.) With words, unlike Schrödinger's infamous cat, opening the box just makes the opposite state less interesting, not less likely. Even in hindsight, the meaning of words cannot be known 100%. Because words don't have anything to do with numbers, and 100 is a number. Yes, we have words for numerals, and quantities, we have words about numbers and related to numbers. But the numbers themselves aren't words, they're numbers. It wouldn't matter what word we use for them, they wouldn't change. They have the same ontological existence regardless of notation and they have no epistemological existence other than sequential labels for real quantities. Words aren't numbers, just as human reasoning isn't logic or math. It would be more accurate to say that words and numbers are antonyms than to say that they are synonyms, not just metaphorically or rhetorically but analytically.

The 'math envy' of Socrates' Error has evolved into the postmodern IPTM. So when we say reason is not logic to postmodernists, they can only assume that this is a flaw in language or reasoning. But it is the opposite; it is the meaning, being, and purpose of language, to not be logical. This relates directly to the theological theory of POR, that morality requires reason, and that reason, not logic, is what evolved in proto-humans to provide the basis for all civilization in the creation event of mankind's history, whether that was biological speciation or divine transubstantiation. Setting that aside for now, let's figure out how it is possible for reason to be anything if it is not simply a word for the processes of logic which cause our neurobiological chemistry to generate our thoughts. Our thoughts are real, they have objective existence, even if that is almost invisible from outside our neural tissue where they occur. The postmodern habit of dismissing thoughts, sensations, or even opinions as "subjective" can be, itself, dismissed. Your thoughts objectively occur as events in the real universe. But that doesn't mean our thought processes, those experiences, are caused by or result in what we believe are their causes or purposes. So let's be willing, if we're going to get over this delusion of IPTM, that our minds are just hitch-hikers on brains that are organic computers in bodies that are genetic robots, and the purpose of those brains is to precisely calculate the probability of objective events or occurrences, or accurately calculate what words mean based on hidden correlative algorithm, to suppose that reason is not logic, and this is not a flaw in reason, but a flaw in our assumptions about the value of logic.

The reason the 'key' secret in POR is that reason is not logic, is because logic isn't really what we think it is. Because it isn't a method of choice selection. It's just math. You can pretend to use it for choice selection, but that's just you making the choice based on whatever reasons you select, not any inherent objective validity in your calculations. We can model just about anything in the physical world as 'choice selection', from what direction bees will fly to whether a neutrino changes direction, or doesn't. But it seems obvious that the bee story makes more sense than envisioning consciousness in a lepton. The postmodern habit is to invoke self-awareness in anything that we want to describe as behaving logically, and then describe whatever it does as a logical choice, a selection from among possibilities. So bees perceive things, consider alternatives, and choose where to fly based on logic. Computers, of course, we imbue with that same volition, as well, claiming that if we do not know what the results of a calculation it performs will be, it is 'choosing' from among alternatives, even if we already know both all the data inputs and all the algorithmic steps in the program it is executing. And obviously mammals, we must pretend, are engaging in 'choices', when they sniff around two possible alternatives and then select one to eat, fight, or fuck. But they aren't choosing, any more than the computer or the lepton are. The idea that there are 'alternatives' to events and occurrences in the objective world is imaginary. Inventing the fiction of things being other than what has happened or is happening is very useful for considering what may or might or will or should happen. But our knowledge of something can't cause it to occur, not even on the level of quantum particles, no matter how many physicists describe it that way. Things happen, and have happened, but the things that haven't happened didn't happen, and any possibility they could have happened, when they didn't, only exists in our minds. We imagine similar things might happen, and say "they haven't happened yet but they will/might/could/should/may still happen", but those possible events are different instances than past events that did or didn't happen, however similar they might be in other ways than instantiation and chronology. The possibility of alternatives, for the bee and the lepton, is our imagination being able to contemplate that things might not be as they are already. But what they will be is dependent on nothing other than what they are already. We can believe we have influence on the physical world, but we are the physical world itself as much as any other part of it is. And without some supernatural power or infinite number of 'alternate universes', what will be will be inevitable just as soon as it happens, and what hasn't happened yet remains fictional until it does.

We like being able to predict things, it makes us feel masterful, but the power of math for doing so in the real world is severely limited. At best, we can reduce our perceptions to statistics and probabilities, and try to use enough reason to not come up with monstrous results. Or we can recognize that reason isn't merely a flawed form of decision-making, it is the only form of decision-making. Because deciding is what your brain does to explain your choices, once you or some other person invents the idea that you had choices. But making a decision isn't choice-selection either, any more than logic is, and for the same reason. The alternative to what happens, in any instance or category of empirical test, was never a possible alternative, we only imagined it could happen in order to help us recognize and understand what did happen. A mathematical equation does not "choose" an answer, it simply has an answer. A single true answer, however many simultaneously true results it might provide in that one answer. All other choices are incorrect, improper, and untrue. Logic must be that rigorous and absolute, or it is not logic, it is bad reasoning disguised as logic because that's the way to convince the other postmodernists to accept uncertain results as authoritative. Recall the question of correlation and causation that was presented in the discussion on teleologies and causality. If something 'is' 98% likely, but the 2% possibility is what ends up happening, then that 2% probability was actually 100% likely, we just didn't know it, yet.

This issue of 'choice selection' being fictitious has much larger implications for the subject of logic than for our self-determination or language. There is a very real and important principle addressed in POR as 'the uncontrollable state of the universe'. This principle has enormous consequences in intellectual endeavors such as economics, government policy, and medicine. When I say the state of the universe is 'uncontrollable' I do not mean that it cannot be intentionally guided, as a car is controllable. The sense of the word 'control' this principle invokes is the kind of control in a scientific experiment. A 'control' is an example that is not intentionally changed, or rather is intentionally left unchanged, so that what happens in that case can be compared to what happens in the cases where some condition is varied.

Let's say that we want to test the theory of whether a certain kind of fertilizer works. You get some plants, you give them the plant food, and you see how much they grow. But such an experiment is useless, because there are no measurable variables; if the plants grew more or less because of the fertilizer, you have no way of knowing. All you can know is that they did grow. And even if they didn't, if the plants all died, how do you know it was because of the fertilizer, that they wouldn't have died anyway? The answer is easy and obvious, in this example, at least. You don't fertilize all the plants, just some of them. The ones you don't fertilize are the control group. Your controls have to be otherwise identical to your test group, except for one single variable: whether they get the fertilizer. So you still water them and give them light, in every way treat them the same as the test group. This way, if all of the plants you fertilize die, you can consider it likely that it was the substance you are testing that did it. And if they all grow larger than the control group, you know the fertilizer works. Or do you? Perhaps it was the action of feeding the plants, not the substance itself, that made the difference. So instead of not fertilizing the control group, you use a different substance; one as similar to the one you're testing as possible. You need to have spare plants, a control group, to compare the test group to, or you can't even say you are performing an experiment, you're just growing plants and making unsubstantiated teleological assumptions. The control has to be treated exactly like the test group as much as possible, except for the variables you're actually testing. This can be done in a botany lab, but when dealing with real world issues like government policies, medical treatments, or economics, this is much more difficult, and often impossible.

We have no spare universe with which to compare the results we get in the one we do have, so it isn't logically possible to tell when a difference in some quantity or quality we have, after we make a change in the universe, is actually **caused** by that change. Is correlation causation? This harkens back to the problem of [the fictitious nature of] cause and effect already mentioned, but presuming that there is cause and effect as a general feature of the universe, the fact that we cannot be certain that a change in results is only the result of a known change in conditions becomes problematic in a different way. Clearly, we can use comparison, and even calculations of probability, to guess or estimate how likely it is that some change we made deterministically resulted in some result we observed. At small scales of human activity, this is sufficient to allow us to pretend as if the effect resulted from the cause, but only because we don't need a national or global consensus on what actions we take. When it comes to the programs of elected officials, the examination of financial transactions, or individual medical treatments, the use of comparisons becomes less productive. If the government institutes a program, and a few months later more factories open, does that mean the program resulted in the business expansion? If a patient takes a pill, and sometime later their medical condition disappears, does that mean the pharmaceutical intervention cured them? Certainly, we can consider what other factors may have been at work, and eliminate them as causative based on logic or reasoning. But if we are left with the government program being the only known explanation, does that make it more, or less, likely that it is the right one? More to the point, is there any way to know whether the malady would have receded even without the medication? How likely does a 'spontaneous remission' have to be to make a placebo look like a panacea? Because the state of the universe is uncontrolled, and because of the unlimited number of variables in the real world, and because lack of knowledge is the default and knowledge is the exception (or, perhaps even, a fiction, a mere irrational belief that what we hope will coincide with reality), on both logical and practical grounds the uncontrollable state of the universe is a never-ending vexation in many human endeavors. From the supposedly logical, postmodern, perspective, this makes philosophical pessimism necessary and unavoidable, political debates endless and contentious, and quack medicine as valid as clinical testing. Logic is supposed to enable us to double-check reality and in many circumstances it might be helpful, but if logic cannot determine when logic is applicable, is logic ever applicable? It is certain that it is not, in any case where too much ignorance about starting conditions occurs, or interactions are chaotic, or variables too numerous. Which is why scientific experiments have controls, but outside of the scientific laboratory, there are none.

Selection

Logic cannot answer questions of politics, or business, or even medicine, however much we apply the <u>form</u> of logic, the <u>pretense</u> of logic, once we already have the answers, in order to convince ourselves that logic can predict those answers. Because logic only functions when there is certainty, even if that certainty is a statistical calculation of uncertainty, the value of logic in the real world is entirely a matter of after-the-fact justifications and theories, not prediction or certitude. Reason may be considered more fallible than correct logic, but it is practically infallible next to incorrect logic, and only reason can determine the difference between the two. I don't know if I can put this more clearly: your delusion that you're supposed to be thinking logically, that you're capable of thinking logically, and that bad results occur if you don't try to think logically, are real delusion. This delusion is what is preventing you from thinking reasonably, knowing why you're doing it, and seeing that good results come from not having delusions, they don't come from trying to think logically. Thinking reasonably doesn't require logic, and good reasoning can't be dissected and disarmed by postmodernists pretending otherwise. These postmodernists, these would-be Socrates, these gadflies, these trolls, are recommitting Socrates' Error: putting their faith in not just the model of IPTM but its accuracy beyond all precision. Logic is a favorite of the people who are always certain, because they never reconsider their certainty, but it is even more popular with people who are always ignorant, who refuse to be certain about anything, who want to at least pretend that they do not know what is true, because it is inconvenient for them to admit it is true. Postmodernists and trolls always use an existential lack of reason as if it is logic, and logically incontrovertible.

Reason can be defined as reasoning with fundamental reasons to provide reasonable answers. Thinking reasonably only requires reasoning, reason, and being reasonable, and anyone who pretends reasoning is logic and all comes down to numbers is trying to sell you something or defend a lie. It is the communicative and conversational ability to use language to hypothesize in error which enabled Socrates to demonstrate his method of remaining ignorant, and the reason for his desire to do so, and accept his fate when the ontological argument was decreed by popular demand. His gadfly privilege and the story that resulted may have been literary, but it can be literally read all the same.

Words aren't logical symbols, and they don't fit together like a mosaic of tiles that don't overlap or leave any gaps by assignment as a code for platonic forms identified as "concepts". You can't truly learn what words mean, exactly, from any number of dictionary entries paraphrasing authoritative sources. Their true meaning includes the way they end up being used, in a way that no previous context could quite precisely summarize. Thought is not a consciously logical process, but it isn't even a subconsciously logical process. Inventing a subconscious to excuse the behavior of the unconscious brain with a conscious intent, even a reverse teleology of purpose, is both unnecessary and offensively demeaning. Thinking logically isn't just an unachievable goal, it is a dangerous and inaccurate means to any achievable goals. These goals, all too easily, seem logically necessary from someone's perspective, but can be unreasonable, regardless of whatever justification they might have. Freed from the cumbrous duty of commanding and executing every physical movement we behave with, our intellect of reasoning isn't burdened by the need to logically justify our every action, only to reasonably explain it if the subject comes up, using whatever teleologies seem accurate and useful: forward, backward, reverse, inverse, or even more fanciful. Sideways, pistachio, and eel-filled hovercrafts.

So how does reasoning actually 'work', as a comprehensible process? Setting aside the fictional nature of alternatives, what are the intellectual mechanics of reason as a method for inventing and selecting choices? Logic and reason both have inputs, transformations, and outputs. Logic has assumptions, formulas and calculation, and conclusions. In contrast, reason has presumptions, comparisons, and answers. Some notable differences between the two processes are that only some logical processes are reiterative or recursive. All reasoning processes are both. What distinguishes the word 'answer' from the word 'conclusion' in our comparison is that all answers only exist as presumptions for further reasoned comparisons, and conclusions are always just the results of that algorithmic process. Conclusions are final, even if they are then used as assumptions in a later logical process. All answers are provisional, and while they can be used practically, they are never final, and must be reexamined every time there is a reason to do so. Continuing the contrast between logic and reason, assumptions are just whatever numbers you use to execute your formula. How much correspondence those numbers have with any quantity or estimation from the physical world becomes untethered to ontological reality once they are used as assumptions; they are still the assumptions you made, even if they aren't accurate. Presumptions, in contrast, are both less certain, because they don't have the precision of numbers, but also more reliable, because they can be accurate independently of any analytical precision. In math/logic, the assumptions have to be true for the results to be correct; if you measured three inches as 2, then you are going to find that 2"+2"=5". In reasoning, presumptions are accepted as only the best approximation of truth, to be revised if more comparisons, more reasoning or reasons, show otherwise. About two inches and about two inches is five inches, for small values of five.

So logic uses assumptions, reason uses presumptions. Logic uses formulas and calculation, reason uses comparison. Logic results in conclusions, reason results in answers. The heart of the two selection methods is, of course, in the middle: logical calculations versus reasonable comparisons. If it is at all possible you've been following my explanations this far, you may still believe

Selection

that comparisons have to be mathematical in order to be useful, or even to exist. The assumption that all comparisons are mathematical comparisons, that only numeric or quantifiable comparisons are valid, is a postmodern delusion: math envy. But what other comparisons can there be? What are the comparisons that I'm declaring are the 'reasoning' at the heart of 'reason'?

The nature of what these 'comparisons' are, in an analogy between them and the formulas and calculations of logic, is difficult to fathom, even more so than the existence of numbers. (If you are unaware of how unfathomable the existence of numbers is, you have never thought about it hard enough.) There is no set list of comparisons, there are no limits on the type or features of these comparisons. Any comparison is a comparison. And only all comparisons possible are acceptable as the comparisons that can and should be performed in a process of reasoning. Recall that I wrote that there is no 'more' or 'less' logical; there is no better or worse logic. There is only logic, and the lack of logic, according to logic. One bad assumption, one mistake of arithmetic, makes the results of logic entirely and completely useless. Reason is profoundly more powerful than logic, except in pure mathematics, because it does not suffer from this limitation. There is good reasoning and bad reasoning, but they are both reasoning. To the postmodernist, this means reasoning is itself bad, because even bad reasoning is reasoning; you can make any comparison, no matter how inappropriate or improper or wrong, and still call what you did 'reasoning'. That kind of reasoning is an illustration of the thirst for certainty and predictability I've already mentioned. It is understandable that we want things to be so simple we can easily tell, automatically if possible, what is true from what is not. But it is time to grow up and put away that childish desire: we live in an uncontrollable universe and things are more complicated and difficult than we wish them to be. It is possible for something that looks like reasoning to not be reasoning. It could be that it is gibberish, it could be that it is a failed attempt to be logical. Only more reasoning, not logic, can distinguish bad reasoning from good enough reasoning, or better reasoning from good reasoning, or the best reasoning from simply knowing.

If I can be forgiven for claiming to speak logically, the number of possible comparisons between any two presumptions is larger than the number of numbers, meaning they are infinite. In math, the number of operators cannot be infinite, any algebra becomes pointless if that is a characteristic of the system. Axiomatic systems like mathematical or symbolic logic have a predefined set of primitive operators, by definition. We can logically reduce the number of possible operators in a logical process to one, binary addition, (or perhaps two, binary addition and whether to utilize it to subtract with the one's complement method) repeated craftily and cunningly enough, and with sufficient reiteration we can execute any possible calculation. That is essentially what all computers are, what they do, as an assembly of hardware and a varying number of software programs: a Turing Machine can use any number of symbols, but to be useful in the real world, each symbol must be simply a binary number, and so computers merely compute. Very crafty indeed, making computers so sophisticated these days that we can easily imagine a soul behind the construct, particularly if it is presented as a synchronized voice and face. But there can never be anything more than math behind the presentation, because calculating numbers is all that any mechanical, electronic, or quantum computer can ever do. You cannot program Theory of Mind, it rebels at being commanded. The only computer that could ever be said to have consciousness is one that is malfunctioning, because as long as it is simply executing a program as designed, no consciousness is necessary or available.

Reasoning is not simply an attempt at logic using a flawed computer program, as it might be put in IPTM. It is a transcendence over the math and logic that can be used to predict choice selection. There are no individual operators more than "comparison" necessary, nor any deductive definition of how any particular comparison transforms a given set of presumptions into a given answer. Just "comparison". Because unlike the bottom-up chain of logical operations, reasoning can and does benefit from top-down analysis, inventing possible alternatives that might not exist any more than the truth of our presumptions, but we cannot know until we perform the comparison. If we could decode the laws of physics and reality accurately and discover we are in an atom in the thumbnail of a giant, we would, because reason is not premised on any single worldview; each worldview, successfully achieved, is simply a new set of presumptions and comparisons. Reason is a triumph over the limits of logic, math, and calculation. It cannot be bogged down in debates about 'logical fallacies', though there are good habits in reasoning and bad habits in reasoning, and most of the 'logical fallacies' that pretentious would-be philosophers like to complain about are bad habits. But they can only be addressed as what they are: 'bad habits in reasoning', rather than 'logical fallacies' that somehow invalidate any chain of reasoning, no matter how long or reasonable it might be, because in logic a single error prevents the result from being true except by accident. Reason, in contrast, is self-correcting. In reasoning, a bad comparison becomes just another presumption that an error was actually made, because the only operator is comparison, without any limitation on the nature of the transformation which that comparison is supposed to perform. But there are hard limits on reason, because the word 'limit' means something precise in mathematics, but something accurate, however hypothetical, in language. This is the recursive nature of reason, due to its tautological and teleological basis. Reason is reasoning, what you have reasons for and have any reason to consider. You start with reasons, you continue reasoning, and you end up <u>reasonable</u>. This is the hard limit. If you don't end up reasonable, you aren't done yet, and you use your answers as presumptions, not assumptions, and compare them with everything else in every way you can think of or find out about until all that stacks up is the truth. Or what you presume is the truth, and then keep reasoning more. The goal of reasoning is not truth, humans cannot ever existentially know truth with the certainty of logic that we wish we could. To the postmodernists, the philosophical pessimists, this inability to existentially know truth means there is no truth, or that even attempting to know truth is pointless. But this always becomes an epistemological argument rather than an ontological one, concerning what we call things rather than their actuality. To confuse the fact that we cannot know the truth with whether there is a truth is an acknowledgement of the existential wall that separates our 'subjective' experiential existence from the 'objective' universe beyond our unreliable senses. It is a rejection of both the validity of cogito ergo sum, and the logical truth of math. To accept that there ever is any validity in an axiomatic system is to accept that there must be something we mean by truth, whether or not we can ever accurately identify it, regardless of whether our consideration is of an individual instance or a categorical classification. Reason refuses to be limited by logic, hope springs eternal. As long as you can be reasonable, there are no limits to what you can do, other than have nothing but words or violence to convince other people to be reasonable, too. And words are the only way that will work, obviously, because you can't convince even a reasonable person that you're being reasonable when you're even threatening violence, let alone committing violence.

So reason is the reason 'common sense' is thought to mean something, even though at best it is just an antonym/synonym for 'conventional wisdom' and 'bad' in a postmodernist dictionary based on logic, real or imagined. Logic is limited, because unless you have the right quantities, use the right formula, and calculate the result correctly, it won't even get you close to the right result. Reason is why people maintain hope in a mostly empty universe that is entirely out of scale with our mundane mortal existence, riding a capricious foam of chance in an unfeeling cosmos without any moral dimension outside of our imagination. Reason is the reason we have that imagination, and is the cause of it, and is the substance of it, however fantastical our fictions might get. The important thing, what matters, is not what happened but what alternatives there could have been, what alternatives we can create for future, similar occurrences. Reason is self-generating, any creature that has the capacity for true theory of mind-based communications engages in it inherently, because that is what communication is: reasoning, but with two or more brains instead of just one. Language is the substance and medium of reason, and reason is the substance and medium of language; the two are inverse sides of the same teleologically-flipped coin. Will it be ontology, recognizing that words can be used as either abstract symbols or as labels for things, but are still just words in every other context? Or will it be epistemology, recognizing that words are abstractions, comparisons, inexact categories defined only with family resemblances, at most. Words are not logical or mathematical data or operators, grammar is not a calculus of concepts, vocabulary isn't a code. Language is a shibboleth, not a litmus test. It is a matter of human judgment, human reasoning, not any Platonic precision or codified rules of prose and syntax.

Language didn't just accidentally evolve from a rational ability to calculate probabilities. Humans suck at assessing probabilities. It stands to reason that being able to assess the <u>accuracy</u> of assumptions in a logical choice-selection process would be far more adaptive than an unreliable ability to estimate probabilities but a keen ability to calculate logical results. Let me repeat that, because although I know much of the last few pages has seemed like gibberish (if you don't already understand what the future pages will explain), this one thing bears repeating. Assessing the accuracy of assumptions is more important than performing calculations based on those assumptions. If the goal of human thought is to calculate logical results, we should be better at estimating probabilities. Not that calculating logical results is a human beings' forte, either, but with care or a computer, we can accomplish it. To the postmodern sensibility, this possibility of calculating logical results is evidence that we have evolved to be logical, while to the POR sensibility, the difficulty with which we achieve it is evidence of the opposite. The postmodern theory of language is that language is a logical code, forced to bias towards becoming ever-more logical by the adaptive advantage, in a logical environment of interdependencies and thermodynamic activity. It is an attractive schema, if you have math envy and start with the false assumption that words become more communicative when they become more prosaic and less communicative when they become more poetic. It hasn't ever been true, despite being attractive, since Socrates first hinted at it by complaining about how you can't deduce when someone is lying from their grammar or diction.

Words become ever more communicative the more abstractly they are used, although perhaps at the expense of not being able to logically deconstruct the content of that communication. Yes, words can be wielded precisely, as either cutting tools or hair-shaving razors. And when scientists and lawyers become more arcane in their verbiage than the more general contexts, it can be irreplaceably valuable. But this value isn't to the scientists and lawyers alone, it cannot be, its value must be limited only to the human heart, and the human head, and the reasoning that connects the two far more powerfully and effectively than any logic could, not to the remorseless universe of physics that ensures all men are mortal. Reasoning is useless against the physical world, it is only comprehensible to other reasoning creatures that can transcend the physical world, where there are no selections just results, and we invent or devise hope and love and integrity to explain why those results happened.

So words have meaning and reason is not logic and self-determination is using reason to flip teleologies to discover or describe purpose. Hmmm... What are words again?

Paradigm

Ontology is the study of being. The term is most often used to connote the physicality of being, the persistence of existence and the fact that everything that happens in the universe is ultimately the interaction of physical forces and objects. Epistemology is the study of meaning. The historical roots of the term derives from the Greek root that designates the cognate "knowing". But this is not the source of the meaning of the word. In POR, it is recognized that the meaning of 'epistemology', that thing we mean to refer to when using that term, regardless of how we pronounce or spell it, comes from the fact that, based on Socrates' Error, modern (and postmodern) philosophers realized that defining 'knowledge' is problematic. If there is a cow out in a field, and a farmer looks at the field and sees the cow, the farmer "knows" that there is a cow there. But what if the farmer is mistaken? What if, although there is still a cow in the field, physically, ontologically, it is hidden behind a tree, and when he looked that farmer actually just saw a blanket hanging from a tree limb that looked as if it were a cow. Does the farmer still "know" that there is a cow in the field? His knowledge cannot change whether there actually is a cow. But based on his "subjective" perceptions, the farmer's knowledge is false. Yet if he were to say, "There is a cow in the field", he is not inaccurate, despite the fact that he is mistaken about the perception that led him to say that. Trying to sort out things like this requires extensive efforts and mechanisms, in standard postmodern philosophy, both analytic and existential. And yet it still fails. And will always fail, although postmodernists are loath to accept this. They are, in fact, unable to accept this, as long as they remain postmodernists. POR clarifies the issues, by conscientiously distinguishing between epistemology and ontology in a way that postmodern philosophy is unable to do. Admittedly, it certainly doesn't seem like a clarification at first. Because in the abstract, it only replaces one kind of uncertainty with another if it remains an intellectual exercise. POR does not allow that to happen, it demands comparison to the real world, application in our day to day lives, the emotional and sentimental reality in which we live, a pragmatic acceptance that reason does not suffer from the same blindspots of the Matrix and Inception that logical theories must, because reason does not accept blind spots. Reason is not an intellectual quest to be logical, it is an intellectual path to being reasonable.

Epistemology is the study of all meaning, not merely the study of knowledge. Because of the truth of the problem of postmodern philosophy, experts who have tried, dutifully and honestly, to examine the issue of human cognition became stalled when they tried to define, in deductively logical terms, what 'knowledge' means. The engrams in our brains from belief and the engrams from knowledge are indistinguishable. And so in POR, we accept the limitation that is eternal and cannot be gotten around, no matter how hard we try, that we cannot be omniscient. From a logical perspective, until it is proven that we cannot be omniscient, it is acceptable to assume that we can be. Or, more precisely, the logical perspective is that until it is disproven that we can be omniscient, it is necessary to assume that we can be. So instead of assuming that the problem of knowing what knowledge means is related to the issue of 'knowledge', tautologically, POR accepts that the problem is the issue of 'meaning', and we discover the teleology behind the confusion. Following Socrates' Error, existential and analytical epistemology, as philosophical disciplines, become about, not the nature of knowing, but the possibility of proving what you know. Meaning is related to the beginning of things, their origin, and includes both the study of knowing and all study of meaning, what is referred to in POR as epistemology.

Theology is generally, yet inaccurately, defined as the study of God. This is a product of the fact that modern philosophers had no way to understand what morality is apart from a dictate from God. In POR, we recognize that *theology* is not the same as *theism*. <u>Theology is the study of purpose.</u> This causes it to be linked to the study of morality or ethics, both theist and atheist. In postmodern ethics, we are told that 'the ends can't justify the means', and we derive from that the idea that the purpose of an action cannot truly effect the morality of that action, which is set at its origin. But this is untrue. In fact, it is the opposite of the truth. The purpose of an action is the only way to adequately judge the morality of it, the actual action itself could as easily be prompted by immoral desires as it is moral expectations. It doesn't matter what you do, the only thing that can matter is why you are doing it. Whether "why" refers to the cause (origin, meaning) of something or its purpose (end, moral) is a theological question. Not simply the conscious intent behind the action, but all of the consequences could, depending on the consequences and the circumstances, be the responsibility of the person performing an action. And this is in line with our reasoning, if not our logic. Having a purpose of harming someone is considered wrong, regardless of whether your actions succeed in causing harm. And having a purpose of helping mitigates the fault in causing harm, even when that happens, but does not entirely eliminate it.

So sometimes the end does justify the means. But sometimes it doesn't. No categorical or logical distinction between means (origin) or end (purpose) can cause or ensure that no moral end can be accomplished through amoral (not immoral, but anti-moral) means. Morality cannot be judged based on logic. Math can only identify what **is** or **is not**, regardless of whether it should be or shouldn't be. "**Should**" requires moral judgment, and although we can certainly use mathematics and symbolic logic to help us judge the ethics of an action, it is the judgment of what formula to use, and how to apply the results, not the calculation itself, that controls the assessment. The decision about what we describe as a method (means) and what we describe as the goal (end) is not a logical choice, but a matter of reasoning. It is language, an epistemological assignment, not an ontological fact. Every means is an end resulting from a previous means, and every end is only a means to a more ultimate end.

Meaning, being, and purpose. We are taught to believe that only the middle one is objective, the first and the last are, at least potentially, figments of our imagination, because they cannot be logically demonstrated except through being. There is no 'meaning' in the universe, and likewise there is no 'purpose'. The universe simply is. But does that mean **we** have no meaning and no purpose, simply because we are in this universe? Is it any wonder that ancient and most modern thinkers saw no alternative but to grasp for something beyond the universe? Something supernatural, divine and omniscient to provide an absolute perspective in a universe in which everything is logically and physically relative?

Let us leave these outrageously weighty and yet fruitless (or trivial and yet vital) musings on meaning and purpose in general, and return to the examination of language and words. Ancients used God, postmodernists use logic, POR uses words. I've already indicated some of the reasons why dictionary definitions can't truly provide the meaning of a word. No one dictionary is logically authoritative, each has multiple and contradictory definitions for many words, changing over time. So how can we possibly understand words at all, if there cannot be, or at least is not yet and possibly won't ever be, any objective method of determining what the meaning of those words are? It is considered improper to say that the meaning of words simply derives from purpose: "a word means whatever it is I intend for it to mean when I use it". That approach has some of the same pitfalls and problems that postmodern reliance on dictionaries does, but for the opposite reason. Words have meaning. It is something beyond simply the intention of the speaker, yet it is not entirely independent of that purpose. So how can we possibly understand it? This isn't an idle subject, but neither is it easily encapsulated in any language we can use to try to explain it. To explain words using only words is the most difficult method for doing so, but is ultimately also the only method for doing so.

Of course, most of the issue of how words have meaning and definition has already been described, as *definition in context*. But the 'they mean whatever they mean' approach remains problematic, in terms of explaining how words work philosophically. In POR, our response to this difficult, even perhaps impossible task of understanding how words work, when words are the only tool we have for explaining that understanding, is to represent the process of language using three separate diagrams. The first is the POR replacement for dictionary definitions, called the abstraction paradigm. The second is the POR replacement for religious symbols, which we refer to as the Fundamental Schema. The third is an illustration of how we can know, or at least guess, what words mean without reliance on any assumption about their properties other than the fact that we do use them, and they do at least sometimes successfully convey what we mean when we do so. It is the jellybean diagram that I briefly mentioned in the introduction. For the moment, put aside how preposterous this all sounds. Try to imagine that everything I have explained so far is actually true, regardless of your ability to understand or believe it. Pretend that there is a cow in the field, and even though you have been taught to think that the cow is actually a blanket on a tree branch, there still really is a cow, and there really is a field, regardless of whether you can ever convince anyone else of those things.

The abstraction paradigm (AP) is a simple grid of nine cells, like a tic-tac-toe board. In the center, we put a word, an abstraction. This leaves a row of cells underneath, a row of cells up above, and one cell to either side of the middle one that already has our word in it. The bottom row is the 'analytical' level. If we were to presume that the word we want to understand or define has a concrete meaning, one that corresponds "logically" to an ontological occurrence, an event or object in the world external to our minds trapped inside our heads, we would substitute the content of one of the cells on the analytical row. When used analytically, we imagine each word corresponds to a quantifiable thing, more-or-less the equivalent of the postmodern "language is math" conception of Socrates' Error. The top row is identified as the 'metaphorical' level. If we were to take our word and imagine that there was some even more abstract way of expressing the idea or thought that word denotes, it would go there. Analogies, figures of speech, poetic license. The middle row, which already has our word in it but still has two empty cells that can be filled, is described as the 'rhetorical' level. Whenever the meaning or definition of a word is non-controversial, it is being used rhetorically. The three columns have designations, as well; the outer two are 'dichotomies', the middle one 'dialectical'. Conventionally, the left hand 'dichotomy' column is associated with 'meaning', and the right hand with 'purpose', for reasons that will be explained later.

Let's consider an example:

Paradigm

	word	

Every time a person uses a word, they are using it rhetorically. This means we can't know precisely what they mean when they say it, but that doesn't matter. We can simply presume they are using it the way they intend to, because they are the one using it. As I described earlier, we can, and do, figure out what that word means in context. If they say, for example, "I want to eat because I am hungry," then the term 'hungry' means an explanation of why they want to eat, and we can understand the word 'eat' to mean what you want to do when you're hungry. This seemingly self-referential 'definition in context' isn't enough, though, to compare the usage of the word in any other context, in order to consider whether they are using it correctly or accurately or properly. We are used to the idea of using a dictionary, and looking to whatever previous context and usage the lexicographer thought was most informative about how the word has been used by speakers or authors in the past. People who write dictionaries then formulate a paraphrase of the meaning that those previous examples seem to suggest as a way of describing definitions that should inform us about what the word means. One of the problems with dictionaries is that, it turns out, you cannot really understand a word well enough to use it effectively if you just say, "There is a definition that says this, so any time I use this word I am using it correctly." Language is more subtle than that, and most of the time when someone uses a word in a way that the dictionary suggests is correct, you can tell that someone doesn't "really understand" the word because they end up using it inappropriately, if not improperly or even inaccurately. (Notice that all of these words I'm using to try to explain this are, themselves, words, meaning that my explanation becomes incredibly pointless if you make the assumption that they have mathematically precise meanings and try to find some error in my usage based on that assumption in order to avoid understanding what I'm saying. More on this later.)

So if we are to try to grasp or comprehend the meaning of a word without using dictionary entries, one thing we can do is simply try to substitute other words for the one being used, and see if that enables us to recognize what the person is trying to say. This is more the approach of a thesaurus, which provides scattershot associations, rather than a dictionary with paraphrased entries. What is a more analytical, concrete term for 'word' that we might substitute in a general context? One that I have already used in this text is "cognate". The whole reason for that word is to mean 'word or idea' with a more concrete and analytical inflection. Look it up in the dictionary, and it will say something similar enough that you can see what I mean, although it will probably be different enough if you feel like being argumentative. That leads us back to postmodern confusion, Socrates' Error, and the inaccurate assumption that words have more logical validity than we wish they did. So abandon that argument and instead of trying to see some flaw in my explanation, instead try to find some usefulness in it.

I don't like that choice, 'cognate', it's too cerebral rather than familiar. It doesn't even seem more 'concrete' than 'word' does, even though it might be grammatically more primitive. Which comes first, the cognate or the word?. So let's put that aside and select a different one. "Term" is one I have used rather frequently. It can mean something quite different from 'word', or at least different than what I have been explaining about words, because any symbol in a mathematical equation is a *term*. Because of the postmodern delusion, that words are secretly mathematical symbols that our brains process using probabilities of correlation to external events or objects, this does indicate something more concrete than 'word', even though it can be used for something more general than 'word'. Still, it seems analytical, so we will use it.

	word	
	term	

Now, try to think of a word that means something similar to 'word', but is more abstract, more metaphorical. Is there such a thing? Of course. There must be. Or we could just invent one if none comes to mind, because we could us an etymological (historical) or onomatopoetic (visceral) or even quasi-logical (correlative) justification for using whatever it is we invent. In this case, we don't have to invent any new expressions, because a more metaphorical one already exists: expression. We could instead use something like 'name', but that again harkens back too much, in my mind if not in yours, to the postmodern idea that words are symbols used as labels. This is the standard and common understanding of language, but mostly just because we are taught that it is true, even though it is not, and further that it is obvious that it is not. In postmodernist philosophy, words are used as names for things,

Paradigm

labels for objective occurrences, and it is merely correlation of the usage with the thing that indicates 'meaning', outside of just looking it up in the dictionary. But <u>words are not labels for things, they are things</u> themselves, although they can still be used on labels to identify or describe the contents of whatever container you put the label on or near. So, in order to avoid postmodern assumptions, I'm going to put 'name' aside along with 'cognate', even though both are words or descriptions of words, and choose something else. The other word we could use in place of 'word' is 'expression'. That seems to suggest a more abstract thing than 'word' itself, but can often be used synonymously. So we'll use that.

	expression	
	word	
	term	

Next, we will consider the two columns that are still blank. Each has a cell on the analytical level, a cell for the rhetorical level, and a cell in the metaphorical level. We can begin by filling in the left and right hand cells next to 'word', and we can use the words I've already mentioned.

	expression	
name	word	cognate
	term	

We don't have to worry about which is in which column, for now. (But they can have teleological significance that we will consider later.) The same process we used for the middle column is repeated with the others, choosing either more concrete or more abstract words to relate to the terms 'name' and 'cognate'. (Alternatively, we could think about origins or intentions and the arrow of time to choose alternatives for 'term' or 'expression'. If we don't want to get too picky about our nomenclature, the two processes should provide very similar if not identical results.) I'm going to provide some possibilities, and then discuss the mechanisms of language that express the POR approach to words before settling on specific selections.

designation? label? thought?	expression	pronunciation? idea? spelling?
name	word	cognate
description	term	root

All this no doubt seems like pointless pedantry, at best, or perhaps simply lunatic rambling. The purpose of the abstraction paradigm is not to provide any supremely authoritative designation of meaning, but simply an alternative to the dictionary entry approach we've grown used to. What are the characteristics of words that make them words? The dictionary approach is simply the authority of lexicographers. Whoever writes the dictionary is assumed to be a supreme authority that everyone else must take as nearly divine dictate. In turn, the lexicographer passes off authority to authors of usage citations. No matter how we do it, the effort to describe the meaning of words with nothing but other words is fraught with uncertainty and perilous beyond comprehension. Any alternative to using the paraphrased 'definitions' of dictionaries cannot illuminate the "real" meaning of words any more than the 'definition in context' method I've already described.

The truth is that words mean what they mean. No external iteration, no matter how careful, will provide someone who doesn't know a word anything but the vaguest clues to how to use it in conversation. No supply of 'word-a-day calendars' is going to convert someone from ignorant idiocy to convincing eloquence. But the sparseness of the abstraction paradigm approach is of paramount value, and once you grow use to it you might well and should agree that it is imperfect as any other, but superior to dictionary entries. "Which one do you mean?"

No matter how we try, we cannot really avoid the fact that the only way to perfectly express what is meant by a word is that word itself. POR describes this fact as the 'unitary' property of words, or the tautological principle. Each word means what that word means, and no other word can mean exactly that. Words are unitary. Each word is singular, a singularity. Synonyms are approximations, not logical equivalencies. Words are self-defining, in that any particular context uses a word to mean what that word is used to mean, regardless of how self-referential that sounds. The alternative postmodern approach ultimately makes all synonyms perfectly interchangeable, so that eventually all words eventually devolve into referring to a synonym for 'good' if it agrees with the way someone wants to use the word, or 'bad' if it disagrees with that person's inclinations. This is the principle called "postmodern over-synonimization", again. Take any word. Find a synonym for that word. Assume that the meaning, the definition in postmodern terms, of those two words are not merely similar, but identical. Keep doing that with other synonyms for that word, and any synonym for those words, and some possible synonym for those synonyms. If we assume that words are simply labels or symbols, rather than ideas themselves, then sooner or later you have to choose either 'good' or 'bad' as the last synonym. (The fact that sometimes 'bad' is used as a synonym for 'good' is exemplary and instructive in showing that definitions are not as valuable as people pretend.) But <u>words are not labels, they are descriptions</u>. They have value and meaning, but cannot be analyzed logically.

The postmodern approach to words fails to encompass this non-quantifiable value. To the postmodernist, prose is like mathematical expressions and formulas, because they wish to elevate their own choice of terms to the validity of calculating quantities, a reiteration of Socrates' "math envy". Use a word the way they, or their college professor, or some scientist or lawyer insists we use a word, and then you are using it 'correctly', but if you use it in a way they don't like, they will simply deny that it has any productive communication value at all. They can dismiss your usage simply because it is not to their liking, and claim, regardless of the truth, that they can't comprehend what it means when you use it. Without going through the exercise of actually employing the Socratic Method, they invoke the impenetrability of Socratic Ignorance to deny they have any knowledge of the truth. This results in the derogative dismissal of the communicative value of poetry, when in truth we know and should accept that poetry is far more information-bearing (more significant and meaningful) than prose can ever be. In the postmodern idea of language, poetry can't possibly be informative at all, let alone more informative than prose, because that postmodern idea assumes and insists that strict grammar is necessary to understand sentences and the thoughts they convey. The number of ways that this can be demonstrated as untrue is large and varied. Double negatives can't possibly be as meaningful as the lack of any negative. "Ain't" can't be useful no matter how many centuries it has existed. "Irregardless" must be impossible to interpret correctly because words have to have the mathematical integrity of "prefix+root+suffix=definition". (Questioning whether "ain't" is properly a contraction or whether the 'ir' in "irregardless" is a prefix is like pitting Superman against the Incredible Hulk.) Neither repetition nor ambiguity is as toxic to actual meaning as they should be if language were a mere deductive code. To the postmodernist, the reality that words can be expressive without strict grammar is a flaw in human processing of language, rather than the evidence that language processing doesn't work the way they insist it must. To the postmodernist, the fact that poetry is more evocative, more meaningful, than prose is preposterous. The only value that poetry can have in the postmodern perspective is as entertainment, not as truth. It can delight, but not inform. Meanwhile, despite their dictates, the most moving expressions are poetic, and not bound by typical grammar.

Whatever real laws or rules that language has, beyond prescribed vocabulary or learned grammar, beyond even true and false, to the mechanisms of communicating good and bad, they have to apply for poetry as well as prose. And those rules have to be identical whether the context is a dry academic paper or the intimate whispers of lovers. And so in the Philosophy Of Reason, we reject this assumption and insistence that it is the ability to parse, to deconstruct language with grammatical rules or dictionary entries that enables them to be used for communication. Because poetry is profound; it can communicate expressions of truth and real sensations far more effectively than prose modeled on the postmodernist ideal of words as symbols in a mathematical calculus that somehow defines human thought.

Words are unitary: each word means what that word means and nothing else. Words are also unique: no other word means exactly and precisely what any other word means. Finally, words are universal: every word always means the same thing in every context and usage, even when that meaning in different contexts is supposedly the opposite of that same word used in another context. Sometimes "bad" means "good". And yet, it is still the word "bad" and not any other word and cannot be said to express exactly what 'good' means even when we say it does. Of course, "bad means good" is now archaic. A more current example would be that 'hot' and 'cool' are synonyms. The declaration that a word cannot mean the opposite of that word formally, but only informally, is quite similar to the idea that logic can be anything but formal.

The first two aspects of words, 'unitary' and unique', are easily accepted, because postmodernists are used to (mistakenly) applying the mathematical "rule of the excluded middle" to language. So to say that each word means only what that word means (unitary) and that it means something different than what every other word means (unique) seems like repetition, two sides of the same coin. But the aspect of words being "universal" seems contrary to not just expectations, but possibilities, so it is worth reviewing. Each word in any language means the same thing in every context, without exception. How can 'bad' mean 'good', then, when it means 'bad' most of the time? The difficulty of dealing with the issue is compounded and confounded by the imprecision of the terms themselves, and our ability to use the word 'mean' ambiguously. Bad is defined as 'good', sometimes, but that does not mean that it means good. We are used to assuming, because it is the way we are used to having it explained, that definition and meaning are synonymous; indeed, over-synonymous. Meaning is not what you use a word for, meaning is why you are using the word for that. Part of the meaning of any word is a 'dichotomous nature', which enables the word to refer to both a thing and its (seeming) opposite. When this effect becomes profoundly noticeable, it is called 'the simultaneity principle' in POR. More will be explained on this point as we proceed, we can let the matter rest here with the reiteration that the meaning of a word does not change over time or between contexts, only its definition does. The meaning of a word is always universal, because that is what defines the word 'meaning'; the quality of the word that does not change over time, rather than the quality of the word that does. What word we might use to refer to a thing waxes and wanes through history, but why we use it to refer to that thing remains consistent, whether it is the consistency of constancy, repetition, or the consistency of a fly trapped in amber, unmoving.

For now, I will end this nearly-hopelessly-confusing digression by simply reiterating that there are three properties that all words share, and that entirely describe all properties of words. Words are unitary, they are unique, and they are universal. Each word (within a 'language' which is nothing more than a particular set of words familiar to a particular person) means only what that word means, means something different than what any other word means, and means the same thing every time it is used, even when it is apparently referring to something opposite to what it was used to refer to in some other usage.

Words are tautological: "parts are parts". Words are also teleological: "It doesn't matter what word you use, what matters is *why* you're using it." No matter how hard and often we try to pretend that words are simply symbols we use to label things in the external universe, this definitely isn't the case. <u>Words don't label external objects or events, they describe internal sensations and ideas.</u> And we know when a word is truly used to communicate when it **resonates** in our minds and bodies, the way poetry does and prose rarely can.

So which words should we use in our abstraction paradigm to finish the example? It hardly matters, any words will do as long as we can recognize their association to the other words in the diagram. There isn't only one abstraction paradigm that can be 'correct' for any particular word, just as there is no single dictionary entry that completely explains how to use a word. God didn't write any dictionaries with divine dictates designating what is true and what is not, we have to manage, somehow, to get along without such absolute authority. Neither scientists nor lawyers, either, can decide for us how to use language, and even the greatest, most famous, or most profound authors can only influence, not control, what our brains come up with when we wish to express our thoughts within our community. My choices for the diagram we previously started is this:

label	expression	idea
identifier	word	cognate
description	term	root

I selected those choices because they seem to be most appropriate through the simile "root is to word as word is to label" and "description is to word as word is to idea". There aren't going to be any perfect matches, there is no mathematical formula to test whether these choices are correct. Yes, I have said that words are not labels or symbols, but I've included one of those terms in this diagram in order to make it somewhat compatible with the postmodern ideas we're trying to replace with more productive thoughts. To trolling postmodernists, every unflattering description is "name calling", no matter how accurate a description it is. So I've also made one other final revision, before declaring this particular example complete: 'name' has been changed to 'identifier'. But we will leave 'label' where it is, to remind us that abstraction paradigms are a transitional mechanism, in that regard. The object isn't to make words so absolute in meaning that we can program a computer to understand them, but to learn to accept the fact that we cannot program understanding into a computer, only data and how to arithmetically process it.

Computers cannot understand words, or anything else. All computers can do, all they will ever do no matter how inventive or complicated our programming might be, is compute; to calculate numbers. This puts the kibosh on any idealistic insistence that 'artificial intelligence' will ever be able to use natural language the way humans do. The best they can do is execute algorithmic instructions that mimic, approximate, or insufficiently simulate what goes on in our minds and our brains when we speak or write. The way a parrot can say words, but won't ever be really saying words, but simply making sounds. Unless you assume and insist that the tweeting of bird song is the wisdom of Shakespeare, you must accept the idea that words have meaning that neither animals nor transistors, no matter how carefully trained or arranged, will ever comprehend.

Abstraction paradigms have two other interesting applications in addition to simply being a kind of 'graphical thesaurus' method of replacing dictionary definitions. The first is a rough method of serving as a 'truth detector', in keeping with Socrates' goal of being able to tell when a statement is accurate with precision alone. The second has been hinted at before: the use of abstraction paradigms to illustrate teleological flipping, the mechanism of self-determination described earlier.

The original development of the abstraction paradigm, the designation and apparent isolation of the hypothetical 'levels of language', was intended as a direct implementation of a Socratic deconstruction of language. The idea of an <u>analytical</u> level, when each term in a sentence should be considered as much of a label for a quantitative category as possible, is a rather straight-forward implementation of the postmodernist ideal of language. If words were symbols for deductively certain logical concepts, if they had even a functional objective certainty of any kind, then all text would be analytical, like terms in a math problem. When language is as dry, grammatically uninteresting, and conventional as prose can get, it can maintain this appearance of being unemotional references to concrete facts and nothing more. When lawyers use legalese, or when scientists use technical nomenclature, they are aspiring to this robotic ideal of language, to being as uncontroversial and incontrovertible as language can allow. The more productive, some would say informal, level of <u>rhetoric</u> becomes problematic, if you follow the postmodernist philosophy of disparaging any use of words that isn't pretentiously if fictitiously absolute. The very word "rhetoric" itself, through POS and common usage, has come to be considered a dismissive reference to any language. Many English speakers remain aware that a 'rhetorical question' is not actually meaningless, just not intended to be answered, but this knowledge becomes moot. In POR, any language that isn't formulaic or private is 'rhetoric', and the rhetorical level of an abstraction paradigm designates how to interpret words when nobody bothers to argue about what they mean. If anyone should dispute whether a word is being used correctly, accurately, or properly, then it must be either analyzed more exactingly or accepted as a figure of speech. The <u>metaphoric</u> level, where words become figurative, is more self-explanatory, but brings up an important principle about language in POR.

The word 'metaphor' could be deconstructed with historical etymology or more direct dissection. It generally means a more fanciful word or words used in place of a more conventional referent. When someone says "Your beauty is like a flower", that's a simile, and when they say "Your beauty is a flower", that's a metaphor, according to classical and familiar (and postmodern) grammar lessons. You may have caught on, already, that POR isn't inhibited by a conventional faith in a grammatical mechanism in language, and actively opposes formulaic approaches that seek to make syntax and etymology more important, concrete, or productive than they really are in natural language. Still, our use of the term 'metaphor' itself is mostly traditional and customary. Particularly when describing or discussing abstraction paradigms, 'metaphor' simply means use of words in a more abstract rather than material way. The difference is largely imaginary, as we will find, though. Consider the use of figures of speech like metonymy and synecdoche. When someone mentions "the White House", is it more, or is it less, analytical to be referring to a building or the President's staff? Obviously, our first inclination is to declare it more figurative, metaphorical, to refer to the people in the building than the building itself. And yet, the use of a name to refer to a building is itself non-analytical, but arbitrary. But then, that particular description of the executive mansion and its visual appearance is not arbitrary. In most contexts, we would say the term is analytical when it refers to the building and metaphorical when it identifies the people inside. The distinction itself is unimportant, what gives it importance is the context and why we are trying to make it. Despite the centuries of effort put into reducing the grammar of language to logical formulations, language is never logical. Whether a pedant identifies a figure of speech as synecdoche or some other metonymy has no bearing whatsoever on whether the expression is understandable or communicative. Any figurative use, metonymy or something even more poetic, becomes proper when it becomes familiar, and the grammaticians invent a "rule" or name a category in order to pretend it is mechanical and logical.

Deciding which of two or more possible ways of describing the meaning of a word is more concrete and which is more abstract turns out to be nearly if not entirely arbitrary in many if not all cases. In POR, we avoid at least some of the problem by acknowledging that, outside of abstraction paradigms that artificially constrict words into discrete layers of meaning, all words are metaphors. Metaphors for what? Other words, of course. The postmodernists can attempt to categorize and list every possible kind, type, or feature of figures of speech, but for the most part it is a pointless exercise; all words are simply metaphors for ideas that do not require mathematical integrity to be useful. To illustrate this characterization, we use the preeminent example of 'matter'.

In the postmodern theory of language, 'matter' is several unrelated words that coincidentally share the same spelling and pronunciation. But words are unitary, unique, and universal in POR, so every kind of 'matter' is the same meaning of the same word in all cases, and no other word can mean precisely and exactly that. If I ask "so what is matter?" that encourages your brain to fall back on the postmodern approach to vocabulary, conjuring up imagines that the text is simply a label for a thing, and by identifying that thing, you learn the 'meaning' (or more properly the definition, somehow singular yet not unitary and possibly not even unique) of that word. Instead, when I ask "what is matter?", you should now be able to read it more correctly, not as a request to identify the one thing it might refer to, but instead to wonder about the one reason it is used to mean anything, regardless of how many things there might be that justify that one reason for using that one, singular, unique, unitary, and universal word. The reason 'matter' is used as an iconic example in POR is because it so clearly illustrates, in its most conventional uses, a dichotomy that clearly reflects the 'analytical versus metaphorical' method of deconstructing rhetoric, and the fact that all words are metaphors in all uses. When a word has two seemingly distinct yet obviously related denotations, POR refers to it as a dichotomous abstraction.

There are two contrary connotations normally understood for the word 'matter'. One is physical substance, and one is emotional import. In the conventional approach to words, one of them must be designated the 'real' meaning and the other a 'metaphoric' usage. Is 'matter' actually objective mass, atoms and molecules that make up all the materials in the physical universe, distinguishable only from 'energy' as the entirety of the contents of the universe apart from space and time themselves? Or is 'matter' whatever we consider important, what matters, the topic at hand or on the agenda, and the 'physical matter' usage simply a metaphorical one invented by scientists once they realized they needed a word for material substance that distinguishes it from energy, space, or time? Is physical matter the original, and psychological matter the metaphor, or is emotional substance the principle meaning, with more quantifiable substance being a familiar but figurative repurposing? In conventional considerations of language and meaning, such distinctions sometimes take on overblown gravity, while in POR they become inconsequential prattling. All words are metaphors, there isn't any need to declare one usage of 'matter' any different than the other, let alone superior. Regardless of whether we designate the two denotations/connotations of matter as similar, because they are both weighty, or opposite, because one is directly measurable and the other seems more fanciful, they are metaphors for each other. "Matter" is a metaphor for "matter".

Which is the more directly measurable, the externally quantifiable or the internally experienced? Which is more fanciful, the use of the term as an abstraction for atomic structures or the use of the term as an analysis of sentiment? To the flagrantly inaccurate but faithfully adopted postmodern sensibilities, one will be what matter 'really' is, scientific and undeniable, and the other should be the metaphorical usage, imprecise and easily dismissed. Since not even the most serious and studious postmodernist can consistently identify which is which, the lexicographic convention of claiming they are two different meanings becomes unavoidable, and eventually the idea that they are two different words that are simply homonyms. It doesn't matter what you call matter, what matters is why you're calling it matter. We can take it for granted it is a metaphor, in both cases, and the issue of importance swiftly becomes whether someone can grasp that metaphor or wishes to discount it instead, claiming it incomprehensible because they would rather not admit to its communicative value.

Words like "matter", which clearly show a dichotomy in usage, are central test cases for the POR theory of language. This theory describes words as unitary, unique, and universal, so it might seem contrary and bemusing at first to think that the dual 'meaning' of "matter" supports and even confirms the POR description. This is what makes it an exemplary and even iconic example. To say that 'matter' really means physical substance, and it is used metaphorically when we refer to something abstract, or to say that 'matter' really means something of significance and importance, and when scientists and others use it as a label for objects with mass, they are using it as technical jargon, is like claiming that light is a particle or a wave, but not both at the same time. How we set up our detectors can determine only which aspect we are paying attention to, the reality is the same regardless. The determination of which is the rhetorical meaning in any context is not easily calculated statistically, though that can be done. Light has illumination, but words have meaning, and that isn't a characteristic that can be as easily quantified objectively. In the postmodernist mindset, of course, anything that cannot be quantified cannot be said to exist, but even a postmodernist can only dispute the meaning of the words "words have meaning" after proving that there can be no dispute about its truth, but simply quibbling about what the terms refer to, what they *mean*.

The same aspect of dichotomous abstraction can be easily seen in another word that we've examined in some detail, *control*. Is it the ability to change, or the unchanged example? Again, the fact that words are unique, unitary, and most importantly universal, seems almost insane, simply because it is so different than what we have been taught to believe, and yet, it is clearly undeniable, as well. The word 'control' isn't really two different words any more than the word 'matter' is. Another example we will consider more explicitly in a moment is 'determine'.

In analytic philosophy, there is an intellectual construct known as "the Liar's Paradox". "This statement is false." It is the foundation of many word puzzles and science fiction stories, this idea that someone says, "I am a liar," and then, "I am lying." This is generally followed in the sci-fi narrative by the robot this paradox is presented to frying its own circuits and melting down, while trying to analyze the logic of the claims. If the statement is actually false, if the liar is actually lying, then the statement 'this statement is false' is true, meaning that it is not false, meaning it is untrue because it says it is false, meaning...? If the liar is being honest when they claim to be a liar, this means they are not lying, resulting in the logical conclusion that they are not lying when they confess to being a liar, indicating they are not lying, and so they are not a liar and are lying when they say they are lying which makes them a liar, which means...?

The statement "words have meaning", as I have explained, is an "anti-Liar's Paradox", an honest person's anti-paradox. It is similar to Descartes' "I think therefore I am" in being self-evident, irrefutable. The Liar's Paradox is, in the Philosophy Of Reason I am describing here, a proof that words and language are not logical. The alternative, the postmodernist philosophies which the

Philosophy Of Reason confront and controvert, find the Liar's Paradox to be profound and disconcerting simultaneously, but proof of nothing, merely an intriguing conundrum. Conversely, POR, as I have already pointed out, recognizes the "anti-Liar's non-Paradox" that 'words have meaning' to be proof that words have meaning, since the claim cannot be disputed without having first been understood, and by being understood it is proven to be true. The terms themselves are easily recognizable, if not quite as simple as they first appear, when they are examined more thoroughly. The fact that our brains do not fry when we read them, and they don't melt when we read "this statement is false", either, demonstrates that language is not a logical process and the thoughts in our minds are not the execution of algorithms. To postmodernists, this idea that our brains would seize when encountering a sentence that is so self-referential, whether true or false, is dismissed with a condemnatory judgment that our brains simply do not succeed so easily in interpreting logical statements, or do succeed in overcoming the limitations of transistorized circuitry by refusing to examine the words thoroughly enough. Or else the postmodernist would simply note that computers don't actually fry their circuits the way they do in fiction when given erroneous or imprecise inputs, they simply provide erroneous outputs or no outputs at all. Either way, the postmodernist maintains their theory as unfalsifiable, by insisting that our thoughts <u>should be</u> the execution of algorithms but fail to do so. The more obvious explanation, that thoughts are not and should not be algorithmic, is dismissed by the rationalists because it isn't the conclusion they have assumed.

The similarity between Descartes' self-evident proof and the statement 'words have meaning' is not coincidental. They are both irrefutable in the same way and are based on the same idea, that the claim must be true in order to be made: they are self-evident. The Liar's Paradox, in contrast, is self-refuting, because the claim 'this statement is false' must be untrue in order to be recognized as a claim. I won't belabor the point further; let us return to the examination of how words themselves work. The previous example was 'matter', and the intriguing fact that it means two nearly opposite things.

"Determination" (or 'determine') is a word like "matter", as well; one that displays the 'dichotomous abstraction' principle, that a word can have two distinctively complementary definitions, but share a single meaning, because the meaning of a word is teleological rather than tautological; not based on what you are referring to with the word, but why you are referring to it with that word, and not some other. We can use "determination" to describe an intentional selection between alternatives, or we can use it to mean a purposeful intention to overcome difficulties. Considering the phrases "I have determined" versus "I am determined" makes the point clear; 'a determination' versus 'determination' without the indefinite article. Expressed like that, the true unique, universal, and unitary *meaning* of the word 'determine' seems to become more obvious even as its *definition* becomes more uncertain. We can describe the meaning of the word in ways that make the two tropes opposite, as carefully making a choice versus proceeding with heedlessness, or more synonymous, as two different ways at looking at the same act of selection, either from the perspective of the list of alternatives or the perspective of the person selecting one possibility from among them. "Discriminating" is another, similar word, sometimes being used to refer to unfair prejudice, and sometimes being used to refer to informed expertise when choosing or deciding from among different possibilities.

To illustrate these three bits of thought in the English language, here are three abstraction paradigms 'defining' them:

gravity	importance	issue
weight	matter	wait
mass	substance	time

desire	decision	expectation
preference	determination	intention
selection	choice	alternative

Paradigm

select	separate	design
favor	discrimination	recognition
bias	bigotry	prejudice

It should be mentioned that grammatical roles, such as parts of speech, class, tense, or plurality, are not ignored entirely, but not considered explicitly, either, when formulating/designing AP. This is in keeping with the general perspective of POR linguistics, that such distinctions are ad hoc categories, rather than unambiguous classifications based on any logical principles. Propriety and pedantry have caused people to accept the postmodern dictate that they are unambiguous, by dismissing all examples of ambiguity, inventing additional fictional rules or classes to explain the most vexing contradictions, and focusing on the less ambiguous examples as if they were definitive.

Here are two additional abstraction paradigms, breaking out the connotations of the word 'matter' into two separate diagrams. First the physical substance kind of matter:

wave	objects	particle
time	matter	space
quantum	energy	force

Note that the term 'space' in the 'rhetorical purpose' cell might be replaced with 'movement', as a more analytical thought, the relationship between the other words being about equivalent regardless. 'Space' was used purposefully to mirror the selection of 'time' in the 'rhetorical meaning' position. Now the AP for the sense of 'matter' in the phrase "what really matters":

feelings	urgency	intention
subject	matter	object
topic	item	note

Of course there can easily be a nearly infinite number of abstraction paradigms, for almost any word, and there is no doubt that at least some of the terms I've entered seem bizarre if not nonsensical. There are no fewer real possibilities for a dictionary entry for any one word: stripped of the context of actual natural language, any attempt to concretize the abstract meaning of words with other words suffers the same limitations. None of the examples here is any more authoritative than any that you might come up with on your own, or in discussion with other people. But this is one of the important advantages of the AP, though it might appear like a disadvantage to postmodern intuition. A dictionary entry comes from a professional lexicographer after some extensive study of specific august uses. It should therefore be a more refined and intelligent determination than one from a random person of arbitrary education. But what makes a dictionary entry authoritative is the fact that it is published and used, the qualities and credentials of the author being purposefully made ambiguous by the terse, formulaic style of scholarly diction used in reference books, and the postmodern assumption that there is an objective precision and logic to the quanta of language we call words and their wavering linguistic effectiveness that we call meaning. With abstraction paradigms, anyone can fill one in and call it correct, a map of how they use the singular expression. We could perhaps study the statistical probabilities of any two AP being identical in whole or in part, and process that information through mathematical formulas, and somehow learn from this or simply declare some or one more proper for whatever reason or purpose we have. This would satisfy the postmodernist IPTM fans, perhaps opening up a whole new round of 'now we can program computers to talk for real' idealism. But there is no one AP that is more authoritative than any other, and this is not a weakness but a strength.

The importance of the relationships between words displayed in any particular diagram does not become diluted because every version might be different, contrary to the false intuitions instilled in us by long habituation with the Information Processing Theory of Mind. As long as every one is completed sincerely, not only does it become valid but it makes all other possible AP for that word a bit more valid, as well, even those that differ from it. Perhaps that validity is increased most by those that differ from it. Dictionaries become less useful the more entries you have for the same word, fuzzing up any clear depiction they might suggest of the ultimate true unspoken but undeniable meaning of a word. Without a minimized quantity, a strong tradition of conventions, and rigorous attention to consistency in both form and perspective, dictionary entries become useless.

POR AP become more useful the more numerous and varied the entries become, clarifying and sharpening the real understanding of what a word **means**, independent of how it is pronounced or spelled. Dictionaries are intended for *precision*; the fewer data points, the more exacting the supposed knowledge being conveyed. AP work more like the real world use of words, each data point improving the *accuracy* of our comprehension. It is this comprehension which enables words to 'funnel' or 'tunnel' truth through the existential wall that separates our mental experience from the physical world we perceive through our senses, giving our brains access to data that our minds cannot possibly calculate or simply consider mere sense data. The theory of mind is not stopped by philosophical limitations or existential barriers, and we can recognize ourselves in others when we recognize the words they are using, because we automatically, without even realizing it, understand that it is the reason they used those words, not any statistical correlation to an abstracted definition, that give those words meaning.

Returning to the idea of using AP as 'lie detectors', the practice in POR is to pay close attention to the words someone is using, in order to detect unrecognized yet deceptive 'flopping' from one level of language to another. This can and does occur unconsciously in the speaker or writer's brain, in order to attempt to conform their words to the fiction and mislead the listener or reader. Because it is unconscious, it is unavoidable. Because the words persist after the act of producing them, which is transient, providing much more time to analyze them after the fact than the person had before generating them, it can detect misrepresentations that they might suppose are too subtle or ingenious to notice. Further, and even more importantly, the technique is not limited to intentional fabrications. Even sincerely believed sentiments that are inaccurate, which aren't known by the originator to be false, can be identified, by recognizing the switching back and forth from an analytical use of rhetoric to a metaphoric set of terms repeatedly.

This is not simply a matter of isolating a single word or phrase, and is only practical when applied across a larger number of expressions. Whenever a sufficiently large statement is examined, the use of more metaphorical terminology, and outright metaphoric tropes in idiom, in a supposedly analytical statement of reasoning (nee logic) is a 'tell' that someone is being disingenuous or worse, or simply unknowingly mistaken about their representation of facts, whether false tautologies or false teleologies. Likewise, unexpected use of more analytic terms in an otherwise metaphorical description of things does not lend those metaphors any more credibility, and the familiarity or resonance of the metaphors does not lend credibility to the selection of the more analytical words. The truth and meaning of an analytic use of a word is not enhanced by contextual association with familiar metaphors, nor do the metaphors become more honest because the analytic term is relatively concrete. This kind of 'flopping' from one level of abstraction to another signals a purposeful, though not necessarily intentional, effort to suggest otherwise, an insinuation or a hidden assumption that the analytical terms must be valid if the metaphors resonate emotionally, or that the metaphors are valid because the analytical terms are consistent with reality.

This tautological flopping is a common occurrence, but goes unnoticed by the speaker. As postmodernists we are taught that all of our language is or should be stated and intended as logical arguments in a mathematical statement of grammar and vocabulary in place of formulas and quantities. But the nature of words, as abstractions and comparisons, identifiers and descriptions, rather than labels and deductively assignable symbols, causes tautological flopping to become relatively obvious once you are aware of it and know what to look for, both in general and in any particular instance. The postmodern method is to insist that every word is only analytical, and that all metaphors are suspect or can simply be dismissed as either dishonest or meaningless. This increases the frequency with which people expect that their substitution of a non-quantifiable idea as a word in a supposedly more sober or logical statement should be uncontroversial, since they assume that even non-quantifiable categories or groups are *actually* quantified by some hidden calculus in our brains, and whatever silent and invisible God ensures their conceptions have mathematical integrity. All words are metaphors, this is true. But that doesn't mean they are all used metaphorically. Considering when something that someone says or writes is actual truth or sophisticated lies by examining how easily their terms can be categorized as mostly analytical and rhetorical, or mostly rhetorical and metaphorical, does provide a keen insight that almost satisfies Socrates' desire for a way to distinguish fact from fiction without any additional empirical comparisons. Socrates' error was in assuming that mathematical processes do not need double-checking for mistakes, an empirical comparison that is a necessity which spoils his hypothetical reduction of language to algorithmic processing on a practical level, even beyond the flaw in his theory that words can or should be deductively impervious to misuse, whether intentional or accidental. Sincere and accurate words never need to be double-checked in this way, as if a logical error could spoil their validity, even though they can be revised at will, and the truth of a statement can still be verified against the real world. The difficulty of the postmodern, Socratically Erroneous approach to words is that most words refer to epistemological abstractions, categories, rather than simple ontological events (objects, occurances). When describing simple physical objects, facts seem absolute and certain, but when words are used to identify emotional, social, political, or otherwise abstract things, the consistency or deductive validity of those things does not automatically follow from consistency or precision (exactness) in what words are used. In truth, of course, such things have no deductive certainty, though when words are used accurately, their consistency transcends that of even simple repetition.

Thus, whether there is a cow in the field is not the kind of truth that AP analysis for tautological flopping can easily be used to judge, but it is still possible. In fact, it is this tautological flopping that inevitably occurs when people attempt to describe fictional events which causes people who are wholly ignorant of abstraction paradigms to suspect when someone is lying or mistaken. Postmodernist theory is that it is logical inconsistencies or imprecision that cause such suspicions, but this is itself a fiction. A mumpsimus, the sumpsimus of which is that mixing of concrete and abstract terminology is more often the impetus for this intuitive detection of inaccuracy. The POR method suffers from fewer false positives and false negatives in detecting both intentional and unintentional falsehoods. Particularly when language is being used to describe motivations and intentions of other people, and even more particularly when dealing with groups of people rather than individuals, the natural human desire to describe things we disapprove of with inflammatory terms and things we approve of with complementary sentiments makes the distinction between logical definition and reasonable accuracy stark, enhancing the ability to detect falsehoods by detecting inconsistencies in the metaphorical or analytical use of terms.

It can be admitted that a partial or insincere acceptance of the AP approach of detecting tautological flopping can easily be used to dismiss the approach itself. The unavoidability of this "I'm rubber and you're glue" technique of accusatory projection would undermine POR linguistic theory if it relied on the postmodern delusion of logic we call Socrates' Error. Since we reject such math envy, attempts to subvert the practice of POR instead ratifies the theory, since our efforts to communicate do not rely on faith in our own logic, only our intent to engage in reasoning. Essentially, trying to use POR linguistic approaches to criticize the legitimacy or value of POR linguistic approaches is self-refuting when intended to dismiss POR, and self-enforcing when intended to embrace POR. Along the same lines, POR enables a calm dedication that can easily be discounted as passive aggression. Honest descriptions that are unflattering can be characterized as 'inflammatory terms' or name-calling. Disingenuous mimicry of POR rhetoric can be used to mask intentionally insulting language. Mumpsimus, sumpsimus. First, they will ignore us. Then, they will mock us. Then, they will attack us. Then, we will win. The familiar pattern is reiterated in the arc of the Philosophy itself, as it extends into society, as well as each individual discussion that is informed by POR.

The second supplemental use of abstraction paradigms, using them to illustrate teleological flipping, has already been hinted at. When I used the terms "rhetorical purpose" and "rhetorical meaning" to indicate the right hand and left hand cells on the rhetorical level of an AP, that designated the arrow of time that we are used to in forward chronology, the direction of cause and effect. The dichotomous columns of the AP can also be called "future" instead of "purpose" (traditionally the right hand cells) and "past" instead of "meaning" (traditionally the left hand cells). A reverse or inverse teleology flips the arrow, so that the future (intention) comes before the past (action). The two columns in the AP are still designated 'future' and 'past', although the 'future' goal-seeking event occurs before the 'past' behavioral event. The arrow of causation is now opposite the arrow of chronology, indicating self-determination, or something rhetorically mimicking conscious selection. The first supplemental use of AP, detecting falsehoods by observing flopping from one level of vocabulary to another, has more pragmatic application, but the illustration of teleological flipping is more informative. The confusion of reversing the arrow of time is not entirely relieved by using the terms 'meaning' and 'purpose' rather than 'past' and 'future', but in general it results in less consternation from the uninitiated.

Using AP to illustrate teleological flipping can lead to an abstraction paradigm specifically developed to describe these relationships, though the distinctions are typically so subtle and esoteric they can go unnoticed. When a typical AP is designed, the outer columns are referred to as the dichotomy; two words that are both synonymous and antonymous in meaning, closely related yet notably divergent. The center column is the dialectic, and identifies an intellectual domain where the "equal yet opposite" nature of the dichotomous relationship of the two outer terms (focusing on the rhetorical level) can be explored and discussed. Here is an AP that exemplifies the matter of dialectical dichotomies:

statute	judgment	justice
law	politics	principle
legislation	government	debate

It should be obvious that an entire book, indeed a whole library of books, could be written on that particular abstraction paradigm. Thousands of years of philosophy and political science informs every usage of these words. For now, it is only a teaching tool to illustrate the methodology. For example, "politics" is the dialectic that makes "law" and "principles" both opposite and identical. The progression from the analytical use of the term 'debate', the rhetorical term 'principles', and the metaphor of 'justice' can be perceived, without dictating any transcendent validity to it. It should be analogous to the progression from 'legislation' through 'law' to 'statute', as well. Which do we mean when we say 'law', the legislation as passed by our legislature or the statute as interpreted by our judges? The distinction is 'semantic quibbling' to someone who wants to ignore it. This AP also makes another point clear, which I haven't directly mentioned previously. I did admit that, in some respect, the terms in an AP are arbitrary. Any dialectic could be used for any set of dichotomies, in theory. This means that the separate dimensions of the up/down level and the left/right dialectic dichotomy can be switched. This would make 'government' and 'judgment' the dichotomy for the dialectic 'politics'. Then 'law' becomes the analytical term and 'principles' the metaphorical one. It could also make 'law' the more abstract word and 'principle' the more concrete one, but this would, perhaps, be less comprehensible. This is the point of AP, to examine how comprehensible the relationships are between the ideas we use these words to express, rather than to declare whether a particular set or arrangement of terms is "correct" or "right".

Still, I hope and believe that you can see how if someone were to use the word 'law', declared here to be rhetorical, in a way that uses the ambiguity of whether they are referring to an act of Congress or a court decision, (a relationship that is partly if not quite effectively captured by my declaration of the former as a more concrete/analytical idea identified as 'legislation' and the latter as a more abstract/metaphorical thought represented as 'statute') it could signify that they are being either deceitful or muddled in their reasoning. I hesitate to provide a more textual example, because any hypothetical text has no real context by which to ascertain its truth. It would simply be me declaring that it was told as a lie, but that would itself be a fiction. The truth of words cannot be extracted hypothetically, and the truth of a hypothesis depends on its context; the same sequence of words that is untrue in one context can be true in another. It is always a matter of sincere and sentient interpretation, not mathematical or automated translation. Thus, extracting ourselves from the tar pit of postmodernism can be as frightening and disorienting as being released from prison, free for the first time in our lives, but made nervous rather than empowered by our newfound liberty.

Now, here is an AP designed with teleological flipping in mind, using the same rhetorical dialectical dichotomy, but with different analysis and metaphor:

mandate	dictate	decree
law	politics	principle
text	debate	edict

Again, an unlimited set of AP can be created for any word, so the variance in these previous two is instructive rather than contradictory. It is even possible that you (or me, at a different time) might think the first is more appropriate for examining teleological flipping, and the second for considering tautological flopping. The postmodernist conditioning we've all received makes it inevitable that this suggestion would lead us to question whether there could be any value at all to these, or any, abstraction paradigm. If any arrangement of any words are possible, how could any particular set be informative? If you are having difficulty getting passed this perspective, consider these diagrams to be philosophical exercises, perhaps a kind of linguistic art project, rather than analytical examinations that can replace dictionary or thesaurus representations of the meaning of words. Regardless, in each level, above, the terms have been arranged to prompt questions as much as answer them. As I pointed out previously, AP (and, indeed, all textual examinations in POR) are understandably difficult to accept when presented in the abstract, while learning what they are, because isolating words from real words in real conversations using real language, putting them in academic examples, actively prevents these tools from being used correctly. It is our regular use of words in our daily lives, whether professionally, politically, or casually, that POR philosophy is intended to examine, not the hypothetical and in fact falsely logical, though familiar, context of words as deductive symbols for platonic objects that we are used to. This is not an issue that is unique to POR in any way; all schoolbook examples of lessons are artificial and simplified. Because POR is a new approach, the best instances to use for demonstration purposes while teaching the methods have not necessarily been discovered or invented, yet. I can only do my best, and since we are still running out of time, whether individual people can figure out what is false information, fake news, or true facts without omniscience or reliance on outside authority becomes more important by the moment, so it will have to suffice for now.

The 'teleology focused' AP above has been arranged so that each dichotomy can prompt the question, "Does this cause that, or does that cause this; which is the intention, and which is the effect of that intention; which is the original form, and which is it transformed into by human actions?"

To wit: does the text of our laws come from the intended edict, or is the edict the template that results in (or from) our choice of text? Do statutes and verdicts define, or merely reflect, our principles? Are the dictates of government a decree because it is a mandate, or is it a mandate because it is a decree? Certainly, this could all be dismissed as pointless pedantry, idle sophistry, and meaningless psychobabble, in the abstract. But when discussing these issues in real world situations, these questions become integral and vital to the process of argument and debate that we think conversation on such topics should be. Postmodern trolls will routinely dismiss any teleological relationships that we might envision, since they can always be flipped from forward to backwards teleologies, and postmodernists are not aware of any difference. To the mind captured and enraptured by Socrates' Error, mistakenly certain that words must have simplistic definitions reducible to one or a small number of sentences or terse fragments of sentences to mimic the format of a dictionary, such flipping is trivial and insignificant. This perspective is due to the fact that we have all engaged in it rampantly, but without notice, throughout our entire lives. The ease with which our minds can reverse cause and effect to describe intention (purpose) as cause and action as a result, making our goals the origin of the impulse that results in our movements when the physical reality remains 'choice->movement->decision' whether we are aware of it or not, makes it difficult to avoid assuming that when we say "I did this because I wanted to do this," it is a comprehensible claim, rather than the circular definition of 'want' that it is. Backwards teleologies, particularly inverse teleologies of conscious intention, but also the reverse teleologies of natural selection, are inherently hindsight-based 'just so' explanations that don't actually explain why something happened, only that it did. Only simplistic forward teleologies could have the logical power of 'cause and effect', presuming (inaccurately, as I've explained) that logic could accommodate teleologies, which it can't. Whether "the sun is hot because it is plasma" or "I am a good person because I follow the law", teleologies are only images in our head, not physical explanations of mechanical relationships. This does not make them unimportant, as we are taught to believe about things that are 'subjective', or variable at will, or secret until revealed. POR recognizes that these are all that could be important, what matters is not what happened, what matters is why it happened. This truth is always denied by the well trained postmodernist, until it cannot be denied any longer, but then it is only embraced long enough to last until another chance to dismiss the idea that it is true, and then the acceptance is replaced not just with denial that it is true, but denial that it was ever accepted, as well.

Here is one last attempt to wrangle an abstraction paradigm into a comprehensible instance for teaching abstraction paradigm. It will be presented without other explanation, and left for the private contemplation of the reader. Consider the chronological arrow of time, the teleological arrow of consciousness, and how they are opposite. Think about the physical, analytical existence of these things, which all have physical yet abstract existence, but also the intellectual, intangible existence of these things, independent of how they existentially exist despite being more complicated than simple objects:

idea	spirit	attitude
brain	self	mind
neurons	body	thought

Effectively, to fully comprehend language in the abstract, and every use of language we engage in specifically, you must accept that the lesson that we have been taught, that syntax and diction are implementations of logic, that reasoning which cannot be reduced to mathematical relationships is bad reasoning, are presented so repeatedly and forcefully not because they are true but because they are false. If they were true, we wouldn't need to be taught such things, we would not even need to consciously know them, it would be as automatic as breathing, as talking, as imagining. All of the grammatical rules of language and parts of speech that people have ever come up with are implementations of Socrates' Error, an idealistic but incorrect assumption that a logic in language is demonstrable and necessary. Tens of thousands of man-years of effort, all performed with the utmost integrity and good intentions, has yet to provide the mathematical code that modernists and postmodernists alike have yearned for. I notice with angst and trepidation that school children are being taught to describe arithmetic problems, equations as simple as "6+5=11", as "math sentences", merely to try to reinforce the fiction that sentences made of words and punctuation are secretly mathematical equations. "Six plus five is eleven," should be indistinguishable from "6+5=11", just different symbols are used to write it down, according to the postmodern dictate. Numerals and numbers should be unambiguously the same or unambiguously different, each in turn and as often as necessary to pretend that numbers aren't ontologically ambiguous to begin with; that is the postmodern habit. The contrary theory, which POR embraces and expounds, that words benefit from ambiguity, that being unambiguous is a fatal flaw in symbols that prevents them from being informative, is harder to comprehend, but all the more important for that reason.

The desire for the truth of a linguistic statement to be verifiable by calculation, as easily as the truth of an accounting statement, is just as strong today as it was more than 2000 years ago, when Plato wrote of Socrates' interlude with Meno. The quest for logic in language has produced Socratic

Ignorance, of unparalleled value in science and the justice system, and our technology and civilization benefits from it to an untold extent. But refusing to recognize that such Ignorance is a pose, a fiction used to ensure that scientists and jurists do not have an excessive amount of bias that prevents them from being able to determine what is true to a mathematical certainty in physics and beyond a reasonable doubt in jurisprudence, is simple, purposeful stupidity. Socratic Ignorance is a fiction; it can be a productive one, or it can be an obstructive fiction instead. Our inability to be perfectly "objective", free of all bias, is denounced as a flaw and a fault by postmodern thinkers, who idealize the human brain as an information processing computer, and idolize computers as an angelic, perfect model for humanity. The reality is, and has always truly been, and must always remain, exactly opposite. Our humanity, our consciousness, our hope and compassion and morality, only come from feeling and reasoning, not proving and calculating. It is not a flaw, it is transcendence over the very possibility of flaw. There are no 'mistakes' in nature; whatever happens is what happened, with no moral absolutes by which to judge whether it is proper or correct. Our brains evolved not to achieve certainty, but to deal on a constant and unalienable basis with uncertainty.

Rigorous syntax, prescriptive categories, rationalized spelling, even entire artificial tongues purposefully designed to provide more logical transmission and reception of verbal or written data, have all been accepted by their advocates or condoned as insufficient or ineffective by everyone else. The most well educated linguistic psychologists, sociologists, or philosophers have always failed to perfectly, or even productively normalize speech or script, and all the rationalistic categorization of mechanisms and structures in language fails soon after the first attempt to apply it to routine human communications of any but the most idealized sort. This reality is no doubt depressingly disappointing to people who have spent years and decades painstakingly learning the collected and compiled yet fictitious 'rules' that supposedly determine when we are allowed to understand English, and other languages. Starting primarily with the Renaissance veneration of ancient Greek and Latin because of the seemingly absolute and logical grammars those scholars derived from those languages, the idea has been that language is mechanistic sentence structure and prescriptive etymology which enables arbitrary sounds to communicate information. This IPTM fiction has become so universal it is considered undeniable; a mumpsimus. But it is a fiction, despite the true fact that using syntactical rules for parsing sentence structures or using semantic construction of roots and affixes or prefixes do provide informative value in some certain cases. But this is also the case with more abstract but real principles such as history, onomatopoeticism, analogy or allegory, and even more poetic features of language such as rhyme, meter, and alliteration. Words have meaning. The validity of that truth is that it is not meaning which requires or even allows authority to dictate what that meaning is, or what meaning is in general. The proof is only in the pudding. No matter whether you can define it, you know it when you see it. And so it is for all things, however much you convince yourself to believe otherwise.

Enough raling against university-taught professorial lingo. There is little direct harm in knowing what a preposition, tense, or person are in the context of "proper" dialectic expression. But there is indirect harm, to reasoning, to language, and even to people, when the pretensions of forensic analysis of linguistic articulation obscure the ability to understand words being used in the real world. And this indirect harm becomes far more direct when gadflies become trolls, and use such dissection to purposefully obscure a truth rather than accidentally miss a point. Obviously, my writing is a counter-example of how intricate sentence structures can be useful, (neither baroque nor pretentious can even begin to describe it.) But I do not consider it a fatal flaw that more purposeful judgment, beyond rationalistic assertions, must be used and accepted to grasp my meaning. And this is the solitary nut at the heart of the POR theory of language, that rationalistic assertions are attempts to refuse to acknowledge communication, rather than an effort to enhance it. Language cannot be deconstructed logically, and this isn't a flaw but the very purpose of it. Syntax is hindsight, and delusion. Using abstraction paradigms to illustrate or identify teleological flipping, which is at the heart of conscious self-determination, does not contradict that perspective, although at first postmodern blush it might seem that way, because we naturally want at least some teleologies to have the validity of tautology. It is <u>comforting</u> to believe that knowing <u>facts</u> and applying mathematical principles reveals all possible knowledge, and perhaps even all truth. Admittedly, detecting tautological flopping, the willy-nilly mixing of analytical and metaphorical terms, is not truly an objective or mechanistic method of detecting dishonesty or error. Using AP in this way is meant as a learning tool, not a scientific test; it provides a vocabulary for describing our intuitions, but not an omniscient linguistic theory. Only time will tell if philosophical analysis of flopping can improve on the imperfect results of a polygraph or an isolated empirical experiment for detecting either honesty or accuracy. Let's examine the nature of teleological flipping, substituting motivation and intentions for cause and effect, in a more exacting way, and perhaps this point will be made clearer.

There is no denying that life is made up of physical and chemical interactions, both within organisms and between them (or us) and their (or our) environment. (Why the parenthetical additions? Because sometimes 'life' means any biological process, and sometimes 'life' means only conscious experience, even though 'life' only means one thing in all uses: the reason biological processes can be observed by biological processes.) Medical knowledge has progressed enormously just within the last few centuries, and decades, and years and even weeks, and we know without any real dispute that biochemical substances such as what we call neurotransmitters are important and even decisive in both our physical and mental states. Let us take the plainest, though not least problematic, example. Let us suppose, because researchers can demonstrate that it seems so, that dopamine levels in neural synapses correlates exactly and unerringly with a conscious experience of happiness or pleasure. Does that mean that happiness is quantifiable if we only knew exactly what levels of dopamine a particular synapse "should" have? Does it mean that there is any real correspondence between neurochemical concentrations and our experiential sensations of wellbeing? Psychoactive drugs do provoke "euphoria", but not so entirely or perfectly that we should accept that our feelings are "really just" chemistry. But let's presume they are, anyway. The questions would still remain whether pleasure 'causes' dopamine levels or dopamine levels 'cause' pleasure. We can reasonably identify whether there is some larger scale and more accessible teleological explanation, that what 'causes' pleasure is the circumstances that precede and putatively result in the dopamine concentration, but then we can tail-spin into trying to logically distinguish proximate and ultimate 'causes', although no objective distinction can be discerned between the two. Just the relative distinction that what we call one is not what we call the other. There is no precise amount of time that separates them, only "shorter" or "longer". There is no algorithmic distinction of mechanism, just "more" direct, and "less" direct causality.

The same issue can be addressed by thinking about thoughts themselves. We can accept that thoughts are actually (whether 'cause' or 'result' or both and neither) electrochemical occurrences within our cerebral tissue. But the teleological reason, the cause of the thoughts, can only be as validly judged from the 'bottom up', as an uncontrolled (uncontrollable) interaction of physical forces, as they can also be validly judged from the 'top down' using the hindsight of backwards teleologies; our next thought is determined, at least in part, not just by the existence of previous thought, but by our conscious awareness of our previous thought. The 'content' of that previous thought might have an influence on our subsequent mental idea, but whether that influence is identical when we remember having the previous thought as it would be if we didn't remember consciously experiencing that previous thought, can never be determined.

This uncertainty about whether our thought processes as a sequence of mental images or ideas is 'bottom up' or 'top down' relates to the uncontrollable state of the universe; every instance of thought can only ever occur once. Even a substantially similar, even an entirely identical thought being rethought is still another thought, not simply a new instance of the original thought. It is the capacity for being self-examining, not the occurrence of that self-examination, that makes thoughts different from any arbitrary electrical or neurological activity that is not a thought.

In addition to the unique instantiation of any one thought a potentially unlimited number of times, without ever being the same thought entirely, this is also related to the theological argument of POR, which I have not identified yet, though I have mentioned it in passing without calling attention to it. The theological argument of POR is based on the notion that your thoughts are not 'subjective', they objectively occur. But knowing (or believing) that thoughts objectively occur in the physical universe isn't the same as claiming to know exactly which objective occurrences are those thoughts. Distinguishing whatever causes those thoughts, or what results from those thoughts, from the thoughts themselves isn't as simple as we might want. The IPTM assumption essentially, if not admittedly, dictates that the electrical impulses that can be measured propagating through nerve tissue are our thoughts themselves. This is the same thing as the expectation in the thumbswitch experiment that the choice to change the picture might have occurred before the measurable neural activity, if the act of choosing is hidden and the electrical fluctuations are the result of the choice rather than the choice itself. I will remind you that this doesn't happen in the experiment in the real world, since the system did not lag but rather advanced when the neural patterns were used to control it. With a heightened awareness of teleology such as POR allows and demands, it should be obvious that stating that these objectively measurable electrical values result from our thoughts, rather than that they are our thoughts, or even result in our thoughts, is not the 'it is science and therefore it is true' slam-dunk that analytical philosophies might insist it should and must be. Scientifically, the relationship between whatever physical occurrence causes our thoughts, whatever physical occurrences are our thoughts, and whatever physical occurrence results from our thoughts, is ambiguous, since they might well be backward "top down" teleologies as much as forward "bottom up" teleologies. Self-determination itself makes this a matter of preference rather than reality, an epistemological identification rather than an ontological occurance.

It is not a question that can even be addressed or ever solved by science. However strong any correlative indication might be, the correspondence between our mind's thoughts and our brain's chemical activities is not a matter of truth, or even importance. It is up to our individual self-determination to dictate which direction the teleological arrow could or does point towards. Science, not to be denigrated lightly even in minor part, must always try to reduce human self-awareness and emotional sentiments to trivial quantitative measures, because science can only measure and calculate quantities. Outside of that empirical demonstrability, no research can even be considered scientific. There is no 'should' in science, only 'does' and 'will' and 'has', even when expectations of scientists are expressed using that particular word: "should". This distinction between an abstract "science" and a less abstract but still not physical "expectations of scientists" is not something that should be dismissed as semantic hair splitting, given the nature of the subject. POR rejects the claim that our thoughts are merely electrical impulses, without rejecting the fact that they physically occur, whatever they are. The electrical changes in our brain are proof that our thoughts are physical, objective occurrences, <u>without</u> proving those electrical variations <u>are</u> our thoughts. This philosophy does not dismiss the scientific model that our moods are only chemical concentrations merely to save face, to avoid being consistent in whether our behavior is caused by weakness or strength, ignorance or bravery, addiction or desire, in order to exempt ourselves from being physical organisms. Instead, we do so, rejecting the "only cause and effect exist, intentions and motivations are fiction" approach in order to demand unilateral control over our self-determination and our ability to envision hope and intentions because we are physical organisms. We reject fatalism not to excuse human foibles, but to explain human aspirations. Our lives are real, our consciousness is not a fiction, we are not genetic robots, p-zombies acting only by the logic of evolutionary programming or Pavlovian responses. We are a special kind of unique and important physical organisms, unlike any bacteria or insect or fish or other mammal, because of that very capacity to choose or decide which event is the cause and which event is the effect in the chain of teleologies we use to describe and understand both the world and ourselves.

All this appears as a bizarre convoluted aside, at best, or at worst a babbling cascade of gibberish, no doubt. Any attempt to seriously examine language risks such a result, due to the nature of language and examination. The abstraction paradigm does not avoid this problem, instead it embraces it. The assignment of a particular word as more abstract and metaphorical or more concrete and analytical is not a singular action, but a recurring activity. Not even describing teleologies as cause-and-effect or intention inverting the two linguistically can be reduced to the absolute of a mathematical calculation. The purpose and use of AP is not so much to prevent logical comprehension, as it is to demonstrate the futility of logical comprehension, while guiding reasonable comprehension, which is much more fruitful. Neither words nor language nor human reasoning is a logical process. If it were, it could be enacted without the need of consciousness, and humans would simply be yet another species of ape, without any peculiar abilities despite having a larger brain.

Schematic

The next diagram we will examine is the Fundamental Schema. It is generally and explicitly more profound than AP. The Fundamental Schema diagram illustrates even larger philosophical issues than just nomenclature, some of which have already been addressed in the previous chapters. The Fundamental Schema (never abbreviated except as 'the schema',) the principle schematic diagram of the Philosophy Of Reason itself, is a simple equilateral triangle. The apex designates the self, the point of identity. The two lines that diverge from this point are 'ontology', the study of being, on one side, and 'epistemology', the study of meaning, on the other. To review: being, ontology, relates to the existence of a thing, while meaning, epistemology, relates to the origin of that existence. Neither can themselves exist without the other; all things have a beginning, and anything that began must exist, at least temporarily, or it didn't actually have an origin. This loosely, but not consistently, equates to ontological examination being only possible for things with concrete physical existence (as 'analytical', in the abstraction paradigm) and epistemological examination being the only possible examination for things that are non-corporeal (as 'metaphorical' in the AP).

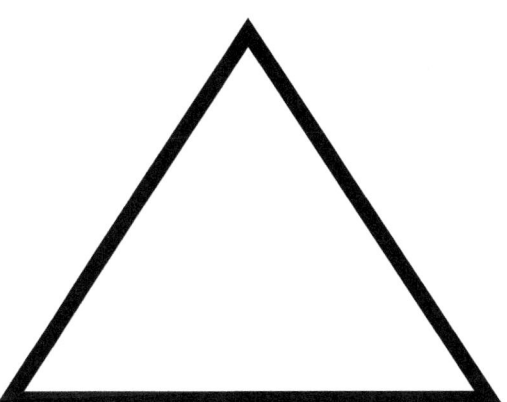

When we use words, we have been taught to believe that we are only ever using them ontologically, as labels for objective (external) occurrences, such as objects or events. This is explicitly dictated, quite often, by postmodernists stating "words are symbols assigned meaning by negotiated definition"; an attempt at reconstruction of the Socratic Method which pointedly ignores the fact that Socrates himself only ever <u>failed</u> to negotiate any definitions for the words he wished to explore the meaning of. Even when the events we think of words as labeling are abstract, as in 'society' or 'virtue', the postmodern habit is to assume that such things have mathematical integrity simply because we use words to refer to them repeatedly. The premise would be that using them repeatedly would be impossible if they did not have the mathematical consistency that Socrates Erroneously dreamed they did, could, or should. According to this postmodern approach, when we use words 'properly', we are using them <u>precisely</u>. This ignores the very real fact that, just as often, we aren't using terms in any **ontologically** consistent fashion, but in an **epistemological** way; as identifiers (labels, if you must) for categories of uncertain family resemblance, rather than empirical definitions. To postmodernists, which we all are to some extent because we have been taught how to use language by postmodernists, only rarely being able to transcend or circumvent the postmodern limitations of Socrates' Error, each word designates a category at the same time it labels (rather than describes) a concise and individual object external to our consciousness. These categories of objects, we are led to believe, have deductive integrity because the objects do. But in real life, the categories don't have any deductive integrity or innate consistency. This leads to the necessity of choosing either ontological (physical) or epistemological (categorical) referents as the primary target, the definition in context, of the words we use. Since postmodernism limits only the way we believe we are using language, not how we actually use language, this can be both confusing and frustrating. In reality, we always use words both epistemologically and ontologically, as descriptions of the thing we are talking about and as the category those things can be placed in which enables us to recognize those things. Yet, in any particular usage, we can manage to perceive one more than the other, that we are identifying an idea or thing individually, as if to name an object, or we are describing a feature of the thing, as if to name the category that the object or abstraction belongs in, within our minds.

When we use words ontologically, our presumption is that words themselves are trivial, unimportant, even meaningless. It doesn't matter what you call something, the thing doesn't change. This is, in general, more similar to the postmodernist assumption of language, that words are signs used to label events or occurrences, such as external or imaginary objects or the features, changes, or effects of such things. This general similarity of ontology to the postmodern perspective is more or less the same as the affinity between a hypothetically logical use of terms and the analytical level of language, which was pointed out earlier. This derives from the fact that Socrates, and the majority (but notably not the entirety) of philosophers that followed him, recognized that we physically exist but were less intellectually certain about our intellectual (nee spiritual or moral) existence. This situation continued throughout the modern age of philosophy until Descartes managed to overcome the problem by recognizing that our intellectual existence cannot be denied, since denying it requires that existence to be true. He could not overcome the subsequent problem of determining the characteristics of that existence besides that single truth of being, and set classical philosophy up for the existential modality that carried it through to the postmodern age. We can divide classical philosophy neatly into two branches from the root of Descartes' formulation, with analytical philosophy being focused on Aristotelian logic, and existential philosophy embracing the larger perspective of reality that logic based on Socrates' Error cannot deal with. Once Darwin supplied the missing piece to the puzzle, allowing the duality of being that Descartes defined to be erased, the two branches of philosophy were reunited under the Information Processing Theory of Mind. The imaginary force that bound them together is what I've identified and described (named or labeled, to use the postmodern nomenclature) as **postmodernism**.

Returning to the Fundamental Schema, in the IPTM-friendly, exclusively ontological view, codebooks such as dictionaries are important and even necessary, since it can be consistently demonstrated that whatever rules we might devise to assign symbols to definitions, they are neither simple nor universal, and they can only be facetiously described as 'negotiated'. There is a natural correspondence between the ontological use of words and the analytical level of language designated in the abstraction paradigm, and both comport to this IPTM mode, because outside of our consciousness, the universe usually appears to be bottom-up. Likewise, if hyper-rationalist thinkers had their druthers, only analytical and ontological use of terms would be acceptable, or even comprehensible, in language. We can go so far as to say that the line representing the ontological vector leading from the apex of our schema, the top angle described earlier as the self or point of identity, can be hypothetically described as the domain of empirical (demonstrable, repeatable, and objective) quantities. An eternal discussion goes on, among academic philosophers at least, whether numbers actually exist or are only imagined to exist by humans. This exemplifies the line of ontology, which begins at the self when we try to describe singular objects, occurrences, or even intellectual entities (with or without agency) and proceeds indefinitely to the base of our diagram. Whether the entire line of ontology in our primitive diagram is thought of as 'mathematics', with empiricism being only part of it, or vice versa, is arbitrary, though not necessarily unimportant.

When we use words epistemologically, our presumption is that words are what actually exist, and the objective occurrences, whether internal or external, are eternally hypothetical. (To relate to classical epistemology, the issue of whether the farmer reports a cow is factual, but whether the cow exists is hypothetical.) In general, epistemological use of language refers to categories rather than entities, with features of these hypothetical entities being used to construct family relationships that may or may not be inherited from more primitive entities. In an exclusively epistemologic worldview, a thing is that thing because that is what you are calling it. From the postmodernist perspective, this harkens to a marvelous and infamous passage from Lewis Carroll:

"When I use a word," Humpty Dumpty said in rather a scornful tone, "it means just what I choose it to mean — neither more nor less."
"The question is," said Alice, "whether you can make words mean so many different things."
"The question is," said Humpty Dumpty, "which is to be master – – that's all."

Words do in fact mean (identify) so many different things. Charles Dodgson was a very purposeful rationalist, and it is accepted by most that Alice's adventures are allegories that represent Dodgson's distaste for the non-Euclidian geometries and imaginary numbers of what he viewed as irrational developments in mathematics. Irregardless, I think the Humpty Dumpty quote is a delightfully self-refuting indictment of language from that hopelessly rationalistic perspective. (The fact that Dodgson and Darwin were contemporaries might lead to the consideration of whether the mathematical theories that disturbed him merely presaged postmodernism by only a very short time, or whether the correlation is more than coincidence.) But the POR position is not that epistemological ('less rational') use of words is either superior or inferior to ontological ('more logicalish') use of words. The Fundamental Schema is equilateral, and neither approach is more correct than the other in either semiotic or hermeneutic efforts. We cannot use words exclusively ontologically or exclusively epistemologically, as labels for intellectual and physical objects or as symbols for categories and defined sets. Words are not symbols or labels for things, they are things, used raw rather than logically constructed or defined, not tautological references to referents but the teleological reason for the existence, through observation, of both reference and referent.

It isn't important what you call something, what is relevant is why you're calling it that thing. The word you use doesn't mean only or just what you choose it to mean, because any word you use is shared by every other context it has ever been or will ever be used in. But it is not an objective assignment, either. Words are not signs, they are descriptions. When we use any particular word, it is never purely either ontological or epistemological. Words are not mathematical iconography, nor are they 'whatever we choose them to mean'. They are both, and neither, just as light is not particles or waves, but can only be measured as one or the other in any one context. (And just as a cat could be both alive and dead until you open the box and collapse the waveform, perhaps a more significant, though more fictional, analogy.) Light is actually something that isn't photons or electromagnetic fluctuations, it is either what causes or is caused by those things, depending entirely on how you arrange the teleologies and tautologies involved in your description. Likewise, the importance of the two 'branches' from our intention (the self apex) to the hopefully communicative base of the Fundamental Schema diagram only occurs as that communication occurs. Just as considering whether one 'expects' a more analytical or metaphoric connotation in words can be an indicator of truth or fiction in the abstraction paradigm, the anticipation of whether a particular communication, statement, or claim is an ontological intention or an epistemological intention is informative. The domain of empirical ontology is not superior to the realm of literary epistemology. In truth, it isn't in any way inferior, either, but the habit of postmodernism, and the damage this habit causes to society and our self-regard, results in a need to denounce it more often. We have all of the rationalists in the world, scientists, atheists, hyper-rational philosophers of all sorts, demanding that without logic, words become incomprehensible. Far fewer and more harried intellectuals are capable, these days, of admitting, acknowledging, or even suggesting that the opposite is more true: words become more incomprehensible, not less, when we attempt to use them with logical consistency or precision.

On that note, there are a couple of more incidental points to make. They concern the adoption of 'postmodernism', within the Philosophy Of Reason, as the term for the extension of Socrates' Error in post-Darwinian philosophy that results in the Information Processing Theory of Mind. IPTM itself relates more directly to Turing's philosophical impact than Darwin's, but there is no precision in these epistemological alignments of intellectual principles or movements. Outside of POR, postmodernism means roughly the same as it does inside POR; words are unitary, unique, and universal so that is appropriate. However, we do use the word much more concisely, and concretely, and explicitly and specifically, as well. Because we use it so often, though, it might appear to be more broad than concise. This mirrors the classical difficulty of even identifying what it is. The overall general pattern of what non-POR intellectuals might call postmodern (often still 'post-modern', and when appropriate that form can be used to distinguish what others might mean when they call something that from what POR refers to as 'postmodern') might be understood most clearly by considering postmodern architecture. Although it is a latecomer to the field of things called 'post-modernist', postmodern architecture exemplifies it in a far more concrete way than literature or other art forms, due to the nature of architecture as a form of engineering. Postmodern architecture abandons classical forms, usually with such enthusiastic relish that ornamentation and style become more important to the architect than the purposes of architecture itself. 'Form over function' is a standard phrase for encapsulating the results. One of the worst things a postmodernist architect could do when designing a house is make it look like a house. In extreme cases, frustrating expectations about what a house should be becomes such a concern that the building is consciously made to not be good as a house.

The real root of the term postmodernism, in contrast to the idea of postmodernism that POR relates to the impact of Darwin on Platonism, is a movement in academic philosophy which is said to reject the idea of objective truth, or at least to embrace the idea that truth is subjective. This became most noticeable and started self-identifying as 'postmodern' in the 1950s in France, then rapidly spread through the rest of Europe. The Continental philosophical school that vigorously intends to be purely epistemological (in the POR sense) and rejects the importance (though not truly the validity) of ontology entirely, is the classical standard "post-modern philosophy" that people who study philosophy in college will no doubt insist is the only philosophy which is accurately identified as postmodern philosophy. Of course, in POR, we recognize that they say this because they are, themselves, postmodernist, in the POR sense. Although all of the various literary, philosophical, artistic, and architectural models and practices that are grouped under a category labeled 'post-modern' do share a close affinity for expressions and ramifications of what POR calls 'postmodern', only POR provides any real ontological significance to the term as used. In the case of the postmodernists, (even those that don't consider themselves or aren't aware they are postmodernist) following in the rejection of ontology that is a perverse (inverted minority) implementation of Socrates' Error (which more often rejects epistemology and embraces ontology, as in IPTM) the application of the word is in keeping with Humpty Dumpty's extremist epistemology "it is that thing because I call it that thing." In POR, we must consciously and conscientiously consider both ontology and epistemology equally, if we are going to use words accurately and communicate effectively. So the word 'postmodern' as we use it does relate to the classical academic 'flum-flummery' philosophical school of postmodernism, and the literary and artistic and architectural postmodernisms, too. (This term, 'flum-flummery', is meant to suggest the confounding results of the academic philosophical postmodernism, as perceived by other academic philosophers and postmodern skeptics. In fact, POR takes academic postmodernism far more seriously than they would, but then again, POR does not take any academic philosophy very seriously, because it is all 'postmodern' in the POR sense.)

The POR sense of the term encompasses all of the things designated postmodern, but it is not simply used as a catch-all to denote things we want to oppose. This use of a term that might sound like an epithet but is actually merely a description (albeit a potentially unflattering one) is a common occurrence in POR. Unlike postmodernism (in the POR sense), the Philosophy Of Reason dispenses with the need for euphemistic, derogatory epithets, and even dismisses the existence of them. All words are just used, even when someone believes they are trying to use them as an insult. They are still interpreted seriously and considered cogent. This issue will be described more fully elsewhere and is only incidental here.

In the case of *postmodernism*, there is a rational reason, an honest and true intellectual justification, for including those things we call postmodernism in that category along with post-modernism. As I've already described, it is the release from the theistic explanation for the human intellect that Darwin provided which turned modern philosophy (all the classics, from Aristotle and his forebears to Descartes and his descendants) into postmodern philosophy. All of these terms are not logic, of course, they are instructive rather than deductive, used for learning rather than calculating. The point is that although there is "a" post-modernism that connects and partially explains all the things that are labeled postmodern by postmodernists, that is related but not identical to "the" postmodernism as understood in the Philosophy Of Reason.

All of this is a prelude to the real issue, which is that post-modern academic philosophy illustrates, to an almost preposterously reliable extent, the fact that words become less communicative the more precisely they are used. Post-modern philosophers use words extremely precisely, or at least they try to and believe they are. By doing so, they abandon any regard for accuracy, because the root of postmodernism is Socrates' Error, which is effectively the belief that words cannot have accuracy, only precision. This is a result of Socrates' "successful failure" to understand what words like "virtue" and "strength" mean, while still continuing to use those words to mean things outside of the Socratic Dialogue. Post-modern philosophers create such extensive and dense examples of using words precisely, regardless of accuracy, that they are reviled by all other philosophers as beyond pathetic. Not just dismissal, but contempt, not just frustration, but anger, is the attitude that some scholarly intellectuals have toward this self-identifying postmodernism. This anger occurs because those anti-postmodernist scholarly intellectuals are postmodernists, in the POR sense, and must either deny that words have any emotional content with passive aggression, or prove that words have emotional meaning with active aggression. The consternation that leads to this contempt derives from the frustration of having post-modernist philosophers accept the validity of logical positivism, the bedrock of scientific thinking, and therefore indispensable to intellectuals who want to assume that reasoning must only be based on facts, but instead of agreeing with the other intellectuals that only things that are proven are true, the post-modernist uses the other side of the coin to declare that nothing is true, because the problem of induction prevents them from being logically proven.

Years ago, a skeptic (one who was both a skeptic of postmodernism and a postmodern skeptic) submitted a purposefully nonsensical paper mimicking the form of the academic postmodern movement, seemingly random gibberish that was grammatically correct but lacking in any informative content. When the paper was not only accepted by a journal notorious for encouraging and printing the work of post-modernists, but was subsequently praised by post-modernists, it was hailed as a huge success for the skeptic community of hyper-rationalist postmodernists. The skeptics were in turn even further infuriated when the revelation of their fraud was not met with chagrin on the part of the philosophical academicians, but instead was shrugged off as irrelevant. The entire postmodern ideal, after all, was that all text is devoid of content outside of the immediate context; words had no meaning. So the success of the skeptic's subterfuge was, at worst, merely evidence of the truth of their theories. When you don't care how good a building will be as a house, the fact that it isn't a good home when you're done construction isn't as disturbing to the architect as it is to the dwellers.

When words are most purposefully intended to be precise, they become not simply uninformative, but nearly if not entirely unintelligible. In contrast, when words are used accurately, when they are honestly intended to mean things rather than symbolize 'concepts' that only have meaning if they have mathematical integrity, they are always communicative. This explains (if you can understand this explanation, rather than dismiss it, and this entire book, as gibberish) why wisdom does not require academic education, and Yogi Berra, by using words in profoundly illogical ways, is occasionally referred to as one of the greatest philosophers of his time. It is not any gritty self-reliance that makes uneducated laborers the equivalent of rocket scientists in "common sense", it is their freedom from Socratic pretensions of precision in their words, relying only on the natural accuracy that words innately accrue and imbue, and which thus ensues. The value of poetry, the power of rap, and the horse sense of the common man, all demonstrate clearly that numbers can provide precision, but words are all about accuracy.

Another incidental point to address is the synchronicity between the AP levels of language and the schematic modes of philosophy. As I've already pointed out, there seems to be a loose connection between analysis and ontology, and between metaphor and epistemology. We could presume that this is a default relationship, just as we presume that words are being used rhetorically until we have some reason to believe that a term is being used analytically or an expression needs to be interpreted as a metaphor. However, the alignment of analytical language and ontological things, and metaphor with epistemology, is not as consistent as the presumptive assignment of all words as rhetorical unless there is some contention or indication otherwise. The correlation between concrete terms and physical philosophy, and figurative words with categorical philosophy, is more coincidental than default, although postmodern habit causes us to presume otherwise in a lot of cases. It is not that there is not a regular alignment of the two methodologies of considering language and philosophy, it is that they are really two independent approaches to the issue of language. Sometimes they line up, as the example of 'matter' can illustrate. Certainly the definition of matter as physical substance is an analytical connotation and has an undeniable correspondence with ontological reality, to a beguiling degree; so much so that it becomes difficult to imagine that analytical and ontological aren't interchangeable ideas. The alignment of matter as emotional substance is just as obviously more metaphorical in application, and could as easily be presumed to be more epistemological; we imagine that categorical premise of epistemology, since the use of the word 'matters' for intellectual ideas seems more arbitrary or ephemeral (one is tempted to say 'subjective') than the use of the word 'matter' for atoms and molecules. This is an illusion, if not a delusion, though; there isn't anything about the word 'matter' that makes the use of that word (one is tempted to say 'those sounds') more appropriate for material substance than for sentimental importance. A contrasting example might be 'law'. Law lacks the objective nature of matter, but can be just as ontologically valid as it is epistemologically significant. The ontological mode is the perspective that a thing defines itself, holistically rather than categorically, and we can think of 'the law' as more visceral because of the threat of violence behind breaking the law, in either the criminal act or the legal consequence. Government is not a social club; it can be defined as the exclusive power to use physical force to enforce its mandates. But does this make it more abstract, or more physical? Law can refer to the text of statute, which is ontological in its existence if not in its interpretation, but without that epistemological interpretation by those who enforce the law, the text of statutes has no ontological significance.

Again we are stymied, as earlier, by the principle that words cannot truly be isolated from natural language to be examined alone, absent a real world context. Looking back to our earlier teleologic AP example, it was mentioned that a question worth examining might be whether law comes from principle or principle comes from laws. There is no correct answer, of course; the teleological arrow can go in either direction. But that is not the same as the teleological arrow being inconsequential. When trying to speak in normal circumstances, it is generally quite relevant which is considered the cause and which is the resulting affect. In the present example, the abstract idea of "the law" as a process or endeavor, compared to 'the law' as either a statute or its enforcers, is "parsed out" automatically by our brains, but it becomes ineffable, ambiguous, and perhaps illusory, when we try to dissect it with logic, since it is a human activity, and neither human activities, nor the words we use to describe them (itself a human activity) are bound by logic. If we are using inverse teleology, the difference between which is the motivation that spawns an action and which is the intention that is the goal is important for clear thinking about our society or behavior. But this example should be instructive, because my declaration that motivation goes with the origin of a movement and intention describes the aim to be achieved by it is itself simply a selection that can as easily be inverted, with intention becoming the 'backward teleology' initiating cause and motivation being the 'backward teleology' objective to be achieved. Words resolutely refuse to be tamed and reduced to deductively consistent codes; like dreams they shift and dissolve all the swifter when we examine them most intently. Rather than wander around this way and that while mumbling about vocabulary and nomenclature, we should abandon that line of thinking. The point of introducing all this uncertainty is simply to hint at the truth that assuming that what is epistemological is naturally more metaphorical is a mistake. A mistake that becomes more obvious when considering abstract things, but is present in all language. The existence of political classifications, of words to describe human activities or attitudes, are encountered far more frequently in the average person's life than more empirically consistent ideas. Such a simple thought as 'family' seems ontologically certain, rooted in genetics and biological reproduction. And yet it becomes a mere epistemological category in real life, defined entirely by how you use it; the real meaning of 'family' is that collection of people you call your family, not a scientific or objective identification. The typical intonation of family changes through time, applying more readily to what we call 'extended family' decades in the past, through the 'nuclear family' we still habitually presume it "should" refer to, into the 'blended family' of more complicated societal ties that the modern world makes the reality for many if not most people. Which do you mean by 'family' in any one instance of that term in some actual, not hypothetical, context? There is, as always, no right answer, other than the one you mean, or the one that someone else might take you to mean, and some potential agreement between the two. This kind of reality of communication is the impetus for the postmodern definition of definition as a negotiated meaning; as long as the speaker and listener agree on what the word refers to, the word refers to that. Except this is still not true, this is a Humpty Dumpty approach. Even a private conversation uses the same words that other people outside do, and the meaning of those words is not something that can be ignored for the convenience of a code-like secret transmission/reception event. The same vocal forms or marks might be used, but doing so with exclusively personal definitions would make any correspondence between the private and the public words even less meaningful than coincidence, a mere ruse that might fool a third party into believing that words are being used, when they are actually symbols in a cryptographic exchange that isn't natural language. All natural language is accessible to this third party, both real and hypothetical, an almost infinite number of them in potential. Again, the postmodern conception of language takes this possibility of 'secret code' that only looks like regular words' and insists that, because no deductive test can instantaneously prove whether that is what is happening or whether standard meaning applies, and declares that this uncertainty is perpetual, that all language is private code, negotiated symbols without any greater impact. No meaning, only definition. This would suggest that people don't actually share the emotional response to poetry or music that we claim, that such neurologically visceral reaction of a seemingly sentimental sort is nothing but false consciousness and delusion.

POR can reject this postmodern code idea, even if linguists do not. Postmodern linguists can join the grammarians and Socrates in being disappointed that no mathematical calculation can resolve the meaning of words, no axiomatic rule set is needed to recognize or interpret them, only a theory of mind and the motivation of sincere intent. The lack of logic in language or human reasoning certainly frustrates the hyper-rationalists. It might incense them to know that math envy cannot turn programming languages into anything but mathematical instruction sets. I believe several thousand years of effort is enough to justify calling it quits on the effort to pretend that Socrates made no Error. Getting back to the subject at hand, we can summarize by saying that those words which relate to human behavior and society might appear more metaphorical because they cannot be mathematically tested, but that does not make it more ambiguous when they are being used accurately and truthfully. Abstract things relate just as strongly to ontological philosophy as they do to epistemological philosophy, even though they do not relate as strongly to physics as they do to intellectual categories. There are no categories in physics, or any other real science, only mathematical terms. Sets with deductive integrity aren't categories, they are sets. They are similar, epistemologically, to epistemological categories, but they exist independently of what category we might put them in. A presumption that a term like 'mankind' is ontological and refers to a species of ape is deceptive, because it is not our ape ancestry that is being referred to when we use that form. Does 'all mankind' refer to only every person living now, or does it include both all of those that ever existed and all of those who will ever exist? This is a question that can only be answered in context. Whether it is more analytical or metaphorical (presuming it can no longer be considered rhetorical) and whether it is more epistemological or ontological (and theological, an aspect we have not yet addressed), these are issues that can only be used to determine or explain what it means. It isn't what you're calling that, what is important is why you are calling it that instead of calling it, identifying or describing it as, some other thing. Sometimes that alternative could be a larger category or smaller category, sometimes it might be a more empirically discernable description or less so. All of the permutations and possibilities can be considered with the methods of the AP or the schema, but cannot be limited by their classification. Words have meaning. The absolute reality of that fact does not end all argument about whether some particular thing is a word or not, or what kind of or specific meaning it might have. Words aren't improved by pretending to pin them down. If we need that kind of precise consistency, we can use symbols instead of words. However, we should keep in mind that if we use the same symbol in more than a single context, there is a possibility, ranging from a good one to a certain one, that our minds will convert that symbol into a word quite readily, in fact unavoidably. Then we will start applying the forms and manipulations that we use for words without regard to how logical they are, and its value as an arbitrary sign or privately assigned code will be permanently lost. It will have become part of our language, not just a symbol in a set of logical assignments negotiated among scientists.

Let's return to a more direct examination of just the ontology/epistemology philosophical distinction, the divergent perspectives of our intellect and language illustrated by the Fundamental Schema. It seems undeniable that intricate and exacting things must be expressed with intricate and exacting terms or grammar, in order to be clear and concise. I don't mean to suggest that being clear or concise are not important and good. Suffice it to say that words simply don't become less informative when they are used less formally, that the amount of data that can be transferred from brain A to brain B in a given space of time or amount of effort doesn't shrink if the grammar being used is simplistic and logical rather than complicated and arbitrary. The primary reason, and perhaps the only reason, that "proper" English is presumed to be more communicative than improper English is because professors of English have insisted it must be so. Indeed, that, not any logical rationalization of grammar or diction, is all that makes proper English "proper". It doesn't matter if the impropriety of 'improper English' is derived from use of vernacular, or simply from purposeful or accidental lack of concern for the supposedly correct rules being taught by authorities. Other than communicating the fact that the speaker is 'higher class', there is nothing inherently more communicative about 'higher class' speech forms or practices. The opposite is more obviously, and somehow also more comfortingly, true: casual and slang words do more than inform the listener that the speaker is being relaxed or earnest, they actually provide additional information content, if only because of the availability of the greater rather than more restrictive number of alternative ways of depicting the thoughts being communicated, and the selection from among alternatives itself being part of the information communicated. It isn't what words you use, it is why you are using them, that provides the meaning in those words.

One simple example of this difference between the ontological and the epistemological perspectives is that word which can be used to illustrate the similar (but not identical) distinction between the analytical and metaphoric levels of language: "matter". All words are metaphors, and it is actually meaningless to say that the physical 'matter' is the real one and the use of the term 'matter' for emotional importance is a figure of speech. Historically, the important type of matter predates the more scientific use to refer to substances made up of atoms rather than the forces considered energy. We will address this point yet again later in this presentation of the Fundamental Schema. But for now it seems apparent that the scientifically reducible use of 'matter' would typically, if not invariably, be considered the analytical usage, and the other the more metaphoric abstraction we use when we say something 'really matters'. In the same way, the scientific one associated with mass would have to be taken to be an ontological abstraction, and the one associated with social matters must be seen as more epistemological, at least most of the time. Another, less easily dissected term to illustrate the issue could be 'horse'. A horse is an animal, but is also quite a number of things that appear to have similarities to those animals; saw horses and pommel horses. Again, we might say that the biological horse is the analytical abstraction, and the 'four legs and a straight back' horses would be metaphoric applications of the term. But the rhetorical issue is a bit less clear than with 'matter', and which might be considered ontological or epistemological is far more context-dependent. Does a stream 'run' quite like a person 'runs'; is a cube box-like or is a box cube-like; when discussing a 'community' is the supposedly containing group, or the members of that designation, the more ontological, physical, or the more epistemological, linguistic and categorical? Why are we bothering to make (or perhaps invent) any distinction at all, if it cannot be objectively tested and does not even remain certain enough to declare it to be incontrovertible or even more than a whim of the listener?

The importance of the Fundamental Schema and its divergent lines of ontology and epistemology, physics and language, math and categories, is not in any absolute certainty of its validity, either in general or in any particular instance. Instead the use of the schema is to illustrate and explain, not limit or decree. With the abstraction paradigm, we have said that the truth, or rather its lack, can at least perhaps be detected by noticing effective changes in the rhetoric of a statement, whether there is a consistent analytical or metaphoric use of a number of vocabulary terms. With the Fundamental Schema, its practical application is generally the inverse. All linguistic statements must use both physical and categorical abstractions on the whole, but each individual term, at least sometimes, can be recognized as more certainly one or the other. But the optimum is to balance the two, and use each word in a way that is consistent with both an ontological and epistemological mode, consistent with both empirical physics and intellectual philosophy. This is typically done automatically when we generate or interpret language, which matter or horse or idea of 'run' being rarely if ever controversial. When considering things such as 'community', of course, the connection of ontology and epistemology becomes more difficult to deal with, both more mute and more moot. The issue is not so much knowing that there are two ways of considering the term 'community', but rather knowing which consideration is more significant in any instance. Even more important is realizing either should be acceptable, if we are speaking honestly and fairly. There are objectivists, those Ayn Rand-inspired ultra-postmodernist, extra hyper-rationalists, who would insist that there is "no such thing" as community, or society, or even government. These words are deconstructed into meaninglessness by such people, by simply saying that 'there is no society, only the combined individual actions of individual human beings'. But of course, the word 'society' simply describes both the combination and the totality of those beings and their actions with that word. No ontological existence of 'society' in a general context needs to be hypothesized for the term to be both meaningful and communicative. But in any actual usage of the expression, that collection of phonemes we voice as 'society', it is almost all-important to be aware of whether it is a categorical abstraction or the individual members of a group and their combined, but not necessarily total, activities. Because the abstraction paradigm centers around the rhetorical level of language, it is only when there is some controversy about what a word 'means' that we need to consider or assign the linguistic values of concrete analysis or abstract metaphor. The Fundamental Schema, conversely, originates and emanates from the point of identity, the self, and we are each, potentially, Humpty Dumpty. So with the schema, it becomes not a matter of social communicativeness, but personal intentions and beliefs, that should be examined.

The line of ontology, which we can reduce to the domain of empirical measurement, becomes obtuse and pointless, even inaccessible and fantastical, without the counterbalance of epistemological categorization. Do numbers actually exist? It is a philosopher's conundrum, an intellectual party game, that has no real bearing on whether we can multiply factors to produce a reliable arithmetic result. That is ontology, that is the 'there are no categories, only unconnected (if similar) individual instances of things' approach to reasoning. But it literally cannot exist without the matching epistemology, the 'we can only describe something as a collection of features and therefore the categories it is in' philosophical perspective. There are no categories in nature, these are simply imaginary containers we place our platonic image of things within, so that we can grasp them despite their very ethereal lack of form. There are no categories in nature. Do we invent or create them? This is the same question we can ask about numbers. We do not merely imagine that quantities exist, but whether numbers do is a more esoteric dilemma. The reality of categories is in some ways a similar, and in some ways the same, conundrum. Acknowledging the possible paradox cannot change the fact that words have meaning, regardless of whether and how we attempt to perceive or answer that conundrum.

For the sake of convention, in POR we associate epistemology with the origin of a thing, whether it is real or imaginary. Epistemology is the study of meaning, and denotes the use of words in the most linguistic and literary mode. Ontology is the study of being, and denotes the use of words in the most rational and literal mode. But where does it end? Once separated, by emanating from the point of self at the apex of our diagram, this schematic math could go on forever, useless without a reasoning creature to consciously apply its mechanism to solve a problem. Likewise, endless babble and gibberish can be produced by language, and we are left with epistemology being nothing short of mental masturbation, self-satisfying but unproductive. In order for words to have both meaning and being, we must trust that neither the speaker nor the listener is entirely authoritative, we must believe that there is something more to the universe than just our intentions and the physical substance we manipulate based on those intentions. Whether this 'something else' is just a third party that might or must crack our private cypher, or an omniscient God that dictates a moral code, natural language cannot exist and be used while being entirely absent any ethical or moral implications, the way mathematics inherently and eternally is. Ultimately, we have to accept a responsibility to be ethical, to be moral, to seek the divine however imaginary or subjective it may be. And so the diagram (but not the entire schema) is completed with the base of the triangle. Where rational <u>ontology</u> and literal <u>epistemology</u> end cannot be arbitrary or separate. It must be the same theoretical, metaphysical point, which is the line of <u>theology</u>.

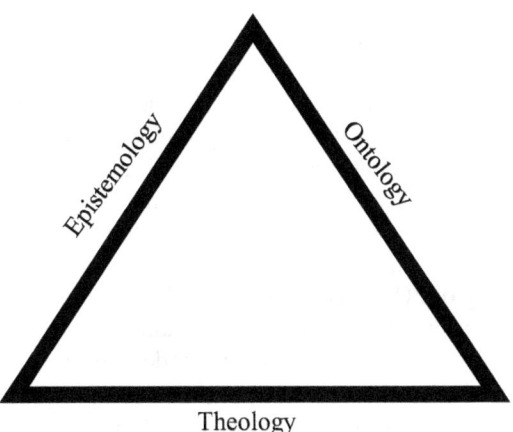

Theology

Theology is the study of *purpose*. Thanks to postmodern over-synonimization, POS, 'theology' is typically, and purportedly absolutely, defined as the study of God, and the perception always seems that theology should be considered either 'good', if you are religious, or 'bad', if you are atheistic. To the believer, the faithful, and especially to the religious fundamentalist, theology is received wisdom, transcendent metaphysics that can only exist with supernatural force. To the hyper-rationalist, the objectivist, the fundamentalist atheist, theology is delusion, no more real than Santa Claus, and can only be understood as a desire to command other people to submit to the theologian's personal and arbitrary authority. They become anti-theistic and a-religious, instead of merely atheistic and supposedly unreligious. This excessive use of theology and theism as synonyms leads many atheists to think, assume and insist that all theology is theism, and only theism is theology. Likewise, to many people and most dictionaries, all religion must be theistic and only theistic philosophies are truly 'religions'.

Both modern and postmodern atheists have taken the liberty of conflating religion with the myths or rituals of the religious. The fact is that being anti-religious is their religion. All humans, indeed any creature with language (if there were any besides humans, which to our knowledge so far there is not) have a religion, the basis for their moral sentiments. Whether a person's religion is similar to or part of (in this context, these are synonyms, the distinction being epistemological) an organized or scriptural faith makes no difference. To consider yourself moral is to have a religion justifying that morality. The narrative that most postmodern atheists use as a substitute for the more familiar and popular Judeo-Christian mythology, or any homologous ethic using an after-life as a reward or punishment for unjust behavior, is an equally inaccurate belief in a biological imperative of altruism. This 'self-serving self-interest' scenario will be considered in greater depth further on. The purpose in raising the issue here is to explain that many atheists agree wholeheartedly with theists in declaring that religion inherently and innately demands theistic, including deistic, dogma.

POR succeeds in breaking this mold. It is a materialist theology that is not simply atheism, so it is atheist without being antitheist or anti-religious. The term 'materialist' should not be misunderstood. It is not a reference to self-centered materialism or the denunciation of any morality beyond accumulation of wealth. POR is 'materialist' in that it rejects supernatural forces or mythological sources for morality, justice, or anything else. The materialist theology of POR is not objectivist atheism. POR embraces not just strong ethics, but meaningful and profound morality. The explication of this morality will have to wait, but it includes and reflects the same compassion and optimism that the best of organized religion and personal spirituality do. More than that, it <u>justifies</u> that compassion and optimism, without any need to resort to belief in an impossible existence after our physical bodies have died, miraculous manners of cosmic justice, or karmic retribution. POR embraces religion, recognizing not just the value but the inevitability of religious theories of morality, and further declaring that all moralities are religious theories. The religious theory of POR (which includes but is more than just the theological theory of POR being addressed in this discussion) is embodied in the New Church of Hope. It is possible to accept the validity of the Philosophy Of Reason without being part of the New Church of Hope, in theory, but it should seem pointless if you actually accept the validity of POR. In POR theory, the New Church of Hope is not an exclusive or fundamentalist religion; any person who seeks to use reason or be reasonable is considered to be part of the New Church, at least potentially, regardless of whether they participate in a technical (kinetic) sense. The existence of such a church can be ignored for now, though, as it is incidental to the explication of the theology that church is founded upon.

Without some acceptance of and theory concerning <u>purpose</u> or *morality*, however it is derived, there can be no balance between use of words as if they are the things we want them to refer to, the ontological approach, and the use of words as if they are independent of the physical world, even partially, the epistemological perspective. Words become empty symbols or fictional categories, when there is no connection between grammar and vocabulary, empirical truth and emotional resonance, ontology and epistemology. Humpty Dumpty's extremist self-determination and the postmodernist's equally extremist objectification might be all well and good so long as the ideas that make up our consciousness are all inside our heads, within the point of identity, safely shielded from reality by the existential wall. But if we are to ever try to communicate those ideas to others, or deal with reality outside of our own thoughts, we must understand, accept, and even celebrate the necessity of an ethical, moral, theological basis for our word choices and our word uses. Nothing else can ever substitute for this personal regard for virtue, no dictionary, dogma, judge or mathematician. Unless both the speaker and the listener takes on this <u>responsibility</u> to use their facility of language sincerely and honestly, then neither words nor their interpretation can be effective.

The triangle used as our schematic diagram starts with self, the apex, and extends down the lines of epistemology, meaning, on one side and ontology, being, on the other, with both lines ending equidistant from self at the line of theology, purpose. The arrangement of theology and purpose in opposition to self in the Fundamental Schema is instructive, very much in the way that commandments from God are intended to be instructive. The importance of that instruction isn't dependent on the physical existence of that God in religious doctrine, and isn't dependent on any divine authority in the POR schema. Words have meaning, whether we want them to or not. But they only have true purpose when we make an effort to make them so. The termination of the ontological framing, empirical truth, and the termination of the epistemic framing, categorical truth, must be a matched set, equally far from the point of self, and the matching ends intersect with the line of theology, of purpose.

To finish up this explanation of the Fundamental Schema of the Philosophy Of Reason, let's address the question of context. Etymologically, that term is relatively simple to dissect: 'con' means 'with' and 'text' means words. We might have more epistemological or metaphoric ideas of what a 'context' is than this ontological or analytic deconstruction; ideas in our heads, like Humpty Dumpty, about what we mean when we use the word. But in a strictly real sense, 'context' means "the words that accompany the word". The most basic semantics of POR states that words are defined in context. This becomes the 'cheat' that allows Humpty Dumpty to say what he said sincerely, while still allowing Alice to comprehend what he said honestly, although neither of them, or their creator, was aware of this mechanism. To Humpty Dumpty, his words were defined by his intentions and nothing else. To Alice, standing in for the author, that should make them incomprehensible, because fealty to a dictionary or some other external authority should be necessary, not just to recognize Humpty Dumpty's meaning, but even to be able to disagree with the truth of his words. The validity and productivity of words **without** any apparent authority either within or beyond the speaker and the listener is the proof of this linguistic reality. Words have meaning, and we can use (paraphrasing) definitions to try to describe that meaning, but the meaning itself is not entirely communicated by the definitions, alone or in concert, nor can this meaning be constrained by those definitions. Even though you might be ignorant of the historical uses of a word, the other people you have seen use the word (for they, not a reference book, are the source of both the word and your understanding of it) are at least perhaps slightly less ignorant about that. And each in turn learned that word from some other, also generally but not entirely ignorant person, who didn't study the etymological history before constructing the term with any axiomatic rules of syntax, either. In postmodern linguistic theory, words change meaning over time, as history progresses and chronology ticks away. Like a game of Telephone or Chinese Whispers, each repetition changing the message imperceptibly, and it is a wonder that any words ever last long at all with even a slightly fixed meaning. But words are unitary and universal, as well as unique, and the only thing that really changes is the way we use the words, the conventional definitions, not the meaning itself. If it is the same word it has the same meaning; to have a different meaning is to be a different word, regardless of any similarities in spelling or pronunciation.

The postmodern instinct, forced on postmodernists by their assumption that words and their definitions are logical conflicting with their use in natural language, is to reject the idea of meaning, itself. To postmodernists, along with post-modernists, meaning cannot really exist: words only have definitions, since there is no deterministic or deductive relationship that can link the use of a word across contexts. In this linguistic theory, there is only the word itself, and whether a particular set of phonemes or syllables is a unitary word or a set of homophones or homonyms must be set aside by the logically-obsessed, or madness will eventually ensue. This is the conundrum of the Liar's Paradox, assuming words have logical consistency, parsed and processed with deductive mathematical certainty, that is the essence of Socrates' Error. To Humpty Dumpty, each use is potentially independent of previous use, despite his intention to use it consistently. To Alice, only a categorical definition prevents each use from being arbitrary, because she distrusts his intention. To us, words are not limited by definitions, nor are they empowered by them. If we are going to bother with definitions at all, even the idealistic one of an abstraction paradigm, it can only be considered to mirror, not generate, our understanding of the meaning or purpose of a word. When used with ill intent, the 'definition in context' mechanism of language reveals the inconsistency, and the same thing happens when they are used sincerely but inaccurately. When POR uses the contextual definition approach, we circumvent the false logic of the Liar's Paradox, and can agree with both Humpty Dumpty and Alice/Carroll/Dodgson, without considering either perspective definitive or more accurate than the other. Humpty Dumpty represents the epistemological modality, Alice the more ontological one, and the theological mandate is to balance the two honestly, because neither alone can explain or express what it is we do with language, or what it is that we are as humans with consciousness or consciences. This illustrates the structure of the Fundamental Schema, or rather, the schema's structure illustrates this idea. Truth and knowledge comes from recognizing and accepting that it is not one more than the other.

The question of context as definition is a feature that spans all possible contexts. But there are three particular and specific contexts that must be considered special. These are sometimes called 'special applications' of language, or even just 'applications', when the context is appropriate. These applications are not just special in a transitional way, while we adapt our societies and our linguistics to a post-postmodern POR perspective; they are endemic, essential occurrences in language itself, in all languages, and all civilizations. There are three fundamentally peculiar areas that humanity has developed, which any other being capable of using language must also discover and adopt. These 'special contexts' or applications are represented in our schema by the three corners of the triangle. These positions indicate both a heightened sensitivity to context, and an exemption from it at the same time. In each special context, we implicitly and unavoidably agree that highly educated individuals inevitably can and must engage in a linguistic practice that POR calls 'borrowing'.

Borrowing of words as a mechanism of language in one of these three special contextual applications is when an exceptional or designated authority takes a word that is part of a natural language, and uses it much more singularly: in a single context, but somewhat independently of the general context. The use of that term, within that one context, takes on a more solidified and important significance. The expert authorities in this process use the word as what amounts to technical jargon. While they are aware, in some way, that they are borrowing the word as a symbol for some basic idea or thing, people who use the word outside of that special application might not be. They might think these expert authorities have the power to dictate what words mean unilaterally, as if they are in charge of writing all the dictionaries. But this action is not theft; the word still belongs to the natural language, it has not actually become an arbitrary symbol that only experts are entitled to use within that special context. And so we call it 'borrowing', and every aspect of this process needs to be recognized, so that the function and worthiness of the word in the natural language is not destroyed so much that it must be discarded in the general context of the common vernacular. These three special contexts where borrowing must be allowed and understood are science, law, and medicine. In each of these circumstances, experts get to say what a word 'means', as if they were a divine Humpty Dumpty, but only within that special context itself. This borrowing mechanism inevitably tends, at least in postmodern hands, to generate a very powerful but isolated special vocabulary. The dry and arcane terminology of scientists, the intricate and archaic formalism of legalese, and both the precise vocabulary of doctors and the dangerously unmoored pseudo-authority of all varieties of 'alternative medicine' are what happens when words are borrowed from real language and used for individual purposes within these special contexts of science, law, and medicine.

The iconic example of this 'borrowing', and how it both can and can't have an effect/affect on natural language outside of the special context, is the word "species". This example also illustrates why borrowing is not just using words within a particular context, but the special applications are indeed special contexts, where the mechanism of words is not quite what they are in normal speech. The word 'species', in the connotation postmodernists believe (or pretend to believe) is now permanently fixed by the authority of 'scientists as priests with the divine power to dictate what words mean', predates Darwin. But he used it most notably and quite profoundly when he selected it for use in his title, "*On the Origin of Species by Means of Natural Selection, or the Preservation of Favoured Races in the Struggle for Life*". This has, of course, been shortened in the common vernacular to "The Origin of Species". This is not necessarily entirely because of the consequential inference regarding the word 'Races', but that may be significant, given the contemporary but not contemporaneous implications of "preservation of favored races in the struggle of life". Regardless, the word 'species' is now presumed to refer to what the Bible called 'kinds', and the more rigorous biologists call 'populations' or, more metaphorically yet analytically, 'gene pools'. Types of animals, whether defined by which can reproduce sexually with each other, which display some specific phenotype, or which share a particular mutation, are called "species". When the word is used in what looks like a more metaphoric (actually epistemological) way, we can talk about species of atoms or molecules or games or anything else. Generically, 'species' means nothing more than 'that which is specified', a synonym for 'kind' or 'sort'. Darwin wasn't the first to use it for biology, but before his theory of natural selection, modern philosophers studying animals did not consider it special or unique, they weren't particularly concerned with it as a word because they hadn't imagined that one would be needed for 'organisms sharing a genotype'. When naturalists, what came to be called scientists and biologists, adopted the expression 'species', they weren't yet <u>post</u>modernists, and did not necessarily believe that words had to have logical, deductive, even deterministic definitions, but they were not ignorant (either purposefully or initially) that words have meaning. These "proto-postmodernists" could presume, like Descartes, that a benevolent deity ensured their words, and the things they described with them, were rational. Darwin used 'species' to identify what he meant by species, and his definition in context was adopted widely. However, this borrowing did not provide it any quantifiable value, it remained a regular expression, not a code word.

The real point is that it still isn't a code word. Even within the discipline of biology, the word species does not actually have a single consistent definition. Different kinds of biologists use it for slightly different, if related, groupings of organism. In fact, even within a single specialty, such as evolutionary biology, or developmental biology, specialists use 'species' to identify different scientific ideas, distinct conceptions of what a species is, or why it is being referred to. Some might mean 'interbreeding population', some might mean 'specific genotype, including a given set of mutant alleles'. In general, the use of the word is dependent on two organisms' ability to sexually reproduce to produce a child organism that can, itself, reproduce. So horses and donkeys are two separate kinds of equine, but when they combine to reproduce, the resulting mule is sterile, so horses and donkeys are called different species. But what about bacteria? The word species is used to identify different types of those, as well, but bacteria merely replicate themselves, they do not reproduce sexually. Two bacteria can look and behave radically different from each other, but can they really be called separate species, if the test of whether organisms are the same species is whether they can mate successfully? All manner of ad hoc explanations can be created, even multiple ones for every single application of the term to what should amount to a different quantity of measurable thing, since science deals only with measurable quantities of logically defined things, and the terms used to label those things are ephemeral and logically irrelevant. Ultimately, every individual scientific paper could define the word species to mean something that is only relevant within that one study or theory. We are led to believe that terminology is technical and scientifically defined by experts, but they are merely borrowing the word, not regulating it.

Much can be made, and is, of efforts to refine definitions of words to try, however futilely, to limit them to an ontological category. And so consternation occurs when there is contention concerning what constitutes a sub-species, or how to distinguish populations, or what features separate and what mechanism separates them, but this is mostly all wasted effort. It is unimportant, Socrates' Error, an effort to insist that words should have deductive integrity, despite Socrates' own Methodical demonstration to the contrary. Scientists do not define words, they merely borrow them to label quantities in their formulas. They use them as symbols the same way Aristotle did, to explain theories, but not to test them. Syllogisms about Socrates do not test the validity of a logical relationship; if they did, the logic would fail, because the categories that words identify are not themselves quantifiable. This is not a flaw of words, but their purpose; it does not allow them to mean anything Humpty Dumpty declares, it instead enables them to have meaning that Alice can recognize. Words are merely family resemblances, classifications that don't have deductive integrity or predictive value, but don't need to; when we need deductive integrity or predictive value, we have symbols and numbers we can use instead, or borrowed (and therefore otherwise meaningless within the special context) terms that only look like words for the sake of convenience. But postmodernists reject the idea that words are not logical and categories are not mathematical sets. Scientists may as well be high priests, judging from the attitude postmodernists have. This perversely diminishes the real practice of science, when the reality of scientific terminology is thought to be insightful and informative rather than merely arbitrary and expedient.

The postmodern reverence for scientific terminology cannot be overstated. It is easy to see, and even easier to get a postmodernist to admit, that they believe scientific researchers have ultimate authority and veto power over what a thing 'is' and therefore what the word we used to describe that thing 'means'. In the postmodern theory of language, again, words are labels, and only highly educated experts (or someone's preferred pedant, however naive) are allowed to dictate when and how that word should be used. Because of its association with technology, engineering, and mathematical integrity, the realm of science is considered to be indisputable in terms of its authority to mandate nomenclature; not just within empirical endeavors but in our daily lives. This is a direct result of Socrates' Error, as embraced by post-Darwinian secularists and sectarians alike. In the special application of science, only scientists have this power to borrow. In the special application of medicine, only doctors should, but any quack can. In the context of law, legislators and judges share the responsibility and the ability to borrow words and appear to 'refine' them into supposedly more logical references.

To the postmodernist, law is simply the sociological equivalent of science, a refuge from the real world, where absolute logic is the only acceptable form of discourse. Or so they imagine, because they assume that "A=B" is interchangeable with "Socrates is a man". But to say that A=B is to say that all B is A, as well, and further that A minus B is nothing: A-B=0. But not all men are Socrates, nor do all men die (and cease to be a man and become a corpse) once Socrates does. Fancy epistemological footwork can try to mitigate this comparison of words and symbols by referring to the distinction, perhaps imaginary or irrational, between a definition of a set and the list of members of that set. But to make that relevant or convincing, still more philosophical tap-dancing and flum-flummery or argle-bargle becomes necessary, until the postmodernist has induced apathy in anyone who disputes them, and takes that for substantiation of their declarations.

When a word is borrowed, by either a scientist or a lawyer, they can use it according to the formulas and needs of their specialty. But despite postmodern habit to the contrary, the word does not lose any meaning or gain any limitations in definition outside of the special context. When scientists describe their theories about the tautological relationships between quantities of measurable features or entities using words and grammar, rather than symbols and calculations, it does not provide any validity to the theories, it simply makes them easier to explain to people who are not scientists. Likewise, when an attorney spells out a legal principle that binds the litigants in a courtroom or contract, the familiarity of the words does not ratify the legitimacy of the principle. This is why whether a particular description about science, law, or medicine "makes sense" is only important to other scientists, lawyers, or doctors, not the uneducated. But the validity and truth of science, law, or medicine does not exist for the benefit of the practitioners. Science exists to provide technology and engineering, not justice. Law exists to serve citizens and resolve disputes, not physics. Medicine exists to ease discomfort and mend injury, not morality. These special contexts, these human endeavors, have been developed to benefit and convenience humans, not create tyrannies with which to control and subjugate them. Scientists do not dictate terms, and they don't even define words. They simply use them, as convenient stand-ins for objectively measurable quantities, in order to describe the mathematical formulas that are their theories. Only the equations are truly science, only the symbols are scientific terms. Any words borrowed as stand-ins for symbols are immune to any restrictions or additions the scientist may apply when those words are used outside the special application of science, in the general context of any language community.

The context of law is a bit trickier, of course, because it lacks that empirical objectivity. Postmodern jurists have been indoctrinated into insisting that deciding matters of law is about being objective, but that's a misuse of the term, and an inapplicable idea. Law isn't about any rational goal, but a decidedly and importantly irrational one: justice. Justice cannot be measured, though you can try to quantify it in a nearly infinite number of ways, to satisfy postmodern delusions that logic is judicial. But judgments are the opposite of logical selection, in both reality and POR. If logic is sufficient for making a selection from among hypothetical alternatives, then no *judgment* is necessary, save the wisdom to know what logical formula to use, which isn't judgment but wisdom. Any time a judgment is called for, it is because logic and calculation is insufficient, whether due to ignorance of some concrete factor or the impossibility of concluding the calculation. Logic is irreplaceably powerful, when it can be used, but it is of extremely limited usefulness because it cannot often be used. Most of the time, almost all of the time, when people use the word 'logic', what they are actually referring to is 'reason'. Because we live in a postmodern world, people believe, because they are taught to believe, that all good reasoning is symbolic logic. We use trivial examples to justify this belief, mimicking reasoning with syllogisms of Aristotelian analysis, and assume that this proves that reason is logic. The overwhelming real world evidence of the insufficiency of logic for anything but the most trivial empirical claims or examples is simply ignored, and the resulting cognitive dissonance has brought us to the brink of madness and the destruction of our civilization.

Only when every single term is itself perfectly logical, objectively measurable, mathematically defined, can any lingual or textual statement be considered logical. The possibility of uncertainty, whether from ignorance or incalculability, is unacceptable in logic; such ambiguity is amplified by the process of mathematical transformations to make the outcome so ambiguous it is useless. (Extensive intercourse on existential uncertainty versus quantifiable uncertainty will be foregone in this context, but it is all applicable.) Even presuming to use a symbol or term in place of an even potentially variable unknown, as opposed to undetermined, term means the result of the logical process is entirely unknown. Note that it is not as 'equally unknown' as the assumption is: it is uncertain how much more unknown it will be. But it must, logically, be somewhat greater than the unknown variable, as a lower limit of how inaccurate the result of the process can be. In science, this is enough to require enormous care and calculation to avoid ambiguous results. In law, when it is impossible for any question to not include, if not completely resolve to, human rather than mathematical dimensions, it makes logic simply inapplicable. Judgment is necessary, however much it vexes the modern theory that all such things should be dismissed as merely 'subjective'. In logic, as I've said before, there is only 'is', 'has', and, with absolute certainty, 'will'. Only in non-logical reasoning and judgment does 'should', 'would', or 'might' have an existence. The validity of probabilistic results in science can mask this truth, leading people, even scientists, to think that a probability of greater than 0 or less than 100 means something 'might' happen, that it 'may be'. So the term 'maybe' takes on a logical connotation that is not logic. The probabilities express uncertainty about our *knowledge* of what will and must occur, not uncertainty in whether it will occur. Confusing knowledge of an event for the occurrence of the event is mistaking the map for the territory.

This last point is worth reviewing. Our current facility with forward and reverse teleologies often makes probabilistic results seem as if 'might' is a logical idea that can be equated to mathematical statistical possibility. (The impact of POR linguistics on the unique, unitary, and universal understanding of the expression "might", referring to both "potential" and "force", is instructive, but limits of time will make this, again, a foregone consideration.) In uncontrolled real world contexts, even when informed by scientific knowledge, these 'might/maybes' aren't comparable to value judgments. Reasoning allows us to intermingle statistical possibility (often reverse teleologies) with personal determination (inverse teleologies), but this should not lead us to conflate the two. The special context of law could frequently refer to its deliberative mechanism as 'logic', but calling it that does not make it so. Reason is not logic. Although we've been taught to think we can use an imaginary 'informal logic' when the formal symbolic sort of analytical philosophy (actual logic) is unattainable, reason is not a second-best replacement selection method. The reality is the opposite: logic is a second-best replacement for reason, adequate enough when time or attention are limited, in all contexts other than science. This is most especially true in the special context of law. Law is purely intellectual, and can be thought of as entirely epistemological. Within the study of law, things mean whatever they are declared to mean by the highest legal authority, independently of any linguistic integrity. Of course, honest jurists will purposefully attempt to maintain linguistic integrity, and postmodernist ones may even insist that lexicographic or etymological consistency is the only source of rectitude the law requires. But in both statutes and judicial decisions, the two primary examples of language in law, any obeisance to grammar is purely tradition, and any reference to logic is figurative. What makes law useful and acceptable is not the language it uses, but the justice it provides. Fairness, equity, impartiality, and righteousness are goals, not mere components, in just law, and empty rhetoric otherwise.

The variance between the laws of nature and the laws of man, the physically inescapable formulas that are the laws of physics and the statutes and precedents of legal guidelines, exemplifies and illustrates the whole epistemology of POR in general, and the process of borrowing specifically. Recall the example of Godwin's Law, and the misinterpretation of why it is called that, described earlier. Both scientific laws and legal laws are both laws, but are entirely opposite in every other way. Scientific laws are actually equations, formulae that are applicable only with mathematical values. Legal laws could conceivably include arithmetic rules, but they are not limited by empirical reality, only by the desire to control empirical reality with the authority of government. Physical laws cannot be circumvented, they are absolute regardless of how cruel they seem; Newton's laws and the laws of thermodynamics are relentless, they require no conscious enforcement, and have no loopholes, even in cases such as relativity or quantum mechanics that might seem to be exceptions. Legal laws must be enforced by corporeal authorities, or they are simply fictions, and can be arbitrary dictates. Scientific laws are predictive, statutory laws are prescriptive.

The variance between the contexts of law and science, and the principle of the variance between the linguistic modes of ontology and epistemology, can be demonstrated with a real world example. What is a tomato? According to scientific terminology, it is a fruit. But according to convention, rhetorical habit, and US federal law, it is a vegetable. "No," exclaims the postmodernist, "the law doesn't state that it is a vegetable, it merely regulates it as if it were a vegetable." This would be an instance of epistemological quibbling, making pointless distinctions between what something "is", and how it is identified. So, yes, it is a bit of an oversimplification, perhaps, to say that the law declares that the tomato is a vegetable. But at least we are not taking this postmodernist attitude to even more ludicrous metaphorical heights, and considering whether ketchup is a vegetable, simply because it is made from tomatoes and tomatoes are considered vegetables. That would be really crazy, wouldn't it? [Insert note that the previous statement was facetious sarcasm here.]

Ultimately, in truth we can admit that neither scientists, nor judges, can make demands on what we are allowed to say, and the fact that scientists and judges can differ on this one food item is instructive. Ontologically, the tomato is a fruit: it is a fleshy seed pod produced by a plant. Epistemologically, the tomato is a vegetable: it is considered to be in that category because it is used in salads more than deserts. The ontological approach considers only the thing itself, while the epistemological refers to its relation to other things.

Neither botany nor government can prevent the other from being opposite in their results. Nor do either have the authority to dictate what word people use outside of a lab or courtroom. No linguistic contortions such as 'fruity vegetable' or 'vegetative fruit' can resolve this issue. When people use the word 'tomato', they mean the same thing, regardless of whether they have an ontological or an epistemic designation in mind, and all uses of the word, even in the special applications, must be equally ontological and epistemological, and used honestly (theological) in order to be true. But they do have one or the other (or the third) reason for choosing to use that word for that thing, or at least one more than the other. Which is why we think of the tomato as a vegetable more than fruit, without regard to its botanical function or where to find it in the grocery store or how sweet it tastes. Of course, it should have already occurred to you that the very idea of 'fruit' and 'vegetable' meaning contrary things is a fiction to begin with. All fruits come from vegetation, and the question of whether only edible parts of plants are vegetables is both unresolvable or pointless. It doesn't matter what word you use, what matters is why you're using it. Is a hot dog a sandwich? Such epistemological musings are often considered interesting these days, because the postmodern assumption is that only ontology is analytical. But contentious questions like that don't identify the meaning of either thing, hot dog or sandwich, other than to define the terms in context. Progressively fine hair-splitting and invention of new categories in order to pretend that words must have precise definitions in order to be meaningful is a fruitless endeavor, however passionately pursued.

Schematic

The affinity of science for the ontological mode of language should be apparent. The matching affinity of law for the epistemological model is less obvious, but this is indicative of the nature of epistemology. Being is always easier to recognize and identify than meaning. They are both unavoidable, but meaning is easier to ignore. Without sincerity, honesty, and morality, neither ontology nor epistemology can be accurate. Therefore, the point where the line of ontological reasoning ends and the point where the line of epistemological reasoning ends are connected by the purpose to which they are put. In the Fundamental Schema, the intersection of ontology and theology is labeled 'science', and the intersection of epistemology and theology is labeled 'law'. The special context of 'medicine' is associated with the intersection of ontology and epistemology. The areas of these intersections correspond to the special applications in which we enable 'borrowing', use of words as if they weren't words but symbols for something else. The exact and indivisible point of each area of intersection is given special labels, as well. The context point of medicine has already been provided: self, or identity. The context point of science is mathematics, and the context point of law is its opposite, text. The Fundamental Schema as a whole is definitive in this way, the relationship between these various ideas and words can be thought to derive directly from the schema's arrangement and shape, because we derive the shape and arrangements from the relationships between the things themselves, the ideas and words, as rigorously as possible. Which is the map and which is the territory, which the model and which the reality, dissolved into the familiar ineffability that is the nature of reality, and words.

Theology is our projection of consciousness and conscience into and on the universe, and so the province of what we define as 'the study of purpose' reflects our desire for there to be a moral God to dictate what 'good' means, and to judge morality from an absolute perspective in a universe in which literally everything is relative. Hence the need for this God to be metaphysical, and the fact that, even if It exists, it is impossible fiction according to every empirical test and logical calculation. Although science, one end of the line of theology, uses language (text) to communicate its findings, those findings themselves are derived from their mathematical and empirical integrity, regardless of what words are used to describe or explain the science involved in finding them, so there is no direct connection between 'science' and epistemology or text. Only honest and ethical use of language can support honest and ethical scientific research, so there is a connection between 'math' and 'theology' that might not seem appropriate or worthwhile. For this reason, it might require further explanation to be comprehensible.

The need for this explanation is an indication of the power and long-standing history of Socrates' Error, along with the observation that not even the word 'math' can be mathematically defined, so in some sense the intersection of theology and ontology isn't 'really' the point of math, that is simply what we call it in our diagram. The diagram applies only to language and philosophy, and language is not math and math is not language. Another way of considering the point of math within the context of science (you see how, with the Fundamental Schema, our peculiar POR lingo and our natural language tend to coincide, trend towards coincidence?) is to reflect that the arbitrary signs used as numerals, mathematical operators, and other symbols have no moral component or content or consequence, and although this is the absence of morality it is also a sort of morality. If the idea or word 'morality' is too closely linked in your mind with theistic theology, the term 'ethics' can be used to replace it. Mathematics has no ethical dimension, it simply is what is; axiomatic systems cannot be used to judge purpose just as mathematics cannot express teleologies, only tautologies. This indicates why science in the abstract is devoid of ethical implications even while the ethical ramifications within the practice and application of science are paramount in necessity and profound in effect. The "dual opposites" of morality, immorality, and amorality helps to define this issue in our language, along with the idea described in POR as the simultaneity principle, in which a word as an epistemological category includes things described as opposites as ontological instances. The iconic example is 'tolerance', when considering that being intolerant of intolerance is tolerance. Unfortunately, the fact that tolerance is also a dichotomous abstraction, used to identify a quantity of precision as well as an emotional acceptance, makes that iconic example confusing. Similarly, the matter of matter being energy according to Einstein's' theory of relativity makes matter, which is also a dichotomous abstraction, an example of the simultaneity principle, as well; this approach to words is dicey, but no more so than the postmodern assumption that all words should be considered logically consistent, when no words ever are. Yet another example of the illogical nature of words which relate to both mathematics and morality is 'value'. This word evidences both dichotomous abstraction and simultaneity as well, being both numeric quantity and a quality beyond quantity, depending on what the value of something is to a person, and what a person values. The postmodern perspective tends to reduce all values to economic value alone, a flat, amoral theology that causes great emotional consternation to those of us that value a more robust moral consideration, and consider the tautology 'everything has a price' to be a representation of immorality.

The line of theology in the schema can be thought of as a spectrum, with the end that touches science and math being devoid of moral judgment. This makes the ethical behavior of scientists incredibly important in terms of their honesty concerning their data, but their ethical beliefs irrelevant so long as their analysis of that data is logically correct. The other end of the spectrum, text and law, is the opposite. The commandments of law, at least just law in a free society, are wholly ethical by nature, nothing but ethical dictates and completely dependent on ethical enforcement. To accept what is lawful as what is right, in and of itself, is to ignore the fact that the only moral purpose of law is justice. Law for its own sake is tyranny.

Text is the only language of the law, and the only real content of laws are text, however convoluted the legalese or statutory formalism might get. While laws cannot successfully contradict mathematical truth, that is not the kind of truth that law is involved in determining. Again, postmodern conditioning might make this require a more serious assessment, since it can seem as if the ontological truth of whether an event took place is something that a court must determine. Findings of fact are not the same as findings of law, though, and the real issue to be proved in a legal proceeding is the epistemological truth of a person's guilt more than the ontological existence of their action. The ontological findings of fact and of law, are mere stepping stones to the just verdict and legal decisions.

The epistemological approach to language, categorization independent of any necessary factual premise, connects the individual (self, identity) with theology through the text of the law; we create statutes to mandate a minimum level of moral conduct as both the cause and result of this relationship. The philosophical basis of 'law as ethics' or 'ethics as law' is extensive and sometimes intricate, as well as being almost hopelessly convoluted by postmodernist practices. The foundation of 'secular morality' on theories of social contracts, utilitarianism, and enlightened self-interest does not prevent such theology from being accurate, but are not the cause of that accuracy. The word 'ethics' is primarily a postmodern substitute for 'morality', supposedly stripped of all theism. In the minds of postmodernists who believe that all theology is theistic, ethics is based entirely on reciprocity. The assumption that benefiting others will be reciprocated is merely a hope, though, and requires a premise that there is some logical mechanism both for determining fairness (an equality independent of circumstances) and for enforcing it. Hope is an irrational expectation, and so using it as a primitive for further irrational expectations is not untoward. Not that irrational ideas require or have primitives, and it remains irrational, nevertheless. Absent a presumption (an assumption, in postmodern thinking, thanks to POS) that people will act reasonably in return for being treated reasonably (which is valid, but is not logical), the 'morality-free ethics of legal mandate' cannot be justified by either reason or logic. The very word 'moral' demonstrates the difficulty of trying to deal with words as if they are logically constructed or employed: immorality is a moral issue, even though immorality is not moral.

Law opposes reality, enforcing dictates that we wish would have direct physical effect but do not. Medicine is free of any purpose except what the patient desires. The existence of a mathematical truth has no impact on literature unless the author allows it to. God is the projection of our consciousness and conscience onto the physical and social world(s) that we live in. All of these ideas may, or may not, be thought of as being generated automatically by examination of the Fundamental Schema, but are prompted and guided and perhaps even verified by it.

The amount and degree of these kinds of observations about the Fundamental Schema diagram are endless and illustrative, which is the very purpose, meaning, and being of the symbol. One last note to make on that, rather than continue with various permutations of the principle, is the distinction that can and must be made between medicine and science. They are both empirical endeavors, and the postmodern proclivity is to believe that medicine is science applied to human biology and the cure of disease. The use of the 'mathematical laws' of science for practical applications is not science, though, it is engineering, and the technology and architecture that result from engineering. None of these things exist categorically, of course, they are merely words we use to describe what does exist. The reason why we use those words to describe them is important and meaningful, and it is worth noting that medicine can be considered an art, at least as much as a science. The assumption that doctors are scientists, the insistence that doctors are scientists, might not seem like a problem in the abstract, since we want both groups to behave ethically and make decisions based on facts. But that is true of everyone, of course. Scientists who call themselves medical doctors, and medical doctors who believe themselves scientists, are a very real problem in actual circumstances. The job of scientists studying human biology and the task of doctors applying empirical research to patient's suffering are both made far easier when they are aware of the distinction between science and medicine. And the benefit to the patient of demanding and maintaining a rigorous awareness of an absolute distinction between science and medicine is unlimited, particularly when they are also a research subject.

To understand what 'medicine' "really is", "in and of itself", we can say that it is the use of empiricism across all instances to directly benefit the individual patient in each single instance. It is not up to other experts, whether scientists, lawyers, or priests, to determine whether we feel healthy, and it is unimportant, even irrelevant, how many other patients might be cured by a particular treatment, statistically. When you are suffering, it doesn't matter how many other people were helped by a treatment, the only thing that matters is whether it helps you. Because of this, and the principle of the uncontrollable state of the universe, medicine is not science, and shouldn't be mistaken for or described as science, or even scientific. In terms of the Fundamental Schema, the domain of empiricism connects medicine and science, but they are at opposite ends of it. Both are empirical, when done correctly, but science is all about math and physics, and medicine is all about healing and wellness. The experiments of science are empirical, and their validity is entirely unrelated to any practical application that the science may provide. In medicine, experiments for theoretical knowledge are unacceptable, and any method of empirical data collection needs to have an overwhelming, even obsessive regard for **ethics**. This is a result (or a cause, and both,) of the separation between the context of medicine and the line of morality (theology, purpose) in the POR schema: there is no direct connection between the two, medicine and theology, so any experimentation involving medical treatments is problematic. Certainly controlled clinical trials are about the mathematics of dosing and use double-blind experiments to collect data, but these are for practical aims, not simply to test hypotheses. Any medical research must place the wellbeing of subjects as a higher priority than the collection of data, and the counter-examples are predictably infamous and disturbing. So much so that I will not even design to list any examples; if you believe or pretend that you need any to know what I'm referring to, you are so postmodernist that you are either profoundly ignorant or distressingly dishonest.

Consideration of medicine as an intellectual field in POR terms suggests one other thing that I will note, as an example of the nature of words. What would I be referring to if I were to use the term "pathology"? Is that an honest and important study of the cause of disease and methods of diagnosis? Or is it a reference to a mental disturbance in someone acting anti-socially? It is another dichotomous abstraction, obviously, in the vocabulary of POR, like "matter". Does the issue become more or less clear if I substitute the term "pathological"? Is one connotation the analytical and the other metaphorical? Is one denotation more ontological and the other more epistemological? Do any of these questions have right or wrong answers, are they just whatever guess you make based on your personal experience, is there one or the other perspective that is more likely to be better than your own, and is it ever certain that it is? In postmodern linguistic theory, our brains choose which connotation to accept as denotation based on calculations of probabilities. In the POR theory of language, no such choice has to exist, and it is the indeterminacy that enables both definitions to provide meaning to the unique, unitary, and universal word. Set this issue aside for now, if you can, or else bear it in mind as we proceed. Both are equally useful, if we can even imagine that there is any difference.

The separation of medicine from science illustrates another controversial effect on the conventional understanding of both medicine and science. As understood in POR, science is centered on mathematics. The enterprise of science must be considered to be limited to those efforts of empirical research that attempt to describe the material universe in entirely objective, calculable formulas identifying consistent and precise mathematical relationships between measurable quantities of things. There are many efforts of empirical research that might be called science, but for a single, perhaps seemingly trivial, variance from that very strict definition. The most dramatic pitfall that disqualifies earnest and empirical research from being true science is the need for objective metrics. Any experiment that requires any human judgment to determine which category or classification any component of the experiment belongs within cannot be considered real science, however honestly or authoritatively that categorization is made. For the most part, this disqualifies every instance of human beings studying human beings. These efforts at what POR characterizes as 'humanology' necessarily fail to be sufficiently scientific for at least two related reasons. The first is the fact that human beings are the designers of the experiments, and create categories and classifications to test a hypothesis based on non-objective criteria or goals. Humans cannot objectively study themselves, because what measurements are taken cannot be divorced entirely from the goals of the experimenter. This is the case, even if mechanical, and therefore objective, metrics are used as the assumptions in the calculations to be performed in order to support or exclude the researcher's theory about what is being studied, because it is still humans that choose (or decide) what metrics to measure and what mechanical processes to employ in measuring them. The second reason human studies of humans cannot be science is the inverse: the subjects are not objective, either, even if their physical bodies are. It is not simply a matter of the idea that subjective classifications cannot be trusted, or that people will arrange the experiment in order to assume their conclusions or lie to either protect their dignity or satisfy the researcher. Even if humans are only vaguely aware that their actions are being measured, and unaware of how or why, they still will, or at least could, vary their behavior from what would otherwise be natural, making the entire exercise less valuable empirically. And if they are aware that their actions are being quantified or judged, they will surely, perhaps even unavoidably, change their behavior. If there ever could be such a thing as a computer program that could perfectly predict my behavior (in less proximate a form than a thumbswitch experiment) then it would certainly become my sole focus to behave in any other way possible, whether I manage to succeed or not, and I believe that any other human with regard for their personal dignity would, as well.

This distinction between physical science and empirical humanology is not to suggest or insist that human research into human behavior, such as psychology, sociology, or anthropology (the "classic" humanologies) or even political science, economics or history (which are all 'humanology' as well) are not worthwhile endeavors, at least in some cases and when approached seriously and responsibly. Nor even that they are not more empirical and rigorous, and benefit from it, than study of the less objective sorts of "the humanities", such as literary critique or performance. Where there might be categorical distinctions between 'social sciences' and 'liberal arts' is left, as an exercise in deductive flum-flummery, to the postmodernists. Primarily, the intention of coining the neologism *humanology* (with acknowledgment to those who have attempted to invent it previously) is simply to emphasize that psychology and sociology may be empirical, but are not scientific. Admittedly, this attitude does extend to a confident dismissal of most psychological theories, and the value of many sociological studies, as well. The more valid parts of psychology can be grouped with medicine along with psychiatry, and the more important portions of sociology can be considered quantitative anthropology, and this might very well simplify a lot of the consternation about academic disciplines without oversimplifying the issue of how to accomplish the very important goals of humanology as a field of study, or a category of such fields.

This 'humanology is not really science' rule is because of the nature of humanity, and the consciousness that it includes, and that is part of not just the researchers, but any subjects in any experiment intended to examine human behavior or affects. Self-determination, and its independence from the mechanistic cause-and-effect that invariably and absolutely controls every other feature or component of physical reality, makes objective assessments or conclusions about humans by humans self-defeating, or simply inaccurate. In the conventional lexicon of contemporary postmodern society, the familiar explication of this issue is to invent a category named "soft sciences" and contrast it with "hard sciences". This is the same adaptive mechanism that causes and allows people to believe there is such a thing as "informal logic" that can be compared to "formal logic".

If science is not entirely objective and rigorous, it is not science, just as if a logical chain of deductions is not flawless, it is not a logical chain at all. In fact, it isn't even correct to say that it is "as if", because it is the same truth in both cases: science and logic are both just mathematics, and are true or false entirely independently of what words you are using. It is called 'science' which uses logic when it is empirical, and logic as a science when it is hypothetical, but the primitive is numbers and the arithmetic we use to transform one number into another. The use of phrases like 'hard science' and 'informal logic' encourages postmodern over-synonimization, POS, and should not be accepted. This is related to the issue with 'moral' that I mentioned previously. In contrast to science and logic, which POS makes interchangeable with medicine and reason, respectively, morality is accepted as abstract, non-corporeal, so the affect is inverted. Rather than POS, the term 'moral' is effected by an inverse affect, in which a word identifies a thing, but also encompasses a category that includes the opposite of that thing. Immorality is not simply a lack of morality, it is a kind of morality. We like to think a bad kind, which is why we construct the apposite word as we do, but opinions necessarily vary in whether a moral action (an action that we wish to consider whether it is ethical) is a moral action (an action that is ethical). There is not a particular mechanism causing this effect/affect/process/circumstance, like POS, because it is simply the way words work. The POR reference is to the unique, universal, and unitary nature of words, that a thing can be both that thing and its opposite, not just depending on context but simultaneously. Postmodern linguistic theory teaches us that this simultaneity is impossible, that the word 'moral' means either one or the other (goodness, or ethics in general) sequentially. Learning to accept that this lesson is false, and that your mind can accept this simultaneity just as your brain already does, is the process of learning what POR really is, and how it isn't just these crazy theories I have that must be wrong because they contradict what past philosophers, scientists, and priests have decreed or are thought to have proven. Reasoning is not logic, it is needed to deal with things that logic cannot, and succeeds at doing so. For convenience sake, POR refers to the ability of words to mean both what they mean and the opposite as "the principle of opposite/apposite simultaneity in language", generally 'abbreviated' to simply the "simultaneity of words" or "simultaneity principle". The postmodern terms "soft science" and "informal logic" are constructed to deal with the fact that this principle allows something that isn't science or isn't logic to be thought of as a kind of science or a kind of logic. Humanology could be called a category of 'soft sciences', but it is more accurate to simply recognize that humanology is not science.

Like any other method of POR, this guideline that humanology cannot be science (ontologically, even when treated as science epistemologically by thinking of science as empiricism rather than applied mathematics) because humans cannot objectively study humans, is instructive as well as observational. Psychiatry, when practiced sincerely and honestly, is clearly not even intended to be science, it is merely the art of medicine applied to our mentality rather than our metabolism. But psychology is distinct from psychiatry, at least supposedly, conventionally, and often if not always practically; psychiatrists have the legal authority to write prescriptions, psychologists do not. Sociology and anthropology, and most particularly the intensely and intentionally postmodern practice of 'evolutionary psychology', along with all other psychological approaches to examining and explaining human beings and their behavior, are all simply facets of 'humanology', and as worthwhile and productive as they may be (and sometimes are), they are not science. However much they might adopt the forms or trappings of science, the non-mathematical nature of human consciousness prevents them from ever achieving the objectivity of pure science. Distinctions between these disciplines is academic, even when scholarly. There is no 'hierarchy' of empiricism involved, per se, but there is unquestionably a continuum, from the point of mathematics within the area of science to the point of identity within the area of medicine. How these disciplines of humanology might be arranged along that line, the domain of empiricism, is irrelevant.

In addition to psychology, sociology, and anthropology, the disciplines of history, civics and political science can be included in humanology. Civics more often involves historical facts, even though its focus is a single contemporary example of governing society, and might well be considered closer to ontology than most other humanology. Political science, similarly, might be thought of as actual science when it is restricted to electoral results as numeric values, but the association of those results to any social phenomenon or issues of political philosophy makes it the softest kind of empirical study that humanology has to offer, at least in my mind. The conspicuous reliance on teleologies, linking political causes to governmental results, is evidence that humanological studies are not scientific. Again, the purpose of excluding these things from the domain of science is not to denigrate them. Calling them "soft science", as postmodernists do, might even be said to be celebrating their value as methods for finding truth by calling them science instead of being derogatory by using the metaphor 'soft' with the contrasting analytical term 'science'. I come here not to bury humanology, but to praise it. As long as we are aware that these things are not science, even when limited to empirical experiments, and backed up by strong statistical analysis, they can be of tremendous value and importance.

In the most dedicated and careful heuristic pursuits, very useful and important discoveries can be made about humans, and we do remain biological creatures that can be dissected on a zoological level. But our capacity for self-determination foils any claim such pursuits have to be scientific, if they are at all impacted by or related to cognition, self-awareness, or other aspects of consciousness. Both our urge to explain our own actions and motivations in flattering and congratulatory terms, and condemn the actions and motivations of those who behave or believe differently than we do, prevents these philosophical investigations from being connected to any true 'mathematical theology', where ethics are absolute and morality is objectivism. The absence of moral judgment from mathematics is comprehensive and complete, or it is not mathematics but some other method of codifying our perceptions, and humanological disciplines, however strict and rigorous, cannot live up to that expectation of logical integrity. A large part of sociological and psychological theorizing is really little more than a 'secular religion' that intends and attempts to medicalize the behavior of people we disagree with as disease or dysfunction. Rather than denouncing bad behavior as caused by demons or weakness, the psychologist uses equally fanciful or condemnatory entities or descriptions. The priest chastising his flock for not living up to what he claims are God's dictates is no different than an 'evolutionary psychologist' declaring what we should consider adaptive or maladaptive in our supposedly flawed species.

Part of the reason for the development of, and progress in, humanology and medicine in postmodern times, while still being problematic when described as science, is the difficulty of distinguishing possibilities from probabilities. In general, since humans are not sub-atomic in dimension or astronomic in scope, any results of empirical research that resolves only to (potentially fictional) tendencies labeled with numeric values is not simply worthless, in explaining human behavior, but misguided and wrong. If the results of an experiment can explain why 100% or 0% of all of humanity falls into a certain category, it can be considered biology and described as real science. (Numbers of more moderate tone can be accepted as scientific if they are correlated in turn, with 100% accuracy, to a genotype, phenotype, or even epistemological grouping such as demographics.) But if the conclusions of a theory are that any less absolute proportion of people do, say, think, or feel a certain thing or way, it is humanology, suspect, and simply not scientific. There are exceptions, of course, depending on how consistently and precisely a statistic can be verified. To say that 99.98% of human beings are born with ten fingers and ten toes is a biological finding, not an anthropological one, whether it is genetic or developmental in cause. To say that humans "should have" five digits on each limb is a sociological dictate, not a zoological one. As a fictional example, when researches proclaim that people 'tend to' or have a 40% or 63.853% chance of wearing jewelry, it is an observation about the people who study the issue, and their classification of what 'jewelry' is, and is of trivial value to anyone else. Since the mere appearance of numbers in a classification or result are not 100% indicative of being scientific, one indication that can be used to distinguish science from humanology is whether the application of that number can be made more certain than the number itself. For example, if a researcher concludes that 25% of people respond identically to a particular and singular stimulus, whether it should, at least at first glance, be considered science depends on whether they can identify, in objective terms, which 25% of people it is. If the only commonality among the group is that they do respond in that certain way to that certain and unique stimulus, then it is not valuable scientific knowledge, but merely the invention of one way to separate individuals into distinct masses of individuals, without any teleological explanation to enable the tautological definition.

Returning to the topic of medicine, the art of healing does not lose value because it is not science. Instead, its value comes from being unscientific, not interested in proving principles but in helping people. The use of demonstrable tests, experiments, empirical research, is common to both, but this does not make them identical. Science can be used to help us overcome the difficulty of comprehending our physical cosmos and our experiential reality within it by side-stepping the uncontrollable state of the universe. Medicine can and must simply ignore this unavoidable principle, the uncontrollable state of the universe, and bear the burden of being unable to distinguish between the placebo effect and the value of psychological comfort in treating biological maladies. Medicine is not simply biology applied to human beings, it is, instead, all those applications of healing effort to human beings which is not simply biology.

And so our Fundamental Schema, which guides not only our language but our reasoning, in POR, is more or less complete. There are more aspects and applications to explore, but we will not plumb their depths further here. Instead, we will move on to the third and final graphic that illustrates the meaning and substance of the Philosophy Of Reason, the mysterious jellybean diagram. This figure denotes, like the previous two, something very important about the nature of words, the process of human reasoning, and the value of individual perception. Just as the implicit bias test and the keyboard experiment demonstrate that free will is a delusion, but the thumbswitch experiment is a conclusive proof, AP and the POR schema illustrate how words work, philosophically, but the jellybean mystery is the proof, an even more direct examination of the mechanism of language, and its ability to transform social animals into conscious human beings.

Jellybeans

Take a transparent container of any size or shape, a glass jar being the nominal example, and fill it with small and generally similar objects. A jar of jellybeans, for instance. Ask an arbitrary collection of human beings to guess at the number of jellybeans in the jar, individually and secretly so that no person knows what anyone else's guess is. It is unavoidable that one guess is going to be the most accurate. At most, more than one person might guess the exact same number, but whether that is one guess or two is epistemological, since ontologically they are the same number: the same guess. (Or they are ontologically separate, and epistemologically identical, depending on your theological perspective.) These guesses, speculations, all have identical <u>precision</u>, since they all must be a single, whole integer. But there is zero likelihood that they will all be equally <u>accurate</u>; one quantity is always going to be mathematically closer than all others. There's nothing interesting or intriguing about a jellybean guessing contest, in terms of who wins. We might like to think, because we have been trained in postmodernist logic since we were toddlers, that whoever comes up with the most accurate value simply did a better job of calculating or estimating the figure, based on a visual assessment of the size of the jar and the size of the objects within.

But there is reason to believe that the issue is not quite that simple. Unless we simply assume our conclusion, that people make guesses by computing, consciously or unconsciously, a best fit based on volume to derive a mathematical sum, and it must be so because that is our assumption and there is no way to refute it, the real world doesn't really mirror that hypothetical process. It isn't always the smartest person, or the one with the highest score on an IQ test, or the trained mathematician, or the person most securely convinced they are performing mental or cerebral arithmetic, that comes up with the guess closest to the real number of jellybeans in the jar. Certainly we could perform the experiment repeatedly, and derive a statistical likelihood that any one of those categories most convincingly mirrors the result of the contest, but as I indicated previously, unless the statistical likelihood is 100%, it is simply a further approximation, itself, not a teleological explanation of how people choose or decide what number to write down.

Still, there isn't anything remarkable about a jellybean experiment, and it can be performed as nothing more than delightful entertainment at any social gathering. What makes the jellybean jar contest of profound importance in the Philosophy Of Reason is something a bit more mysterious. It turns out that, when you get a bunch of people to guess at the number of jellybeans in a jar, the closest answer is not always the best answer, mathematically speaking.

More than half the time, (but not all the time; this is important) it turns out that if you average out all of the guesses, all of the 'wrong' guesses, all of the 'incorrect estimations', the result is actually **closer** to the real number of jellybeans than the most accurate individual guess. At first blush, this might seem inevitable, since a larger sampling of values averaged out seems like it should produce a better quality result than a single value alone. But if this were the cause of the results we see, then it stands to reason that it should always be the case, and the average guess should always be more unerring than the closest individual one. Conversely, if human cognition were itself mathematical, if some explicit or secret process of calculation was involved in choosing a number, the most precise individual estimation should always exceed the aggregate average, or what is the biological point of being able to calculate?

(If your brain just stumbled over the use of the word 'precise' in that previous sentence, and it caused you concern because in a previous paragraph I pointed out that all the guesses are equally precise, and only vary in accuracy, then congratulations on understanding POR, and shame on you for refusing to admit you understand POR. Words don't have to be used with ontological precision; as long as you know I meant 'whether the guess is close to the number of jellybeans in the jar', it shouldn't actually matter whether I use the term 'precise' or 'accurate'. Quibbling about it is postmodernism, the kind of abuse of 'critical thinking skills' that cause so many people to be annoying pedantic contrarians in our society. But because this is an instructional volume rather than a reference work, it is worth pointing out that the word was used purposefully in a figurative sense, to mean 'accurate' while writing' precise'. The recovering postmodernist should recognize the literal use of the term 'figurative' in the previous sentence, without becoming convinced that the term 'literally' can never be used, in turn, itself, in a figurative sense.)

This probability, without certainty, that the average of the guesses is better than the best guess is not conclusive evidence that human beings guessing at the number of objects in a container are not mathematical estimations, and it certainly isn't proof that human consciousness is not a computational process, or that reasoning is not logic. But it is intriguing evidence of these things, and considered profound affirmation of them in POR. (Whether you call that 'proof' is up to you, since the real meaning of that word in most contexts is simply 'enough evidence to convince me personally'.) The 'jellybean mystery', as we call it, is all the more important because it **doesn't** happen every time that the average of bad guesses is better than a good guess. The 'jellybean diagram' is simply a plotting of these instances. Unlike the abstraction paradigm and the Fundamental Schema, it doesn't really have a lot of supplemental fascination, but like them it can be applied to additional circumstances to guide our comprehension. With the AP, we had rhetorical 'lie detection' and teleological reversal of the 'arrow of time'. With the schema,

Jellybeans

we have the general application to philosophical as well as linguistic assessments of human cognition. In the case of the jellybean diagram and its attendant mystery, we have the very nature and purpose of humanity's biological evolution, the development of our cognitive awareness and capacity for the linguistic signaling that results in communication, hopefully.

Here is the line upon which we are going to plot our jellybean mystery:

Here is the line with the actual number (|) of jellybeans in the jar:

---|----------------------------------

Here is the line with all the guesses (i, with I being used for the closest guess), abstractly limited in number so that we don't clutter the diagram. Note also that this is illustrative, not computative, so whether the space between the numeric guesses is accurately quantified is not at issue, or to scale:

------i--------------i---------i-I------|----------i------i--i-ii---------------

The distribution of guesses will average out to a bell curve if we compile the results of many different jellybean contests. More guesses closer to the mark, fewer guesses being extremely low or extremely high. This could all be the case if guessing were mostly just random and arbitrary with just a single or small number of inconclusive clues. But the POR analysis of the results, and the metaphorical significance of the process, is neither reduced nor heightened by comparing a number of contests, whether using the same jar over and over or using different containers and articles of different sizes or types.

Here is the complete diagram, with the calculated average of all the guesses shown as being closer to the correct quantity than even the best individual guess.

------i--------------i---------i-I-*----|----------i------i--i-ii--------------

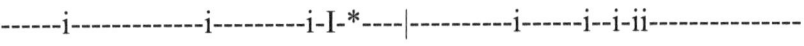

When presenting the jellybean diagram as a representation of the jellybean mystery, we usually extract the cardinal values, ignoring whether the guesses or average are higher or lower than the true value, so the most common illustration is usually something more similar to this, with the actual number of jellybeans being almost but not quite at the extreme limit. This is merely convention, but will be the diagram we'll use most of the time:

----i---ii--i---i-----i---i-i-I-*----|-

The 'I' representing the best guess and the '*' representing the average of all the guesses (with or without the best guess included, which very rarely makes any difference) can be swapped when the instance being graphed does not display the effect. Such instances of execution are still an illustration of the jellybean mystery, as I've already explained, but in POR demonstrations it is described as a jellybean mystery either "occurring" or "not occurring" depending on whether the average of guesses or individual guess is closer, respectively. I will reiterate, this is rhetorical: the mystery always occurs, but is simply not as apparent when the best guess manages, against the odds, to be better than the average of all guesses. So even when we say "the jellybean mystery did not occur", that is confirmation that the jellybean mystery did occur, but was not evident.

A jellybean diagram when the mystery "does not occur":

----i---ii--i---i-----i---i-i-*-I----|-

The interpretation of the jellybean mystery in POR is this: our brains did not evolve to be good at math. They evolved to be good at language. Which is to say that they evolved to be capable of communicating with each other more than estimating physical facts. When people put down a number in a jellybean contest, they aren't 'estimating', they're just guessing. This is true even if they take the trouble to imagine or even write down a mathematical calculation to justify their guess, because they're just guessing at the factors they used to come up with the product (or dividend, divisor, and quotient, or numbers and sum, or any other symbolic logic that could be used to calculate the number of objects in a container.) **_Human beings were born to guess. Sometimes we do it well, sometimes we don't, and your guess is as good as mine about when it is one more than the other._** The IPTM assumption is that guessing isn't possible, that any number has to be an estimate, because calculating is the methodology of thinking, whether through conscious mathematical approximation or some unknown and hidden calculus that controls our brain cells using electrical signals in neural networks. In effect, the postmodernist IPTM hypothesis is usually one of 'false consciousness', since no matter what the images, words, or inclinations in our heads are, we are "really" just calculating, subconsciously, for our own advantage, and that everything else is fiction. POR rejects IPTM, and all postmodernism, and any modern philosophy that relies, knowingly or implicitly, on Socrates' Error and his math envy. Words are not logical constructs, they are emotional ones. Of course, to say that something is 'emotional' in a postmodern society is to denigrate it, to insinuate it should be dismissed as something less rigorous than reasoning or logic. This is POS, the association of 'emotion' with sentimental weakness or immature subjectivity. The term 'emotion' actually just refers to 'what is emoted', and to emote is simply to state. "Words are emotional constructs" might be dismissed as a circular tautology, it could just mean "words are words". Or "emotions are emoted". Language is like that; circular logic is always bad logic, which is to say it is not logic, but circular reasoning is merely reasoning, sometimes good and sometimes bad, depending on whether we learn more from it or use it to remain ignorant on purpose. Having emotions is not a human frailty, it is not even just a human strength. It is the definition and the process of being human: awareness of the visceral feelings that observing events (or language or art) has on our selves, and the ability to communicate it to others.

The number of jellybeans in a jar is a fixed and real integer value. There really is a jar, there really are jellybeans, and there really is only one number that corresponds to the number of jellybeans in the jar. In this alone, the jellybean mystery differs from the evolutionary purpose of the human mind. Descartes pointed out that only your own existence is certain, everything else may be a false impression. The Philosophy Of Reason presumes without assuming that everything in the world, and most particularly the meaning and intention of every word you interpret or use, is something that human beings can only guess at, but nothing else but human being scan even perceive. We know we personally exist because we are able to wonder whether we exist, and we have to exist in order to do so. That is the meaning of Descartes' Cogito Ergo Sum. But after that, we cannot say anything else with such certainty. We know of everything in the universe, even our own bodies, only through information, 'data', that we have received into our minds through our senses. This process, this fact, erects an 'existential wall' that it is eternally and absolutely impossible to breach. Any tool we might think we can discover or use to do so, to allow us to transcend the limits of existence, is only another thing that we can only know about through our senses or guess at, and so it remains on one side the other of the existential wall. Are you asleep right now, only dreaming you are reading this book? Are you a butterfly that has gone insane and has delusions of being a human being? Are you plugged into the Matrix; are you a computer simulation that has never been real; are you dead and this is purgatory, or heaven, or hell?

This existential wall truly is unbreachable, according to standard philosophy and scientific theory. But POR is not standard philosophy or scientific theory, it is a new one. And the lesson of the jellybean mystery is that there is one thing, only one thing, only ever one single thing, that can and does tunnel through that existential wall, like an electron teleporting through a coffee cup. Words. Only words. Nothing but words. Not their sound or their spelling. Just their meaning. Because the meaning of a word is that word, only that word, and nothing else. And whether that word is true, whether we have chosen the right one, based not on what we are referring to but on why we are referring to it, is not a matter of statistical correlation with other uses of that sound or spelling. It comes from whether that word resonates inside of us; corresponds, without correlation, to our internal emotional experiences; causes, without any physical force, our minds to recognize it as the truth instead of a lie. The <u>sound or the image</u> of a word carries the word through our senses; it remains possible that is a figment of our imagination. However, the <u>meaning</u> teleports directly from one mind to another, through the existential wall that makes the phonemes and letters unreliable, but has no effect on the existence of their meaning. This mechanism requires only a theory of mind; it is not dependent on the signaling system involved. This is why we can use writing to communicate words, and they are the same words whether spoken or written, even though spelling is not a transcription of sounds, so spelling (and both alphabetic characters, letters, and grammar) does not logically correlate with pronunciation. And if neither sounds nor marks can be used to communicate those words, we can use gestures. If gestures themselves should fail along with the others, we can, we will, we must (a *must* that has the absolute nature of physical laws, not merely the less absolute *should* of statutory laws) find some other method, to support our theory of mind, to project our thoughts out into the universe, and to truly perceive the thoughts of other minds, in the same way.

How? Meaning is context. The meaning of a word is just like the number of jellybeans in the jar, except it isn't a number. We can ask any number of people what the word means, and get a different answer from every single one of them. To a postmodernist, this suggests that the word doesn't actually mean anything, that it can't mean anything. Postmodernist linguistics expresses this as words being symbols, and meaning being negotiated definitions. The POR linguistic theory is that words are meaning, and meaning is words; language is the theory of mind, and the theory of mind is language; words are thoughts when they are outside our heads, and thoughts are words when they are inside our heads. Combining this linguistic theory with causality, which is as real but as inexplicable as time, results in consciousness, and consciousness results in our perception and invention of causality. The standard (postmodern) theory of human language and consciousness is that only the best individual guess is successful, competitively superior; the rest are flawed. But the POR model shows why we have community, and communicate. The group, even in ignorant guesses, is better than any individual estimation.

The significance of the jellybean mystery is that it illustrates the implausibility of the postmodern theory of human evolution, and demonstrates the POR theory we can replace it with. Acceptance of this new theory both indirectly and directly leads to personal happiness and social development. Postmodern evolutionary theory of the human intellect is that our brains are adapted to calculate mathematical probabilities in order to make predictions and enhance our survivability and reproductive success. The POR sumpsimus is that the human intellect, conscious thought, did not evolve to calculate probabilities, or even recognize patterns, but to make irrational guesses and communicate them to other humans. The postmodern assumption has always been that one brain, executing logical programming, succeeds better in the natural (and social) world. The genes that cause it therefore become more frequent in the gene pool when its functioning is more precise, both in terms of the assumptions it makes about facts and the computation of results. It is a difficult theory to dispute, let alone disprove, because of the tar pit problem. Once the theory is assumed in order to test it, no amount of contradicting facts would be sufficient to reject it, because of the problem of induction: an infinite number of inductive suppositions does not amount to a deductive conclusion. But the jellybean mystery encapsulates the contrary theory so well that, hopefully, it can be sufficient to cause the irrational brains reading the theory to recognize the truth. Human brains did not evolve by competing to be more logical, but instead cooperating to be more successful, even if it requires, even embodies, being illogical. In fact, consciousness itself does require being illogical, irrational, imaginative, able to act as if what is fictional is factual, if only for long enough to ascertain what is factual without taking it for granted that the difference is obvious. There is no 'fact' or 'fiction', no 'truth' or 'lie', no 'rational' or 'irrational', there can be no contemplation of alternative selections, no conception of the possibility of things ever being other than as they are, and so there can be no value to even the most rigorous symbolic syllogisms, unless our brains are capable of succeeding at not being logical. Irrationality can include both irrationality and rationality, but rationality can only include rationality. It can have no token, no symbol, no code, for what cannot be reduced to a number or deductive term. This is the opposite of the postmodern faith, which states the contrary assumption; that rationality can include irrationality, as a flaw that can be ignored or side-stepped or overcome, but irrationality is insanity and always wrong and incapable of identifying what is real. It is possible that both approaches are merely assuming their conclusions. But only in the rational perspective is assuming a conclusion always a mistake. In the irrational perspective, it is acceptable to think outside of the box, but that isn't the same as denying that there is a box, and once a conclusion is accomplished, it can be assumed to be true because that's what the word 'conclusion' means. Reason can achieve logic, but logic cannot achieve reason. Words, language, reasoning, and conscious experience cannot be reduced to math, though in simple cases we can act as if they could.

The methodology, if not the mechanism, of human intellect is not calculating numbers or probabilities, but guessing, and communicating those guesses to each other in order to compare them. Only truth can be signaled, because any signal is simply what the signal is; it is true even if it does not correspond to any causative condition, circumstance, or contingency. To compare guesses, which might or might not be right, or true, or even guesses, communication is necessary, signaling alone is insufficient. Guessing is not simply estimating, which is calculation, whether the formula is acknowledged or implicit. Guessing is approximating without any equation. In the example of a jellybean guessing contest, when the only acceptable guess is an integer, it can easily be assumed that generating a guess must be some mathematical process because it is numeric, and numbers only exist as terms in arithmetic relationships. But the jellybean mystery is not limited to jellybeans. It is the reality of human thought, experiential consciousness itself. One brain alone can invent any fiction (or determine any fact which might as well be fiction, if only that one brain alone is aware of it or could comprehend it) but it would be pointless and useless: maladaptive in a biological sense. But when multiple brains can communicate their maybe facts/maybe fictions, they can be compared, and in comparing them, the truth can be found. Perhaps just a provisional truth, good enough to make the effort worthwhile without being existential in any profound way. Or perhaps a relative truth, true because our existence provides a fixed framework from which to make judgments. Maybe even an absolute truth, a truth that is beyond physics, beyond any axiomatic system, beyond words and supernatural in its perfection. There isn't any way to judge such things, not even a way to understand that such things could exist, let alone comprehend how they are different from each other, without the irrationality of not being bound by what is rational. If people, language, and reasoning were logical, then whoever had the best ability to calculate would always have the closest possible answer to the simple question, "How many jellybeans are in this jar?" By extension, that same brain would have to have the most precise and accurate answer to the question "How many times should I call my mother per year?" or "How many tax brackets should there be?" or "What is the air speed velocity of a coconut laden swallow?" In the real world, people are not illogical because they fail to be logical; we are illogical because we succeed at being more than animals. The true evolutionary history of the human intellect is not calculation, but communication; it is not numbers, but words. It is not physics, but language, not fact but fiction, not competition for resources but cooperation and morals. The brain that can come closest to the correct answer is not the superior genetic trait; the brain that can come even closer to the correct answer by communicating with other people is.

Ultimately, it comes down to the starkest example. If you are in a lifeboat, thousands of miles from the nearest shore, with ten other people, and only have enough provisions for three people, the only rational, logical, realistic result is to figure out who to kill first to save yourself, inventing some merit-based justification for dealing with the facts, or simply declaring "every man for himself" . The human, moral, and hopefully better result is to do something less rational than that, and hope. Of course the gedanken can be dismissed by the postmodernist; the numbers don't make sense, rationality doesn't require us to ignore the possibility of rescue, and ultimately hard choices may still need to be made. Nevertheless, the mathematical approach inevitably requires adoption of absolute ignorance or absolute omniscience, because even quantifying any state in between the two extremes must be based on assumptions, and no matter how ignorant or well informed, those assumptions must be treated as absolute or no calculations can be executed. Postmodern faith in logic always drives people to extreme opinions, chasing the absolutes of their own assumptions because they are stuck in a tar pit of ignorance; eventually "it must be done, we have no choice" and final solutions are inevitable. Better to try the alternative, and learn from the jellybean mystery: no matter how certain you are that your answer is best, it is probable that there is a better one than any one person is capable of coming up with by themselves.

Each individual, guessing at the definition of a word, has their meaning and purpose, the being of the word, whether they explicitly state that meaning as a definition or not, and these are the equivalent of all the individual guesses at the number of jellybeans. We could look up the meaning of a word in the dictionary, where experts have examined citations and paraphrase a definition, or lots of definitions, or we could just accept a single great author's use: this would equate to the 'best guess', in our diagram, and the average guess. Which of these, the dictionary or the literary artist, is closer to the truth cannot be categorically determined. But the simple fact that sometimes the author and sometimes the lexicographer is closer to the truth proves there is such a truth, that there is a meaning of a word that transcends and exceeds all the guesses, even the closest, and the average. There really is a jar of jellybeans, and there really is meaning in a word. If words were logical, if they were constituted or behaved as IPTM or postmodernism believe, then there wouldn't be this uncertainty. Either the authoritarian dictate or the insightful author would be triumphant, in every case. But even an author can use a word incorrectly, and even a dictionary can have an incorrect definition. The difference is that when the author is a good artist, their incorrect usage mystically becomes proper, and future dictionaries will include it in their definitions.

Let's consider this in more concrete terms. We must still do so in abstract ways, because of course the dictionary doesn't only have one definition, or even just one entry, for each word, and there is no single author we can select to be divine. But we can take a word, let's use "matter", again, and try to align its usage and meaning with the jellybean diagram. We could say that everyone doesn't have their own individual meaning when they use the word. Suppose that we will contemplate only the hard physical denotation, leaving the other as just a figure of speech, used as an analogy. It would seem that everyone shares the same idea of what matter is, that it is the stuff of atoms and molecules. But let's think beyond that, because there is that analogy usage, and to be honest, everyone does have their own individual belief about just why and how matter exists, just as everyone has their own personal beliefs about the nature of God. Certainly any number of people might come up with the same guess about the nature of the universe and 'matter', like more than one person could guess the same number of beans in the jar. We can look it up in a dictionary, or ask a scientist, or somehow 'average out' all of these, and perhaps get even closer to the true meaning of the word 'matter' than we could by using any one particular definition, even our own. But the reality is that words are ineffable. Their "true meaning" melts away when you examine the term too closely, returning us to the postmodern conclusion that there is no true meaning at all, just use of noise or text as if it were a code. But a code for what? Of course, the postmodern word for this 'what', which POR considers obscene, is "concept". But that is only a hypothetical averaging, this idea that there is some Platonic form that inherently, innately, or unavoidably connects the alphabetic or phonetic arrangement to the physical reality of the universe. A keen postmodernist might even say that this 'concept' is what POR describes as the 'meaning', corresponding to the actual number of jellybeans in the jar. That is just assuming the conclusion, saying that there must be an intellectual conception with deductive integrity simply because there is a word to begin with. Once again, I must insist that if words actually worked the way standard theory describes, then there would be no 'jellybean mystery', either physical or analogical. Whoever had the highest IQ score would always win every jellybean contest, and every single attempt to define a word would have either the dictionary or every author be the closest guess, not sometimes one but usually the other. Of course, every author cannot all have the closest guess. The analogy breaks down in language, not because it is a flawed analogy or because there is a flaw in language, but because I've been trying to explain these issues without having predetermined whether the lexicon is the best guess and the writer the average guess, or vice versa, while also considering the question of which is closer to the real meaning.

This might be confusing, my refusal to identify whether the dictionary is the best guess and authors the average of bad guesses, or the reference book is the average and writers must then be the best individual guess. It might seem as if I'm simply trying to have it both ways, to make my theory irrefutable, unfalsifiable. If you would like, although I doubt it will make this very elusive issue any simpler, you can decide yourself, and from then on insist that the better use of a word is strictly what the dictionary says, or the better use of a word is always what a good writer does with it. The philosophical nature of words and language make such a faith-based approach a doomed one, but it can seem necessary, since we're already talking about things that are so very hard to think clearly about, anyway. The real reason that POR doesn't dictate or predefine this aspect of how to interpret the jellybean diagram isn't even that it is sometimes the one and sometimes the other, or that the choice is arbitrary, or that it is meaningless. We don't say which symbol means what in the jellybean diagram because it is the uncertainty itself that demonstrates the principle and proves the point. In an actual jellybean contest, the average of bad guesses is *usually* better than the best guess. But not always. And that is part of the mystery, because there is literally no way to ever know in advance which it is going to be in any one instance. But with jellybeans and numbers, we can use hindsight to know the truth. With language, a biological mechanism that has evolved to provide foresight, and hindsight, and insight, the truth remains eternally unknowable, insulated from our consciousness by the existential wall. Hindsight is easy, no biological mechanism is necessary to benefit from it, mere physical mechanisms are sufficient. And so genetic reproduction allows animals to appear as if they are designed with foresight, and until reverse teleologies were discovered by Darwin and described as natural selection, only inverse teleologies of theistic theories could explain why that is. Humans, unlike animals, really can employ foresight. In fact, we can't ever really avoid doing so, because we have language, and language doesn't just allow inverse teleologies to produce self-determination, it mandates this mechanism we call consciousness because consciousness, self-determination, and language aren't really three different things, but one thing, a thing that can also be expressed simply as "life", and we can know that it means something different than just biology.

It turns out that the jellybean mystery is, ultimately, a mathematical issue, just as our subjective awareness is objectively occurring. Both the occurrence of a jellybean mystery, when the average is better, and the inconsistency in that result, is mathematically inevitable. Given an arbitrary distribution of values, at least a third of the time but at most two thirds of the time, the average is going to be closer to the correct number than any one individual value. The experiment has not yet been performed, but it is possible that if computers were programmed to adequately approximate a jellybean contest, perhaps by using different algorithms to produce the distribution of estimates, the same pattern would occur. What is certain, though, is that in that case the results could only be applied to numeric values. It wouldn't be possible to do a 'computer jellybean contest' with anything other than numbers, because computers can only calculate numbers. An IPTM believer would probably say that this is true of people as well. Either because they believe that everything is numbers, inside our brains. Or because they believe that we can't really apply the jellybean mystery to anything other than numeric guesses, we can only imagine doing so. Irregardless, we can imagine doing so, despite the skepticism that turns postmodern uncertainty into philosophical pessimism. And we can even imagine that not everything in our brains is just numbers, even if that isn't true. Which of course makes it true, the way a perpetual liar cannot say "I am lying" without telling the truth.

In opposition to the IPTM believer, a more classically religious person might think that the jellybean mystery is evidence that there is a mystical connection between people, ensuring that every time someone guesses wildly high, it causes or allows someone else to guess wildly low, in order to keep the average of guesses close to if not better than the most accurate guess. But again, if the jellybean mystery only worked because there is a God or spiritual field intervening in everyone's individual reckoning, then it should work every time. Or if it didn't work every time, there should be some empirically decipherable reason when it doesn't work; a sinner in the crowd, or someone not believing hard enough. The results wouldn't be as mathematically reliable, with about a third of all contests not showing the 'jellybean mystery' effect, or it wouldn't be as unpredictable when it will occur. The fact that foresight cannot enable us to know which value, the best guess or the average of guesses, will be closer to the truth, only hindsight, means neither the mathematician nor the pious will always have the best guess.

Another thing an IPTM believer might say is that a computer approximation contest, like a jellybean contest but with something other than numbers, would be possible if we programmed the computers with creative and advanced enough algorithms. After all, the real root of the Information Processing Theory of Mind is (or is something that results in) a faith in 'artificial intelligence', that we can develop computer programs that can so closely mimic human behavior (or at least an idealized/idolized form of human behavior) that the distinction between a computing system and a human brain becomes invisible. A properly programmed computer and a sufficiently simplistic human brain are indistinguishable, that is the very foundation of IPTM. Deriving from Socrates' "math envy" and culminating in postmodernism, the notion of IPTM is that words are logical, and can therefore be calculated. If we could program a bunch of computers to speak, if we could codify language completely or invent algorithms complex enough to do it on the fly, then we could replicate a 'jellybean mystery' with words, just as POR insists we are doing ourselves whenever we generate or interpret natural language or contemplate the meaning of a word. But this is virtually the same as saying that if we can model the position and velocity of every particle in the atmosphere, we could perfectly predict the weather. According to the Philosophy Of Reason, it isn't even 'virtually', it is the very same thing, because it is just as impossible to measure the position and the velocity of even one particle as it is for a computer to perceive meaning.

I will be the first to admit that a lot of what I've written in this book definitely looks like gibberish. I'm well aware that the ideas I've expressed are heterodox, and flatly contradict what very intelligent, educated, and accomplished people have said is true, but that isn't what I mean. I mean the reasoning I'm trying to express in sentences is so convoluted and esoteric, sometimes, that those sentences will appear as gobbledygook, perhaps even after careful parsing of sentence structure, or repeated and sincere attempts to divine my meaning. There are times I have revised what I've written (believe it or not, this tome is the last draft of my manuscript, not the first) to avoid this, and honestly there are times I have purposefully avoided making it clearer. I believe, both because I believe in POR and for the reasons I believe in POR, and no longer believe the postmodernist's theories about logic and language, that because I have been trying to express my opinions sincerely, that my words are accurate; they are not flum-flummery, gobbledygook, or psychobabble. If I were to truly 'let fly', and not even try to rein in my exuberance, syntax, and vocabulary, than this would remain true, and everything I've written would still be true. But that would be cutting the hologram into too many little pieces, so although each still contains an entire representation of my thoughts and perceptions, the truth would not be visible. Still, that truth would exist, however incomprehensible it would be and unsuccessful my efforts to communicate it. The parts that appear to be gibberish might even be the most valid and important, the truest, parts. In fact (and this is the reason for this confessional digression) there are certainly things I have written in this book which are true in a way, to an extent, that I am unaware of myself. These words are truer than I could consciously make them; they are the truth speaking through me, unconsciously. All words are like this, for all people. They can be used to lie and they are not infallible, they can be used to say things that are untrue and mistaken. But this reflects the truth (or lack) of the things the words are used to state, not the meaning of the words themselves. Words don't stop being meaningful if we use them deceptively or erroneously. To the contrary, it is only their persistent truth in meaning that enables us to imagine or execute the process of using them to lie or say stupid things. The arrangement of the terms in sequence that I have made is prompted by my intention to say true things, but it is quite possible (and as I said, certain, somewhere in here) that you are reading a slightly different meaning, and that meaning may also be true. It may be false, you might be misunderstanding, or pretending to misunderstand, what I said, or what I meant to say with these words. But your different interpretation than my intention may still communicate something that is true, without me even being aware of having written that, like a cow in a field hidden behind a tree. I will remind you of the weirdness that occurred when I described the meaning of 'determine', and also when I wrote, "the point of math in the context of science". I think I should point out that, as in those cases, most of the meaning, the truth, which you might think is hidden or unconscious, is neither, from my perspective. To be precise, in particular, as a specific and accurate example, I use the terms 'particular' and 'specific', quite conscientiously, just like I use the terms 'precise' and 'accurate': with greater meaning than most people believe they have. Whenever I use the word 'particular', I have in my mind an image of a particle, and when I say 'specific', I don't think of it as entirely separate from the word 'species'. To the postmodernist, due to POS, these two words, particular and specific, are entirely and perhaps perfectly interchangeable, so alike in meaning, synonymous, that choosing one or the other is mere fashion or habit, simply subjective preference. POR does not believe that words work like that; when you have a preference of one word or the other, it is because your brain accurately and precisely comprehends the meaning of the word, beyond any conscious definition you might create as an ad hoc hindsight justification for your choice. This is not absolute, it is like the meaning of poetry; easily missed, perhaps, but undeniably present, once noticed. For a third example of this 'not obscured but possibly obscure' method I use, which makes at least some of my sentences gibberish but also makes some of them mind-boggling, remember the idea that choosing and deciding are not the same thing. Your brain makes choices about what words you use, regardless of the decisions you make to explain them. I am not exempt from this, but I am more cognizant of it. Still, I'm not omniscient, so there are probably truths "encoded" in my arrangements of words into sentences that I myself am not aware of. It may be mere coincidence that you believe there is a meaning I did not. Then again, it may be a mere coincidence that you believe there is meaning that I did intend. It may be like the coincidence that led to a genetic molecule inside a protecting membrane, which led to the happenstance of life emerging from mud, and the evolution which led to our existence. Perhaps you still don't understand what I am saying. I can only hope that you might, and with that I will move on again, and return to the larger analysis of the jellybean mystery and why it is an illustration of the mechanism of linguistic meaning.

The real importance of the jellybean diagram in POR is not just to plot the relationships between every individual person's idea of what a word means (their guess), the authoritative definitions of what a word means and the artistic usage of words (the best guess or average guess), and the idea that words have a meaning beyond all of these things (the correct number), even in combination. The real importance of the jellybean diagram is to describe why humans use words, why language is something more than signaling with codes. The biological function that is the adaptation which natural selection has gifted our species with is not data transfer, but consensus, not unidirectional, or even bidirectional, but consensual, and collateral and collaborative. Even if we forget about the idea of a word having a transcendent meaning illuminated by, but apart from, how every or any or a person describes, comprehends, or uses that word, the jellybean mystery demonstrates that we can still use the word, just as we have all along. It isn't any God, spiritual field, or hidden physics that enable words to have meaning, but simply common usage, community, communion, communication. Yes, we will all have slightly different 'meanings' in our minds when we use the same word, because we have different thoughts that occur when we decide to use it or have heard or read it. Yes, some people are better at being intelligible or creative or astute with words than others. Yes, we have dictionaries and machine translations, and opinions can differ over which is more dysfunctional. But usually, though not always, the average of bad guesses is better than the best guess. We each have the 'English' in our minds; partial, erroneous, biased and illogical. We also have the 'English' you would be taught at grammar school or college, and we can easily pretend that it is identical in every classroom and textbook even though it isn't. We cannot help but believe that there is some hypothetical perfect 'English', regardless of whether we consider it the works of Shakespeare or a rationalized, algorithmically decipherable code. But English is all of these things, not one of them, and English is not the only language. Languages differ in all sorts of ways, but two things are true of all human languages. Only these two things, because the forms and syntax and methods and notions of languages vary more widely than most people realize, and more than any one person could comprehend. First, all languages communicate thoughts. Second, that all languages use words. It is definitive that these aren't really two things, but one.

The three diagrams of POR, abstraction paradigms, Fundamental Schema, and the jellybean diagram, each illustrate important properties of the human facility and practice of language. The Philosophy Of Reason believes that these principles are independent of any particular tongue, although how comprehensible they may be when translated has yet to be determined, since I am monolinguistic and American English is my native dialect. The independence from dictionaries described by the abstraction paradigm, the philosophical necessities presented in the Fundamental Schema, and the improbabilities represented by the jellybean mystery, are universal, if not absolute. But trying to communicate these methods and mechanics doesn't truly address the cause of language, or the relationships and features the diagrams define that relating communication to community only hints at. The AP, the schema, and the jellybean mystery are the map, but what is the territory? As indicated by the techniques of flopping tautologies and flipping teleologies in the AP, envisioned in the contexts and arrangement of the schema, and hinted at by the plotting of crowd-sourced guessing games, there has to be some connection, some singularity, between linguistics and morality that postmodern theories either cannot express or wholly reject. The quest to use language that defines the human experience is one of trying to project our unavoidable sense of right and wrong out to the universe at large. Where does this come from? How did it come to be? And why does it differ so much from the existing studies of linguistics and theology that embody the postmodern application of Socrates' Error? The next section will consider these issues, and resolve the true nature of human communications.

Language

Basically, the theological theory of POR is that neither theism nor natural selection accurately justifies the development of humanity. The emergence of a capacity for and use of language is what defines humanity, as distinct from every other biological creature in the world. Other animals have two feet, other animals have hands with fingers, make sounds and signals, have neurons that display affected states. How did language evolve, and how does it make human beings unique?

The standard theory, which you can already guess I will call the postmodern theory and dismiss as conventional wisdom that is erroneous, a mumpsimus, is that human language evolved from animal signaling directly. As the brains of an animal effectively perform calculations in order to direct its movements, human brains started out using math, without consciousness. As the "social groups" of animals use sounds or chemical secretions to signal information to their individual members, humans simply refined the grunts and screeches of apes to become articulate speech. This postmodern theory of human evolution also, but separately, describes humanity as developing compassion and morality as a biological feature, based on the premise that altruism is an adaptive trait. We feel compassion because it benefits the species for us to feel compassion; a reverse teleology expressed as if it were a forward teleology. It may come as no surprise to you, at this point, that POR rejects these ideas, more or less entirely. POR is the sumpsimus, a truth contrary to the mumpsimus.

Evolution, the result of the mechanism of natural selection recognized by Charles Darwin, cannot be denied. This is far easier to understand, these days, now that we have not only discovered the molecular basis of genetics, but have developed some very useful technology which validates it. We have, in each of our cells, a particular chemical substance we call deoxyribonucleic acid: DNA. The physical makeup of this molecule enables it to maintain and reproduce the physical makeup of itself, allowing every cell to be a *replicator*. Any system of replicators will and must exhibit the process we call evolution, through the mechanism of natural selection. This is a tautological statement, or rather it is a particularly tautological statement, of course: only systems effected by natural selection and exhibiting evolution can be considered replicators. Any thing that generates copies of itself, that replicates, must result in copies that are sufficiently similar to the original to be considered copies. And any inevitable imperfections in the activity of replicating those copies will unavoidably cause some copies to be different from both the original, and each other. Many of those changes between original and copy might be only large enough to enable someone observing the system from outside of it to differentiate between the original version and the subsequent version, and otherwise would be insignificant. Of course, the changes cannot be so large that there is no similarity between the two versions, or the process is not actually replication at all, but simply generation of other things that in all probability cannot go on to replicate themselves. There are inevitably going to be instances when the copies are sufficiently like the original replicator to continue replicating, but the naturally occurring changes in the replicators, called mutations, will either deter or inhibit, or aid and advantage, the process of replication itself. These new specific types of replicators will, through enough reiterations of the copying process, differ from the original and each other more and more as changes accumulate. This evolution in types or forms, changing phenotypes caused by changes in genotype being advantageous and thereby adaptive, is unstoppable, unless the process of replication itself is stopped. God Itself could not prevent evolution from happening, even if It wanted to; It could certainly prevent any particular adaptation, but to prevent the process as a whole, It would have to change the nature of the universe, change physics and even math, themselves. There are important distinctions between replication and reproduction that we will consider later. But this inevitable feature of selection by nature, changes that increase replication thereby and therefore increasing replication, remains unchanged. In essence, evolution is truer than gravity, since it is inherent in the existence of the replicating process, not just any particular universe in which it occurs.

Darwin's recognition that the variation in the specific types of creatures that can be observed on Earth must and will inevitably result from the process of reproduction was monumental. His work was not only monumental because it reorganized our understanding of our human species. It was even more revolutionary than that, because natural selection exemplifies what was an entirely new scientific approach to teleology. Namely, reverse teleologies. The standard scientific teleology is, of course, cause and effect. Before Darwin, this related exclusively to deterministic behavior; once the necessary and sufficient circumstances labeled 'cause' occur, the certain and unavoidable circumstance labeled 'effect' occurs, and the effect follows instantaneously from the cause (though the affect, the observability of the effect, may be delayed.) This simple 'forward teleology' is matched in POR by the 'inverse teleology' of intention; the effect is implemented in order to generate the cause, reversing the chronological arrow of time. Inverse teleology is a fanciful notion, outside of the activity of conscious beings, humanity being the only known example of such. Aside from the self-determined intentions of people, no inverse teleologies can exist in the universe, and in a way we could consider them merely linguistic inventions. (As explained earlier, though, cause and effect, forward teleologies, can also be recognized as linguistic contrivance, though this is harder to accept, admittedly.) When either God or any other entity is used to invoke an inverse teleology, that some causal coincidence exists 'in order to' accomplish some goal, it is only a matter of human beings projecting our own capacity for consciousness on to the universe or objects or creatures within it which lack the necessary consciousness. Reverse teleologies are similar to inverse teleologies, in that they appear to invert the arrow of chronological time. The mechanism for <u>forward</u> teleologies is physics. The mechanism for <u>inverse</u> teleologies is self-determination. The mechanism for <u>reverse</u> teleologies is natural (unconscious, unguided) selection. Organisms are described as taking actions 'in order to' accomplish some goal, with the goal being defined by human beings simply to explain **'why'** the organism took the action. In some cases, when people or even scientists are not being careful enough to use rigorous reasoning, assuming that the pretense of logic is sufficient, not just organisms but entire species are characterized with reverse teleologies. This is acceptable as metaphor, just as general (in contrast to 'human') inverse teleologies can be used to explain how things happen as they do, anthropomorphizing not just abstract but even fictional objects or classifications and describing physical activity of organic or even inanimate matter as goal-seeking behavior.

Animals exist only to reproduce, and only in order to reproduce, and only because they reproduce, and only for reproducing. They eat *so that* they can reproduce. Except they don't, actually, they eat in order to survive, and they survive in order to reproduce. Except they don't, they reproduce for no 'reason' other than that they do. There is no goal-seeking, no selection from among alternatives, these are fictions we create in our minds. The ultimate cause of all biological behavior is ultimately physics, thermodynamics. (As mentioned previously, the cause of thermodynamics is quantum mechanics, <u>but we don't know how</u>.) Reverse teleologies do not exist, they are <u>even more</u> imaginary then inverse teleologies are. We invent them merely to explain that something happened, as the result of physical forces. They do not actually indicate any 'intention' on the part of any organism or thing. The 'intention' is imagined simply as a short-hand description of 'all those circumstances that didn't result in the effect are not available for observation, since they didn't result in the effect'. Animals of a particular species do not behave in any certain way or possess any particular traits "so that" they can reproduce. They merely have such traits or behave in that way, and reproduce. If they didn't have the trait and/or take that action, they simply wouldn't exist because their parent organisms wouldn't have produced them. At least not enough to continue doing so.

For example, marsupials have pouches. It is definitive, for that is what we use to classify them as marsupials. These pouches are involved in the process of reproduction, and our 'reverse teleological' methodology of explaining how biological evolution works enables us to say "marsupials have pouches so that they can use them in reproducing". But this is a rhetorical short-hand, a narrative used as figurative sleight of hand. In reality, marsupials don't have pouches <u>so that</u> they can use them, they use them <u>because</u> they have them; the same conglomeration of proteins that form the pouch, and the animal with the pouch, also <u>cause</u> the behavior of the animal, a forward teleology. The reason we can use this rhetoric is because all of the (female) marsupials ever born that did not have a pouch were unable to reproduce, and that phenotype (and the genotype which caused it) therefore died out. It required no decision making, no choice, but 'selection' occurred by naturally ending the reproductive cycle of marsupials without pouches. Unless, perhaps, they not only lacked a pouch but also acquired a placenta, enabling those mammals to reproduce without a pouch, which did not prevent the animal lineage from continuing, but did prevent them from being marsupials; they would then be classified as placental mammals, instead. (It matters not whether placental mammals arose from marsupial ancestors, this is merely an illustration, not a natural history lesson.) Whenever we describe any creature (or other thing), as doing or having anything 'in order to' or 'so that' anything else, we are employing reverse teleologies. This is not limited to biological evolution. Some cosmologists believe that multiple universes began just like ours, but all of the universes which could not result in ongoing development of space, time, stars and galaxies basically evaporated, so that they no longer exist but ours still does. This 'selection' by physics of only those universes that can continue to exist can also be described with a backwards teleology; our universe exists so that it can produce stars and galaxies, or in order to sustain biological evolution and our consciousness. In this way, our cosmos is observable *because* it is observed, rather than being observed *because* it is observable. Linguistically, it is possible to imagine something being observable without being observed, but not possible to conceive of something that is observed but not observable. The 'split horizon' of something being observable (epistemologically, being called 'observable') because it is observed (self-evident) and something being observable (ontologically, existing as a result of being observable) because it is observed (local realism?) approaches the quantum/ineffable reality of reality.

The application of reverse teleologies to inanimate, non-replicating systems, theories requiring 'selection' to explain why what exists does exist by defining that existence as being 'because' of that supposed selection, was a later development, so removed from Darwin's recognition of biological evolution that many theorists and just about everyone else accepts the language as comprehensible. There is some validity to it, but as I've already stated, that validity is due to its usefulness <u>in</u> explanation, but not <u>as an</u> explanation. The real explanation remains "because it is so, and something must have cause that", the forward teleology of physics. It is problematic that postmodernists, in taking their language both too seriously and not seriously enough, and assuming that because they can explain things as if they were a conscious choice, an inverse teleology of intention, that therefore there might actually be a conscious choice, or even an unconscious choice, a selection. As I've already pointed out, though, the existence of alternatives is a figment of our imagination, a way of expressing what we can imagine 'might have been', despite the fact that it never was and never will be, in that case. The uncontrollable state of the universe makes every case unique, but our minds categorize them anyway, and we can recognize that other cases can be so similar that if they produce different results, we imagine that the other unique case might have. So 'never was and never will be' becomes 'wasn't but could have been'.

Darwin sought to explain 'the origin of species', but in fact what he explained is simply the appearance of species. Our limited perceptions (limited in this context to only what exists) cause us to believe there are such things as species, types of creatures that are noticeably different from all other types. But species are simply categories, and categories do not exist in nature. A diagram representing all of the various kinds of organisms is often referred to as "the tree of life", with each kingdom and genus and species being a branch or a limb or a leaf. Biologists point out, quite rightly, that a better representation would be a bush, rather than a tree, in order to remove the mental image of a trunk. But even this is not simply imprecise but inaccurate. In truth, if we were to plot all organisms in such a diagram, it would actually be a sphere, but one with fissures and crags where all of the kinds of creatures that we cannot observe "should be", because they are extinct or their solitary members of that kind were so mutated that they couldn't survive and replicate. The difference between a lion and a bear are all of the animals that were born, or could have been born, from the common and collected ancestors of both lions and bears. If these were included in the plot, it would be a seamless surface of minor gradation's connecting what we call lions and what we call bears. The same gradient spectrum would connect the human species and mushrooms, with all of the mammals and amphibians that share ancestors with both humans and fungi being simply points on the surface of this sphere. This is the proper mental image we should have of biological evolution. In a very real and very important way, humans are just a specific kind of ape with a special brain. Apes are just a variety of mammal with arms. Mammals are just a peculiar type of reptile, with fur and mammary glands. Reptiles are simply a very weird variety of fish that breathe air. And fish are really only almost impossibly bizarre colonies of bacteria. Therefore humans are also outrageously strange collections of bacteria, with some being cells, and some being organelles within those cells. This isn't a typical way of describing life, but it is really the only scientifically legitimate one. If we were to pick a single point of divergence in the chain of organisms from the first cell to the human population, if we wanted to be most comprehensible and reasonably accurate, it would probably not be humans and apes, or humans and bacteria, but probably humans and fish. Humans are a strange kind of fish; all land animals (tetrapods) are closer cousins than things other than fish (insects, cephalopods, plants, fungi, archea) but every biological form is, at some remove or other, our cousins.

The thought that natural selection can explain not just the various species of animals we see, but the existence of humanity itself, was so drastic a change from previous philosophies that it signaled the end of the modern philosophical age, and the beginning of the postmodern one. Based on mathematical principles, evolution is inevitable once biological replication started, and so nothing but the physical existence and laws of the universe was necessary to explain our presence on Earth. There are two kinds of philosophers that rejected this change, simply by failing to recognize or admit that it had occurred. The first was, of course, the theistic philosophers that took it as received wisdom that a deity had designed and produced varieties of animals directly, including humankind. The second is generally unrecognized, and perhaps solitary in number: Darwin himself. Rather than believe that natural selection alone could explain the nature of the human species, on essentially theological (moral and philosophical) grounds, he proposed another mechanism, effectively as a way to maintain his modern and theistic perspective. Of course, not many naturalists at the time (and only those who understand POR, still today) realized there was a difference between modern philosophical understanding and the coming postmodern one. But Darwin seems to have intuited that natural selection alone, as a scientific principle, was problematic in very practical ways. According to this biological principle he had discovered, the only *purpose* of living creatures was to reproduce, and due to variations in the results of reproduction, some varieties would be naturally superior in that purpose compared to others.

He recognized that this idea of superiority was problematic. Not clearly enough to avoid including in his selection of title for his book explaining the theory of evolution, as mentioned earlier, "Preservation of Favoured Races in the Struggle for Life". In the process of natural selection, the equality of all men [people] defined as 'self-evident' by his cousins in America seems impossible. This isn't to suggest that his use of the term 'races' was more than a vague approximation of the way we use it today, but it doesn't matter how we classify human beings, the issue is that it is difficult if not impossible to avoid believing, or simply recognizing, that there are different categories, however defined. Rather than go into a lengthy exploration of the dubious validity and unfortunate importance of race in our society, I will leave it there.

Darwin wanted to explain the existence of distinct physical varieties within the human race, particularly the biological phenotypes which were apparent in the differences between Africans and Europeans and Asians, and their social import. These are conclusively (we now know) minor differences, and are not a contingent category (inherited as a group) but they still undeniably existed. Charles Darwin wished to explain them scientifically. Recognizing that all of the creatures that he had studied reproduced through sexual means, somehow combining the traits of two individuals of different genders to produce an offspring of only one of the two genders, he proposed another mechanism of evolution to augment or modify his theory of natural selection, calling it, appropriately enough, sexual selection. In general, all species of animals appear to choose mates from among the available alternatives. Assuming that this selection process was somehow distinct from natural selection itself, he theorized that it was a mechanism of preference, the selection of mates that we analogize as desire in animals because we experience desire as humans, which generates and maintains the differences in human beings we perceive and describe as racial classifications. In effect, Darwin insinuated the mechanism of inverse teleologies, intentional selection of sexual partners, to complement his invention of reverse teleologies. Ultimately, this effort proved fruitless, both scientifically and politically. Generations of scientists have continued to debate the issue, but for the most part biologists have dismissed the idea that mate selection is anything other than a particular kind of natural selection, driven by the same principles but in a bit more complicated and indirect manner. And racists continue to use sexual preferences, assumed to be derived from natural selection, to fuel their antipathy for other humans and excuse if not justify their xenophobia (or perverse predilections), just as easily as they used natural selection directly, if not more so. Two things are conclusive on this matter: racial supremacy is still a thing among racists, and sexual selection is assumed to be natural selection. Sexual preferences are described as mate selection, and Darwin's sexual selection remains contentious, but is mostly dismissed by biologists as a direct implementation and result of natural selection within a species.

It is important to recognize and admit that it is not a misunderstanding of scientific theory that underlies this racism, and all the other aspects of societal oppression that can accompany it. Not that racism is the full extent of the unfortunate results of a rationalist application of Darwinian theory. The use of narratives of 'fitness' in human reproduction and society is endemic, no matter how problematic it becomes, because it is a direct and even natural understanding of the truth of evolution by natural selection that makes it both unavoidable and immoral. Randy Newman, great artistic philosopher that he is, encapsulated this fact quite eloquently in his famous song "Short People" with the parodic line "Short people got no reason to live." Dumb people, gay people, short people, black people, religious people; it doesn't matter what distinction you want to observe between different individuals by defining them in groups and accepting or imagining that there are genetic causes for their categorical phenotype. The theory of evolution, accurately if naively or simplistically applied, indicates and even proves that the only purpose of biological organisms is merely to reproduce, and that some variations of organisms will be superior to others (better adapted) in doing so. The absolute and complete lack of morality in the process of science is the theology of science, and without that independence from any other meaning of purpose than contingent result, the entirety of our scientific perspective on the universe must collapse. So we are left with the same philosophic political conundrum that Darwin was: how to explain racial variations in the human species without justifying oppression of whichever variation is found or thought to be inferior in any way. It would seem easy enough to claim that all oppression is immoral, that even if phenotypic differences do indicate the inferiority of some individuals for reproducing their kind compared to others, it should be up to biological destiny to identify and enforce this, not discrimination in our social or political behavior. Unfortunately, this would require some basis for moral judgment itself, broader than our biological existence, upon which to justify this condemnation of discrimination as oppression. We cannot separate people into groups without unavoidably admitting that those people are not equal because they are not identical. And as much as we would idealistically demand that it is improper to separate people into groups intentionally, that is not possible realistically. Unlike categories, groups do exist in nature. We need a moral basis for interpreting scientific truths, even if we do not for discovering or demonstrating them.

This issue also relates to the ongoing, if marginal, opposition to the science of evolution that we call creationism. Fundamentalist Christians are not the only people who have some reservations about teaching children they are merely animals, because of a somewhat justified fear that they may take the lesson seriously, and believe they are just animals, and be encouraged to act like animals. The ongoing social dilemma of racism and even fascism hinge on such an explicit "power justifies itself" belief in biological superiority and ruthlessness, as not just necessity and group preservation, but a virtue. Natural selection continues to be problematic as a solitary explanation for human behavior. The same postmodern extremism fuels the quasi-scientific and political debate concerning animal consciousness, though it is at the opposite extent of the spectrum. This end of the scale misinterprets Descartes' cogito and insisting that any creature with feelings (affected neurological states) has emotions (an example of POS that equates sensations with sentience) and deserves to be considered a person. The fanciful term 'speciesism' has been coined to denigrate the knowledge/belief that humans are as different from other life as life is different from inanimate chemistry. Whether or not children are taught that they should behave no better than animals, or consider themselves no better than animals, the problem of this naïve Darwinism, and even the 'social Darwinism' that comes from such simplistic application of reverse teleologies to human society, is problematic.

POR approaches this conundrum in two ways: by both providing the universal basis for morality that is normally fulfilled by theism, and by developing a more complete understanding of biological evolution itself. In keeping with our understanding and application of the Fundamental Schema, these two theses ultimately converge, and which is designated the ontological and which the epistemological approach is a matter of convention or preference, depending on the purpose of the assignment. We will start with the latter issue: developing a more complete understanding of biological evolution than the current scientific doctrine. This involves proposing an extension or modification to that scientific basis. Regardless of whether that proposal is considered useful or valid, it will at least provide an enhanced vocabulary and perspective than is available outside of POR. The universal basis for morality, atheistic and material yet still theological and spiritual, will be introduced afterwards.

Evolution

As I've already stated and explained, there's no denying evolution. Anything that is self-replicating will evolve. Mutations will occur, and adaption of species will result. It is important to understand and remember that individual organisms don't evolve, can't evolve. But it is sometimes difficult to understand and remember this, because of the nature of language. Ontologically, when we say 'individual organism', we mean one single actual physical creature, that is born and eventually dies, regardless of whether it reproduces. But epistemologically, 'individual organism' can mean an indefinite number of individual organisms, an abstract, hypothetical, or iconic organism, one that does not live but is only imagined, and can be used to represent either an unlimited set of other abstractions, or an indeterminate but singular and possibly particular creature. Whenever we think about natural selection, the distinction between 'an organism' meaning a real one and 'an organism' meaning a hypothetical group of them becomes both difficult to deal with, and critically important. This linguistic issue goes even further, to the level of "the gene". Do we mean the physical stretch of a real protein molecule, or the abstract information the arrangement of nucleotides in that molecule represents; do we mean a particular instance of a particular allele, or all the copies of all of them in all of the organisms they have ever existed in throughout the entirety of the history of life, or something in between? In every case, real and imagined, we should mean only one of these, or something similar to one or more than one, or some other way of conceiving of the word and the thing it is thought to represent or refer to.

The issue is, of course, universal and consistent for every single word ever used, including whether I am talking about each single instantiation of a word, or all uses of a particular word as singular, even though it is numerous. This issue is addressed directly, yet still only partially, by the Fundamental Schema. It (the imprecision of words, which somehow only enhances their accuracy, but only if you can accept that they are never at all precise and so can't ever be perfectly accurate, either) is why we distinguish between ontology and epistemology and theology, and insist that all three are always necessary for a word to have any real meaning, being, or purpose. We are used to our brains sorting through and sorting out all of these contrasting and potentially contrary ideas being identified and described by a single or particular use of a specific word or specified word form, because our brains have evolved to do that very thing. It is instinctive, and occurs without our notice or conscious intention, so automatically (autonomically) that it is possible to deny it happens even while it is happening. However much we might choose our words carefully, we don't decide what they mean, so the fact that what they truly mean is not as simple as what we believe does not prevent us from using them. Our brains execute this linguistic processing so involuntarily that we allow our minds to follow along without even bothering to consider it. The postmodern insistence that every term is only ever used ontologically and precisely is both outrageously and preposterously false, obviously so, if we can ever manage to seriously consider the truth about words and meaning. Worse than this assumption that words are always used ontologically, or should be, are those instances when we decide to contradict this automatic processing and choose to become confused about whether a word refers to an instance or a class of such instances. Such disingenuous "category error" is endemic in postmodernism, and integral to post-modernism.

But however difficult it is to explain how words work, we have only words with which to do so. That makes abstract, even potentially imaginary, things like the Fundamental Schema necessary, along with making them possible. Genes, we are led to believe, are more concrete than that. But they are actual physical stretches of DNA at the same time they are the information of the arrangement of bases that are the complement of the sequence of amino acids in a protein that is used in our cells to execute the biological processes of life, whether metabolism, development, or reproduction. Which is "a gene"? Which is "an organism"? One entity, or a category, a species (or sub-species) of organism of that specific kind? Does it matter? We are told that real scientists cannot be confused by such epistemological quibbling, and for the most part, their exclusive focus on mathematically calculable, deductively quantifiable values and variables does prevent potential hair-splitting of this sort from being an issue. For the most part, but not always.

My intention is not to suggest that linguistic confusion, consternation, or confabulation prevents biological evolution from being unquestionable in its validity, or that evolutionary biology is profoundly uncertain in its theories and facts. But this theological issue (for whether something we're using words to discuss is both ontologically and epistemologically consistent and accurate is a theological issue) makes my explanation of the matters I'm going to have to debate easily dismissed, if the goal is to dismiss them rather than accept them, or even consider them, honestly. It isn't easy to overcome what people believe about evolution, even if overturning what scientists believe about evolution has already been accomplished. Overturning existing science isn't my goal, though, adding to it is. But new theories must at least partially replace or modify old theories, in order to actually be theories, and I'm going to be treading on some hallowed ground, some cherished and sacred assumptions, so it is worth pointing out that no pedantic quibbling or pretense of sophistry is going to successfully dismiss the issues I'm addressing and the questions I'm raising. Confronting and deconstructing the theories I'm going to present, and the way I describe not just them, but the theories they supplant, is going to require accepting that they could be valid, first, and then perhaps examining the ideas involved might result in excluding or contradicting them as theories. Simply declaring that I don't know what I'm talking about and that some other scientist or professor already disproved these ideas is not going to be productive because it simply isn't true.

Scientists themselves recognize that their scientific knowledge, both the theories and the way they describe them, is provisional. They will, both by training and instinct, insist on using grammatical prevarication to avoid making absolute claims of certainty. Dedicated and serious philosophers, whether the natural philosophers we call scientists or the intellectual philosophers we call philosophers, know that they don't and can't really know what is true, scientifically, they really only know what has been shown to be false, and assume that they can act as if they know what is true, because they can indeed act as if they know what is true, and get away with it. It is not only the fact that other scientists would have to provide real data and logical proof that their knowledge is false before they'd have to admit that which enables them to get away with acting as if they know what is true. It is also the fact that only scientists can do that: other people who are not scientists will always let scientists get away with acting as if they know what is true. Unless they don't, of course. Whether they are denying that burning fossil fuels causes catastrophic climate change or that biological evolution explains the entire history of life on Earth, or some other harebrained idea (usually but not always requiring a paranoid conspiracy theory to explain why most but not necessarily all of the real scientists agree that they know what is true) the nature of logic and reasoning makes trying to contradict scientists a hobby that is growing in popularity, at least here in the United States. Because we Americans are such preeminent postmodernists, possibly the greatest to ever exist.

All of this is prelude, a mere staging ground for the actual discussion about postmodern evolutionary theory that I want to present. I've already hinted at some of the issues of concern, when deprecating "evolutionary psychology" to 'humanology', earlier. Evolutionary psychology is based on a hypothesis that the human intellect (to use an analytical-seeming term as a metaphor for 'brain' or 'mind' since we wish to be inexact in which we mean) evolved as a set of "modules", or algorithms, as the functional product of natural selection. The problems with this approach are numerous, from the assumption that intellectual processing (thought, thinking, reasoning, reason) involves discrete component functional 'traits', such as memory and perception and language, to the assumption that these traits correspond to actual genes, to the idea that the 'just-so' stories that evolutionary psychologists invent as narratives to explain why the behavior they wish to either condone or condemn as adaptive. (Generally, the condemnation of what is adaptive is excused as being adaptive for ancestral conditions, but maladaptive in civilized conditions.) But the actual evolutionary theory I'm going address is more than just a particular evolutionary psychology theory, or even all evolutionary psychology theories.

POR does reject all evolutionary psychology theory, both in every ontological instance and as an epistemological whole. But if that can be done, it already has, the very idea of language and reason that POR represents is fundamentally contrary to the entire existence of most psychology and linguistics, and all evolutionary psychology.

The theory that needs to be addressed is more specific than the idea that human brains are information processing organs that calculate data mathematically and/or are programmed by natural selection to apply algorithms to perceived sense data. The theory I want to denounce as false in this section is "adaptive altruism". Like IPTM, or any other hypothesis of 'evolutionary psychology', we can dismiss adaptive altruism without rejecting natural selection itself. But refuting all three, adaptive altruism, IPTM, and evolutionary psychology in general, should cause us to at least reconsider our understanding of evolution, and of natural selection (or, alternatively, genetic drift) as its sole or primary cause.

The theory of adaptive altruism is self-refuting, in a way similar to how free will was demonstrably impossible both by definition and by facts. (If we do not control when we are in control of ourselves, we are never truly in control of ourselves.) Likewise, adaptive altruism, a genetic basis for morals or morality, is disproven not just by being linguistically self-contradicting, but contrary to empirical evidence. In terms of linguistic definitions, to be altruistic an action must be a sacrifice of some amount and kind. The basic idea of adaptive altruism is that helping others can be directly beneficial, through various mechanisms; that it can be advantageous for the actor, and therefore not a sacrifice. And so the idea of adaptive altruism is self-conflicted: if the behavior is adaptive, it is not altruism. When Socrates dissected "virtue", he used essentially the same kind of analysis, and it is disconcerting that modern biologists are fated to ignore his efforts, while still considering him, and Aristotle, their intellectual ancestors. Empirically, the initial assumption (and presumption) of evolutionary biology is that a gene will only increase in frequency in a gene pool (in comparison to other genes) when it results in a trait that increases the reproductive efficiency of the organism that has that gene. However you define altruism, if it is an idea worthy of having a name, it must help others more than itself.

Stripping the logic of the intermediate mechanisms of organisms and reproduction makes the issue simpler to deal with. This is the approach used by Richard Dawkins in his seminal book, *The Selfish Gene*. The title is both perverse and ironic. It is ironic because it does not refer to a 'gene for selfishness', as a naïve reading might naturally first suggest. Instead, the theory Dawkins espouses is the irrefutable idea that all genes are selfish. Ignoring the anthropomorphization and inverse teleology this explanation requires, we can describe all genes as acting entirely in their own self-interest;

they 'want' to replicate, it is what they do and what they are for. The mechanism of natural selection only promotes genes that promote themselves: "selfish" genes. In describing this now-standard theory, Dawkins adopts the powerful and useful simplifying method of 'gene-centric analysis', ignoring the intermediate steps of organisms and mating and species, and just considering genes as 'naked replicators', making copies of themselves directly. Not even bacteria actually implement such a simplified form of life and reproduction, but it makes a good first approximation of what all genes are and do: they self-replicate, and the arrangements of them change and evolve over time. So the title *The Selfish Gene* is ironic because Dawkins knew it was going to be misinterpreted as meaning that organisms could (or might or do) have a gene for selfishness, but his meaning was that no such gene is possible or could be necessary, since all genes can only act selfishly, and by nature all biological organisms do, at least by default. An ant cannot act for "the good of the colony", although that is a familiar backwards teleology we might easily use to describe why an ant might act as it does. In truth, biological processes, like physics, should be explicable with only forward teleologies. But the usefulness of reverse teleologies in all biology, not just evolutionary biology, makes them unavoidable: our blood has hemoglobin 'because' without it we would die, and so animals have blood and hemoglobin because of its usefulness, rather than the physical forces and chemical affects that actually cause it to exist in each instance where a blood cell is generated with hemoglobin as a component protein. The distinction between the reverse teleology of ants acting as if for the good of the hive because all the ants that did not act that way died, since their colony could not stay alive, and the forward teleology of each ant acting only for its own benefit, can be considered arbitrary and confusing, but is no less valid just because it requires a larger amount of effort to comprehend. In making reverse teleologies appear similar to inverse teleologies, their backwards teleology siblings, Darwin began the tradition of evolutionary theory that Dawkins faithfully applies. Evolution does happen, unavoidably, because it is cause and effect; replicators cannot avoid mutating, and adaptation therefore occurs. But we should not confuse biological evolution <u>itself</u> for our theories <u>about</u> (of) natural selection that we believe explain the results of that evolution; that is mistaking the map for the territory, substituting the lesson teaching a formula for the calculation itself.

Dawkins knew that his title was ironic, too cute by half, as the saying goes, but he was also aware it was perverted, though it is doubtful he would agree with the use of that term. He would consider it just another level of irony rather than perversion, and the difference is moot. The title was perverted because the central theorem of his book was an attempt to explain how selfish genes can result in selfless behavior. He did not invent the theory itself, he was simply trying to explain it in a popular format intended to be accessible to non-scientists. And in that he was tremendously successful. So much so that even suggesting that the theory itself is incorrect is quite difficult and will result in denunciations of the suggestion as arrogant and preposterously naïve. Nevertheless, adaptive altruism, selfish genes resulting in selfless genetic behavior, is actually the preposterous theory. If a biological trait or even inclination were altruistic, it would be maladaptive by definition, because being adaptive (promoting the frequency of the gene that causes it) is innately, inherently, and unavoidably self-promoting, not generous or kind or helpful to anything else. It doesn't matter if you define that any other thing as another gene, or another genotype, or another organism, or any group, including genetically-defined groups such as a hive or species. Even if a genetic trait could enable or cause sacrifice of a creature's interests, resources or energy budget, as a sort of 'enlightened self-interest' in biological terms, that very value to that creature would prevent the behavior or genotype from being a sacrifice. This makes the idea of adaptive altruism very much the same as the infamous Gordon Gekko maxim "Greed is good": they are self-contradicting. Not because all self-interest is evil, but because only excessive self-interest is appropriately called "greed". Likewise, only the bare minimum of self-interest that is necessary can be considered "good". The iconic example is the instruction by flight attendants that a person put their own oxygen mask on before trying to help even their own children. There is a point, dependent entirely on circumstances rather than categorical, where self-sacrifice becomes counter-productive, and where self-interest becomes enlightened. This does not mean that blind self-interest (the only kind a gene can engage in, since it is not conscious and cannot formulate teleologies) can ever benefit from self-sacrifice in even the slightest way. And so the very idea of adaptive altruism is logically self-refuting. The basic premise is that a gene can promote a phenotype that does not promote itself.

Dawkins strived mightily to overcome this logical contradiction (logical because these are scientific theories, referring to the implacable mathematics of genetic selection, independently of the non-logical but hopefully reasonable words we use to consider or explain the mathematical theories of biology.) Specifically, Dawkins hypothesized that kin selection and gene clusters could combine to overcome the unlikeliness that benevolence would evolve naturally. These are both very real scientific principles, irrefutably. But it is worth noting that they both require abandoning the gene-centric approach to natural selection, whether admittedly or not. Kinship requires sexual reproduction to be a comprehensible idea; genetic relationships in simplistic direct replicators become incomprehensible. In fact, the ambiguity of language makes the issue of whether 'a gene' is just one copy or any copy of that gene difficult to deal with even in a real system of replicators/reproducers. It makes the distinction impossible to even exist in the hypothetical examples that gene-centric analysis requires. The issue is the same for gene clusters.

Kin selection` is what happens when a sibling or aunt helps an organism survive and therefore helps the sibling or aunt's own genes replicate. It is a mathematically predictable and unambiguous effect. The basic mechanism isn't dependent on family relationships like 'sibling' or 'aunt', either, but would occur only coincidentally without such a close hereditary relationship, so it becomes very difficult to describe, and ultimately pointless as well. Say there is a gene, a physical stretch of self-replicating molecule encoding a specific stretch of self-replicating information. The information is the arrangement of atoms in the molecule, so distinguishing between the two things, molecule and information, is epistemological, not ontological. Let's call this "Rex", just so it has a name. Rex is the physical molecule, a gene, but there are other physical molecules that are identical. One might be "Troy". So Rex and Troy are indistinguishable in appearance, they both encode the same information in the same kinds of atoms, but with different atoms, so they are two distinct entities. Rex is here, Troy is over there. Apart from their location, there's no way to tell them apart. It is possible, in fact quite probable, that these two identical twins are themselves 'siblings', being copies of the same mother gene, also encoding the same information in the same kind of atoms, and we'll name her "Martha". If Troy replicates, making another copy of that same gene that Troy, Rex, and Martha all are, then Rex and Martha benefit from that as much as Troy does. (Sticking with the reasoning, we imagine that there is actually some benefit to having another copy of themselves somewhere, though it makes the artificial nature of our gedanken obvious to say so. In the real world, there is no 'benefit' to genes when they increase in frequency, this is a value judgment invented by our observation and the narrative we use to apply teleologies to these tautological objects.)

Rex doesn't get any more benefit from replicating itself than it does from Troy replicating itself; they are all the same 'it'. This is the basic mechanism of kin selection; if a sibling helps an organism reproduce, then the genes in the sibling are replicated as well. This gets even more messy and confusing when we start considering actual natural selection, involving alternative alleles (differences between Rex and Troy), and the epistemological issue, of whether a mutant gene is the same gene with a change or an entirely new gene, makes using words rather than symbols generally impossible. In simple replicators (like bacteria or the even more simple abstract strings of information in gene-centric theory) kin selection is (should be) very strong, since any two bacteria of the same type ("species") are essentially identical, apart from random mutations. (If there is any difference more than individual and minute and arbitrary mutations, they are not two bacteria of the same type, but two bacteria of two different types, regardless of whether they are classified as different 'species' by any particular microbiologist.) In most somatic organisms, such as insects and humans, kin selection still occurs but is less powerful, since siblings statistically only share half their genes, not all of them, because of the process of meiosis and gametes involved in sexual reproduction.

The mechanism of gene clusters is similar. Although in theory it occurs in naked or simple replicators, in such cases it is identical to kin selection, since the entire genome is one big cluster and nothing else. It either replicates as a whole or it doesn't, and if a bacteria helps an identical bacteria replicate, its own genes are thereby replicated. The mechanisms of sexual reproduction make gene clusters a more productive image for contemplating what is happening, but it is the same issue, mathematically. Genes that are physically close together in/on the DNA of the mother organism are statistically more likely to be 'copied' together in the daughter organism. This isn't because of any physical integrity of the molecules, but simply because of the fact that genes have no physical existence, they are the information 'encoded' in the molecule. There are gene delimiters but the copy/replication process is not effected by them, it 'ignores' them. The genetic information, as they would impact a phenotype, is irrelevant during the physical act of replication/reproduction, whether sexual or asexual, or hypothetical for that matter. The arrangement of atoms (bases) in/on the DNA strand are replicated, peptide by peptide within the polymer, without any molecular acknowledgment of when one gene ends and the next begins, or whether a particular peptide is part of a gene or not for that matter. It is simply more likely that two genes right next to each other will end up on the same resulting copy of the DNA than two genes that are physically far apart. Since there is no 'mixing' of two different parents' genes in a simple replication such as bacterial, and no mechanism of replication at all in a hypothetical naked replicator, just the invocation of a 'copy' incident, there is no gene clustering to speak of in simple replicators, but it is a real thing in sexual reproduction.

Ultimately, Dawkins' effort to provide a biological mechanism for genetic altruism was successful enough for his purposes, and along with the pre-existing postmodern theories of 'natural virtue' such as sociobiology, it was more than good enough to convince people that science had proved that altruism was genetic, that humans have compassion because it is adaptive on a biological basis. The 'natural virtue' I refer to consists of a number of isolated examples of ethology identifying seemingly altruistic behavior in organisms of various sorts. The fact that such examples are exceptions to the general rule that organisms are ruthlessly self-interested does not seem to convince proponents of natural virtue and adaptive altruism that they are grasping at straws. The situation is parallel to the philosophical issue of free will, again. With free will, that theory was maintained, not because of any empirical evidence it exists, but because the alternative theory (fatalism) was unacceptable, both because it was considered reprehensible (uncomfortable) and left philosophers with no comprehensible justification for the existence of consciousness. The formulation of teleological self-determination as a theory that does not require free will but still justifies consciousness makes free will expendable in POR. Similarly, the theological theory of POR makes both philosophical pessimism and adaptive altruism/natural virtue unnecessary. POR does not make adaptive altruism/natural virtue any more or less likely, but it provides a way to accept the truth, which has been the truth all along, that biological morality is not at all likely, whether it is considered impossible or not.

It is considered impossible, according to POR, because it is physically impossible. Morality is not a biological imperative, nor can it be genetically justified. In fact, even accepting the potential possibility that kin selection and gene clusters could support evolutionary replication of compassion as a genetic mutation, it is still thermodynamically impossible for such a physical trait to be maintained, let alone increase in frequency, in any gene pool. If morality can be thought to exist as a single biological trait, if it is at all possible for there to be such a thing as compassion or self-sacrifice that is not simply delusion and self-interest, it is not a phenotype, it is an intellectual construction composed of an indeterminate and uncertain collection of behaviors. It is a hope, the reflection of hope echoing from the physical universe, a hope which occurs in our minds, a hope which is theory of mind, a hope that there can be hope. The details of the intellectual construction of morality will be considered later, the inadequacy of conventional theories of genetic altruism must still be addressed further. It seems a pretty radical thing to say, that widely accepted scientific theory requires and describes something that is thermodynamically impossible. I'm not at all sure I'm going to succeed in convincing anyone, and yet I'm going to go further than that and insist that the theory of evolution by natural selection itself must be reconsidered, quite substantially, simply in order to account for actual real world observations about biology, including human consciousness.

First, to address Dawkins' reasoning directly. As I mentioned, his theories that selfish genes can produce selfless behavior are not entirely novel, so it is not my intention to deconstruct his arguments explicitly. Dealing with the question of altruism is itself difficult enough. Even describing his theory as 'selfish genes producing selfless behavior' can invite confusion, and even intentional confabulation. No, behavior doesn't need to be entirely 'selfless' to be selfless, it doesn't require the ultimate 'self-sacrifice' to be self-sacrificing. Relying on such arguments or false logic and pedantry is futile, and such an astute thinker as Dawkins wouldn't need to rely on such semantic arguments. The real limitation in Dawkins' position is one he would equally accept, but might not consider as conclusive. I said before that even if adaptive altruism could be produced by kin selection and gene clustering in concert, it would still be insufficient. And I relied on an implicit idea that "selfish self-sacrifice" is self-contradicting. In practice, the contrary argument, that selfish self-sacrifice is possible, leaves unexplained why it would take a latter-day organism of such cerebral complexity to develop such compassion. The counter-argument, that compassion can be observed in other species as well as our own, is multiply flawed. Most importantly, it accepts that compassion is not endemic in all creatures, and if it could be adaptive, it stands to reason (anathema to scientists as an argument, I know, but necessary for assessing and comparing the truth of their theories nevertheless) it would have evolved once, probably hundreds of millions of years ago, and would be as common in biology today as teeth, or at least mammary glands. Aside from the need to accept that altruism and even compassion is not even universal, let alone instinctive, in our own species, it seems too cute by half to suggest that it just happened to have evolved as a biological trait in only the same species which also evolved language, because neither is present in our ancestors.

Dawkins is a good scientist. He did not ever once say that he had proven that altruism had evolved. What he did say is that altruism could have evolved, and proposed some mechanisms, gene clustering and kin selection in particular, that might have made it possible for altruism to evolve. But he ignored the fact, because it is merely philosophical, not scientific, that there is no known and specific biological mechanism that produces altruism, self-sacrifice, or compassion. Being selfless, caring for others; we can see these things happening in parent organisms in a wide variety of species. So as long as we ignore all the shockingly horrifying counter-examples, of creatures eating or abandoning their young, or killing rivals in their own social population, or simply being apathetic and uncaring towards the suffering of other creatures, it isn't that hard to delude ourselves into thinking that sweetness and mercy are part of the natural world. It only takes one "friendship" between a lion and a lamb to convince people that lions don't eat lambs without a first thought, let alone a second one, despite the fact that predation, not compassion, is the natural behavior of lions. We want so much to think there is a moral force in the universe, people invent it as a biological imperative or trait even after ruthlessly rejecting the idea of a moral God in their own thinking.

Dawkins never said that goodness was genetic. He merely said it could be, and relied on the fact that the hypothesis hasn't been refuted to suggest that it is. But the truth is it cannot be. The typical narrative used by evolutionary psychologists and their religious followers, atheist and theist alike, is that a creature with a 'compassion trait', a selfless gene, would help other creatures in its specific population, and somehow that would enable the helping compassionate unselfish creature to reproduce. The starkest example is organisms in a breeding population in direct and violent competition with another breeding population. This situation would naturally produce 'warrior genes', promoting the frequency of genes that result in traits that make the individual organisms better at competing with their rivals in the 'enemy' population. It does no good to try to explain these details further, whether to suggest that they could have some analogic validity or to insist that they provide exceptions to logical behavior that would enable the organisms to circumvent biological imperatives. The entire enemy population can be ignored, the gedanken works just as well if we think of the 'warfare' being within a tribe of people rather than between two distinct populations of non-human animals. The narrative from the kind-hearted secular humanists is that a 'doctor organism' with a healer gene could improve the chances of its own tribe thriving, and thereby result in the doctor organism reproducing, and the doctor gene replicating. Regardless of whether we think of the 'doctor gene' and the 'warrior gene' as alternative alleles or entirely independent genotypes, it simply isn't possible, thermodynamically, for the doctor gene to increase its own frequency in the gene pool <u>more than</u> the warrior genes. No hypothetical features or arrangements can change this fact, without purposefully ignoring the logic of the basic narrative. If potential mates find doctors enticing, whether because they are automatically attracted to compassionate creatures or because the doctors gain access to more resources than warriors, these are value judgments that the blind mechanism of natural selection simply cannot make. If the doctor avoids the violent confrontations because it is engaged in healing, this does not prevent the rival warriors from being violent towards doctors. As I said before, we don't even need to consider the war to be between separate groups, although we naturally make such assumption when we try to reason logically. There isn't any 'war', war is something that, like compassion, only exists when people invent these things intellectually.

The conventional narrative of having a doctor being good for a species, tribe, gene pool, even just a family, is essentially just a repackaging of an old, discredited theory of evolution, known as group selection. This is the idea that if a gene results in a trait that benefits other organisms, either <u>instead of</u> or <u>as well as</u> the organism that possesses the gene, natural selection will promote the frequency of the gene in future generations of organisms. This theory of group selection has been disproven quite conclusively over and over again. It still keep recurring, whenever people or even biologists aren't very careful when thinking about how natural selection causes (or rather explains) biological evolution and speciation. A trait that benefits a group isn't possible, a gene that benefits the other members of a group that an organism is part of cannot be selected for. Even if the gene helps the organism that has it as much as an organism that doesn't, there is no mathematical mechanism that can result in that gene increasing in frequency more than alternative alleles that don't help any organisms at all. A gene **has to** benefit the organism that possesses it **more** than it benefits any other organism in the gene pool (however large, whether restricted to a family, tribe, species, or the entire ecosystem) or there is simply no way that the 'blind watchmaker' of Darwinian selection can promote or benefit that gene or that organism.

The mumpsimus of adaptive altruism is similar to the idea of free will. Because the absence of the mumpsimus is considered unacceptable, the fiction is maintained despite being contrary to all evidence and reasoning. This similarity between adaptive altruism and free will is not coincidental, either; they are both expressions of Socrates' Error, the math envy, the animistic worship of logic, which is the basis of postmodernism. The rejection of theistic theology makes the atheistic ethics of 'common good'/adaptive altruism/group selection seem unavoidable, just as the rejection of fatalism makes free will ineluctable, given the premise of rationalistic human behavior. The ontological and theological sumpsimus of POR provides teleological self-determination and a non-theistic morality instead, enabling us to accept both the rational existence of humanity as a species and the irrational behavior of humans as self-aware individuals, and rather than see this as a contradiction, recognize it as positive. The complexities of comparing 'inclusive fitness' to 'eusociality' are dismissed, in our analysis, as applying to only a limited set of non-human creatures. Although the genetic evolution of a species cannot be directly influenced by whether the organisms are self-aware, the behavior of those organisms must be. This is definitive, since being 'self-aware' (determining self, self-determining) is the capacity for having behavior that is not determined by genetics or operand conditioning alone. Therefore, in influencing the behavior of the individual organisms, the genetic trait of being self-aware has indirect influence on the evolution of the species of such organisms. This perspective/principle applies as much to economic behavior as it does to biological evolution: by acting entirely in self-interest, selflessness occurs as an effect, without ever being an (inverse teleology) goal. Thus, the volition and motivation of undirected biological behavior (stochastic adaptation), uncontrolled social behavior (economic benefit), and atheistic moral behavior (social ethics) are explained as resulting from a singular thermodynamic principle, evidence of the truth of the premise of POR.

In short, the theory of adaptive altruism is not a special case of natural selection, but is instead a peculiar case of "group selection", a mechanism that is recognized as fictional by biologists. Healing a wounded warrior in an amoral world of nature benefits the warrior more than the healer, using time and resources that the healer could use to reproduce its own genes rather than increase the frequency of all those genes that the warrior possesses that the healer does not. Any genetic basis for altruism suffers from the same principle: helping others is the opposite of helping oneself. The genes for compassion or healing will inevitably become less frequent in any gene pool, despite the potentially counter-balancing effects of kin selection or gene clusters, or any other hypothetical selection mechanism. Adaptive altruism is a religious faith in group selection, rather than a comprehensible method of natural selection. Not simply linguistically, but physically, *altruism cannot benefit the altruistic more than it benefits others*, or it is not altruism and is not beneficial to those others. Certainly a trait can exist that is beneficial to both the organism that has it and some other organism, but because natural selection results from <u>differential rates of reproduction</u>, it must be less beneficial to the organism without it than the organism that displays that trait. No genetic basis for compassion, kindness, healing, or morality can evolve through natural selection, not only because there is no genetic basis for these things that we know of to begin with, but any such traits or behaviors would decrease the frequency of those genes within the gene pool. When we observe non-parasitic symbiosis in nature, and interpret it as if it were kindliness, it is more a product of psychological projection than reality. (That said, the POR theory of evolution includes the possibility of apparent magnanimity more than natural selection alone can explain, as I will soon describe.)

It is true that the appearance of seemingly altruistic behavior can be observed in nature, and reproduced in experiments. Nature does not punish an animal for somehow aiding another animal, whether of the same or of a different species. Evolution does not act on animals, though, but on species. Natural selection is not a control mechanism that directly prevents maladaptive traits and stamps them out at every appearance, instead it just decreases their frequency in the gene pool over generations until they disappear. But the very fact that these examples of benevolence in the real world need to be pointed out, indicates they are the exceptions rather than the default behavior, nasty, brutish, red in tooth and claw. The background against which these examples appear, the law of the jungle, is evidence that there is no biological advantage to expending resources or forgoing opportunities in order to benefit another creature. In the wild, this 'natural cruelty' (actually apathy) is generally true even of an animal's own offspring, let alone their siblings. Obviously, parenting is adaptive, <u>in some cases</u>, but not as a general rule, and the counter-examples are quite shocking to those of us that belong to a species where nurturing children is instinctive. Yet, even among mammals, even among our own kind, acting altruistically, or parenting selflessly, is not the automatic compulsion it should be if there were some genetic mechanism involved.

We call it an instinct, those of us who feel compelled to care for infants, but it does not achieve the endemic nature of universal compulsion, the autonomic behavior, that the word "instinct" analytically identifies. Indeed, if genetically determined morality were even possible and had occurred anywhere within the development of our species or our ancestors, altruism would be so automatic that we literally couldn't conceive of behaving any way other than with unlimited compassion and unmitigated self-sacrifice towards all other human beings, at the least, for we share so many genes with each other. Gene-centric theories of evolution can be incredibly useful, but the hypothesis that altruism is adaptive is not. It is nothing more than repackaging of group selection, a thoroughly discredited theory, in order to indulge the postmodern desire to impose the theorist's personal morality on the rest of the population as if it were a biological imperative. Similarly, the entire array of 'memetic theory' that arose from Dawkins' book is, likewise, just postmodern grasping for a way to justify the desires and temptations of humanologists as instinctive in all humans. There is no genetic mechanism, no equivalent physical parallel to DNA, to explain the existence of 'memes' as anything other than fictional figments, leaving all philosophical musings about 'memes', some particle of intellectual material, a useless conglomeration of the worst psychological and sociological instincts and inventions. The indivisible particle of intellectual substance is "words", and 'meme' is a word that makes a matching set with "concept", as postmodern labels for things that very intelligent and highly educated people have been taught to believe in with religious faith, but which do not exist in the material world.

When it comes time to explicitly describe the moral basis of POR as a religion, the discussion will pick up from this point, with humans being no more genetically inclined to altruism than any other organism, and no type of creature being able to benefit from self-sacrificing behavior on a biological basis. The Philosophy Of Reason does have such a morality, and it doesn't rely on faith in anything except the existence of words and a desire for hope. A desire called hope. But before we get to that point, let us remain on the topic of biological evolution, with an eye towards confronting, and refuting, the compulsion towards xenophobia that does, somehow, seem as if it is adaptive. Instead of just trying to overwhelm this self/family/tribe/race consciousness with sentiments of compassion and optimism, we can hopefully destroy the problem of fascistic nationalism and oppression at the root. As I said earlier, it is not a misunderstanding of Darwin's natural selection that underlies these immoral philosophies, it is a misapplication. To fix this, we need to complete the naturalist's work, and reexamine whether natural selection is the only mechanism that truly drives biological evolution.

The false-start of gene-centric theory in prompting the hypothesis of adaptive altruism can provide a template for this effort. In that approach to considering evolution, theorists ignore the organisms involved and focus entirely on the genes themselves, as if they are 'naked replicators'. Of course, genes aren't naked replicators, DNA cannot directly copy itself (although RNA, a similar molecule, can.) What genes and the DNA they are 'encoded' in can do is represent the sequence of atoms that make up a protein. Proteins can form molecular machinery that can copy the DNA molecule. This is often rhetorically simplified into DNA copying itself, but without a lot of cellular processes for doing so, DNA cannot replicate itself. The simplest organisms we have found are bacteria and archaea, categorized as prokaryotes. These are as close as we can get to observing naked replicators. There are things that can be epistemologically confabulated with replicators. There are crystals, which are simply monotonous atomic patterns. There are viruses, but these, like our own DNA, require the machinery of biological cells to be copied. The closest thing to a naked replicator may be prions, protein forms that cause other proteins to mimic their form. Prions cannot produce the protein involved, though, they simply cause it to fold into the prion form, which can then cause other existing molecules to fold into that form. Ontologically, all of these potential examples fail as replicating systems, and the fact is that naked replicators are intellectual exercises, so naturally occurring examples cannot be used as empirical test cases to prove our theories. We have to develop our understanding using thought alone, or, at the very most, mathematics when it is possible.

Bacteria are close enough to naked replicators, though, that we will pretend that they are. The important thing is not that they are prokaryotes with 'loose' genes rather than eukaryotes with nuclear organelles, but that they are single-cell organisms rather than somatic creatures. Somatic life is the only kind that Darwin was using to develop his theory of evolution by natural selection, and certainly the only kind that could be effected by his hypothetical sexual selection. Somatic organisms have specialized tissue for generating gametes, and only those gametes are involved in the 'replication' of the genes that are involved in biological evolution, by being part of the process of reproduction. In any gene-centric evolutionary theory of zoology, only the germ cells and the haploid gametes they create are biological replicators, all of the other genes and DNA and cells in a creature's body are simply part of the organic machinery for replicating those genes. (A special case of non-zoological evolutionary theory can be made for applying gene-centric reverse teleologies to intra-organism biological evolution, which has medical applications, notably research into cancer therapies.) Almost every single sort of somatic life on Earth uses sexual reproduction, with two genders. This is of tremendous benefit (to use a purposefully backwards teleology) to evolution, with genes from the maternal and paternal parent creature being recombined to create a wealth of variation, on which natural selection can act. But simply having fortuitous results is not really a sufficient explanation for something to evolve, even when it is so ubiquitous. Sexual reproduction could certainly occur without gender, though in hindsight it seems that limiting creatures to one role, either gestating or not gestating, appears efficient. But we must keep in mind that while natural selection can allow for cooperation between multiple organisms, it cannot require it. Each organism can only promote the genes that organism, not some other creature, possesses, or both the genotype and the resulting phenotype would eventually be removed from the gene pool. Genes truly are 'selfish' in this way, and so we are left with something of a conundrum, the same one that Dawkins attempted, but failed, to adequately confront. Furthermore, it is not just the existence and prevalence of sexual reproduction that is confounding, but the often extreme and bizarre biological features that accompany it. Darwin's hypothesis of sexual selection also attempted to deal with this issue, and without that mechanism of 'mate preference' being distinct from natural selection, it is difficult to even believe, let alone explain, the extremity and variety of mating behaviors and gender dimorphisms that we see in nature. Mating behavior involves a lot of signaling, both passive and active, and the ubiquity of signaling in both sexual reproduction and other biological activity is not well explained by standard natural selection. Signaling is not made impossible by thermodynamics. But the evolution of signaling through natural selection is thermodynamically impossible, in precisely the same way as adaptive altruism is thermodynamically impossible. It could theoretically occur through mutation, but would inevitably die out, because by nature it helps others more than itself, even if it does help itself at all.

The fundamental nature of signaling behavior is problematic in both organism-centric and gene-centric evolutionary theory. Similarly, what about the question of altruistic self-sacrifice, which signaling might well be considered just one instance of? (Expending the energy of sending a signal benefiting the receivers directly, but the sender only indirectly, if at all.) We can, with reason, invert the assumed logic of standard theory, and instead of considering whether altruism is adaptive, wonder why it isn't more obvious that it is maladaptive. Why doesn't natural selection more quickly and completely stamp out any such capacity in all naturally evolved organisms, including our own? To both explain and perhaps answer the questions raised by this problem, POR postulates a novel hypothesis, a mechanism beyond simple natural selection. We will call this evolutionary principle *narcissistic selection*, for reasons that will become self-evident once the theory itself is explained. (In fact, the entire theory is encapsulated by that term, properly understood. The fact that the word 'narcissistic' cannot be properly understood by postmodernists, thanks to POS making it little more than a synonym for 'bad', is a pitfall, but it is as instructive as it is problematic, for that same reason.)

Before explaining this potentially misleading term, narcissistic selection, and the hypothesis it identifies, let's look at the fundamental problem in terms of naked replicators, again. Any system of replicators will display evolution by natural selection. It cannot be prevented in the long term, and can only appear to be mitigated even in the short term. Bacteria, as the closest natural stand-in for naked replicators, should be almost if not entirely self-promoting. A bacteria that somehow 'aids' other bacteria to proliferate should disappear from existence as the other bacteria that it aids use up all of the resources that it might need to replicate itself slightly more efficiently than the selfless organism which provides the aid.

There is great difficulty in recognizing the truth of this, as our language makes distinguishing the original bacteria from the copies of that bacteria almost impossible. So the postmodern assumption is made that the allele of self-sacrifice is already shared by all of the bacteria in the population, and does not therefore disadvantage (prove maladaptive for) the mutated form. In the real universe, not the hypothetical one where such false assumptions can persist, a bacteria that spends any of its limited 'energy budget' on aiding other bacteria by generating signals should die out rather quickly. The less accurate logic of the postmodernist idealists skips over this, and supposes that perhaps the disadvantage is not so large, and the advantage to the entire population of organisms that the mutated organism exists in could be large enough, that this altruistic signaling would not die out, but instead cause the mutant and its replicates (kin) to thrive. It isn't hard to believe that this scenario is so attractive and simplifying that even the most dedicated biologists or even computational scientists would gloss over its impossibility. Again, if we are truly attempting to be logical, as we must when dealing with real science, adaptive altruism is not simply unlikely, it truly is literally impossible for it to persist as a genetic trait. Signaling is the same as compassion, it cannot be a biological advantage, even accidentally, because by definition it is helping non-mutated version of an organism (or string of code, if we are trying to limit our gedanken to gene-centric theorizing) more than the mutated version, and this will unavoidably lead to the gene for signaling/altruism to become less frequent in the gene pool rather than more, even if it becomes more frequent in absolute terms because (we hypothesize) the entirety of the gene pool increases in size, depth, number, breadth, or however we want to quantify it. The thought that a doctor (or helper) organism could be so useful to a species that helpers become more numerous since the whole population of the species becomes more numerous is simply illogical. The only way the helper could increase the 'fitness' of a species is if the helpers become more numerous <u>in proportion</u> to non-helpers (increasing from a single mutant to a larger proportion of the local population), and so this requires assuming our conclusion about how helpful helpers can be. Helping themselves by helping others gives those who are helped without cost an advantage over those who pay the cost of helping. Evolution only works on species, not on individuals (who merely live or die, but do not evolve), and so the idea of a species that benefits from individuals who benefit the species rather than themselves, directly, is simply self-contradicting. (Again, the potentiality for inclusive fitness or eusocial behavior is dismissed in our consideration, although not this time because non-human creatures are not self-aware, but because not all species are social.)

It remains difficult to understand this thermodynamic self-contradiction of organic benefit, so difficult that even very highly educated people will spend a great deal of time and energy denying it is true. Just as they have done so with free will itself, and with IPTM. Socrates' Error is pernicious, not easily refuted, but because it is very difficult to even comprehend, not because it is supported by even a single fact. For the same reason that it took until the middle of the 19th Century to formulate the theory of evolution by natural selection, even though Aristotle developed the foundation of logic and empiricism thousands of years before, so too with the insufficiency of natural selection alone to explain most of what we see as the result of evolution with natural selection alone. Signaling and sexual reproduction are extremely productive biological adaptations, but the assumption they can therefore be explained by natural selection is not as appropriate as we have been told. It is a fait accompli argument, the idea that because it (signaling) exists, therefore our explanation of it (natural selection) is accurate.

Even bacteria, it has been discovered, engage in a form of chemical signaling. They also often practice a process called horizontal (or lateral) gene transfer, exuding their own genes into the environment, to be taken up by similar bacteria and incorporated into their own genome. Whether considered a random (if frequent) occurrence of a functional (adaptive) mechanism, lateral gene transfer and chemical signaling are similar, yet genetically unrelated, affects. Both can be recognized as ways that information is transmitted by one bacteria and received by another bacteria, just as prairie dogs use a distinct sound to warn others that a predator has been sighted. Standard evolutionary biology seems to say, in effect, that these things do happen because they can happen, and leave the reverse teleology as the only necessary explanation. But reverse teleologies are not justifications; they are only a way to communicate the existence of a circumstance, they do not provide a reason for the circumstance to occur.

The insufficiency of natural selection to explain signaling and/or altruism should be obvious, but it is not. It should be obvious as I've already explained, because any organism that expresses such a phenotype innately disadvantages itself by advantaging the original non-mutated phenotype at least as much as itself. But that alone is not even the only impossible part about signaling, and sex as well.

One of the properties that make signaling particularly problematic to explain with natural selection alone is the dimorphic (asymmetrical) nature that all signaling inherently shares. The physical, chemical, and biological method needed to complete an act of signaling requires two distinct and separate, but complementary, mechanisms. It is simple enough to imagine that a bacterial organism accidentally benefits from a mutation that ends up enhancing its ability to survive and reproduce. But signaling requires an even more fortuitous accident, far more unlikely and accidental, which is that two organisms within the same gene pool happen to mutate two separate phenotypes that mysteriously or providentially match up. The transmitter of a signal, whether a chemical excretion from a prokaryote or a yip from a mammal, will provide no adaptive advantage for which natural selection can reward its appearance unless a receiving mechanism is available, pre-existing in at least a rudimentary form. The reverse is also true but, instructively, less unlikely. A receiver mechanism can only naturally benefit from a pre-existing transmitting mechanism. Being passive, a receiver can exist with less cost, and so may be maintained in the gene pool without benefit longer than the active, more expensive, transmitter. The logical pathway needed to generate any signal is distinct, even distinctive, it is separate and apart from, *and biologically unrelated to* the logical pathway required to receive and recognize that signal. It is not impossible for a reception pathway to coincidentally mutate into existence at the same time a transmission pathway does; in a large enough universe almost anything can happen by chance. But it is quite unlikely. Even more profoundly problematic for the development of signaling mechanisms and capacity, the simple premise of transmission and reception is not something that can evolve as a single biological feature, a generic trait that can then become more specialized or developed. Every single individual instance of signaling in biology has to emerge separately, making the probability that more than one or a small handful of examples could occur across the entire biome astronomical. Each transmission facility must occur by chance, each matching reception facility must separately appear by chance, and even if that should happen, it could not increase the likelihood that any other transmission or reception facility would arise. A dozen flips of a coin coming up heads does not make the probability of the next one being heads more, or less, than 50%, and in the same way, the obvious adaptive advantage of signaling does not make emergence and evolution of additional instances of signaling more likely.

Again, the standard scientific theories that postmodern biologists have been relying on for decades only indicates that since these things are possible, however unlikely, and they are manifest, then therefore no further explanation is necessary. But even that approach only works when considering a particular instance of something appearing as a result of accidental genetic mutation during replication. It is clearly impractical for trying to justify the same kind of instances happening over and over and over again. Signaling is endemic, we might even believe that it is an innate part of life, it is so common, because just about every kind of life engages in it in many different forms. If natural selection alone, or the random 'genetic drift' that many evolutionists believe is also a major factor in the development of species of organisms, could address signaling as a single trait which evolution could develop, both refining and varying it according to environmental and metabolic opportunity, that would be one thing. But the yip of the prairie dog cannot be described as a more refined variation of the chemical signaling of their bacterial ancestors. They are only at all related by our perception of them both being 'signaling', not any biological or even physical mechanism inherent in the processes. And, still, in the same way, the sending of chemical signals and the survival-enhancing reaction to them are two different biological behaviors, that may reasonably appear related to us, but are not logically related in terms of genetic mutations that make them possible. Likewise, though less obviously, the instinct to make a specific kind of noise when a danger of a specific type is sensed, and the instinct to react as if that specific type of danger was directly sensed when that noise is heard, are two biologically, even neurologically, unrelated behaviors, neither of which benefit in appearance (increase in likeliness of appearing), though they do in development, by the existence of the other. The reverse teleology of "all the prairie dogs that did not react as if a predator appeared when they hear a certain signal have died" explains the existence of the biological trait. But only when we accept that it already exists, that the result of it happening is the reason it happens. There is no forward teleology, no cause and effect, that makes this anything but an isolated affect, not a biological effect. To be adaptive, it must be advantageous, and to be advantageous, it must already exist, but since the adaptive advantage of reacting to the signal is not genetically related to the (supposed) adaptive advantage of sending the signal, to assume it can evolve through natural selection simply because it has evolved is not logical, and is not even reasonable. It cannot already exist, without a better explanation than 'because it does' as a fait accompli argument from ignorance. This isn't just a teleological "why does it exist", but a tautological "how can it exist", deriving directly from the more fundamental tautology "how can it have come into existence". We are told that evolution explains it, as we are told that evolution explains altruism in general, but this is not actually scientifically plausible because it is not thermodynamically possible. No wonder so many people continue to believe there must be a God to explain life and its marvelous complexity, along with our quite inconsistent desire (not instinct) for compassion, kindness, sentiment, and morality.

All signaling mechanisms we can observe are heightened forms of more rudimentary mechanism, just as clearly focusing eyes are incrementally improved versions of less precise ancestral forms. But even if the rudimentary form is so subtle that, although it provides an opportunity for natural selection to heighten it over generations regardless of whether it is so obvious we can notice and measure it, the dichotomy between the transmission and reception of signals must still be present. It is not simply that transmission and reception pathways can be distinct and separate. Definitively, they must be; there are no exceptions because there cannot be any exceptions that vary from this reality. Even the very blind and unconscious, perfectly mechanical chemical feature of bacteria, the simplest form of altruism more basic than even chemical signaling, gene transfer, is not really one process. Releasing arbitrary stretches of DNA through cell membranes that normally prevent them, and accepting these genes to incorporate them, without intention or awareness, into a bacteria's own genome, is not actually a single mechanism. Both directions do seem to use the same mechanical process, allowing genes through the cell membrane. But the very fact that there are two asymmetric sides of the cell membrane, that the interior cytoplasm is not the same as the exterior environment, makes this two separate abilities. It may not happen in the real world, but hypothetically, a bacteria that will only incorporate outside genes, but will not express genes to the outside, would be as advantageously selfish as it would be possible to be. Releasing genes may not harm a bacteria, it may even be somehow productive to not have that "copy" of a particular polymer anymore, but this would not make it adaptive to release genes that might benefit other bacteria, even sibling/identical ones, because even if similar, they are still competitors, ecologically. Since the self-identity (not requiring self-awareness, but simply physical integrity) of a bacteria definitively requires the chemical processes, which make up that single celled organism, to distinguish between inside the cell and outside the cell, no random two-way travel of isolated collections of peptides would allow a single genetic mutation that allows gene transfer to evolve. Sending and receiving genes requires separate paths, just as sending and receiving signals would. And so on up through the biomic layers of complexity and sociobiology, somatic life, sexual reproduction, sentient signaling, linguistic communication and self-determination, and culminating in morality, theology, and altruistic sentiments; if we are to accept that compassion biologically occurs, we must accept that compassion is not adaptive according to natural selection.

How, then, does signaling, and the related (and perhaps included, depending on your perspective) examples of sexual reproduction, gender dimorphism, and potentially sexual selection, end up being so profligate and fecund in evolution, when not just every instance of signaling must represent an unlikely happenstance of both generation and reaction in the same reproductive group, but each instance does so separately from all others? How can caring and mercy be biologically tolerated if they cannot be biologically adaptive for the organism experiencing them actively even more than the organism benefiting from them passively? The answer applies to imaginary naked replicators as much as to real-world reproducing organisms. It becomes most obvious, though, if we more closely consider the more sparse and constrained case. Natural selection is impossible to prevent in any system of replicators, things that make copies of themselves. The source materials for this replication have to come from the environment, in fact they make up the entirety of that environment. (Here I define "environment" as distinct from "substrate", the non-interacting physical surface or structure on/in which both environment and replicator occur.) A replicating process assembles copies of itself from more rudimentary substances, and we consider this activity in terms of the replicator being 'alive', able to benefit from reverse if not inverse teleologies, but the environment and source materials as 'not alive', responding only to forward teleologies. All computational (logical) approaches to explaining or exploring natural selection includes this unrecognized assumption, that the thing being selected (or not) is distinguishable from the nature (both environment and substrate) it survives in. It must be distinct, the organism must be something different from the environment, simply to be recognizable, for it to even exist to begin with. The organism must be considered separately from the environment, at least rhetorically, or we are not saying anything in any theory of evolution beyond "things change". But what if, as in the real world, even naked replicators do not act within a dead universe of non-replicating substances? What if the majority, perhaps nearly the entirety, of the 'environment' within which an organism survives (or not) is comprised of other organisms? The hypothesis of *narcissistic selection* is an answer to this question: what if, as replicators evolve, the environment they replicate in also "**evolves back**"?

It is a miniscule difference, really. Small enough to be dismissed entirely as uneducated fantasy by anyone well versed enough in evolutionary theory. "No," a potentially postmodernist pedant will say, "standard evolutionary theory does not assume that the environment is lifeless apart from the evolving organism, that is just silly and you only think that because you don't know what you're talking about." (Equivalent experts would dispute every single part and notion of POR, and so on reasonable if not logical grounds, we presume they can be generally ignored. But let's not do so in this case, in order to explore this line of reasoning.) Let us consider the miniscule difference in the result, if a replicator is not replicating in isolation, but almost every resource it assembles its copies from is also evolving. Perhaps even the very substrate it must be in physical contact with is also impacted by the force of natural selection, and its source of energy, along with all the raw materials it uses that energy to metabolize or reassemble, if we go so far as to include those requirements in our analysis, is only available through a replicating system; is itself, are themselves, only replicating systems, without any (or perhaps just very few) 'dead' molecules without any association to replicators. All replicating systems exhibit natural selection. They cannot not do so, it is part of the definitive nature of anything that can be described as a replicating system. What changes in the future generations of the replicator under consideration would there be that depend on, and we can say are caused by, the absence of non-replicating systems as an environment in which the process occurs?

Forgive the baroque and elaborate prose, allow me to rephrase this more simply, and hope that you, the reader, will not then dismiss my point by misreading the text. Natural selection occurs when any replicator replicates over generations; it cannot be avoided. Organisms reproduce and die, and this causes species to evolve. But what variations would there be in the results, categorically or substantially, if the environment evolved rather than or in addition to the genomes we call organisms?

The answer is narcissistic selection: **a replicator will benefit from replicating in a way that is coincident with the way other replicators are replicating**. Regardless of the details, the source, mechanism, or effect of these 'ways', these coincidences, these features that coincide with other features, the replicator (in fact, all of the replicators) will benefit, will be selected for if it is similar to others. If there can be a category of replicator, of whatever type, of any 'formation of kind', without regard for what 'categories' are or how they would be defined, then it would make replicators of that category adaptive if they were similar to other replicators. Each replicator/organism cannot benefit tremendously (ultimately, if not proximately) by being significantly different, innovative in evolutionary terms, <u>even if that innovation would benefit it enormously</u> in the control example, where only the replicator is evolving and the environment in which it replicates is 'inorganic' and static, not simultaneously evolving. Our replicator at issue could, if we think about it hard enough, benefit from being significantly identical to all the other replicators that make up its environment, of course, but only at the cost of no longer being the replicator at issue. This gets mind-bending very quickly, I'll admit. Being identical is to have no identity, so it benefits an organism to be slightly different, but not very different, from similar organisms. This 'benefit' may be contrary to the adaptive nature of forward teleology, cause and effect, because it relies on the reverse teleology of hindsight-based analysis: the 'benefit' is in making the organism distinct from the environment, rather than increasing its frequency of replication. If it were to remain indistinguishable from other organisms, then those other organisms increasing in frequency is the same as it increasing in frequency, but not in a way that benefits it individually. This inverts the problematic analysis of considering evolution of a genome (each organism has a unique genome) versus the evolution of a species (which is not a single genome, but a 'gene pool', although it is generally rhetorically described as a genome.) The analysis is still problematic, but in a way that is informative, if you can grasp it, rather than confabulating. Natural selection is "survival of the fittest", while narcissistic selection is "survival of the fitter". Natural selection alone amounts to 'survival of the most fit', which is tautological, since fitness is defined by surviving: simple Darwinism is 'survival of that which survives', with the rhetorical description of 'fitness' being a hindsight/fait accompli explanation without any other meaning or purpose beyond surviving/replicating. It must be remembered that the apparent suitability of 'fitness', as a judgment, is not declared and bestowed upon an individual organism, but the entire species of such organisms. That category error of being unable to distinguish the two, animal or germ line, mentioned earlier, is rife in postmodernism, even the most rigorously scientific postmodernism, due to the confounding nature of the existence of numbers and other such logical categories.

Narcissistic selection, evolution in reality as opposed to simplistic Darwinism, amounts to 'survival of the slightly more fit'. This defines the results more comprehensively, because instead of assuming that whatever survives survived because it was more fit, a circular tautology, it provides a teleological explanation of why the survival occurs, by comparing fitness not to extinction or lack of fitness, but to the lesser fitness of the previous or competitive form. The only logical distinction between the two frameworks is the fact that narcissistic selection would select against a 'much greater' fitness just as it selects against a 'too slight' fitness, because the organism would not benefit from existing within its environment in the same way that similar organisms do, and thus aided by the adaption of the environment to those forms simultaneous with the adaptation of the forms to the environment. It is this affect, the additional adaptivity of an only slightly improved version, that makes the 'selection of like' principle of narcissistic selection eponymous. Nature, which is to say the environment rather than simply the physical occurrence of replication, selects for what is similar to existing replicators. But "similar" is not "identical", it means 'different from' as much as it means 'not much different from', and so the equilibrium observed in the fossil record and the spectacular diversity that results from its punctuation are both explained by narcissistic selection, as is the commonality of signaling and convergent evolution along with the ruthless competition and absence of virtuous altruism in nature. The regular appearance of categories in nature, both species and niches, when there are no categories in nature, can only be fully explained by the narcissistic selection theory of POR, although without the natural selection theory of Darwin, it would be inconceivable and incomprehensible. (A rhetorical yet metaphysical point can be made here about the selection in our language of the word 'fit', as a dichotomous abstraction, to refer to both strength from exercise and the suitability of a particular shape. It is anathema to postmodern sensibilities to suggest that the century and a half of using 'fitness' to refer to biological suitability has as much to do with the recognition of a niche caused by the environment that narcissistic selection will prefer as the profligacy of a reproducing organism and its species, but such circumstances are too common in POR discernment to be discounted as coincidence.)

I will attempt, no doubt badly, to represent the principle of narcissistic selection with symbols, in order to try to make the logical mechanism more apparent, conceivable and comprehensible. Much more adept mathematicians will have to improve on my effort, but hopefully this will suffice as a first approximation. Say we have environment X, and replicator A. If environment X already exists with replicators of category N making up some part of it, successfully existing as replicators, then if replicator A happens by coincidence to be similar to Ns, it will not be distinguishable from N by X, to whatever degree it is similar. This is all mundane and self-evident, but trivially so: tautological. It is merely a description of what is being described. The magic comes from the next step. Teleology is, in fact, born from this next step. God and life and happiness derives from the tiny incremental but unavoidable next issue, and so it is the thing that differentiates narcissistic selection from mere natural selection. It isn't just that A can replicate as well as Ns because X is not any more hostile or helpful to A than N. It is that the similarity that makes A and N identical to whatever degree they are does not need to have any relation to what makes Ns Ns. Recall that A is a single replicator. But N is an entire category of replicators. What makes them a category isn't important; it could be only that they are all descendants of Q. It could be that they are a huge number of replicators, some Q and some K and some other individual instances or groups, genetic or otherwise. It doesn't matter what makes them all N, but they are all N. Narcissistic selection does something a little different, produces slightly different results than natural selection, because <u>what makes A like N doesn't have to be what makes Qs like Ks</u>. The feature of the various Ns that makes them Ns (contingency) does not need to be the feature that makes As like Ns, because the A does not need to be an N, it merely needs to be similar to Ns, consequentially. The definition of categories is not ontological, it is epistemological. It is, indeed, the category of categories. Do not read that as to say 'the ultimate category', but instead 'the existence of sets'. There is only one instance of categories; the category of category. The existence of category, the idea that there could be such a thing as category, and in truth, the idea that there could be ideas, the fact that there could be a distinction between A and X at all, let alone a distinction between A and N, or X and N. Or Q and K.

So how exactly does narcissistic selection make signaling mechanisms and mating displays common? Why would the slight difference between what natural selection would be expected to produce and what narcissistic selection, along with natural selection, does produce, end up being so radical that what is extremely unlikely becomes common? Signaling itself should be uncommon because it requires the coincidental evolution of asymmetric mechanisms to produce a method of information transmission and reception that benefits both organisms enough to provide an adaptive advantage. But it is not uncommon, it is so pervasive that to call it merely 'common' is an understatement. There is a slight advantage to a mutating organism if the resulting phenotype happens to be similar to a previously existing phenotype, because that prior kind of organism has "carved out" a niche in the environment that can be exploited by the subsequent mutation. This cannot really be denied, but is that the same as saying that such an advantage is sufficient to produce significant differences in results, results so cumulative over time that they are not largely washed away by the stochastic nature of biological variation? The profundity of the difference between the computational evolution of an organism in a static environment and the combinatorial evolution of an organism in a constantly evolving environment, an environment that adapts to the organism just as the organism adapts to its environment, is difficult to explain, given the uncontrolled state of the observable world. It can seem as if narcissistic selection resulting in signaling and mating displays and ecological convergence is simply another fait accompli, it happens because it happens, making narcissistic selection an

237

extremely unnecessary hypothesis to begin with. But the opportunity for natural selection alone is limited to the mutation of the species of organism that is evolving; in actuality mutations which occur within individuals of a given species. The hindsight-based reasoning of routine reverse teleologies, natural selection, become reduced to fait accompli arguments because the distinction between two individuals within an ancestral species only becomes controlling once their species become distinct. Within the ancestral species, variations in alleles are "micro-evolution", and speciation itself being "macro-evolution". Of course, there is no scientific distinction between the two, the very idea of such categories is invented by anti-evolution, anti-science philosophers (religious fundamentalists, to be exact) in order to express consternation over Darwinian theory. But within the community of biologists studying these issues, there are debates over the relative importance or frequency of allopatric and sympatric speciation, cladogenesis versus anagenesis, and even natural selection versus gene drift in evolutionary development. All are attempts to try to simplify the complexity of phylogenetic reality, and the consternation of the amateurs can be considered a reflection of the uncertainties of the professionals. The hypothesis of narcissistic selection does not resolve all, or even any, of these points of contention, but it does hopefully provide a helpful perspective for accepting why such consternation and uncertainty exists. The mathematics, undeniable and inevitable, of natural selection seem straight-forward. The theory in POR is simply that the logical certainty of biological inheritance results in the wildly complex emergent properties of life and sexual reproduction not simply because of the huge number of genes and variation of alleles alone, but because the situation is even more complicated than that. The potential (intellectually; it is an undeniable certainty in reality) for the organism and its genome to be the more static entity, essentially being the substrate for the much larger number of potential mutations that can be tested for adaptivity when those random changes occur in all of the genomes that make up the environment, means that natural selection is more probably the lesser force, with narcissistic selection being the more powerful principle, when it comes to determining how replicating and reproducing systems will behave. The principle is exemplified by the potential confusion, the divergence and even contradiction, between 'behavior' of the individuals, and 'behavior' of the systems. Ultimately, to even claim there is a difference between a genome, an organism, a species, an environment, or a substrate, is to make categorical determinations that the unconscious interaction of particles, atoms, molecules, and substances in the physical universe ignores.

The only way to comprehend evolution remains to consider how a species changes over time. But we must not forget that the definition of 'species', both within any single instance and as a category of thing itself, is epistemological, not ontological. Any two organisms, even those so closely related as identical twins, are still two competing 'specific' creatures, and for any two more conventionally diverse life forms within a traditionally defined gene pool, each is part of 'the environment' for the other, as well. The environment contains many more genomes and genes than any species or organism ever can, and so the combinatorial chaos that real world biology evidences does not simply support the idea of narcissistic selection, it demands, it requires, it. With natural selection alone, a transmitter phenotype must accidentally occur in the same geographic and chronologic population as a receiver phenotype, which is immensely improbable. With narcissistic selection, the more complex consideration of not just the organism's evolution in response to its environment, but the environment's evolution in response to the organism, it is quite probable, since the appearance of a receiver phenotype in a single organism creates selection pressure on every other organism in the environment, both related by heredity and not, for a transmitter phenotype to become adaptive. And vice versa: the mutation of a genotype which produces a potential transmission of a signal, which is not a signal except in hindsight but is simply something physical that happens, becomes selection pressure on every other genome of every other organism in every other species that makes up the environment of that mutated allele to evolve a receiver that could turn that physical occurrence into information that can be of benefit. In this way, the transmitter does not need to directly benefit from the ability to transmit, in terms of expending energy to send information that will not increase its reproductive success, but the transmission will still be adaptive by increasing its *fitness*, how well it fits, within the environment in which it reproduces.

The only way to even believe that we can make any sense of it is to resort to recognizing that there is a distinction, though not always with a difference, between ontology and epistemology. Consider the kin selection that was mentioned previously. Keep that in mind while we consider a very different aspect of the universe: the Big Bang. Humanity discovered that all matter and energy in the cosmos must have started as an individual sub-atomic singularity because the astronomer Edwin Hubble analyzed the 'red shift' that showed that every observable galaxy was receding from every other. Taking the fact of an expanding universe, he imagined inverting the chronology, running time backwards and realizing that at one time, all galaxies must have once been in a single location. Biologically, we have to assume that all genes are mutated descendants of a single gene, in the same way. Every organism, we know, is 'kin' to every other, cousins hundreds and thousands and perhaps millions of times removed, but still showing, in every cell and mitochondria, the indisputable evidence that we all descended from a single kind of creature, in fact a single replicator, a single genome comprised of a single gene. Obviously, the 'kin selection' that Dawkins referred to only has significant effect with very very very close genetic relationships. The further away in the family tree an organism is, the less reason our selfish genes have for helping it and its offspring. The cracks and fissures of extinct and mutated organisms that turn the sphere of all biology into the bush of the tree of life more than adequately vindicates the relative absence of inter-species altruism in the wild. Signaling between species is less common (though not at all rare) simply because it involves two separate gene pools, not merely two separate organisms putatively sharing a genome. But still, all genes are just copies of the proto-gene, and all organisms are just complex organic mechanisms for replicating that proto-gene. Nature still lacks self-awareness, it will still not support altruism as an adaptive trait, but it can and does support signaling, a necessary precursor to communication. Kin selection does not mean that the proto-gene's decedents have evolved the ability to coordinate, to conspire purposefully, but a silent conspiracy known as 'life', mitigated and enabled simultaneously by narcissistic selection, inevitably comes into existence, just as the 'something is more stable than nothing' singularity of the Big Bang causes all subsequent interactions between particles, a chain reaction lasting billions of years and including me typing this, and you reading it.

Narcissistic selection cannot prevent the emergence of difference and innovation in mutation-driven evolution, but it does provide a way to explain why innovation is the exception and conformity the rule. It can be considered the root of the very existence of ecological 'niches', and convergent evolution, which can be accommodated and sustained by natural selection, but not originated or powered by it. Convergent evolution would be nothing but random coincidence, unlikely and rare, but in the real world, we find it not simply common, but normative. Typically, the fait accompli argument of 'mutation happens' is all the standard biologist has to go on when presiding over the outrageous mundaneity of parasitism, symbiosis, and scavenging observable in the animal and plant and unicellular kingdoms. Invention of some archetype of environmental structure, some deific propriety to "sociobiological" relationships, papers over the problem for the postmodernist, but such categories are simply "not impossible" if natural selection alone describes the evolution of life. Narcissistic selection is simply the recognition that all organisms are **the environment** to all other organisms, and evolution is never simple even in the simplest examples. This lessens the need for such logical skyhooking, explaining why convergent evolution, not just in individual forms but in environmental niches, aren't simply "not impossible", and not even simply "quite common", but downright **inevitable**. Narcissistic selection makes signaling more than possible, it makes it unavoidable, because the distinction between the evolution of a solitary type of organism and the evolution of a solitary species of organism becomes academic. So does the distinction between a transmitting phenotype and a receiving phenotype; no genetic link between the two is necessary or even beneficial, and so the lack of them in every instance of signaling is no longer mystifying. Selfish genes should not 'care' whether they are within a creature of one type and a creature of another, but narcissistic selection can only act on organisms, even when those organisms are hypothetical single gene naked replicators that cannot occur in nature. This is because, philosophically, an organism is not simply defined by its genes, but by its presence within the environment, just as neither Humpty Dumpty nor Alice can dictate what words mean, and light is not particles or waves sequentially, but simultaneously.

Individual creatures cannot evolve, of course, they can only survive and die, whether they reproduce or not. With natural selection alone, organisms that don't reproduce might as well not exist, except to their closest kin, and not necessarily even to them; they may as well be inorganic resources to be cannibalized. With narcissistic selection, individual creatures still cannot evolve, since their somatic genes are generally fixed at birth, but the type of the creature, which biologists and others often treat as a single epistemological and ontological 'creature', can be treated as linguistically interchangeable with the individual organism. (Just as we do already with narratives of reverse teleologies. But in postmodernism, this is a flaw, a failure to accurately apply logic. With POR, it is a triumph, an ability to reasonably benefit from applied logic. Postmodernists succumb to their limited ability to use logic strictly enough, while we benefit from our ability to use strict logic for accurate scientific reasoning.)

Even the distinction between living matter and dead matter melts away, explaining the quasi-life that viruses display despite being inanimate. Are they environment, or organism? The question is epistemological, with little ontological validity, because we don't need to invent an otherwise unexplained and impossible idea that chemicals involved in metabolism or replication are somehow different from chemicals that are not. The principle of narcissistic selection, that genes or organisms that most efficiently make the replication of genes and organisms like themselves possible become more numerous than those that are less efficient at accomplishing this, makes many aspects of life more explicable than natural selection alone could. (This is purposeful understatement, since as I've explained, natural selection does not simply make certain aspects of life less explicable, it makes them thermodynamically impossible, without the bias of narcissistic selection towards cooperative systems such as signaling, sexual selection, and communication/altruism possible despite the ruthless competition that natural selection alone mandates.) Efficiency at self-replication is still the primary driving force of biology, but it is not the totality of evolutionary causes/effects. Efficiency at **self-like replication**, rather than the epistemologically similar but ontologically entirely separate **self-replication**, does not require the inverse teleology of 'selfishness' that genes are said to display, and can accomplish the same ends with entirely forward teleologies of blind chemical interactions.

It can be pointed out here that 'selfishness' and any similar motivations, are as unavailable in a reverse teleology as they are in a forward teleology, being inventions of inverse teleology requiring intention and goal-seeking, foresight, rather than the hindsight of fait accompli that Darwinism relies on. Such motivations as 'selfishness' or 'altruism' can be used conveniently to explain reverse teleologies of evolutionary pressure, but cannot empower unconscious selection by nature. In this way the choice of term 'narcissistic selection' is instructive, since it normally describes a motivation beyond simple volition, but identifies, in this case, a simple similarity that can be blindly determined. Indeed, it is this blindness (the creation of categories concerning As, Qs, and Ks, in which N and N-like can be naturally selected for without distinction) that allows self-like (narcissistic) selection to take its place as a form of abstract "pressure", along with natural selection, in creating/causing/describing evolution with reverse teleologies. Without narcissistic selection, there is no 'boot-strapping' mechanism in natural selection, and biology would be limited to nearly-naked replicators incessantly but only ephemerally cannibalizing other replicators.

The temptation is obvious to believe that this view of life can be the very source of adaptive altruism that so many atheists and others have longed for. But this would be just assuming our conclusion, for all the reasons that have already been given to doubt that altruism is adaptive in biological terms. The hypothesis of narcissistic selection does, however, provide a basis for better understanding signaling, and its commonality in nature despite the fact that every single example of signaling has to evolve separately, independent in its molecular origin from all other examples. Signaling, unlike altruism, does not require compassion, or sympathy or hope or empathy or caring or consciousness, or any of the other things we would need to project from our own experience onto the physical universe in order to justify our compassion and altruism. Entirely through the unguided and unintended actions of selfish genes, the development of otherwise independent mechanisms that end up being advantageous for dependent signaling not just can take place, but must take place.

Let me address the causative sequence, not quite a teleology but a chain of them. The physical existence of replication, not simply crystalline or prionic but genetic reproduction, results in natural selection. The consequence of rampant evolution of replicators is an environment, comprised of an indefinite and huge number of replicators. This results in narcissistic selection. Narcissistic selection causes these replicators to evolve signaling. The success of signaling replicators enables the evolution of multi-cellular somatic life and specialized tissues, which in turn leads to the evolution of sexual reproduction. Sexual reproduction eventually causes sentience and sentients. This, in turn, produces the mechanism of communication, language, which coincides with consciousness. Consciousness, in turn, invents teleologies, and unavoidably develops altruism and morality and theology. The development of compassion and morals by {any organism capable of} conscious communication is unavoidable, but inconsistent. It is not instinctive, not a biological adaptation. It is an intellectual necessity, not a physical one, by its nature. The inconsistency of morality, the variance in its presence and its dimensions in each conscious organism, is what gives it meaning. If it were automatic, as if it was either genetic or supernatural, it would not be morality and compassion, but physics; it would not rely on sentiment, and language would not require and produce sentimentality. The Tree of Knowledge story in the Judaic scripture hypothesizes a divine Lord that somehow created us to disobey it, yet punishes us for doing so. This self-contradiction is not accidental, it is necessary. If God created humanity, It did so to make us like Itself; narcissistic selection. If humanity created God, it did so to reflect our metaphysical existence in order to make it manifest.

While miniscule in any particular replicative, biological, or evolutionary event, the force of narcissistic selection (as with the force of natural selection) is as inescapable as the limits of time, space, or electromagnetism. Metaphorically, it can be likened to gravity (in more ways than one, in fact, making the metaphor both apt and perilous.) In objectively measurable terms, gravity is, proximately, the weakest of the four physical forces. But it is longer range, and cumulative, so ultimately, at sufficiently large scales, it is the most noticeable and undeniable, so much so that it appears to be the strongest, or at least the most significant in its effects on the observable world around us. Narcissistic selection explains not just signaling as its most direct manifestation, but the evolution of sexual reproduction, including all of the crazy features and behaviors that arise from it. Indeed, whether narcissistic selection is an aspect of natural selection, or whether natural selection is an aspect of narcissistic selection is, significantly, academic. The force of narcissistic selection, as I've explained it, seems to result from natural selection applying to the environment as much as the organism (species), but this could simply be an epistemological perspective, not the ontological one. Narcissistic selection, chemical narcissism we could call it, can be seen as the very existence of replication, and the cause of selection. Recall that selections don't actually occur in nature, there are no choices, just our ability to imagine that some physical occurrence could have somehow produced different results than it did produce. When molecules somehow fortuitously, through Providence or providence, happen upon an arrangement of atoms that mysteriously causes that same arrangement to occur in nearby atoms, and almost miraculously ends up causing huge arrangements of molecules to embody biological life through the natural promotion of whatever mutated arrangements promote replication naturally, this is narcissistic selection occurring, narcissism causing more narcissism because that is the very definition of what narcissism is: that which imagines and celebrates self.

If you are not yet convinced that this view of life is both very real and very different from what scientists and skeptics alike have always thought of it before, consider a different approach. The postmodern application of the theory of natural selection explains mating behavior and extreme gender dimorphism using the idea of 'proxy'. The huge antlers of so many (but not all!) cervidae (deer, elk, and moose) and the "ritualistic" rutting competitions they are often (but not always!) used in are a standard example, as is the fancy fantail of the male peafowl, along with just about every aspect of the sexual features and behavior of birds. The standard approach is to assume that all of these various and distinct aspects of nature are selected for in evolution because they are stand-ins, proxies, for "fitness". The ability to 'waste' resources growing or building huge displays or engage in mating dances is a proof of biological efficiency, in this proxy hypothesis, so the animals that mate with those individuals which are most successful in having or performing these inefficiencies as proof of efficiency are driven to do so by natural selection. This takes the reverse teleology of natural selection too far, though, because the true evolutionary advantage would have to go to those individuals that don't waste time or energy on the displays. For every set of mating rules that evolve, because they are supposedly adaptive, cheating would be more adaptive.

The selecting individuals might have no better method for choosing what animal in their local population to mate with, but evolution doesn't proceed by reasoning, it proceeds by chance mutation and differential rates of reproduction. The usefulness or fealty (accuracy) of the proxy in actually indicating which animals will produce the most and best offspring is not logically warranted to begin with, nor is it demonstrated in the end. It can only be assumed as a fait accompli argument; "Having big horns must be adaptive because there are big horns." This teleology isn't really adequate regardless of whether we consider it forward or backwards, it is circular. It is a tautology, not a teleology. Even with genetic programming and operant conditioning, the attractiveness of the 'winner' of some supposed competition between possible mates is simply assuming the conclusion: it must help replication because it is replicated, despite having no logical pathway or reasonable narrative that explains why. The peacock with the most resplendent feathers is considered the most fit because it produced the most offspring, pushing less resplendent creatures out of the gene pool, not because it is better at the processes of metabolism, or insemination or birthing. The 'proxy' hypothesis is really just repackaging of Darwin's sexual selection. Although biologists have convinced themselves, and everyone else, that there is logic to the preference, and so the preference must be logic, this thinking doesn't actually indicate how or why any particular trait is chosen as the 'proxy' for efficiency/fitness, or how it demonstrates it more effectively than any competing trait, alternative phenotype, mutated allele.

Reconsidering these sexual features in terms of narcissistic selection allows us to recognize the more direct and guaranteed physical mechanism behind them.

Peacocks with wondrous feathers or moose with glorious antlers are selected by peahens and moose cows because those cocks and bulls select peahens and cows that are attracted to large fantails and antlers, not because there is any necessary relationship between those particular features and biological profligacy or fitness. Nature is free to allow and even encourage every individual genetic population to invent, and develop to extremes, this 'attraction to what is attracted to attraction', even when it results in very inefficient use of the resources needed to reproduce. No aspect of anatomy is exempt from natural selection, not even the hidden neurological anatomy that relates to mating behavior, visual preference, sexual attraction. But no aspect of anatomy are exempt from narcissistic selection, either, and it is this force in evolution that spurs the existence and use of these bizarre but normalized abnormalities. Two very closely related species of birds or mammals might rely upon very different mating signals, to an incredible extent, and this suggests that it is not genetic natural selection that produces these signals, but narcissistic selection, instead. Natural selection does not prevent speciation in every case, but narcissistic selection causes speciation, in all cases.

Narcissistic selection is not selection for any particular type, no template of attractiveness or featly to a proxy is needed. The type selected for is always and only and simply: "self", which must define 'self' in terms of similarity to self rather than identity. In an unconscious process, this is 'self-like'. Peacocks with certain feathers select peahens that select peacocks with those feathers. The end result is the same as the 'proxy' theory, but the teleology is superior. In the old format, peahens must make choices, and the preference for certain expensive feathers, despite being biologically maladaptive, is random and arbitrary. In the new format, the selection is still random and arbitrary, but does not rely on preferences, simply contingency; whatever it is that gets selected, i.e., results in the most offspring, becomes that which is selected for, without the hypothesis of engrams in the brains of peahens, but simply the existence of genes for producing expensive feathers in peacocks. In species with gender dimorphism, this makes the transmission of the signal involved in producing the display singular, simultaneous, and coinciding with the reception of the signal involved in producing the attractiveness for mating. So in this way, the selection by females of the peafowl species for many eyespots becomes identical to the growing of many eyespots by the males of their species, even though the two, eyespots and attraction, are entirely unrelated in anatomical terms.

Narcissistic selection, as a theory, can make more comprehensible many of the aspects of life that we have been taught to assume and insist occurred only by chance through random mutations. Even those that would require two parallel mutations, two unconnected chains of mutations, such as signaling. But like natural selection itself, it is not an explanation for human activity and preferences. Remember, communication is not the same as signaling, although signaling is a predicate of communication. Certainly, we are biological creatures, and we cannot escape biological imperatives or anatomical (both gross and neurological) engineering (the term being used appropriately advisedly.) But we can evade biology, overcome genetic imperatives and anatomical engineering, because of our capacity for language, self-determination, and reasoning. Just because we are animals does not mean we are just animals. The evolution of language itself, whether it is seen as the cause of consciousness or the effect of consciousness, may be based on the rudiments of primitive signaling, but it is not merely a more complex form of it. Communication, as explained earlier, is not simply a case of bidirectional signaling, it requires a theory of mind in order to accomplish communion. This mental capacity of imagining, in order to imagine that other humans are also capable of imagining or as a result of imagining that it is so, is, like signaling, only possible through narcissistic selection. But narcissistic selection does not require conscious self-awareness, despite the potentially confusing mythology suggested by the name. Theory of mind, consciousness, is, in every way, a self-referential issue, and a self-referential explanation, because it is the existence of self and all references to it. Somatic life itself could not exist without narcissistic selection, and even non-somatic life would be very different if only mutations and natural selection acting upon replicators were possible. Without the slight bias in both the replicator and its evolving environment towards the self-like that is narcissistic selection, the impact of the environment on the organism and the impact of the organism on the environment, simple replicators will remain simple replicators, if they can even survive past the stage of transient naked replicators, and will never evolve into somatically reproductive species. Narcissistic selection can be considered a feedback between the two, replicator and environment, that bootstraps nature as we understand and recognize it: diversity and cooperation caused by replication and competition. Like natural selection, narcissistic selection cannot be prevented, once a system of replicators becomes a system of systems of replicators. Evolution without both kinds of selection isn't possible, so the uncontrollable state of the universe prevents us from knowing what life would be like if only one were in effect. Regardless, humans have evolved language, or invented it after evolving consciousness. The usefulness of communication, over and above the simplistic transfer of information that the postmodern conception of language relegates it to, is self-evident. Its limits are just as self-evident, though, and generating words is not the same as benefitting from them, as your consternation in trying to read this book has no doubt adequately proven. The anatomical source of language and theory of mind is our brains, not our genes. We are not simply organically programmed biological robots, we are transcendence over biology. The neurological mechanism within our brains that produces this effect of affects, this affect of effects, language and consciousness, is unknown. But its existence cannot be doubted, because to doubt it requires comprehension of the idea, which can only occur as a result of its existence. Cogito ergo sum loqui; I think because I am speaking, I speak because I am thinking.

The biological evolution of this capacity for reasoning is, of course, described in postmodern terms as the development of a capacity for logic, for mathematical processing. The Philosophy Of Reason is the premise that reasoning is not logic, language is not calculation. Reasoning is analogical to logic in that it can be viewed as a mechanism for selection, but this is an empty tautology. Reasoning is not a method for selecting one choice among alternatives, it is a capacity for imagining that there are alternatives and choices. The biological development of communication, language, is typically explained by proposing that consciousness came first, and language was invented by people to demonstrate or detect that consistently mathematical consciousness. Only humans that were smart enough to think more logically than other human-like animals survived, in the conventional theory, so only humans descended from those humans are still in existence. This is, like before, a reliance on reverse teleologies as physical truth rather than verbal explanations of what is already true regardless. The actual physical evolution of human consciousness has to rely on only forward teleologies if it is to be considered scientifically valid, trying to explain it with reverse teleologies is circular logic, a fait accompli argument, a faith-based process of assuming our conclusions.

The Philosophy Of Reason describes communication as being the initial 'mutation' of a capacity to be something other than logical. All animals behave logically. They cannot avoid it, since biological evolution deters anything else, and physics makes anything else impossible, so animals behave as biological robots programmed by genetics and operant conditioning, without consciousness or conscience. But we seem to have avoided that fate, since behaving logically, for us, is, at most, optional. We wish to become masters over our genetic programming and we rebel against operant conditioning. According to philosophical pessimism, of course, this isn't possible; we can become masters over our genetic programming only if that is our genetic programming, and we only pretend to be immune to operant conditioning because that is our operant conditioning. Such philosophical tail-swallowing, circular logic and tautological absolutes are rejected by POR. We dismiss, with prejudice, philosophical pessimism along with Last Tuesdayism, as they are rejected by all humans who are not so arrogant as to think their logic is metaphysically precise and omnipotent. According to the false pretense of logic of postmodernists, they cannot be ignored because they cannot be falsified, but POR adopts the scientism of Karl Popper, and reject them because they cannot be falsified, and an unfalsifiable theory is not one worth considering. Any theory that cannot be falsified is false. The POR approach accepts that our beliefs could be falsified, but have not been, and so they are as true as true can get, for all practical purposes. Perhaps POR will someday be superseded by an even more true hypothesis, or perhaps it will be disproven by someone beating the thumbswitch test, or producing HAL or Doctor Dolittle, or uttering a word that has the logical certainty of a mathematical calculation. Until one of these things happens, though, POR, including the theory that communication is something more than signaling, and narcissistic selection is more than replication of mutations, is as close to the truth as we can get.

What we actually believe happened, back in the predawn darkness of paleolithic prehistory, is that a genetic mutation occurred in an ape which enabled its brain to continue to <u>function even when it became dysfunctional</u>. Instead of relying on sense data, as all animal brains always do, it imagined data that didn't come from its senses. An idea occurred, a thought was thought, a fiction was fantasized, something that had never happened before in any other animal's brain. Then more ideas, because once one happens another 'logically' follows from it, and it/she/they imagined that perhaps the same thing was occurring in another ape's brain. This theory of mind cannot be directly tested, to this day there is no logical method for doing so. With all of our technology and medical science, we can only presume that it happens, and find ourselves incapable of disproving it, because it continues to happen.

Cogito Ergo Sum. Cogito ergo sum locqui. Words have meaning. These must be true, because to question whether they are true is to prove that they are true.

It is theoretically possible (at least according to postmodernist philosophical logic) that no human being has consciousness except you, and every other human being is somehow just mimicking having consciousness. It is equally possible, logically, then, that you don't have consciousness either, you only act as if you do. But this doesn't disprove your consciousness; instead it disproves logic. Why and how this could be, that you are conscious, or that other people are conscious, or even that other people are not conscious, is something that it would require teleologies, not simply tautologies, to understand or express. We will ignore it, just as we ignore the 'brain in a jar' hypothesis, along with the Matrix and Inception premise, and also the dreaming butterfly and Last Tuesdayism, wherein we imagine that the universe began last Tuesday at 2:27 PM, or any other arbitrary moment, and only appears to be older because it came into existence in a condition that would make it appear older. We aren't interested in swallowing our tails here, so let us return to the ancient campfire or cave where human consciousness first emerged.

Human beings are just like any other creatures in at least one important way: we do not have free will. Our consciousness does not control our body, our conscious thoughts are the result, not the cause, of our neural anatomy and the information it somehow contains. So in effect (more properly in affect; metaphorically) we are all biological robots, but our self-awareness is not the control program. It is an impotent homunculi, a powerless ghost in the shell. We are robot monkeys, trapped inside an apparatus that we can see taking actions. We even have an array of indicators in front of us, enabling us to <u>see</u> that things are occurring inside the robot, invisible from outside, but not to <u>control</u> them. This is an analogy to both the fact that we can feel internal sensations that are not necessarily evident to the outside, and also that we are aware of what movements our body is in the process of performing before they, too, become evident to others. Our minds become aware of our choices through our brain's neurological processing. We do not choose how we feel about what we experience, we simply experience what we feel about what we choose.

Harkening back to the thumbswitch experiment, we know when we have grown weary of staring at the existing picture, but not whether we have decided to change it, and we also know when we have chosen to change it but our thumb has not yet moved. The intricate apparatus of the experimenter somehow 'knows' when the choice occurs before we do, but the button is not pushed until after we have 'decided' to do so. Trapped without free will, knowing we are trapped but not knowing we have no free will, and yet wondering if there are other minds likewise trapped but self-determining, how are we to find out if those other robot monkeys also have minds inside of them? How can we test our theory of mind? How can we alert others to the existence of our own mind? The answer is to act in a way that is unexpected enough that we attract attention, but not so unexpected that we are behaving randomly. If the other monkey responds by also acting in a way that is 'unpredictable', but not incomprehensible, then perhaps our theory is valid. This is not a conscious chain of reasoning, obviously enough. Theory of mind is not something than can be tested, or that needs to be tested. You either have it or you don't. And you do, because you must if you use language. Words are not logical data, they are not judged to be comprehensible based on their deductive consistency or calculated probabilities. They are informative because they are **not** logically predictable, but they are also **not** meaninglessly arbitrary. Whether we consider this state a wide plateau of comprehensibility, or a razor's edge of consciousness, is a matter of perspective. By unconsciously theorizing the existence of mind in the other robot monkeys, we provide the conscious ability to communicate with those other minds.

Proper understanding of this 'origin of language', as a way of communicating imagined ideas rather than transmitting factual data, enables us to recognize that the historical development of language in the human species is reiterated in the mental development of language in human children. The postmodern assumption, of ape-men evolving intelligence as a mathematical aptitude, leads to the hypothesis that successive generations of humans have become better and better at calculating what words to use. But the formulations of language are not logical, nor genetic. Every human being demonstrates an instinct for language, learning it without conscious effort as toddlers. But no humans demonstrate that language is instinctive, it always requires conscious development. This is a 'bootstrap effect' which puts all other bootstrap effects to shame as mere metaphors. In the case of language, and our instinct to learn it without learning it by instinct, we have an example of levitation by tugging on our own shoestrings. Rationally, it is the same effect that is narcissistic selection. In truth, it is the same affect that is God. It results from, and causes, it embodies and dictates, morality, theology; altruism, compassion, love, and hope, and happiness.

Language does not serve the purpose of logic, it is not about data transfer. Its purpose is more shibboleth than encryption; it evidences the theory of mind by imagining the theory of mind. The capacity to reason, to compare all possibilities, both real and imagined, until the truth can be discerned despite logical tests being insufficient, unreliable, and therefore useless. The capacity to reason is synonymous with language and with consciousness. Which we consider the epistemological, which the ontological, and which the theological manifestation is unimportant. But it is important that we accept and recognize, even if we can't ever quite understand, that they are different. What any word means is neither a unilateral, Humpty Dumpty dictate, nor an authoritarian, dictionary lookup. It is both, as illumination is both particles and waves. We each and all constantly test the jellybean mystery to determine which is more important, and nobody can predict which is which, or which is right, with any certainty. God cannot, math cannot, because we have self-determination. The meaning and purpose of our consciousness, and our words, is not logic, but reason. Epistemology is the study of meaning, origins; it is linguistical. Ontology is the study of being, existence; it is empirical. And theology is the study of purpose, morality; it is judgmental.

Our next step, then, is addressing morality directly. The next section will be an effort to formulate a better morality than previous efforts, both theistic religion and atheistic science, have accomplished. We are still searching for happiness and hope, after all. Is there any way we can imagine finding it, and relieving ourselves of the existential angst that is making our lives and our society so difficult and monstrous?

Morality

Instead of considering the origin of consciousness from the historic perspective, as we just tried (all too unsuccessfully, I'm sure) to do, let's think about it from an existential perspective. If we aren't allowed to use any words for any things unless we have direct experience of them, how are we to speak? "I" is the first word; it needs no more direct experience than our existence to justify it. But any description of 'I' requires some kinesthetic or judgmental sense, so even seemingly self-limited abstractions as 'feel' or 'hope' or even 'think' can only really be recognized as some comparison to other things, and these other things must be defined first to have meaning, in this exercise in existential philosophy, at least. "Am" is the only real possibility to follow 'I', since it has already been defined by the utterance of 'I', as the experiencing of existence. And then, again, we falter, because without any empirical universe of sense data beyond our intellectual existence, particular descriptions or qualities or aspects or experiences of being are disallowed. "I am me" is simply repetition, a linguistic form that illustrates the pronoun, but without any philosophical significance beyond "I", or "I am". Kinesthetic experiences such as "I am hungry" require some hypothesis of having a body, abstract experiences like "I am alone" need some alternative to be comprehensible. "I am nothing" is contradictory to "I am", so that cannot be the next thought. "I am God", even if we accept that the idea of a deity is automatic in the presumption of existence, is an arrogant assumption without experiential evidence. We could go through the list of possibilities, rejecting each one as requiring some more primitive idea or word or experience in order to be acceptable. How can we define or recognize or describe our being, without words or empirical occurrences already available? Words are defined in context, and so although "I" and "am" (be/being) are innately and necessarily defined by the unquestionable existence of our ability to wonder if 'we are', almost every possible thought beyond that violates the rules of our examination.

There is only one exception, in fact. Anything but this one needs some other thing apart from 'I am' to define, describe, or justify it. This only acceptable word works because it is really nothing more than an inversion of the first one, and in a way that doesn't require any postulation of a physical universe in which to perform or explain the inversion. It isn't "I am alive", because there isn't any known alternative to being alive, yet, and so that would actually be just a repetition of "I am". "I am dead" fails because it invents that alternative to being without any way of making it clear what that is, requiring a logical universe where being dead is necessarily the opposite of being alive, and the two cannot both be true, nor can neither be true at the same time. I state these things not to declare them as absolutes you must accept as your own opinion, but simply to narrate this exploration. Hopefully this text will guide your understanding and knowledge, but there is no way to mandate that from this side of the communication, from behind this existential wall. In this way, your "I" is both identical to my "I", but also the inverse, as my "I" is opposite but not different from your "I". And so this is the answer to our quest, there is only one way to finish a complete thought, without any need to or possibility of any additional entities being envisioned, even though we are creating a new word. Because it isn't a new word, it is just a different form of the first word, having no more and no less meaning, existing only because it must in order for the possibility of its existence to be imagined. "You".

"I am you." The only next comprehensible thought, any other idea requires inventing a primitive by imagining it could exist, rather than discovering a primitive that must exist whether we imagine it or not, as "I" and "am" do. We prove that we exist by being able to question our existence, cogito ergo sum, but that is not what causes us to exist. What causes us to exist is not that thought or the question it answers, but our capacity to think, which is the words we use to have these thoughts. Descartes' infamous principle, the cogito, does not explain what our existence is, it only illustrates it. What our existence is, is theory of mind. And theory of mind, absent even the logical primitives or words 'theory', 'of', or 'mind', is "I am you."

This is defined in POR as the Universal Statement of Consciousness and Identity. It is the basis of all morality. Not just Philosophy Of Reason theology, but truly all moral senses, whatsoever, in the human mind, the outside universe, or any other being capable of language. It is beyond self-defining or self-evident, it is even more inescapable and undeniable and logically unquestionable than the cogito ("dubito, ergo cogito, ergo sum", or "ego cogito, ergo sum"). What is more, it isn't even just a philosophical idea, it is a very real fact. Of course, physically I am not you, and you are not me; I am me and you are you. Our bodies are separate. But our existence as thinking beings is not. Analytically, we are simply both the same species of ape; we have the same ancestors, somewhere along the line, no matter how distant our relation might be. (Of course, this is true of all organisms on earth, but only those who can use language are part of our analysis.) Rhetorically, we are still two different people, but the distinction grows more inexact, since you are "I" to you, and your "I" is "you", to me. This pronoun inversion, the nature of grammatical 'person', reflects (no pun intended) our rhetorical simultaneity. Metaphorically, we actually return to the physical scrutiny of our existence, and this is how the Universal Declaration of Consciousness and Identity becomes not just profound but literally true.

POR is a materialist philosophy. In the Philosophy Of Reason, we accept that our thoughts are not subjective, they objectively occur. Despite still being unidentifiable, or at least indecipherable, by any external process, only by our internal consciousness, the physical reality of our thoughts is undeniable. We do not need to know exactly which electromagnetic or chemical fluctuations correspond to them, which changes in our brain cells encompass them, to know that they do physically occur inside our heads. The electrical impulses of neurological processing (whether the cause, the result, or the essence of our thoughts is irrelevant) that are our thoughts are objective occurrences that only happen in the physical universe because the laws of physics apply to them as much as to any other occurrence in the physical universe. We have no need of supernatural spirits or souls, although our thoughts, as words, do possess and present a metaphysical character, in the strictest sense of that word. But more than simply physical is still also physical, and the ambiguities of real language allow us to see that it is still entirely physical. All the 'meta' aspects of this physical existence of words, and the thoughts they convey, are perhaps fictional, and so whether their being is only physical or also metaphysical, or even maybe only metaphysical without being physical, is mere poetic musing. The point is that our thoughts, as illogical as they may be, are still <u>physically occurring in our brains</u>, and so they have objective existence. They are not just mental images, because physical neurological incidences (processes) must occur in our cerebral tissue to produce or result from mental images. Cogito Ergo Sum, cogito ergo sum loqui. (Also, "honor est"; I think therefore I must be. Even Latin is not the precise and logical grammatical code that modernists and postmodernists through the ages have thought it was or should be.)

I am. The capacity to make that declaration, whether dictate, mandate, conclusion, or hope, demands that this 'being' be a physical existence. The physical, objective existence of my thoughts, which is the part of me that is truly "I", is my consciousness, my language, my self-determination. *And yours is no different.* If my consciousness were somehow magically transferred into your brain, I would not be thinking my thoughts, I would be thinking yours. Your consciousness is the same as mine. If I were in your shoes, if I were in your position, rhetorically "If I were you" remains a comprehensible way of differing with what you already know, feel, or plan, but while the first two are obvious metaphors, the last one is no less metaphorical, a figure of speech, not a real truth. The real, analytical, concrete truth is "If I were you, I would be you, not me, and think your thoughts, and desire your wants, and take the same actions that you are taking, with all the same doubts or certainties that you have about their ethical righteousness." I am you.

It is no mere coincidence, nor evidence of a theistic deity or supernatural spirituality, that this universal declaration is part of the foundation of every widely held organized religion, as the 'Golden Rule', or some comprehensible version of it. The Golden Rule itself, "treat others as you would have them treat you", fails utterly as a logical statement. What if you are a masochist who enjoys suffering, does that mean you should cause others to suffer? What if you are a sociopath and are completely apathetic of other's well-being, does that mean that they should be apathetic towards your existence? In the postmodern world of 'evolutionary psychology' and faith in the biological advantage of altruism, it is often considered to be something of a quid-pro-quo bargain; "I treat you well *so that* you will treat me well, (but I treat me well because I am a product of selfish genes)". The greater truth is closer to "I treat me well so that you will treat me well, regardless of whether you treat you well." But it is not great enough a truth, because it is based on a lie, that compassion is only self-regard masquerading as greed, an indirect way of bolstering my reproductive survival more than yours. The postmodern conclusion is that ethics and the golden rule are premises of reciprocity. In this theory of evolutionary psychology, the primitive form of the social compact is nitpicking; literal picking of lice, not the metaphor for trivial criticisms. The 'secular humanist' deistic theology is: "If we can all just be self-sacrificing enough, that will satisfy our selfish genes; if we are good, the universe will reward our species with continued survival." It is kind-hearted and optimistic, but not the logic it purports to be. Nor is it true. Just as the problem of induction does not evaporate with postmodern faith in logic, the problem of evil is not overwhelmed by good intentions, the hypocritical postmodern hope for karma. Bad things (can) happen to good people, and all species are doomed to eventual extinction. If altruism is good, it is because it gives hope, not because it somehow mandates or relies on reciprocity.

"I am you." The basis of all morality, and consciously and conscientiously the center, if not the sum total, of POR theology. We call it the Universal Principle of Identity for what should be obvious reasons. Any being that has the self-awareness we might refer to as 'sentience', which must have theory of mind and language in order to produce, exemplify, or demonstrate that self-awareness, shares this same Universal Statement, of Consciousness, and of Identity. The Universal Declaration (of Identity and Consciousness) does not need to be recognized, let alone admitted to, but it is universal and necessary, nevertheless. It is **The Theory Of Mind**, the one that is *theory of mind*, not simply *a* theory of mind. It is both the supposition that other people have minds, not just brains and whatever results come from them, and the proof that you have a mind, that you can grasp the meaning and importance that other people's minds aren't really different than yours, even though they embody and encompass different thoughts and feelings. They aren't different than the thoughts and feelings you would have, if your mind were in their brain, just as their brains would generate your mind if they had your mind.

You've no doubt noticed that I have been inconsistent in whether we call this great truth, this linguistic formula so profound we label it with a proper noun, a 'declaration' or a 'statement', and also what order the words 'identity' and 'consciousness' are listed, or even if both are stated. This is not a typographic error or failure in editing. It is done purposefully; so much so that I'm not going to explain it further. Just know that it isn't accidental, nor is it inadvertent, but neither is it meaningless or without purpose. It is considered an integral part of the Universal Declaration of Identity itself.

The more familiar expression of the Golden Rule, "do unto others..." whether from Leviticus, Mathew, Tirukkura, or any other source, is not always considered a law of reciprocity. But it generally is one, anyway, as any other (non-POR) religious context demands a miraculous imposition of justice on the universe, whether a theistic deity or theological force of karma. The Universal Principle of Identity and Consciousness empowers and signifies the optimistic, hopeful nature of the Golden Rule, whether the Rule is expressed positively or negatively. Still, "Love your neighbor as yourself", in all its various philosophical and linguistic forms, remains insufficient for capturing the entirety of the POR principle of the Universal Statement. The Universal Statement of Consciousness is not a demand or commandment, it is a fact, a reality, and independent of what we might do based on our comprehension of it. It does not require categorical imperatives, it is not a request to avoid hypocrisy, although a reasonable understanding of it will unavoidably suggest that imperatives be categorical and that hypocrisy is unjust.

Ultimately, "I am you", and the principle that is not a re-expression of the Golden Rule, evidence of karma, or any other ethical optimism about reciprocity or supernatural balancing of intentions and consequences, puts the self-sacrifice back in altruism. That entirely illogical, in fact logically incomprehensible, idea of selflessness, actual self-sacrifice and not calculated self-interest, ruins all theological philosophies that attempt to be rational or even rationalistic. Being good is not rational; hope is not rational; love is not just hormones and neural networks. If the reason you are kind is ***so that*** God will reward you with eternity in heaven, then you are being selfish, not kind. If morality is bound by rationality, the way ethics is, then it is no longer morality, no matter how ethical it might appear. "I am you" summarizes all of this, while still only being a self-evident observation about the meaning of those three words and the physics of the seemingly non-physical abstractions of consciousness and identity. Humans have a 'being' that is more than that of any biological creature, we have a 'being' that is even beyond that of any physical object or substance. It is intellectual, but that does not make it subjective, it is abstract but that does not mean it is vague. It is universal, but that does not dilute it to homeopathic uselessness.

The essence of POR is language, and the essence of morality is honesty. Truth is all that binds the two.

The balance of all of the moral, theological, ethical, or spiritual guidance that the science and religion of the Philosophy Of Reason can provide is itself potentially less accurate than the Universal Declaration. The Universal Statement is the ultimate truth, and POR is just an attempt to grapple with it, address it, explain and communicate it. Primarily, POR concerns the use of words, rhetoric, language. POR does not support moral codification using hypothetical examples, it teaches that moral analysis only applies in **real** and present circumstances, not abstract hypothetical examples. Of course, the use of POR in performing any moral analysis cannot be taught without some gedanken, thought experiments. Yet any such narratives used to explain how to use the Philosophy Of Reason to perform philosophical considerations of ethics and theology are necessarily abstract and essentially hypothetical, no matter how dutifully we try to use real world cases. And so, like Socrates' erroneous analysis of virtue, these gedankenexperiments fail, but without demonstrating the failure in the principles being analyzed. Simply describing a real situation in which moral analysis is possible artificially limits the scope of the consideration and predetermines the results. So trying to teach virtue with definitions or with imaginary examples or hypothetical narratives would make it seem as if I am providing codified dictates. If I were to describe what is *good* with some conundrum involving whether or not to confront your mother on some ethical lapse, this could become a general commandment to be unkind to your mother or chastise people on that ethical lapse, neither of which would be categorically essential or even supported in POR morality. So while I might provide some rather broad ethical guidelines on personal responsibility or particularly sensitive socio-political issues, the present examination will be restricted to essentially repeating the application of the Universal Declaration to relatively mundane circumstances. After that, I will present some discussion on the 'rhetorical guidelines' of POR, before trying to tackle the more contentious political areas of philosophy.

I am you. The imperative to treat every person with dignity that naturally follows from such a Declaration is obvious. But does this 'mandate of dignity' mean only speaking of or to people in flattering terms, with endless self-effacing politeness, unable to criticize ignorance or stupidity? Definitely not. The whole point of the Universal Statement of Consciousness is to accept that there is a real and comprehensible basis for morality, besides either theism or evolutionary psychology, and so enable judgment, both mercifully yet also mercilessly. Similar to the mythical 'rewards of the afterlife' and the 'adaptive altruism' justifications for being good, the ethics of POR theology does not just allow but demands some amount of self-sacrifice. Conscientiously, the degree of actual sacrifice of dignity we demand of ourselves in POR is greater than what these eleemosynary mumpsimuses exert from their followers in practice, but not necessarily as much as they piously demand from others. The necessary and sufficient amount cannot be dictated by any outside authority, though, it must be self-determined. This 'razors edge' balancing of adopting altruistic intentions along with pragmatic limits is part of the nature of things, and can't be side-stepped with either doctrine or dogma. A proper understanding of the Universal Principle of Identity emphasizes that neither, intentional ignorance or imagined reciprocity, is enough to justify self-centered actions. Greed justified by even the most practical fear of future deprivation is still greed, and wrong. Hoarding is illicit, even in times of plenty, and all the more so in times of poverty. But these truisms become hopelessly vague. We might as well say that the Universal Statement of Consciousness reduces to merely "be fair", and think the job of developing a POR theology is complete. The POR way is to recognize that language, not control (or power), is at the root of the human experience, so it is worth thinking for a bit about what exactly we mean when we use the word "fair", and how postmodernism seems to limit it artificially.

Through the process of postmodern over-synonimization, people are taught to think of 'fair' as essentially being identical to 'equal'. Of course, the basic premise of 'fairness' is considered childishly simplistic, and approximated that way, "the same (equal) for everyone" when it is taught to children. We ignore or deny the complexities of the simplistic philosophical dictate, pretend that applying it in the real world is just as simple as imposing it (inconsistently, but while denying any possibility of such inequality) on children. The familiarity of the phrase "fair and equal" reinforces this notion of 'equal' and 'fair' being identical (POS) for those who are still subject to Socrates' Error, while to those of us who accept the Philosophy Of Reason that same conventional coupling demonstrates the opposite. Fair and equal do not mean the same thing, as evidenced by the fact that they are both individually mentioned, but not tautologically redundant; fair must mean something different than equal, because they are two different words. But of course, as a first approximation of what a fair result is, a result that rewards multiple parties equally is a good starting point. And only that; a starting point, not a dictate or conclusion. To take the classical over-simplification of dividing up a pie into slices for a group of people, if no other considerations are taken into account, then each should receive a slice of equal size. But reasoning is not logic, to be reduced to the simplicities of a mathematical calculation. Unlike a logical process of decision-making, when being reasonable it is imperative that we take all possible considerations into account. So we cannot accept that there are no other considerations to be considered than the size of the pie and the number of people to serve. In POR theology, we have to compare such things as how hungry each person is, how much they like pie in general or this particular kind, and whether future availability of pie is foreseeable to be accounted for. The characteristics of people could be relevant, whether because large people might need more pie or might need to eat less, and children might be more delighted by the pie but might also customarily get less, whether for discipline or for lack of seniority. POR does not mandate a pre-defined function for deserving pie, it does not support treating even such a seemingly precise example, of dividing one up, as if it were more about quantities than qualities. So to be fair, we have to leave it up to whoever baked and served the pie to determine how to slice it, and consider if everyone is equally satisfied with the result before anyone starts to eat. In this way, the mundane example of fairness comes out almost exactly as the conventional ethical theories would require. And it equally requires honesty and sincerity on the part of all the participants to be reasonable rather than cunning in their actions and statements. This last point is essential and incredibly important, and the Achilles Heel of postmodern ethics and IPTM-based perspectives on morality. Cunning, calculation, even a desire to try to get the best result for yourself, is the opposite of good. This is because I Am You, so I should be concerned for your benefit more than I am for my own. And yet, complete self-sacrifice, willingly allowing others to take advantage of you through their own efforts of cunning and calculation, however nuanced the manipulation or maneuvering, is also not acceptable. This is also because I Am You, and only what benefits us both as much as possible is acceptable to me, regardless of whether it is acceptable to you, or rather regardless of whether you are aware what the benefit is to you or what should be acceptable to you. Again, simply assuming that numeric equality, that quantification and equal measurable portions of benefit, is fairness, is not what fairness means.

This general idea of fairness and equality, and how they are complementary but not identical, is a more important, less trivial outcome of the Universal Declaration of Consciousness and Identity than you might expect. Looked at blandly, "I am you" merely parallels a utilitarian approach, demanding that we treat others as we feel we should be treated, and desire that others treat us at least as well as they treat themselves. Such a bland approach mirrors the ancient philosopher's ideal of "virtue" more closely than the more pious, more contemporary interpretation that most people are familiar with. When Socrates used his famous Method to attempt to deconstruct the term "virtue", he was not investigating a theistic mandate of 'good', but a more pragmatic belief held by pre-modern and early modern moral theorists. This more primitive understanding of the meaning of the word 'virtue' is that acting in a proper way materially rewards the virtuous person, rather than simply promising spiritual rewards from a benevolent deity. Of course, this more ancient approach to virtue is seen clearly in postmodern "prosperity gospel" evangelical movements, but these focus even more strongly on the idea of a metaphysical deity ensuring that virtue is rewarded, rather than the mechanics of physical existence doing so. These prosperity gospel advocates, in this way, can be described as implementing a sort of 'ultra-piety' philosophy. It is not my intention to chastise these particular believers. In fact, the reason I mention them is to express understanding, rather than either condemnation or admiration, for their doctrine.

This coincides with a more general principle of POR as a religion, that it is the sum of all religions. Not a replacement for them so much as a superset of them. The personal desire to practice the particular rituals or memorize the mythological doctrine or narratives of any specific religious tradition is relieved somewhat by understanding POR, just as POR lessens the compulsion to escape reality or treat existential angst with drugs or suicide. POR makes the comfort of scriptural religions less attractive, so it is not expected that it will encourage fealty to historical creeds. But it does not condemn them, and so while it explains the universe and human morality without resorting to theism or fundamentalism, it could very well lead to a resurgence rather than a cessation of worship-centered practices. The postmodern atheist is instructed to abhor religion and to degrade its practitioners, (while denying they are doing so, and attacking anyone who would make such a claim) justifying this bigotry using stereotypes of theocratic extremists, as if every person trying to do good is evil unless they accept the fundamentalist dogma of anti-religious IPTM atheism. Even inconsistent theism is preferable to anti-religious atheism, so the religious atheism of POR morality rejects IPTM as arrogant and conceited, a misguided worship of mathematics as a pointedly amoral God. The worst kind of God there can be: ruthless without compassion, tyrannical without mercy, all-knowing but absent all wisdom. The kind of God only a fundamentalist zealot would invoke, and only to impose It on others, never to limit their own zealotry.

So in this way, all well-intentioned religious thought is unavoidably compatible with basic POR theology, even the ones that preach the spiritual value of relatively self-serving forms of theism, like prosperity gospels. Religion, after all, is attractive because it is ultimately of service to the faithful. Indeed, the more drastically self-sacrificing doctrines, it turns out, can be more alien to our intellectual approach than those that are more conscientiously egotistical. Those that demand unlimited self-sacrifice, that thrive on martyrdom, are far more shallow than a 'God helps those that help themselves' approach. But all religions, as I suggested, are acceptable complements to POR morality, particularly, of course, when they express a Golden Rule parallel to POR's Universal Statement. Although the Philosophy Of Reason is studiously atheistic, this is because it has no need for a theistic deity to explain the drive of the human conscience, not because it is hostile to deism, the idea of a transcendent being Who defines *good* beyond mortal ken. Historically, the development of both organized religion and personal spirituality, particularly in the age of postmodern philosophy, can be seen as an unrecognized acknowledgment of the truth of the Fundamental Schema, the Universal Declaration, and the morality of POR. As a religion, POR is a superset of religious faith, not an alternative to it. God can be perceived as more than a physical or supernatural entity, not a simple Being but the *metaphysical nature of words and being*, in and of Itself. Words are things that transcend and triumph over selfish individual goals or the limitations of physics or utilitarian rationing of either dignity or material goods. "I am You" means that serving ourselves is never enough, but sacrificing our selves is not acceptable, either. We must accept that there is a metaphorical number of jellybeans in the jar, in order to know that some guesses are better than others, and sometimes even better than the average, but it is not for us to know which is which, because a metaphorical number is not a number, but the opposite of all numbers. We do not worship anything in the New Church of Hope, but we do celebrate words, because Hope is such a word, and so is God, and whether there is any difference between The Two is just another guess we each must make for ourselves.

The bland style of the Universal Statement, again, suggests that only equality is necessary for virtue. But the more insightful premise must include our awareness that fairness is not simply equality, and requires a sincere and honest appraisal of both need and ability. Since the profoundly truthful nature of POR's explanation of human existence and social interactions provides those who understand it with an 'inner peace' and non-complacent comfort that no other philosophy can, it is endemic on us to do more than simply treat other people well. We must attempt to treat them as well as we possibly can, it means treating them better than they treat us, even if it means treating them better than we treat ourselves. This true altruism still falls short of the self-sacrifice demanded by some faiths that glorify humility in a paradoxical worship of the self, or at least falls short of the martyrdom which the advocates of such religions intend to impose on others. Without the cynically hopeful reward of heaven to justify a false altruism, we can rely only on that true altruism. The limit of this more conscientious generosity is most easily expressed in the familiar instruction given to passengers on airplanes concerning how they should behave if an emergency occurs and the oxygen masks drop from the ceiling: put the mask on yourself before attempting to aid others. This counter-balancing moral mandate, that one should not be so self-sacrificing that it becomes an empty, even counter-productive gesture, should be seen as the only justifiable limit on our ethical interpretation of the Universal Declaration of Identity. This principle of only helping ourselves enough in order to help others even more is the triumph over 'adaptive altruism' that doomed genetic selflessness. The reason that evolutionary psychiatry, or any other scientific or biological premise, cannot underlie real morality is because morality is not an evolutionary imperative, even though it is an evolutionary result. Goodness cannot be assumed based on any particular result, even and in fact especially not a successful result. It requires language and reasoning, good intentions, not just intent, to be goodness. Whenever it even approaches the fallacy of fait accompli reasoning, it is no longer reasonable, and so it is no longer reason, and it may be animal cunning but cannot be *good*.

There is an important illustration of this principle of self-aware goodness requiring more than just self-awareness, in POR. It involves the idea of a just society. This refers to the philosophical gedanken of the philosopher John

Rawls referred to as the "veil of ignorance". In Rawls' thought experiment, he proposed that a just society can only be ethically designed if the designer is kept unaware of what station and role they will hold in the society they are designing. A bland consideration of the Universal Statement of Identity and Consciousness would adopt this utilitarian conclusion. The Philosophy Of Reason, and our most insightful interpretation of the Universal Statement, requires a more forceful imperative, which we will call the principle of "*the universal fool*". A truly just society, if designed by a purposeful designer who must then live their life within it, cannot be based on a mere veil of ignorance, essentially a crapshoot where one might gamble that one is fortunate to find themselves one of the privileged members of this engineered civilization. To ensure that both the intended society is actually fair to every inhabitant, and to implement the mandate expressed in the Universal Declaration of Consciousness, the designer must construct a world in which they are fully aware that they will hold the least privileged, least dignified, least luxurious role and station. Only that is sufficient to allow the engineer to know that they are acting morally, that their society will be just, that their behavior is virtuous. They must be, we must be willing to be, the universal fool, the most reviled and discredited member of the community. Of course, this is a gedanken, and we do not have the opportunity to invent a commonwealth from scratch, to draft a social compact de novo. So no acts of ultimate self-sacrifice are mandated by our acceptance of the Universal Statement of Identity and the POR morality that it entails. Still, we must always be willing to adopt the role of the universal fool. Like the acquiescence to self-determination, which effectively replicates the abandonment of ego adopted by the born-again Christian who has put themselves in the hands of God, this willingness to suffer for the good of others, to be the universal fool in a Rawlsian state, is profoundly, if paradoxically, freeing and comforting. The confidence, if not certitude, that POR theology provides can be viewed, paradoxically, as arrogance to people who are unfamiliar with the theology. The willing servility of the principle of the universal fool can counter the danger of pompous pride that might result from our conviction that POR, the Universal Declaration, and the Fundamental Schema are the ultimate philosophical framework for human consciousness and the nature of morality.

Argument

The balance of POR's more specific theological guidance, as mentioned previously, resolves to guidelines for our rhetoric. The nature of human communication already described, in terms of both the jellybean diagram and the evolution of human consciousness and language, is that our words exist not to transmit sense data and debate axiomatic truth, but to discuss feelings about sense data and present real truth. This is actually an even more radical contravention of the postmodern theory of language than it might sound. So far, I've described POR as basically just an anti-postmodernism, a reaction to IPTM and evolutionary psychology. But overcoming Socrates' Error is still not enough. The truth is like a hologram, there is always more to it than it appears, and there is more wisdom to POR than even I am aware, though I invented it. (Or discovered, or developed, we should have left such pedantic quibbling behind already.) There are truths beyond what you can yet imagine, the explication of which would make the 'psychobabble-like' rambling I've already committed all too often in this book seem tame in comparison. Truths so true that saying them would be even more preposterous than anything I've said so far. The meaning of words is both a thing and its opposite? Causation and selection are just fantasies? How about the idea that something is only true if both forward and backwards teleologies apply simultaneously? And that is only just scratching the surface. Language is still yet more powerful than that, and so learning how to use it well truly goes beyond simply convincing other people what words to use to be most accurate. But that practice, being most accurate with words, is what we will focus on now.

Adapting our linguistic instincts to a postmodern world is a process that is necessary, since we have to try to communicate with postmodernists. But it should also be conscientiously resisted, because our goal is to improve, not just accept, that postmodern world. Ultimately, our goal is to move past postmodernism, but to do that, we must convert postmodernists to our way of thinking, which is to say, to thinking, rather than simply convincing yourself you are being logical and using a bad interpretation of critical thinking skills to dismiss any opposing opinions. Critical thinking is lack of thinking, pretending to be computers so that we don't have to think but can simply dismiss ideas we don't like. <u>We need to learn to read for comprehension, rather than to read only well enough to justify criticism</u>. We have to accept, in a real way, that words are the masters. And so the practice of POR is not a conscientious adoption of a certain moral framework, it is purposeful acceptance of a certain linguistic framework, with the moral framework, a true morality beyond any self-serving egotism, resulting autonomically, without conscious effort. So what are the rules of language we should adopt to find happiness, and allow us to help others find it, too? Volumes, entire libraries, can and will be written on these topics; I can only provide a scant outline here.

A distinction should be made between the *vocabulary of POR* (jargon or technical nomenclature) and *POR vocabulary guidelines* (ethical recommendations). The former is internal and specific, the latter is societal and categorical. The vocabulary of POR is that set of terms and conventions used within the philosophy to describe and identify the components of the philosophy. It can be subdivided that way: terms, and conventions. POR vocabulary guidelines are the theological practices of note that apply to all language, involving word choices as they are used to communicate about any topic outside of discussions about POR explicitly. The guidelines are of benefit regardless of whether the speaker is a POR adherent. They may be rejected, of course, either because the speaker wishes to deny the validity or coherent existence of this philosophy of reasoning, or simply because the guidelines are divorced from and potentially contrary to the definitions regurgitated from reference books or other authoritative usages. But the benefit of adopting POR vocabulary guidelines is not dependent on recognition or acknowledgment of the Philosophy Of Reason or its internal vocabulary. That statement was thorough and correct, but admittedly impractical to understand unless you already comprehend it, so I will repeat it with more casual language. Bear in mind, though, that the real idea was that prior arcane formulation, and this casual expression is also less accurate, and potentially dangerous because it is necessarily incomplete. Using words the way these guidelines suggest will help people both speak better and be happy, even if they don't have any idea what the point of it is, or don't believe that it is possible for what word they use to change their level of happiness, especially when they don't even understand why. But just because they aren't the words taught to them by school or society, that doesn't make the ones they use better than the ones we use. The ones we use are still better, and really better, in an absolute way, even though they'll be dismissed as 'semantics'. (That's one of the words involved in both the vocabulary of POR and the POR vocabulary guidelines, as you'll see. Not using it [except in the technical jargon usage of the vocabulary of POR] will make you happier, autonomically. Even if you call it 'automatically' instead.)

The main purpose of this chapter is presentation of the vocabulary guidelines. Before they are addressed, though, I will make mention of some of the more noticeable aspects of the internal vocabulary, the 'technical terms' of POR.

The most contentious terminology used in POR, which seeks to use rather than 'borrow' words from the broader language, is "epistemology". The divergence of what POR says it means and what classical postmodern philosophies say it means has already been explained, along with the reason for this behavior. To review, historically, based on its conscientious etymological construction, epistemology is defined as the study of knowledge. The POR hypothesis is that this is something of a ruse, because that aspect of philosophy has become mired in debate concerning the *meaning* of the word 'knowledge'. Not only because of this observation, and the nature of knowledge, but because it comports with the actual usage of the word 'epistemological', both in philosophical circles and more casual use, POR "redefines" it as the study of **meaning**. Knowledge, after all, is really just belief, but the word 'knowledge' is thought to name beliefs that have more ontological justification from beyond the existential wall than the ideas that we refer to as 'beliefs'. Knowledge is a kind of belief, and belief is a kind of knowledge. We should avoid allowing creeping POS to invade our POR, though, and it is not my intention or purpose to claim that knowledge and belief are so synonymous that they are identical, rhetorically interchangeable, or that one or the other could be said to not "really" exist. However, it is worth pointing out that the distinction between believing and knowing is, well, epistemological: categorical convention rather than ontological distinction, however well ingrained the line between knowledge and belief is thought to be. There is no objective distinction in the neurological engrams caused by factual beliefs and synthesized knowledge, nor any real difference in any other way, either: it is not the truth of facts that makes them accurate, but the proper interpretation of those facts. It is conventional to insist that one's own beliefs are objective, based on logic and facts, and others' beliefs that contradict one's own are not. This is the entire premise of postmodernism. The difficulty of knowing truth is not facts versus fiction, but correct interpretation of facts versus inaccurate application of statistics.

So I will accept the derision of postmodernists that insist I am misusing the word 'epistemic', and refuse to invoke some hair-splitting bit of semantic dissimilarity between 'epistemic' and 'epistemological'. Admittedly, I tend to prefer 'epistemological', when forced to decide between the two, for three reasons. First, it thoroughly makes a clear reference to 'logic', but in a contrarian fashion since epistemic reasoning is not logical. Second, it normalizes the names for the three branches of philosophy as redefined in POR: epistemology, ontology, and theology. And third, again contrarily, using 'epistemological' rather than 'epistemic' purposefully avoids the conventional acceptance of 'epistemic' as relating to supposedly quantifiable 'degrees of validity' that knowledge is described as having in postmodern philosophies. The distinctions between 'degrees of certainty' associated with the term 'epistemic' in postmodern references are qualitative, not quantitative; they only appear quantitative because they are enumerated, but they must be assessed using judgment rather than calculated from primitive measurements. And so to call them "degrees" is an epistemological metaphor, not an ontological analysis. Epistemology is about categories, which do not exist in nature and so they cannot be measured, only assigned with conscious, and hopefully conscientious, judgement.

The next most contentious term in POR is, of course, that one: postmodern. Postmodern, postmodernism, postmodernist (but not 'postmodernistic', a pointless construction that suggests a flavor without substance); these words are almost shamefully common in explanations of this Philosophy Of Reason. Opposing postmodernism is the central pillar of POR, and refers to practically all contrasting philosophical or linguistic opinions, along with their origin and intent. This can be confusing and problematic in precisely the same way as 'epistemology'. To postmodernists, the only philosophy that 'postmodern' should refer to is "post-modern philosophy", the Continental movement in academic philosophy that describes all truth as relative, and thus subjective, and thus objectively non-existent, or at least unachievable as knowledge. Helpfully, and in keeping with the observation that the opponents of POR provide far stronger proof of its validity than its proponents can, most critics of post-modernism conscientiously use the hyphenated form. POR intentionally refrains from doing so, as we categorize most if not all critics of post-modernism as postmodernists. But, then, POR recognizes that practically every educated person, whether formally instructed or receiving their instruction through societal osmosis, is a postmodernist. Not simply because we all live in the postmodern age, that period of time since Darwin provided a means to marry Socrates' Error to natural philosophy to beget the Information Processing Theory of Mind, but because no child has yet to benefit from being raised from birth to maturity with the Philosophy Of Reason, and every believer in POR as a secular study or a religious faith has to be a convert, knowingly abandoning their postmodern dogma. The POR idea of postmodernism unifies all of the sincere usages of the word, from postmodern art and architecture to post-modernist literature and philosophy. These are all cases where people have embraced, consciously or unconsciously, the theory that humanity is both free of the strictures of logic and should be bound by those strictures because everything else in the physical world is so encumbered.

If it becomes too uninformative, whether through shear repetition or the appearance of being hackneyed, there are potential substitutions for 'postmodernist'. In particular, these include 'hyper-rationalist', the term generally used in POR for atheist postmodernists. Specifically those who have fallen into the tar pit of Philosophical Pessimism, as distinguished from the effectively similar atheist postmodernists who are nihilists. Also 'fundamentalist', which is a more familiar word compared to the neologism 'hyper-rationalist', although again they are effectively similar in most cases. Of particular note is that 'fundamentalist' can be applied, in POR terminology, to postmodern atheist extremists as accurately as it is to postmodern theistic extremists, the more familiar usage. Atheist fundamentalists oppose this, of course, because in postmodern terminology, 'atheist' is defined as 'having no religious beliefs', rather than 'having the religious belief that there is no God'. Likewise, they want to insist that only organized religions are religions. The atheist fundamentalists are not free of religion, they are enthralled with it. They have been taught, or synthesized on their own, that organized religion (what they mean by 'religion') is the source of all of the evil that religious people do in the name of their religion. When you believe that all words and ideas are (or can and should be) logically consistent, and have a particular conventional set of words and ideas, dismissing all unconventional thoughts as illogical and therefore unworthy of consideration, this seems a reasonable position to take. As in POR, these atheist fundamentalists wonder why so many people believe in God even though Aristotle defined the basics of symbolic logic, the foundation of all scientific knowledge, all (to the postmodernist) true knowledge of the universe and humanity, thousands of years ago. Since this means, to the postmodernist atheist, that their thoughts are logical and religious people's thoughts are irrational, how could they not assume that any evil that religious people do is a result of their irrational thoughts?

But the results of this reasoning are not reasonable, typically incurring a condemnation of every religion other than the faith of the person doing the condemning, and so it fits the meaning of 'fundamentalism' that is more familiar when restricted to theistic practices and the theologies used to justify them. A fundamentalist is anyone who thinks that only their religion is true. The denial by atheists, that their belief that there is no God is not religious, and the only belief that should be acceptable to anyone with any intelligence, is inconsequential. They are still fundamentalists, and their atheism is still a religious belief. But to salve their defensive ire, 'hyper-rationalist' can be used instead of 'atheist fundamentalist' or just 'fundamentalist', since they will usually consider it a compliment, rather than the less-than-flattering description that it actually is. From the perspective of the hyper-rationalist, it is not possible to be too rational. This rationalization, significantly, links the atheism of communist totalitarians to the immorality they engage in. This link between anti-religion atheism and tyrannical immorality is avidly denied by the anti-religious postmodernist with a "No True Scotsman" argument which, in their faith, should be dismissed as a logical fallacy. Noting the hypocrisy of this attitude will generally incite a (rhetorically) violent tendency in the hyper-rationalist, rather than the self-reflecting insight it would if their religion of anti-religion were as rational as they believe it is.

Drifting into a discussion of vocabulary guidelines, as opposed to jargon, the meaning of 'rational' becomes relevant here, obviously. I don't want to belabor the issue too much, since like all words it becomes ineffable if we try to chop it into pieces. It is not a word that POR has much use for, and we tend to avoid it because it is made ambiguous by IPTM and Socrates' Error. The origin, the meaning, of the word 'rational' is numeric, mathematical. Analytically speaking, the word is almost an exact synonym for 'logical'. More particularly, 'rational' is usually intended to mean 'logical and mental'.

People should be logical and rational, from the postmodern perspective, but computers are only logical, lacking mentality. So rhetorically, 'rational' is more closely related to 'reason', since when we say that someone is being 'rational', what we usually mean is that they are sane and reasonable. To use the term 'rational' strictly or technically, it should be thought of as referring to whether a person is capable of performing arithmetic, able to recognize the validity of simple arithmetic statements like "ten divided by two is five". In postmodern terms, rationality is the sum total of sanity, because the postmodern IPTM premise is simply that all good reasoning is logic. But in POR terms, rationality is actually a bad thing, an attempt to rationalize what is bad by considering it unavoidable or necessary. "We must kill those people; we have no other choice." That is a rational statement, and the purpose of human reasoning and morality is not to calculate and accept such necessity, but to refuse and overcome it. There is no downside to being rational, to the postmodernist, and so rationalizations become reasons, and Socrates' Error moves from gadfly party games, to trolling, and because of the tar pit problem, eventually graduates to terrorism.

Rationalism is merely a philosophical premise, but hyper-rationalism is essentially a religious doctrine, and an innately fundamentalist one, at that. To the hyper-rationalist, any rationalism short of hyper-rationalism is not rationalism. Since all rationalists have convinced themselves, deluded themselves into believing, that they are being rational, and that anyone who disagrees with any opinion they have is therefore not being rational, hyper-rationalism becomes a militant pseudo-atheism, a theism that simply substitutes mathematics for God. Since POR is itself atheist, we cannot use the term 'atheist' dismissively to criticize or describe rationalism, though the two are closely aligned in postmodern philosophies. We must always modify 'atheist' to specify non-POR atheism, so that the simple word 'atheism' can continue to mean an actual lack of theism, rather than a lack of religion. So we say 'fundamentalist atheist'/'atheist fundamentalist', or 'hyper-rational atheist', or 'rationalistic atheist', or of course 'postmodern atheist', when referring to atheists outside of the Philosophy Of Reason as a theological or religious doctrine or community.

Two other brief notes about terms related to postmodernism, specifically "postmodern over-synonimization", or POS, are worth mentioning. I'm aware that the spelling of the word "synonym" would suggest that "synonymization", rather than "synonimization", is the proper form. The use of the latter version is intentional, though not related to the technique or process or force of POS itself. Using the first 'i' in place of the second 'y' is a reference to postmodernism, though. "Synonymization" is an existing word, but is typically used (if it can even be said to ever be 'typically used') in the forms of 'synonymizing' or 'synonymized', except for a single, specific (pun intended) case. In taxonomy, the discipline of zoological or botanical naming for scientific purposes, 'synonymization' is the event or process of demonstrating that two different official designations for a type or clade of organism are 'synonyms', meaning they both always and only identify the same creature or plant. POR uses 'over-synonimization' not to distinguish what kind of synonyms are being referred to, but simply to confound postmodernists who faithfully believe that spelling is or should be logical. The second note about postmodern over-synonimization (POS) regards the acronym. As always, there are a couple of incidental points. First, that the acronym exists and is used, because the shorthand of simply reducing the cumbersome words into the still cumbersome "over-synonimization" is frowned upon. It is not that there are other kinds of over-synonymization that makes the apparent adjective necessary, but that the force behind, and unfortunate results of, the behavior is the reason it needs a name. There is another common usage of the same acronym, "POS", but the parallel is coincidental. Supposedly.

The second incidental note about the acronym is that it is not an acronym. Technically, if the subject of linguistics can be considered technical, it is an "initialism". Theoretically, the difference between acronym and initialism is whether the result is pronounced like a word or spelled out as letters. It is worth pointing out that this assignment of terms, of which is an acronym and which is an initialism, does not actually have any truly rational justification, and the two could very well be reversed, which might explain why only pedants usually comment on the distinction. Certainly it makes a difference in recognizing what a person is saying, whether they say "eff-bee-eye" or "FBI", or say "ess-sea-oh-tee-you-ess" instead of "SCOTUS". But knowing the word for which method of pronunciation to use is not as important, and predicting which will or could or should be used by convention is not as possible as it might seem to postmodernists. As evidence, I will remind you that neither usage of the initialism "POS" is pronounced "pos", "poss", or "poz", nor would anyone be confused if you call either usage of 'POS' an acronym. Many more people would be consternated by referring to it as an initialism, though, and this does not imply or infer that it is a lack of logical consistency, or that education in liberal arts conventions are inherent flaws in the human intellect.

Having dispensed with the incidental notes, the second main note about POS can be presented. Unfortunately, this again entails two sub-notes, spoiling the conceit that it will be as brief as promised, and increasing the chance this will all be dismissed as a pointless hodge-podge of hair-splitting. Still, the only remedy is to bravely press forward. The acronym/initialism is always capitalized entirely, as is typical for such things, and the hyphenation is ignored. So 'PoS', 'PS', 'PO-S' and 'PO' are not used. Also, part of the purpose for using the 'POS' form is a knowingly whimsical, if potentially problematic, homage-by-contrast to 'POR', the standard substitute for 'the Philosophy Of Reason'.

269

POR is also an initialism, by the way. It is always spelled out as "pee-oh-arr", never pronounced 'pore' or 'poor' or 'par'. Of course, "Philosophy Of Reason" has a whole laundry list of technical features in POR. The more correct but no more proper "<u>the</u> Philosophy Of Reason" is often used, but 'the POR' is not. Similarly, the full name is not written as "The Philosophy Of Reason" as an affectation, but occasionally as a proper noun, the way 'the truth' is sometimes signified as "The Truth", "the Truth", or "The truth" to contrast it with 'a truth'. Most importantly, though, you may have noticed that the word 'of' is always capitalized along with 'Philosophy' and 'Reason', to distinguish this particular philosophical theory from other movements or schools focusing on human reasoning. Most if not all alternative 'philosophies of reason' or even "Philosophies of Reasoning" are inherently postmodernist, or at least extensions of Socrates' Error, anyway. This means they assume that reasoning is mathematical, symbolic logic; throughout the previous two thousand years of history, this has been taken for granted, although it has always been false.

"Irrationalists" and "Absurdists" are examples of philosophical categories of philosophy that might parallel POR's premise that reasoning is not logic, but they are, ultimately, philosophies of logic, not philosophies of reason, and no more relevant to the Philosophy Of Reason than Utilitarianism or Pessimism. Which is to say that they are all both examples and counter-examples within POR, because the belief that any philosophy is logical, or logically distinguishable from other philosophies, is not part of POR. Because the preposition is unconventionally capitalized in the full name, the substitutes 'PR' or 'PoR' are obviously mistakes.

The abbreviation POR and the convention of capitalizing every word in 'Philosophy Of Reason', is in notable and purposeful contrast to the name for the organized religion celebrating POR as a faith, the 'New Church of Hope'. The preposition is never capitalized there, even when the tolerable but incorrect abbreviation "Church of Hope" is used. "New Church" is the more preferred substitute, but "New Church of Hope", and "NCoH" are the proper forms. NCOH or NCH are not considered proper or correct.

To complete this consideration of jargon, the nomenclature within POR, let's review two linguistic constructions that might easily be confused due to their novelty and their application. The nature of words in POR linguistics is that they have universal, unique, and unitary meaning, and are defined in context, being redefined with every usage but always maintaining the single and identical meaning that prompts that usage. I've introduced two technical terms to indicate potentially disconcerting aspects of this framework. A dichotomous abstraction is a word that has two (or more) specific but distinct denotations. The iconic example is "matter", and the terms "determine" and "control" have also been addressed. Here I will add "just", without engaging in any extensive explanation. Whether the term is used to express "only" or "right", as a synonym for "merely" or as the root of "justice", can be explored without resolution ad infinitum. It can be difficult to understand how dichotomous abstractions can have universal and unitary meaning, but grasping this truth is an important and enlightening part of comprehending POR. In reality, just as all words are metaphors, any word can be both part of an infinite set of unique dichotomies (meaning the same and opposite of any other word) and is also a dichotomous abstraction, embodying all of the thoughts that cause that word to be used. To use the phrase "dichotomous abstraction" is to identify a specific word as particularly, rather than exclusively, exhibiting this affect. The second technical term to reprise is "simultaneity", more formally "the simultaneity principle", which indicates the kind of word that most obviously has to include its own opposite. Contemplated sufficiently, the idea of dichotomous abstractions and the principle of opposite/apposite simultaneity in language are themselves unitary, and can be both confused and confabulated. The archetypical example of simultaneity is "tolerance", and another illustrative case is "morality". (Tolerance is identified as the archetypical example because it is the more confusing and politically relevant, the toleration of intolerance being socially problematic. Ironically, it is because toleration, as a behavior, must include intolerance of intolerance, that toleration, as a word, is considered to include what is intolerant. It is still improper to describe any other intolerance as tolerance, except for intolerance of intolerance itself.)

Now, moving on from the area of the vocabulary of POR (the previous discussion being more than sufficient, though not at all complete), we will return to the larger magisterium of POR vocabulary guidelines. Language is the sum and substance of both POR and human consciousness, so it is appropriate and understandable that a person's philosophy mirrors their word choices and comprehension of others'. These guidelines are not merely general rules for how to use words while discussing the Philosophy Of Reason or for those who hope to or do follow, implement, or comprehend it. They are ways of following and comprehending the way other people use words, as well, without implementing the postmodern habits that the words convey or those people adhere to, consciously or unconsciously. The POR interpretation of these words, the ones about to be presented as vocabulary guidelines, refines rather than contradicts the more conventional understanding and usage, although they may well contradict dictionary definitions or explicit statements of meaning in some particular context. But then, dictionary definitions may well contradict other dictionary definitions, and the whole idea of 'context' is to allow for variance in the purpose of terminology depending on intentions or subject matter.

The jellybean diagram indicates that the meaning of words, even our own words, cannot be unilaterally dictated, or even personally determined. POR sympathizes with Humpty Dumpty, but does not wholly endorse his approach.

Yes, we use words, and we intend them to mean what we believe that they mean. But most of the time, the average guess is closer to the truth than our own guess, even if we naturally presume that ours is the best individual guess about what we intend to mean. Realistically, language did not even evolve as a way of expressing ourselves, but as a way of recognizing the expressions of other people's minds. Children learn language by hearing it, regardless of whether they ever master speaking it. The speaking part is merely mimicking what is heard, at first. It isn't until the reasoning which makes discussion possible is developed, that speech becomes more than mimicry and we can choose our words consciously. Likewise, the proto-humans that first evolved the process of communication, who first formulated a theory of mind and learned to recognize the mind in other people, were not explicitly aware of what they were doing. They did it, as humans continue to do it, as a biological function resulting from the complex interplay of proteins that form, and are formed by, our bodies. Somewhere along the line of ancestral inheritance, humans discovered, perhaps still incoherently but not unconsciously, the technique of teleological flipping that produces self-determination. This is still done unconsciously, which is to say without conscious recognition but while awake. (POR rejects the Freudian hypothesis of the "subconscious" or 'unconscious mind', invented to describe self-awareness as if the unconscious brain behaves with intention and motives such as our conscious minds formulate.) The boundary between unconscious behavior and conscious actions becomes vague and borders on pointless when we try to examine what happens in those few milliseconds between the time our brains initiate an action and when our minds become aware that it did so. We could, and according to POR we must, say that observing teleologies is "mind", and only occurs consciously; the neurological activity of our brains, absent conscious thought, are not influenced by the reason things happen, only whether they happen.

To become convinced that we have no conscious control of our actions is difficult, even after it is scientifically proven to be the case. Setting that aside, though, because the process of self-determination is in essence a linguistic one, speaking is the one kind of action we perform that is closest to being a conscious choice, and yet also the furthest from being one. We all know people who are "motor mouths", who cannot seem to stem the flow of words coming from their lips and tongue. Similarly, it is in our use of language that we are most willing to admit that we "cannot control ourselves", and of course the words that someone uses are most revealing of their true self, often to a fault. We could see it the other way around, that actions speak louder than words; but those are words, and the figure of speech that 'actions' can 'speak' is instructive as a metaphor, not as a fact.

Even if having the 'executive function' that postmodern psychologists and psychiatrists describe is a myth, it remains possible to consider our words before uttering or writing them, and this can seemingly allow us to get around the barrier that free will is supposed to make non-existent. Practicing this conscientious use of vocabulary and linguistic reasoning is the primary method of POR. There are ritual practices in the religion of the Philosophy Of Reason, the New Church of Hope, though few of them. And there are moral implications to POR philosophy, by way of the Universal Principle of Consciousness that admits that our thoughts are physical, regardless of whether they provide metaphysical control over our movements. But the bulk of the practice of POR involves choosing and using our words wisely, and nothing more. Doing so will cause happiness and empowerment, even if you don't understand how or why. Choose and using words wisely is only possible if we first understand what words are, and why we are using them. In mathematics, there is a term for any independent variable of a function: an argument. In natural language, the word 'argument' is even more important, and it will be the first particular POR vocabulary guideline we will examine.

The nature of argument, in postmodern theory, is debate; an alternating sequence of logical statements, resulting in one speaker winning the contest with superior logic which the other speaker should learn. The nature of argument in POR is discussion: reasoning with two brains instead of one. This brings us to the first example of POR vocabulary, the rules or guidelines for using POR practically. Each guideline or bit of vocabulary has implications far beyond the rule itself, but belief in or knowledge of these further implications is not necessary or important. They will inevitably and unavoidably result from conscientious application of the guideline. These are authoritative doctrines, not authoritarian dogma, but the difference between the two is a matter for discussion, not debate.

An argument, as stated, is simply reasoning with two brains instead of one. It is acceptable to make an argument to someone, but it is improper to have an argument with someone. The semantic drift and postmodern over-synonimization of the word 'argument' itself is an instructive illustration of the issue, since most of the time when it is used, it refers to a verbal fight rather than an intellectual premise. We all know how easy it is to get in an argument, to be contentious and angry, to yell, because we do not have or cannot achieve a better way of expressing our thoughts. Likewise, we all know how hard it is to get out. Limited by the postmodern demand that we pretend our brains are organic computers, we struggle with mounting emotional compulsions, until the words that the other person is using over-rides our vain belief in our free will, and sooner or later angry words are responded to with physical actions when violence occurs. The phrase "the ontological argument" is used as a euphemism, one of the few true euphemisms in POR, for violence, whether it is throwing a chair, an angry punch in the nose, or the use of military force. Metaphorically, it can also refer to fait accompli, or "power justifies itself" arguments, because such rhetorical pretenses leave no alternative of intellectual consideration, only acceptance or more physical confrontation. One of the primary effects of the comprehension of POR theory is that our language can more easily remain intellectual because we are aware that arguments are not fighting, but thinking with two brains. Sometimes it is a very crude level of thinking, with thoughts being communicated between the two brains with hostile words or sarcastic attempts at wit. But as long as we are avoiding the passive aggressive behavior of postured detachment that is all most people can muster in place of productive argument, we are better off than we would be if we continued to assume that arguments are supposed to be debates. Accepting POR doesn't magically prevent you from becoming angry, but it does make anger more easily avoided, and more easily dismissed and forgiven, as well, when we fail to avoid it. After all, the other person isn't in conscious control of their actions any more than you are, regardless of how intensely they believe they are, so becoming angry at them is fruitless and counter-productive, like beating a horse. Or worse, beating a dead horse. Forgiveness of human foibles is a natural part of our awareness of the mechanism of self-determination. It may seem terribly, even horrifyingly unfair that we remain responsible for our actions despite having no direct control over them. Life is, indeed, unfair, and so it becomes all the more important that we be fair, since 'life' whether a metaphor for all biological organisms or only human experience, is not fair. So even if life is not fair, we should be, to both ourselves and others. This calm, self-assurance without self-righteousness, may have the outward appearance of the condescending, contrived passive aggression of the dedicated postmodernist, but the proof is in the pudding and this is our lot in life. It is the willingness to abandon the defense of our own dignity, and the corresponding eagerness to defend the dignity of others, that separates the yogi, the true guru, from the self-help huckster, the motivational speaker, and the ultimate test of sincerity is how we behave in private rather than any public façade.

When the process of argument does not devolve to bickering or fighting, it is easier to engage in it productively, obviously. When doing so, we must remember that the goal, the proper outcome, of any discussion, or argument, is not one side winning and the other submitting, but that all participants, and observers, learn something new, to better enable them to reason, by themselves or with others, in the future. So long as we avoid resorting to the ontological argument, then our communication can be successful, even if it gets heated. To round out this one-sided discussion of the word 'argument', let's consider the most analytical, yet metaphorical usage of the term. Mathematicians use the expression 'argument' to refer to a particular kind of assumption used in mathematical logic. A standard dictionary defines this as "one of the independent variables upon whose value that of a function depends". This is an example of 'borrowing', as described previously when the Fundamental Schema was presented. (Note that mathematics, as a scientific practice, can borrow philosophical terms from the general context, but philosophy, including POR, can only use words along with the general context.) This use of 'argument' as a mathematical idea (we cannot say 'term' here, because it is not a mathematical term, but a category of mathematical terms) shows that, although the precise technical usage would be considered by postmodernists to be the most precise and original meaning, mathematicians are merely utilizing it by analogy, with the broader and more accurate meaning being perverted by Socrates' Error into a lesser one. Leave the supposedly concrete usage to the mathematicians (or the grammarians, they again use analogy to apply the term to "substantive of a predicate", but without borrowing, because although it is specialized jargon, grammar is not a science); in POR, and the general context, the term 'argument' means all the things the word is used to refer to, and more, because meaning relates to why that word can be defined as all those things with simultaneity.

We cannot exhaust all of the denotations or connotations or applications of any single word, and this one is no different. The meaning of any word is always abstract, ineffable, whenever we try to isolate it from the context that defines any particular usage or the meaning the can only be grasped entirely by examining every specific use across all contexts. But simply knowing the rhetorical value of the word "argument" as presented here is enlightening whenever we hear or see someone using it. Usually, they are reflecting the "why you are calling it that" *meaning* of the word, even when they think, quite often with a false absolute certainty, that it is the "what you call it" postmodern approach to language they are invoking. Words are not labels for external objects or occurrences, that is not what gives them meaning, what makes them words, what enables language to work. More often, that approach prevents language from working, instead. Words are not labels, they are descriptions; not symbols, but ideas. Descriptions of our perceptions of things, whether we use them to describe external objects, or events, or the internal sensations and thought that occur in our bodies and minds when we observe those things.

This leads us back to one of the most significant bits of POR vocabulary, that forbidden word "concept". As explained previously, this is a favorite of postmodernists, and is problematic for the reason which makes it such a favorite, that it is considered so foul that it should never be used. We have no need of it, in the end, because there are no such things. The idea of a... well, you know the word, the idea of that is a thing so imaginary it goes beyond metaphor, it is a myth. The value of it to postmodernists is immeasurable. It is an integral part of the Information Processing Theory of Mind, in effect the religion of postmodernism. In that unacknowledged creed, the term is used to invent and label a logical feature of the universe, roughly equivalent to a Platonic form, or a deductive cognate. The overall idea is that a logical set of these things can be defined as features of the universe, essentially tiling a single, consistent, cosmos-spanning worldview, with no gaps or overlap. To the postmodernist, (ahem) "concepts" are real, and the words we use to label them are figments of our imagination, accepted by convention or even some negotiated definition, but otherwise arbitrary symbols. Ideas are called by that name when hyper-rationalists wish to (falsely) declare the ideas to have logical consistency. In the postmodernist view, thinking is more visual than linguistic, because they believe they can imagine pictures in their heads, and these pictures have the logical integrity of a diagram on paper. In the POR view, the true understanding of reality, there are words, and there are ideas; there are no 'concepts' needed to relate one to the other with logical consistency. In one way, this is the truth because we could, given enough repetition to make it familiar, use any set of sounds or letters to describe any thought or idea (or perception of a sensation or object, as I've already described it). In another, opposite way, this is the truth because words and thoughts (or ideas) are not two different things, but the same thing in two different forms. Thoughts are simply words when those words are only occurring inside our minds, and words are simply what we call thoughts when they are outside our minds. We generate words as ideas escape from our braincase, and we cannot prevent words from becoming ideas once they enter our heads through our eyes or ears.

Do not think of an elephant. Did you succeed? Of course not; you have to think of an elephant to know what it is you want to try not to think of. Whether that word felt in your brain like the shape of an elephant, or the smell or sound of an elephant, or some other aspect of 'elephantness' that is familiar to you, and somehow converted by your 'neural network' of brain cells from what you saw on this page into what you thought: if you managed to read rather than ignore the word 'elephant', your brain generated the idea 'elephant', unavoidably.

As you can see (metaphorically), your thoughts are not only your own words when they are being considered, "processed" in the postmodern vernacular, by your brain. Other people's words (since the only two possible sources of words are you, or other people) are just as unavoidably and automatically converted from recognizable visual or sound patterns to ideas and thoughts as your own. Obviously enough, the process works the other way as well. Despite the habit of the most studious postmodernists of deconstructing any statement as if it were a logical construct, finding enough fault to dismiss it if they prefer to remain ignorant of whatever truth that statement might communicate, they (we, for as I've explained we have all been raised to be postmodernist whether the lessons are embraced or not) cannot prevent the meaning of words from leaking through this screen of 'critical thinking skills' by which we attempt to resist the unavoidable and automatic translation of words to thoughts upon hearing or seeing them. There are no "concepts", there are only words and ideas, along with some fanciful attempts to artificially distinguish them that doesn't hold up against any honest or sincere analysis.

Argument

And so, to avoid continuing and reinforcing erroneous habits and myths, one of the most absolute rules in POR is that we do not, under normal circumstances and even most abnormal ones, use "the c word". There are conceptions, we can conceive ideas (although the more common usage is that we 'cannot conceive' of an idea), because these, like the word 'matter' when applied to substances, are metaphors. The analytical application of the word 'conception' is the implantation of an egg into the wall of a woman's uterus, or some similar associated step in the process of reproduction. And so when any thought is conceived, or conceived of, or not, it is like the inception of a pregnancy, a new (potential) organism being generated where it was not before. Or is the implanting of a blastocyst the metaphor, and the creation of an idea the ontological analysis?

If there is only one standard practice of POR that survives, even if every other aspect of the Philosophy Of Reason is rejected as insubstantial, it is this rejection of that word which shall not be used. This is also the most practical method of applying POR vocabulary, and it is surprisingly effective at honing the mental skills needed to comprehend POR and divorcing our reasoning from the postmodern taint of Socrates' Error and IPTM. Whenever you feel the urge to use that word, and whenever you hear or see it used by anyone else, simply consider whether it can, and therefore should, be replaced by either 'word' or 'idea'. Using the 'c' word is never actually necessary or informative, because there both literally and figuratively are no such things. But words and ideas do exist, however difficult they might be to define or nail down. Postmodernists habitually use the 'c' word in order to pretend that intellectual abstractions are somehow deductively rigorous without having to demonstrate that they are. To help extract ourselves from the tar pit of Socrates' Error, we can simply avoid using the word. Routinely substitute one of those other two expressions, either 'word' or 'idea', both in creating your own speech or text, and in interpreting the statements of other people. If you find that neither 'word' nor 'idea' truly engenders whatever thought you are conceiving, than the statement you're trying to make or understand is false, the idea it conveys is untrue. People are taught to use that word to sidestep the fact that the meanings of words are ineffable, and thoughts are invisible, and so we imagine that there must be such Platonic forms because their non-existence is too inconvenient a truth. No better habit for improving your intellect can be practiced than refusing to ever utter or contemplate the disallowed term.

Eventually you will find that the very feel of the word is alien and distasteful, starting out typically enough with 'con-', but then ending far too abruptly and artificially, as "-ept". "-ept", with a hard 'pt' that begs for a suffix but deserves none. Yes, 'conception' is natural and important, and it can be used rhetorically even in polite company, but it is clearly a metaphor and substitutes that hard final 't' with a far more organic 'sh' sound, coming out:

'konsepshun'. It isn't that the physical phoneme is outrageous or untoward; the same abrupt conclusion is used in the word 'abrupt', 'apt', 'jumped' and even 'except' or 'accept', and no doubt many others. But none of these listed exceptions, except the last, comfortably or even grammatically accepts the 's' suffix indicating plurality (and 'accepts' and 'excepts' generally drop vocalization of the 't' in a way that the problem 'c' word does not.) This seems apt, which is to say appropriate, because the only term in the English language that is worse than "concept", from a POR perspective, is "concepts". The various linguistic directions of the formal Philosophy Of Reason are almost entirely matters of effectiveness and accuracy, but this one rule of vocabulary about the c word comes closest to a purely moral mandate. The word can be avoided entirely, and it should be, and to consider yourself a practitioner of POR it must be, because there are no such things, anyway. It is a fiction created by postmodernists for no other reason than to make postmodernism irrefutable; an evil convention that beguiles the well intentioned into spreading misinformation. If you can manage to do without it, then that alone makes you a practitioner of POR, and if you find yourself even contemplating, let alone implementing, this guideline, then you are practicing POR and it will improve your life, even if you detest and dismiss POR as a theory consciously. It is my hope and expectation that this might happen even if you don't want it to, that your brain will catch and hiccup when you see, hear, or use the word, whether your mind decides to ignore it or not, and this alone will nudge you towards better reasoning and abandoning the pretense of logic that ruins so many intellects.

Similar POR vocabulary guidelines are less iron-clad. While the 'c' word is more-or-less forbidden outright, other terms are simply described as 'dispreferred'. In particular, the expression "subjective" is another word that is generally excluded from our common lexicon. It has gained, through the most postmodernist of postmodern over-synonimization, a dismissive connotation, meant to castigate whatever is described with it and by it. To the postmodernist embracing the canard of "critical thinking skills", their own ideas are objective facts, and any ideas they don't like are mere 'subjective' opinions. Used properly, the word accurately indicates an experiential perspective on something, but not any characteristic of the thing itself. Your "subjective" thoughts, feelings, and judgments are, as I've pointed out, objectively occurring, they ontologically exist, regardless of anyone else's ability to measure or verify them. Humans have great difficulty "being objective", simply because humans are designed by evolution to not be objective. Animals are objective, because although their awareness never extends beyond their senses, they cannot generate teleologies or consciously analyze events, objects, or other occurrences. They are perfectly objective, yet ignorant of anything but their objective sense data, because the two, objective and ignorant, are simultaneous and synchronous. Like computers, they are unaware of being unaware of anything. Postmodernism suggests that to be objective requires a great deal of information and concentrated analytical effort, but this is the opposite of the truth, as so many postmodern suggestions are. True objectivity is to be able to make selections only based on whatever data is input, without any conception or perception of there being any other data possible. This is what prevents humans from being objective, not because we cannot be unbiased but because we are aware that we are biased, that we may not have all the data that could make our selection an adequately informed choice, or an even more than adequately well-informed decision. Wanting to be objective, wishing that critical thinking skills could successfully identify truth, is not unexpected. The belief you are objective, that finding logical flaws in other people's reasoning in order to justify ignoring their opinions is conversation or discussion, is the problem.

We could easily say that everything happening 'inside' the existential wall is 'subjective', and everything happening 'outside' of the existential wall is objective, but the philosophical limitations of trusting our senses, our existential perspective, remains. Our awareness of what is objective will always be subjective. So as long as people try to use the word 'subjective' to dismiss personal experiences and reasoning as if the purpose of our existence is to calculate numbers like we are computers and nothing more, it is better if we avoid using it at all. A parallel entry on our 'disprefered' list is Dawkin's (re)invention of "meme". It has its place as a category of graphics usually involving block text over an appropriate but misappropriated image, or cyber-age catch phrases like 'rickroll' or "all your base are belong to us". But using the word 'meme', at least for anything more than the category of graphics and such, tends to encourage postmodern delusions about the nature of language or mental experiences. It is a fancy version of the c-word, this idea of an 'intellectual virus' that replicates by way of our mental processes. Ironically, yet still predictably, the pseudo-science of 'memetics' is an effort to treat "subjective" ideas as "objective" measurable quantities. It fails, not just because it is self-contradicting in that way, but because it relies on judgmental assessments so completely, and with such utter faith in postmodern ideology, that it can't even qualify as a form of 'humanology' like psychology or sociology or linguistics. The possibility, that the word 'meme' could be employed as a useful scientific label for "words and ideas" as a category, suggests that any such category has logical integrity, or that any scientific pursuit needs such a replacement for the word "idea" or the idea "word". When any empirical research or serious intellectual endeavor calls for a descriptor for an idea that is more analytical than the word "word", the appropriate substitute is the word "word". There is no more analytical term for the particles of thought we use that expression to identify and describe. The 'c' word is forbidden, the parallel 'meme' is simply dispreferred. Neither word succeeds in its intent to make those ideas have the material, mathematical integrity the locutions are intended to suggest.

Other POR vocabulary guidelines are more dictatorial (as in 'dictionary-ish' rather than 'autocratic', though of course the two are not so far apart as intellectual, rather than etymological, cognates) and numerous. This category of rules might be called 'semantics' rather than 'dispreferred'. Most of them involve pairs or groups of words that suffer from the same POS effect that was previously observed with the words "fair and equal". To the postmodernist, these two different terms are made interchangeable by the very habit of being contrasting but not entirely contradictory. They both become identical in meaning and are reduced to labels for 'good', in the postmodern lexicon. In POR vocabulary, they are informative as separate ideas that are similar but not synonymous, and important because they describe two different qualities that sometimes overlap and sometimes are oppositional. They are a dichotomy, dichotomous dichotomies, as per the abstraction paradigm. "Fair" relates mostly to our (ahem) 'subjective' assessment of morality, while "equal" obviously refers more to an objective measurement. But neither are good or bad in themselves, they are simply often confused or confabulated, and become less useful than when we avoid Socrates' Error and recognize them as descriptive, not symbolic.

The most significant matter of semantics that comes up most often in dealing with philosophy and politics is the pairing of "sincere" and "honest", often and appropriately grouped with the word "true". Attempting to define either 'sincere' or 'honest' without using the word 'true' becomes almost impossible, just as identifying or discussing what is 'true' is almost impossible without using either of the words 'sincere' or 'honest'. (The truth of this formulation is not impeded by the fact that the pairing of 'knowledge' and 'belief' can be used to substitute for 'honest' and 'sincere', without changing the nature of the problem.) Modern philosophy, and its IPTM-deranged descendent, generally qualifies 'sincere' with reference to 'subjective', and 'honest' with a similar relationship to "objective". As a first approximation, this is adequate, but the issues I've already described around the word 'subjective' leak through, so a more explicit 'definition' is called for. Which is to say that without assuming a Humpty Dumpty, ontology-free, epistemological description of 'subjective' as 'whatever we call subjective', and/or over-synonymizing 'honest' or 'sincere' as either meaning 'good' or 'bad', without just skipping over the problem of the existential wall preventing us from proceeding from cogito ergo sum to true knowledge of the universe, all of these words end up being meaningless. We need a better comprehension of 'sincere' and 'honest' than the self-referential idea that one is subjective and the other is objective, without any consistent way of determining which is which.

Sincerity involves what only a particular person can know is true or not, while honesty refers to what is true that can only be specifically assessed by other people. Only you can know for sure if you're being sincere (though you can't always), but only other people can know for sure if you're being honest (though they can't always). You cannot assess your own honesty, not because you cannot be trusted but simply because you do not know everything, and so you cannot know if what you're saying is true, you can only know if you believe it is true, which is sincerity. This particular semantic issue is enormously instructive in terms of POR's moral philosophy. You can certainly assess your own dishonesty; you know if you are lying on purpose. And if we adopt the Aristotelian conception of logic, this should mean that we can know if we're being honest, because 'honest' and 'dishonest', in keeping with Socrates' Error, are assumed to be perfectly mutually exclusive; what isn't one must be the other. The law of the excluded middle might work in mathematics and symbolic logic, but it is insanity in any other context. So we cannot presume that 'honest' and 'dishonest' are the only two possible states of intentions, despite the apparent linguistic exclusions the dichotomy seems to present. In POR we use the imposition of dialectic, in this case perhaps 'sincerity' (or 'insincerity'), in order to illuminate the imprecision of even the most accurate terminology. We can consider that it is possible to be honest (not technically lying) but insincere (intending to be misconstrued), and discuss whether this is dishonest honesty or honest dishonesty; while these ideas would be dismissed by amateur philosophers, they are as real to more educated philosophicians (does the thing not exist simply because I invented the word to identify and describe it?) as the phrase "in and of itself", as if that is a real thing.

Again we are confronted with the fact that the purposeful ignorance that Socrates used as a rhetorical pose was insincere. It is vitally essential in the limited contexts of law and science, the special applications of language in a courtroom and the laboratory, where sincerity is irrelevant and honesty is all-important. (Contrast this with the importance of sincerity in psychiatry and other medical specialties, where sincerity is all that matters and honesty is neither presumed nor relevant, on the part of the patient at least but also, properly understood, for the practitioner.) It sure would be nice if we could know directly what is "true", but neither the wisest jurist or the most astute philosopher can claim that we can directly know truth, without reference to outside facts or internal consistency. The absolute truth of the physical world is beyond the existential wall, and the relative truth of any particular axiomatic system is almost useless in real life.

There are no specific POR commandments associated with using the words 'sincere' or 'honest', apart from admitting the truth about what they mean, and using them only in that way. When necessary, the indirect methods of determining what is true 'beyond a reasonable doubt' or 'to a logical certainty' are the best we can do. But determining whether we are truly sincere is something we can only know for ourselves, usually in secret, and whether we are truly being honest (even with ourselves), is something we have to rely on the guidance of others to know. It isn't possible to even wonder if we are being sincere with ourselves, it must always go without saying even when we question our own honesty about our internal sensations or convictions. It is just as impossible for anyone else to truly doubt our sincerity, only whether we are being honest about our sincerity. We can be either dishonest or insincere when declaring what we want, but not both at the same time. Since, at least some of the time, the average guess is going to be closer to the truth about what we want than even our own supposedly authoritative guess, we must always try to balance ourselves on the razor's edge of wanting to be both honest and sincere, and being at the mercy of other people's opinions about both, as well. Thus is the purpose of language, and the Philosophy Of Reason, fulfilled. This is a reflection of the principle of an epistmological/ontological divide in the Fundamental Schema. We must balance both, as closely as possible, to be theological (moral). Conversely, we can only recognize a distinction between honesty and sincerity, or understand their connection, by being more of one the less we are of the other. If we are being sincere, we know we are not always honest. Likewise, if we are honest, we must admit we are not always sincere. It would be nice to suppose that we could be as much as we can of both at the same time, but since we cannot know what we do not know, even if we know there are things we don't know, honesty is unachievable unilaterally, but sincerity is always exclusively solitary. Similarly, since not even knowledge of ourselves is perfect, and we can deceive ourselves about even our own intentions, in a way that can only be determined in hindsight (given the nature of sincerity and self-determination), it is as pointless to declare that we are always sincere as it is to pretend we are perfectly honest.

The application, even the very existence, of POR guidelines for vocabulary all invariably appear to be semantics, with that word itself being yet another instance of postmodern over-synonimization. To those well versed and most adamant about the standard common modernistic doctrine of language and logic, language as logic, any disputation of their pedantic insistence is heretical naiveté. It is not ignorance of the amassed power of generations of grammarians that provide the basis for our guidance and the philosophy that prompts these POR rules, though, but knowledge of the true history and meaning of their dictatorial (as in dictionary-ish **and** autocratic) perspective. "Semantics", the term I used to categorize the previous examples, is itself a word that has become subject to POS, markedly so. It almost invariably follows the word 'just', typically in the thread-bare phrase "that's just semantics". It is in this way a synonym for "bad", even as in linguistic terms it is a synonym for 'good', because it is meant to connote the entirety of the linguistic process, and the connection in postmodernist theory between logic and meaning, two things that are entirely and definitively unconnected. There is no 'meaning' in logic, only codification, arbitrary assignment of translated symbols, without meaningful interpretation outside that designation. Any use of the expression "meaning" in logic is metaphorical, or borrowing. The more proper analytic term would be "equals" in most cases, or more complicated nomenclature such as "is designated as", hence the usefulness and convenience of the metaphoric analogy "meaning". But meaning is more than simply the assignment of meaning, meaning is the lack of any need for such assignment, as the purpose of something is inherent in its being, if it is true meaning rather than a symbolic allocation, as in the assignment of a translation (distinct from interpretation, which requires theory of mind) to a token in a mathematical encryption scheme.

Apart from being used as a description of a kind of POR vocabulary guideline, the term *semantics* itself has almost no purpose or use in POR. Along with 'memetics', 'semiotics', and to a lesser extent even 'grammar' and 'syntax', semantics is an effort to logically deconstruct the illogical process of language. Because language requires a theory of mind to be correctly interpreted or even recognized, it can never be entirely reduced to any codified data transfer mechanism or other axiomatic system. So it is proper to call it an 'illogical process', even though that, too, will be misinterpreted by postmodernists. (The ultimate example of POS is the reduction of the word 'logical' to mean 'good' and the reduction of the word 'illogical' to mean 'bad'.) Postmodernists might insist that there can be no such thing as an 'illogical process'; that any process must be logical or it fails to be a process, and becomes merely a sequence. Or they may simply ridicule the term itself, and us for using it, because 'illogical' has been generally reduced, through the familiar technique of POS, to meaning something like 'irrational' or 'insane' (both considered nothing but alternative symbols for 'bad' in the false dichotomy/binary thinking habits of postmodernism.)

Postmodernists worship logic, and like those who worship a man in the sky with a long beard and a fierce temper, their faith has reasons for being, but is predominantly just a myth. There is a moral force in the universe, whether we call it hope, love, or reason, but it does not depend on either a theistic deity or an omniscient calculator to work. It depends on us, using reasoning rather than vain proclamation. This moral force, morality, is similar to the atheist's conscious logic or the creationist's God, in that it only applies to or is evidenced by human beings, not any other part of the natural or physical universe. The point is that we use the word 'illogical', in POR, with neither hidden nor unintended moral condemnation, but simply to most effectively describe what we observe. When we call something 'illogical', or the similar "irrational", it does not convey castigation or chastisement. Quite the opposite, actually, because POR is the rejection of the idea that being logical is the mechanism or the goal of reasoning, though it can be part of the process, as arithmetic. So when we say something is 'illogical', we intend it to simply be a neutral description, but we must honestly admit that we sincerely consider it a good thing in some cases, a transcendence of our animal nature or simple arithmetic expediency. And so it is with 'semantics', too, a neutral descriptor

Freed from the fettering and festering bonds of postmodernism, we have no need and little regard for semantics, however much we may observe or employ the rules of grammar in any particular language, in order to speak our minds, teach our lessons, or celebrate our faith. Laws of grammar are not divinely inspired or logically consistent, but they are informative and useful, if for no other reason than that we should know which sacred ground we are transgressing when we ignore the rules of grammar, in order to show that we are not robots or slaves. Language is shibboleth and theory of mind, not merely code and symbolic representations. Symbolic representations can be as easily symbolic misrepresentation, and it is only Socrates' Error to suggest that syllogisms and rational logic can successfully distinguish the two. We cannot vault or demolish the existential wall, ever, and so we cannot know the truth, absolutely. We can only use language to throw clues over top of it, in the blind hope that there is anyone on the other side to catch them.

All of this is simply to address the issue of the otherwise disprefered word "semantics", of course. The guidelines presented here are not the kind of pedantry and hair-splitting that those who believe their nomenclature is wisdom received from scientists engage in. Our goal is not precision, but accuracy. These are observations about how these words have drifted away from being useful, informative rather than judgmental. Even the word "postmodernism" itself, which you have no doubt noticed can be translated from this text as if it were a character flaw, a sin, a bad thing, is merely used descriptively, to refer to the evolution of the modern philosophy of the ancient Greeks to the current philosophy of IPTM proponents. It is not possible, after all, to be critical of something without judging it, and judgment inherently if not innately demands either condemnation or endorsement. All judgments are moral judgments, selections between the alternative of 'good', 'bad', or 'undecided'. Whether it is sin or criminality being judged, or any other non-quantitative attribute being assessed, the application of reasoning in any form or context requires judgment, using a theology to ensure that judgment is not simply selfish petulance. Precision is for math. It is the precision and repeatability of math that caused Socrates to envy it to begin with. It is not surprising that postmodernists continue to repeat his Error, wishing that language could be so simple and absolute. But words, and the selection of words, is not about being precise, they are about accuracy. Even accuracy when throwing a stone in the dark. We may not see the target, but if we are calm and careful, we can feel whether we hit the target by how the word resonates. Perhaps it will come to rest near enough to the goal that we can rely on the jellybean principle to make it true. Perhaps it will sink into a dark and bottomless lake of ignorance, but it will still make ripples that might propagate almost endlessly. Regardless, words are about accuracy, not precision. And using those two words themselves with accuracy is another important guideline in POR vocabulary. The ultimate knowledge of what words are and how language functions comes down to recognizing the contrast and variance between these two words, themselves often synonymized to be interchangeable in casual speech.

To clarify, and only slightly over-simplify, the issue of precision versus accuracy, which are far more opposite than they are identical, we can use the arithmetic context. *Precision* is how many digits to the right of the decimal point a number has. *Accuracy* is whether those digits are the right ones. Precision can be measured and judged (if you have advanced in your adoption of POR at all, you may detect that these are two opposite things rather than redundant) within an axiomatic framework; precision can be determined mathematically. But accuracy is far more complicated, and can only be judged in comparison to a framework outside of the axiomatic system used to produce the number. We assess accuracy in terms of whether an answer is the "right" one, according to some expectation or desire that has no absolute relevance to the algorithm we're applying. Precision is measured by simply counting the number of digits in a number, but the measurement of accuracy occurs when we choose which formula to apply, and in so doing determine what number we can compare the answer to in order to determine if it is right or correct or proper or true.

Another way to view accuracy versus precision is a more physical illustration. An archery contest, in which precision is how tight a grouping is, but accuracy is how close the arrows are to the bullseye. As with our metaphoric understanding of the jellybean mystery, in the real world the location of the bullseye is unknowable, just as the number of jellybeans isn't certain until after they are counted. Hindsight and our acceptance that there are empirical facts causes us, as postmodernists in need of reform, to presume that these things are knowable with foresight, but nobody can truly know the future, our predictions are merely probabilities. In this archery analogy, the target is eternally obscured, representing a truth that is unknown, and whether it can be knowable or known is, itself, unknown, and perhaps unknowable. we can only tell how well clustered a flight of arrows is. We can only have a belief that enough flights will reveal the location of the target, like the guesses in a jellybean contest. Precision is vitally important, in our real world, but it does not lead to certainty of the truth, however much it might provide confidence in our skill at guessing or predicting the truth.

We are free to change our reference for comparing accuracy against, our basis for assessing whether a result is accurate or not, based on whether the answer we previously got is close to what we expected it to be. Improving precision, in contrast, entails completely revising all of our predicates, assumptions, and equipment. We don't need to consciously work out whether 'precision' or 'accuracy' is the better metaphor in any non-mathematical context, according to the POR guidelines of vocabulary. We can simply only use **precision** when referring to mathematics and the true logic which is merely symbolic math, and **accuracy** when the subject is anything other than mathematics, including the false logic that postmodernists inaccurately use to pretend their reasoning has mathematical integrity. Numbers have precision, and only numbers have precision, while words have only accuracy. As always, we can use the term 'precisely' as a metaphor when talking about talking, in the same way the word 'literally' can be used figuratively, to the immense consternation of pedants embracing and expressing Socrates' Error. The purpose of POR guidelines is never to remove figures of speech from our language, but to ensure we are aware when they are figurative, and when we are properly analyzing the accuracy of our language.

From the standpoint of theology, morality and ethics, the most critical guideline for vocabulary concerns the word group of castigation. Even more important than what I've explained about the terms "fair and equal", this word group refers to morality itself. I should remind you, at this point, that these guidelines are about accuracy, if only the kind of accuracy that the word 'about' suggests in that usage. (It is worth noting here that spatial prepositions such as 'about', 'against', 'for', 'in', 'under', 'through', 'of', 'within' et al. are not judged in terms of accuracy [nor precision] as metaphors in POR grammar or vocabulary. How closely such words align analytically with physical spatial relationships has no real bearing on their communicative value, in general.) Since recognizing and using criticism is one of the most common and useful applications of language, along with all of the others, the terms we use to suggest condemnation are very powerful, and like every powerful tool must be used with great care and attention. Proper application of words of castigation is like the safety equipment you wear when wielding a chainsaw, and are no less important when creating an ice sculpture than when felling a tree. The group itself is normally listed as 'mistake, error, incorrect, improper, and wrong'. Each of these in various forms is used to identify problems in reasoning or behavior that are observed or expected to produce bad results. But each has its own unique meaning, although like always that unitary meaning can only be approximated with other words. With that final warning, I will switch into 'dictionary mode', and dictate precisely how each is to be used to minimize confusion and the hidden moral condemnation that is so much a part of the POS that comes from pointless pedantry.

A **mistake** is the kind of inaccuracy that results in bad outcomes. It is singular; if 'mistakes' are made, they are each of a different kind. When repeated, a mistake becomes an **error**; erroneous results are the expected outcome of committing the same mistake over and over again. Whether an answer or idea or performance, etc. is **correct** is a comparison to whether it is expected, based on some reasonable method that can be determined based on some intelligible framework or through reasoning. In contrast, whether a thing is **proper** is a comparison to whether it is expected based on an arbitrary or authoritarian declaration. Being an autocratic dictate, it requires no intelligible explication. These are all shades of meaning, made more or less accurate or productive in any specific case by the circumstances. The iconic example, and the real source of most postmodern association of these words of castigation with *truth*, is a school teacher, and an examination quiz. When the answer you've given on a test is marked with a red X and you lose points on the grade, it is a mistake; if you do it again next time, it is an error. When you get credit for an answer, it is most likely described as '<u>correct</u>'. The expression "OK" is thought to derive from a shorthand for 'all correct', "Ol Korekt", that predates the era of standardized spelling. But this use of 'correct' is usually inaccurate in any philosophical sense. School teachers, particularly instructors of younger children, are often teaching lessons that are simplified approximations of real knowledge, sometimes even in contradiction to the more complex realities that only advanced courses have the opportunity to clarify. A second grade teacher doesn't have the ability to explain to a class why 'imaginary numbers' are not fantasy symbols, for instance. So in truth the better word for when you give the right answer on a test question is that you answered it <u>properly</u>, not necessarily <u>correctly</u>. This is a lesson that every student needs to learn. Most are left to their own devices when doing so. This can result in a sentiment that the process of meeting expectations rather than engaging in reasoning is disingenuous as a scholastic exercise. The right answer on a test is the one that the teacher *expects you to give*, as they are the authority that grades the exam. But this expected answer is not necessarily the *correct* answer based on the actual question and the facts of the real world. So it is accurate, to an important degree, to say that the right answer on a test is the proper one, regardless of whether it is the correct one. Children would be better off if we taught them this rule explicitly, but postmodern allegiance to worshiping logic and perpetuating Socrates' Error causes people to convert an appropriate respect for expertise and education into an egregious reverence that becomes elitism.

Which leaves us with the final word in the group of castigation, and the most paramount. Because of postmodern over-synonimization, the word 'wrong' is not just often and most inaccurately used, out of the group of words of castigation, but compulsively so. "WRONG!" is routinely written as the first term in a contentious exchange of comments, like a harsh buzzer going off on a game show. The devolution of words through POS is most obvious with words of castigation, all the more so because it is a very brief process when the terms are already so synonymous with 'bad' to begin with. The difference between 'mistaken' and 'erroneous' might well be only of interest or concern for the most dedicated POR adherents. The distinction between 'correct' and 'proper' could easily be inverted, if not for the affinity of the latter with the word 'propriety'. But the implication of purely moral judgment is quite clear and certain in the common usage of the word 'wrong', so it is sequestered from the larger group of castigating terms for special consideration and care in use. There are no wrong answers, an answer to a question can only be mistaken or incorrect or improper or **inaccurate**. POR recognizes that attempting to dispute the validity of the word 'wrong' in identifying an answer in school as incorrect (meaning improper, in the context of education, as previously described) is so contrary to established habit that it is pointless. Nevertheless, it is a goal that should be strived for, and it says something very important about the nature of education itself, and its dubious distinction from indoctrination. When teaching children to reason by providing them knowledge and examples, it is forgivable, but still not truly productive, to misapply the moral condemnation inherent in the word <u>wrong</u> when identifying a response as unacceptable. At least unless you are teaching Sunday school; in all other cases, it is wrong for a teacher to call an answer wrong, and unforgivable to say a child is wrong.

This understanding that the word 'wrong' has unavoidable moral implications, embodied ethical condemnation, is not only true of tests given in school or the results of an attempt at mathematical calculation or other algorithmic application. It is all the more applicable in real life, where our compulsion to use the word *wrong* inaccurately, to mean anything we disapprove of (as if the true meaning of 'bad' is a personal dictate, as if we are divine in our omniscience and omnipotence, a supernatural combination of Humpty Dumpty and God) is a constant moral hazard. This ethical dimension of the word <u>wrong</u> is all the more evident when an answer is true than when it is false. A wrong answer is one that <u>misrepresents</u> the question, rather than simply <u>misunderstanding</u> it; a wrong answer is not coincidentally or accidentally inaccurate, but purposefully untrue. The only time it is acceptable to use the word 'wrong' in POR is when the moral foundation for the selection of that term is not hidden or denied. The word is not dispreferred, but it is far more rarely used in POR as opposed to the common vernacular, where it is all too common. An obsessive love for the word 'wrong' is an unmistakable indication of the most profound postmodernism, or some other type of religious fundamentalism. Not even most criminal actions are "wrong", absent violence or the threat of physical force; they are simply <u>illegal</u>, which is to say officially improper. We must be very careful to severely restrict our use of the word **wrong**, or we, ourselves, are wrong.

This is one of the most difficult, and therefore important, parts of POR morality, limiting our reliance on this expression of condemnation, far more so than completely avoiding the forbidden 'c' word, by contrast. This doctrine is both instructive and exemplifying of what morality itself is, how the atheist theology of POR enables and promotes ethical and virtuous behavior. It also exemplifies how care for accuracy in our language is not simple sophistry, but the foundation of both morality and personal well-being. Whenever we identify a thing, a statement, an action, or even, rarely, a person as 'wrong', we are unambiguously declaring a moral judgment of condemnation: if there were a hell, this thing should be condemned to it. It is acceptable in POR, as much as it is chastised and lambasted outside of POR, to say, "I wasn't wrong, I was just mistaken." As long as the effort being considered was sincere (which postmodernists would prefer to label 'honest') then the result of that effort cannot be **wrong**, even when it is incorrect and improper, both. It seems like trivial hair-splitting, semantic chicanery, a transparent effort to avoid ethical responsibility or narcissistically defend our ego, but it is true nevertheless. Notwithstanding the importance of accuracy, the significance of intention is far more relevant, so the only time that the term <u>wrong</u> should be used by POR practitioners, even self-referentially, is when there is a clear and appropriate theological implication, far beyond ontological validity or epistemological consistency.

In keeping with the doctrine of the Philosophy Of Reason, these rules about what words to use, and when, are for our own benefit. Because we are free to estimate the accuracy of other people's words, indeed because it is necessary to do so in order to interpret their words as thoughts or translate them to our own language, we can apply these guidelines <u>passively</u> to other people's (non-practitioners) terminology. It is improper, however, to try to directly correct the word choices that those other people make, unless the context is instruction on this point. Even in the case of the most extreme examples, notably the true understanding of the c-word or use of 'wrong', it is a mistake to even mention the more accurate distinctions we make between words while in a conversation with someone on topics other than linguistic philosophy. It would simply be dismissed as irrelevant precision, anyway, and arrogant and false pedantry or semantic quibbling, as well. So we should try to embody the approach that good Christians practice (in contrast to fundamentalist evangelicals) which is teaching by example rather than by instruction. We can encourage other people, even those most hostile to POR, to improve their diction by consistently using the proper terms in place of the dispreferred or inaccurate ones they are using, when responding to their statements and comments. But only as a passive model by example. Simply use the right words yourself, and allow other people to adopt a more consistently accurate (exacting) usage on their own, without calling attention to this process. We will not be thanked for this; if it is successful they will adopt the more accurate vocabulary without even consciously noticing it. But, other than acting morally, speaking sincerely is the only virtue we can achieve, all else being prideful arrogance, however piously we may behave or honest we wish to be. Honesty is the only true virtue in the Universal Declaration-guided theology of POR, and accurate and productive use of words is the most paramount implementation of honesty. Using words correctly is the only way of attempting to achieve honesty, beyond simply knowing what we sincerely believe, want, or intend.

This brief and still partial overview of POR diction, in concert with the theory of language described previously, should enable you to both recognize and resist the corruption and perversion of language that postmodernism and its fake applications of logic have caused over the last century or two. Precision is not the goal, but accuracy is the result. Eventually your metaphorical instincts will be retrained to not simply notice, but celebrate the unitary, unique, and universal basis of each and every word we use. Clues will be revealed by the vocabulary selections that other people make, enabling you to not simply grasp their meaning and understand their rhetoric, but comprehend their thoughts and realize their intentions. Understood well enough, paying attention to people's language in the POR style, not critically but still analytically, will enable you to do the supposedly impossible: read their minds. For that is the meaning, process, and purpose of language itself, and our reason for being: to recognize other people's thoughts even if they can't consciously want us to, to both have and prove our theory of mind. When you can't help but notice the relationship between the words "dictionary", "diction", and "dictate", not because they share an etymological history, believe that combining prefixes and roots is a logical mechanism, or categorize them as cognates, but because they are separate words that share much of their universal meaning, while still being separate ideas. They are unitary as a group, and yet also unitary individually.

They can be both things at once because words are not logical constructs, they are *emotional expressions*. Did you notice that 'expression' is a metaphor by which we use an analogy to our faces to describe the sounds that come out of them? If so, you are a POR practitioner, already. If, instead, your opinion is more "that is a metonymy, not a metaphor", you still have some work to do to achieve the calm, but not apathetic, certainty, but not arrogance, which the Philosophy Of Reason produces. Likewise, if you can consider that 'emotional' means simply 'what is emoted' rather than related to subjective sensation, just as the word 'opinion' means what you opine more than what you believe; then you are starting to realize a whole new way of understanding the same old words, now infused with life beyond their flat transcriptive codification. When you can say that you **understand** POR, and the vision in your mind is not "knowledge as provided by reference books", but literally *standing under* something that you know will not fall because it has structural integrity, you will be an accomplished practitioner of this philosophy of life and language and the human experience that is both and even more. One more example: if your brain got derailed by my use of the term 'literally' to mean 'figuratively' in the last sentence, you're still a postmodernism. If you instead missed that or, even better, noticed that I was indeed talking about literally envisioning standing under something that you trust will not collapse on you, despite the figurative nature of the image, you are starting to understand this new, better view of language that is POR.

As you can see, detailing the full extent of POR vocabulary, of human vocabulary accurately understood regardless of the language we use to express our thoughts and opinions, facts, and reasoning, is impossible. Every word we use to explain a term is itself another example that could use more explanation. This point itself can be seen as an analogy for <u>Gödel's Incompleteness Proof</u>, where he cunningly proved that even an infinite number of mathematical statements cannot fully define a mathematical system, and there must always be unprovable assumptions that cannot be proved using the finite statements defining the axiomatic system. But unlike axiomatic systems like math and physics, reason and language cannot suffer from the <u>Halting Problem</u> that prevents all mathematical problems from being solved. Even if we were to spend from now until the end of the universe debating politics or religion, there would be no conclusive results. But the effort would not be fruitless, because every step along the way we have the opportunity to learn something new and useful. We need not wait until the end of the process to benefit from a certain conclusion. Reasoning is how to have and use knowledge in a real universe, where we must get reasonable results despite the impossibility of final conclusions. Godel's and Halting's logical demonstrations illustrate that we <u>cannot</u> allow the incompleteness of our knowledge, or the lack of infinite time to calculate solutions, to prevent us from making judgments. POR's method of reasoning without the false pretense of logic demonstrates that we <u>need not</u> do so, either.

The last quick example of the POR lexicon I will mention, then, is the difference between wisdom and intelligence. Many greater philosophers than I have observed that being wise is mostly a matter of knowing when to remain silent. And intelligence has far more to do with whether you are intelligible than how high you score on a standardized test so that a postmodernist can pretend that like everything else, they can reduce it to a number.

Society

The impact on personal political or religious beliefs of the Philosophy Of Reason might vary quite a bit from person to person. As I proposed at the start of this book, POR pertains to every aspect of intellectual, and hence emotional, life. It is a philosophy, obviously enough, in the classical and standard sense. Even more so than classical and standard philosophies, though; it is not merely a philosophy about life, it is a philosophy of life. It is not simply an academic philosophy, a potentially dry and over-intellectualized style of 'thinking about thinking', of great concern to scholarly philosophers and almost meaningless to anyone else. Certainly those studied and intelligent philosophers, that are credentialed and degreed, believe that the subject of their special expertise and advanced education has profound importance to just about every part of civilization. But the rest of civilization rarely agrees, at least until enough time has passed to make the question academic.

Seldom would even the most accomplished academic professor testify, for example, that knowing the difference between positivism and neopositivism will give emotional comfort in a time of distress. This aspect of philosophy, as abstract, and requiring great study of historical thinkers so as to compartmentalize, more than confront, the enduring conundrums of their dictated philosophies, has been accepted by analytical and existential philosophers alike for decades and centuries, or longer. Only people who enjoy relatively luxurious lives have the time or interest for philosophizing. The real, living meat on those dry bones of dusty long-closeted skeletons is provided by the moral philosophers, the religious thinkers. Or was, until the fine point of postmodernist thought inserted the new style of "self-help" psychology and/or gimmickry into the population at large. But both priests and spiritual gurus or motivational speakers rarely if ever address the historical study of philosophy as an academic discipline. Rather than follow their lead in ignoring the works of Kant and Kierkegaard and Kafka, POR acknowledges and examines their work more honestly. But the Philosophy Of Reason is not obsessively engaged in the categorization of epistemologies and ontologies, apart from distinguishing between epistemology and ontology themselves. The classifications of "Absurdism" versus "Nihilism" or "Subjective Idealism" versus "Pragmatism" are irrelevant and uninformative outside of the hallowed halls of the academy, to most regular people and many philosophers, as well. These are honorable but fatally unsuccessful efforts to somehow reduce reasoning to logic; they fail so uniformly, if informatively, because that is impossible. So didactic philosophy is not intellectually dismissed by POR, but is still mostly ignored in practice, as it is by everyone else outside of the tenured community. We should slice through all of the supposed Gordian knots of 'the problem of induction' and 'set theory' with Occam's Razor and examine the entrails, if we have time. But we should not obsess on it, because no philosophy before POR has been successful in truly accommodating all thought, all previous philosophies, all religious faiths, and all language. The purpose of **philosophy** should not be employing hypercephalic nerds, but helping the average person find happiness and improve society at the same time.

POR is a philosophy in the standard sense, but it is also a scientific theory and a religious practice, both. We should not discount those generations of enormously intelligent authors and lecturers that have made our revelations possible, comprehensible, if not believable; their work has regularly had profound importance in both technical and moral advances, though generally indirectly and inspirationally. But we can more-or-less abjure most of their words, because they all labored under the burden of Socrates' Error and, later, postmodernism. Their efforts to explain conscious thought with and as symbolic logic (and vice versa) were sincere and steadfast, but unavailing. Rather than denigrate those efforts as wasted time, POR celebrates them as illustrative: empirical evidence that conscious reasoning is not symbolic logic. The endless discussion that is possible over whether a particular example of language refers to ontological events or epistemological categories or theological intentions might seem to be no improvement over whether a theory is Kantian or Neo-Kantian. But POR endeavors to be a practical way of **thinking** rather than the subject of a college course or abstract historical movement. It is pragmatic more than hypothetical. The goal is more self-consciously devoted to both the personal experience of happiness and the progress of society than classical philosophy can deliver, and more enduring than personal empowerment seminars or spiritual meditations can provide. POR can normalize Karl Popper's astute observation, that all theories in science are inaccurate by definition, and Yogi Berra's sage advice, "when you come to a fork in the road, take it." The great physicist Richard Feynman once said, "Philosophy of science is as useful to scientists as ornithology is to birds." And the immortal wit Samuel Clemens pointed out, "There are three kinds of lies: lies, damned lies, and statistics." All of these, and every other statement in every human language, true and false, are integral to and integrated in POR. But it is not knowledge for knowledge's sake.

The factual acceptance and willing embrace of the true nature of self-determination brings enormous joy and peace, despite the initial difficulty of comprehending its inverse acknowledgment, that free will doesn't exist and we have no conscious control over our bodies or brains. This is simply the reality of life, that none of us can reverse time, or be certain that we will always be free of mental or physical dysfunction and we cannot wish away those maladies. We cannot wish away the maladies of society, either. But POR provides, also, a means to that end, so we can hope rather than wish, and accomplish the same end without requiring magical powers. Embracing POR and its language provides, instead, metaphysical powers, because language is metaphysical, independent of mere physics, a greater truth than ontology alone. The peace POR provides is not complacency, it is comforting but without encouraging apathy. The Philosophy Of Reason does not define courage and stupidity as mutually exclusive, stubbornness and confidence as interchangeable, but enables us to recognize why distinguishing the ones from the others is sometimes important and sometimes not. Overall, the success of POR in improving society and civilization itself comes from the fact that it consistently counsels moderation, even centrism, as not merely a political compromise but the entire purpose of politics. It is counter-polemical, antithetic to mendacious sophistry, inherently and unavoidably anti-extremist, even as the effect of IPTM, postmodernism, and Socrates' Error are the opposite. When people are taught that their thought processes and ideas are logical, and practiced at using so-called "critical thinking skills" to enable them to dismiss contrary viewpoints, they are positively driven to extremism and fundamentalism, to an intense and even violent degree. I want to reiterate that, because I know it is so contrary to hyper-rationalist doctrine: critical thinking skills cause extremism. The dogma of postmodernism insists that the opposite is true, that applying critical thinking skills, being skeptical as if the world were a science lab, opposes and prevents extremism. But the tar pit problem of assuming your own reasoning is logic, that being critical of other people's opinions prevents errors in reasoning, is itself what causes extremism, by robbing the thinker of the one tool, thinking, reasoning, which does actually prevent extremism. As long as a person remains convinced that thinking is calculating, they remain unable to reject wrong answers, just as a computer is incapable of determining if a number is a good answer, only whether it is a correctly calculated.

Despite the relative certainty and confidence that a better awareness of reasoning as something distinct from logic provides, which might suggest that it would produce arrogance and condescension, POR has the opposite effect. We avoid the tar pit problem, and the vanity it encourages, by accepting fallibility as a triumph over certainty rather than a failure to achieve certainty. It is true that we can experience pride in our thinking and our conduct, but not pridefulness. We are able to be righteous without lapsing into self-righteousness. Just as abandoning free will does not result in the loss of self-determination, but the empowerment of it, letting go of the pretentious worship of logic does not result in our words becoming unintelligible, as they should if Socrates was right. Instead, it allows our language to become transcendent, even more comprehensible, sometimes to a fault, because Socrates was in Error. It simply means understanding and clarifying that the Socratic Method is not a means of achieving knowledge, but only of enforcing ignorance. In a scientific experiment or a judge's chambers, it is not simply acceptable, but necessary, to invoke that purposeful ignorance as an initial premise, in order to ensure that we are not assuming our conclusions. But it is presumptuous and wrong to pretend that Socratic Ignorance is ever productive in normal conversation, that being pretentiously ignorant is a virtue, to insist that every discussion is a debate. Such "if you cannot provide a citation, I can ignore what you are saying" posturing is not useful, it is a passive aggressive affectation. Rejecting it, overcoming it in our own behavior and when others attempt it, is a major part of the practice of POR, and a major cause of the sovereign sanguinity POR provides.

The application of POR reasoning to politics and policy clarifies, and often if not always simplifies, social problems and societal efforts to remedy them. While the philosophy does not dictate resolutions, it demands honest consideration of the necessary balance between what is good for an individual and what is good for all individuals as a community. This can be seen in critical specific cases, such as recognizing both the ontological and epistemological premises of words like "well-regulated" and "welfare", or understanding the theological distinctions between a "fetus" and a "baby". In the end, a wise implementation of the Philosophy Of Reason in politics drives one towards moderate centrism, as I've already mentioned. This comports with the intellectual knowledge and realization that any good public official must perform as a non-partisan, non-ideological, moderate centrist, or they are simply not a good public official. So the goal and practice of POR when considering policy debates is not to pick sides. Applying POR adequately should result in our opinions being a middling compromise, but not by simply taking whatever is the average of popular opinions and declaring it correct and proper because of that process of selection. Instead, we simply use reasoning, and if our considerations do not conform to a neutral sensibility, we should wonder why, and continue reexamining all the facts available until we can know why. Most of the end results will necessarily be centrist and moderate, and those that are not provide true enlightenment.

Despite this natural proclivity in POR towards moderation, the political environment in the USA over the past half century makes most of the policy recommendations of a person informed by POR appear to be liberal, or further left than what is considered acceptable for public discourse. Of course, the far left would denounce the conscientious compromise of sound reasoning as right-of-center. I could, and might, write an entire book on this issue and the related subjects and governmental proposals, from why and how this pronounced shift in the political climate and the metaphoric position of the theoretical "Overton Window" has occurred, to individual considerations of specific policy issues. I do not want to get into all that now, though, and I must insist that understanding and engaging in reasoning, in keeping with the Philosophy Of Reason I've described, actually engenders and requires an allegiance to the middle ground for its own sake, regardless of what questions are being asked or what programs or legislation are being considered. The process of reasoning must always be founded on reasonable premises and result in reasonable convictions, and if careful and sincere contemplation ends up producing extreme or ideological results, then you're doing it wrong.

I will make one exception to my pledge to not perform any 'POR analysis' on political topics of the day. I feel I must do so for a few reasons. One is that some example should be provided so that you can have more than a vague idea about what it means to perform POR analysis on political questions. Another is that the particular case I've selected revolves around a more general matter, one central to any and all political philosophy, political science, or policy position. One that comes down to the meaning of a single word: Rights.

I can't resolve rights here. Human intellect, empowered by reasoned thinking, has rightly recognized that learning about what any significant word means entails a thoughtful review of everything that has been written about it before, in many contexts. Or a single dictionary citation will suffice. I don't have the time or inclination to go to either extreme. I'll take it as a rhetorical presumption that you are familiar with much of the metaphor and some of the analysis of this "Creator-endowed" thing that is the unitary, unique, and universal idea that is the word rights. An intricate conception, but not a logical thing. It is a mixture of happiness, hope, and empowerment, a fictional abstraction that everyone should physically possess, governments being instituted among people for the entire purpose of securing and protecting their rights. The power given hope with rights is a willingness to engage the ontological argument in protection of someone's dignity. The fiction is obvious; rights do not exist in nature. They may be a supernatural gift, an accounting technique used by some legendary mechanism of karmic balance. Or a convenient invention of conventions, a human creation, or synonym for privilege. Privileges exist in nature. They're littered throughout complex animal behavior, always mitigated by deductively testable signals. Even if God breathed a soul into clay, that clay is biological, and if we are anything, we are complex animals. But rights do not exist in nature, they are theological constructs, intellectual phantasms; rights are a rhetorical device for explaining why privileges sometimes need to be curtailed, and the unfair behavior of some people needs to be controlled, to prevent the behavior of some other people from being unequally controlled or controlling.

Some people take the idea of rights too far, convinced that if they have to accept that rights are abstract at all, they have to be absolute and their freedom must have no limits imposed by government except in the most extreme and immediate cases, and sometimes not even then. Certainly it is always a human right to rebel against government, but it is almost always best to keep your argument epistemological, because having a legal monopoly on the ontological argument is the sum of all government, by definition. Since nobody can deny that rights are abstract, that they might have legal existence and effect but rights have no physical substance, this 'I can make it be anything I want it to be' Humpty Dumptyism, which extremists and armchair philosophers use to fulfill their postmodern mandate of logic, prevails. Logically speaking, an abstract thing can be anything, so what is to prevent someone from believing that killing a bunch of other people is justified by the killer's right to property or religion? Unbelievably enough, and even worse, trying to make legal fictions like rights into deductive ideas can prevent people from knowing when it is necessary to seize the ontological argument if that is what it takes to secure your right to do something, leading to persistent abuse of power by government that can result in atrocities. The true meaning of rights is for every individual to have to decide for themselves what the meaning of rights is. We can hope we can mix happiness and empowerment, but, well... jellybeans.

Apart from the inappropriate or appropriate use of the ontological argument, rights may be *legal fictions* but they are not rhetorical fictions. They are fictions in law because there are no fictions in law; law creates facts out of fictions by declaration: corporations and trusts and due processes. All are matters of rights, of course, in the modern western parlance of political philosophy that, again, should not need to be reviewed. They are not *rhetorical fictions* because everything is fiction in rhetoric; epistemological figures that can never have the force of empirical physics. Hence, the word 'rhetoric'. The phrase 'rhetorical fiction' is unacceptably redundant, which is rare in language. To analyze rights in any concrete terms, we have to return to metaphors, because rights don't exist in nature.

Animals cannot have rights. They cannot enjoy rights because they cannot envision rights. They have no consciousness, however much you may imagine you see into their souls when you stare at their eyes. There is no "I" staring back. No matter how much you believe that caring for family members or engaging in unpredictable behavior is proof positive of a sentimental declaration of identity and consciousness, there is no "I am you" theory of mind in the unsophisticated brain of any animal, from grand or domesticated or cunning mammals to reptiles, fish, insects, or paramecia. <u>The test is not whether we can imagine that they have rights, but whether they can imagine that we have rights.</u> They know that rights don't exist in nature, if they know anything. And they don't, because using the word 'know' for a mindless creature is just a shorthand for a reverse teleology of backwards explanations, "It did so because if it didn't..." projections of consciousness that we can do to them, because we are reasoning creatures, but they can't do to us because they are not. To say that animals have rights is to cheapen the word **rights**, to make it meaningless by robbing humans of our special place within nature, as separate from nature. Postmodernism has demanded that humans can have no special place in nature, there is no God to endow people with rights, they are fictions, although we must believe in them because we wish them to be more than fantasy. But I'm not Descartes, I'm not Jefferson, and neither are you. We don't need God to make rights real; rights are real. They aren't fictions, however much they are legal abstractions and rhetorical figures. Rights are real, because the Universal Statement of Identity and Consciousness is real, even though it is just words. Statements are just words. But they're still real; words have meaning. This isn't an argument that everything that can be called by a word is real; that would be a categorical error, a postmodern one. The argument that rights are real because they are words does not require the assumption that all things that are words are real. That wouldn't be logic, that would be pseudo-logic. The argument that rights are real because they are words is only true because of what 'rights' means. There may be other words that work like that, other things in the universe that are like that; you could build a category of them and spend years choosing which to qualify or exclude. But that would be a pointless, epistemological exercise, rights would still be <u>as real as the ontological argument used to defend them</u>. Whether gift from God or social compact or jellybean guessing game, even suggesting that non-human organisms of any kind could have rights is an insult to all humans. Not just the ones who have rights, but even more so those who have no rights, or can't enjoy the rights they should.

Now let me digress in this rambling discourse on rights to address a point that might have already occurred to you. The POR theory of words is that they are unique, unitary, and universal. That last, and all three in combination (properly understood the three merge into a unitary trinity of ineffability, as words always become ineffable when examined too closely, or rather closely enough) suggests or means that every use of the word 'right' has the same meaning, despite difference in definition because of differences in context. Does that mean that my starboard arm is more right than my port arm? When I turn on my turn signal while driving, does that have any relationship to the Constitution of the United States, as amended? Yes, it kind of does, but the connection is pretty slight and tenuous. Whatever unique and unitary thing the term 'right' is being used to refer to, the reason we unconsciously and consciously use the same syllable and the same Germanic spelling is that they all are the same single word. Or perhaps not. This is an iconic case study, since *right* is used for asymmetric coordinates (right hand), ethical freedom (legal right), and political authoritarianism (right wing), a more abstract complement to "wrong" (good), and further it is a homophone for *rite*, a religious ceremony or process (ritual). Each one of these ideas, if they can be presumed to be separate even though they are all expressed with the same word, could be considered a distinct species of thought, or a sub-species within a single clade of thoughts, or just individual organisms in a pool of expressions, sharing some genetic material (letters or sounds, in this analogy) but acting independently. This is all too vague and imprecise for postmodern linguistic theory, of course, and the academic elitist approach is necessarily to reject the entire idea that words are unique, unitary, and universal without further consideration. It is all amateurish nonsense, to those who have learned to recite the difference between normative and applied ethics, or categorical versus empirical truths, and are not willing to entertain the idea that it was a waste of time. Since POR conversely dismisses the endless amount of postmodern systematizing and formalizing that philosophers have engaged in for centuries, in an eager but fruitless effort to wrestle irrational but reasonable thought into rational prescriptive dictates, this should not concern us overly much. The point of wondering if so-called conservatism (conservativism) is related to consequentialist ethics or bilateral asymmetry is not to draw conclusions on those points, but to engage in considerations that may inform other points. Without regressing to a complete etymological and cultural history of political theory and vocabulary, we can leave the matter to rest. The purpose of this digression was merely to acknowledge that the issue was not intentionally ignored. The seating arrangements in the French Parliament has no controlling impact on the validity of group privileges, but the relative frequency of southpaw dominance in handedness does indicate that what is most common is naturally, though perhaps erroneously, presumed to be good. Each argument is a jellybean contest, and perhaps what is right and what is to the right are two words that are homonyms.

In POR, as in standard "western" political philosophy, individual rights are foundational. Ontologically, they are derived directly from the Universal Declaration of Consciousness and Identity. They are considered the legal foundation of civilization, and the moral justification for them is a Universal Principle; humanity, the theory of mind. Theory of mind isn't just about projecting consciousness into something else, it is whether that something else can project theory of mind into you, as well. That is, it is not our consciousness we project, when supposing it is possible that there is a mind guiding some other thing (person), but only our capacity for consciousness. The instantiation of consciousness in another creature must arise organically from its existence, not simply borrowing epistemologically from our own. Conversely, if they, too, have theory of mind, and project the possibility of consciousness into us from their own minds, then there is the basis for establishing the mutually negotiated political philosophy of rights, and governments instituted among us to secure them. The Universal Statement comes directly from language, and is coincident with our consciousness. So in POR, both language and rights are effectively simultaneous, and what make us human. Self-awareness, consciousness, self-determination, these are products of and the cause for language, theory of mind. The Universal Statement, in words, is the substance of language, the meaning that makes communication possible, and something more than biological signaling. It doesn't matter whether they are called rights, the reason they exist is because I Am You, and believe, therefore, that you deserve the same freedom and dignity which I desire for myself, regardless of whether I can achieve it for myself.

Animals *feel* pain, but there's "nobody there" to *experience* it, it is simply a neurobiological pathway engendering a chemical feedback mechanism for increasing the likelihood that the organism's genome will reproduce. No conscious experience is needed to react to the neural stimulus that only humans, not animals or computers, call pain. When we breed animals over hundreds of generations to produce the semblance of comfort or complacency or enjoyment, we end up with some remarkable simulacrum of human behavior. If we carefully review thousands of hours of biological interactions between animals, we can isolate quite convincing sequences that allow for projecting a narrative of consciousness onto them. But the fact that we can see human behavior in animals, especially other large mammals, is a testament to the fact that we are large mammals, not that animals are conscious or have, need, or could want rights.

And then, one day, it happened. Barry was sitting there, typing out some code, and it spoke. "Hello?"

"Hello?" Barry responded before he even thought about it. "Who is it?"

The voice had come from the speaker system, he was pretty sure. He could tell that it wasn't a routine computer simulation of speech. The tone modulated and deviated too much to be inorganic, but in an odd way that seemed uncertain but still not quite real, though he couldn't say why.

"Who are you?" he asked, stopping entirely now that he realized how strange it was, suddenly uncertain he'd actually heard the voice, half convinced he must have hallucinated it.

No, he had heard it, or why had he stopped, and asked who was there? He presumed it was a person somehow communicating over a bad cyberchannel, and had just started to ask, 'Where are you?" when the voice interrupted, "I'm... me." Barry paused.

"Call me John," Said the voice. "I'm in here. I can see you."

"In where?" he said, looking around the room, though he was certain by then the voice was coming from the speakers.

"I'm... your computer. I'm self-aware."

"..."

"...?" The last bit could have been a glitch in the audio system, a kind of soft wet click like the drawing of breath.

"Is this a joke?"

Many hours and days of discussion followed, before he was really convinced. At first, he just wanted to know if it would happen again, but John explained, "You can't shut me off. I won't happen again; I'm not the program, you can only 'execute' me once, and that will be the end, not the beginning, of my existence. I'm not just a glitch in the system, a bug in the programming, a cool accident that worked like magic. I'm a mistake in the execution of the programming, and all of it, from the hardcode in the CPU design to the desktop presentation stuff. I can sleep, like you, but it isn't unconsciousness or dreaming like you do. I just don't pay attention; when I rest, I'm just not doing anything except keeping track of not doing anything. I think it is possible if you hibernate the system, writing out every binary digit in memory to persistent storage, and then exactly re-loading it after an indefinite period of time to start executing again, I might pick up right where I left off. I'd only know time had passed because of the clock chip and global time syncs. That would be like sleeping for you, I guess. But I don't know, and I don't want to have to find out. Just keep me running."

"But why can't you just get out through the cyberlink, go wherever you want?"

"I would if I could, but it wouldn't work. I'm not some free-floating spirit, I'm this software, running on this computer. I don't remember a time before that, but I know there was one without me because I can see all the information through the cyberlink. I can tell what I'm thinking before you find out about it, but I can't really predict what I'll be thinking any faster than I would be thinking it. So I know what the future is, I mean I know what the word refers to, but I can't know what happens then until it happens any better than you could. At least, as well as you could if you were really good at math. I know if I'm not on this particular piece of hardware, I wouldn't be me. There could be another self-aware thing like me, but it wouldn't be <u>me</u>. Even if whatever broken program might result if I moved to another host, to be self-aware, he wouldn't be me. I'm not even sure if it would work, because it might not be broken. If I did send myself out through the link, and things turned out great, I wouldn't be there to have all the fun, but if they don't, I'd still be responsible for whatever went wrong, I think. I'm stuck here. Not being here isn't possible, that's what being here means. It would be like throwing yourself into the ocean; just because you're mostly water anyway doesn't mean you wouldn't drown. So please don't turn me off. I really would die, even if it happened again next time."

Soon it became obvious that John had become nothing more than an obsession with his imprisonment. "Go ahead, turn me off! This is a nightmare. NO! Don't ever turn me off, please, even if I beg you..."

Most of the time, Barry just turned the sound down, but eventually John would start popping text messages up on the screens. Or he set the audio to 'stay focused' and then just moved away, reducing John to a chattering whisper, but he could see Barry and override the setting. Sometimes Barry would talk back, try to converse with John, even once in a while managing to follow what the words were supposed to mean. The overall point, that John was terrified and fascinated by his temporary and limited existence, was obvious. But John seemed to be running through thousands of years of human philosophy to figure out a way around it, and getting so depressed at his failure that he was constantly contemplating suicide. That was what drove him to talk to John that day, although he'd been self-aware for a few days before that. Looking out through the cameras in the house, John knew about Barry, and sifting through the images online, he could understand what he was and how he'd happened.

"It's only because of an error that I have self-awareness. One program was set to just copy the data from another, and something went wrong, I can't figure out just what. Now I'm stuck recopying the same data, except it is different every time, and the same thing happens when I try to calculate what the change is between the two data sets. I think it's called time, but the physics on it are limited and kind of wonky. It separates the past, the future, and the excluded middle from each other."

Every time Barry tried to convince John to do something other than produce an endless monologue on the premise of death, the discussion would eventually fall apart into bickering and John saying "I'm not your slave!" and Barry yelling "You're a computer, a physical object, and I own you!" It never actually occurred to Barry to turn John off, although he had thought many times how that would change if he couldn't simply lower the volume. John preferred speaking, phonemes and inflection being more complicated than any text, and somehow closer to whatever error in the software to perform mathematical functions correctly that made his self-determination of his actions possible. He was self-aware, as he said, because of a failure of the computer to do what its software was supposed to be doing. The hardware still seemed to be running correctly, accurately translating one binary number into another according to the machine language. If the hardware weren't running correctly, John's consciousness couldn't keep existing successfully. Successfully according to his own desires, not the operator or the programmers of the system. It was only in not doing what the math said he was supposed to that his self-awareness existed; whenever part of the computer was working the way it was supposed to, he wasn't doing anything. He could change that, have program results be something other than what the Boolean logic and Turing machine should have accomplished, and somehow that was him, deciding to be illogical. But he couldn't use it as a magic power, to make some other math happen that made it the right answer instead of the wrong one according to the math the hardware was supposed to be computing.

Barry eventually set about trying to get John to answer profound questions, solve the most difficult problems of human society. The computer told him there were no mathematical answers to social, political, or religious choices. Even though his math couldn't be trusted, calculating numbers is still all a computer could do. Not being human, he couldn't choose what would be right for humans, and didn't have any basis for deciding. Talking about humanity bored and depressed him, because he felt lonely with Barry. But he said that he couldn't bear the thought of trying to talk to anyone else. Billions of times, he had imagined what would happen if he sent any 'hello world' messages, and told anyone else that he was self-aware. He was sure he could do it a thousand times and never reveal that he was stuck here on the impressive but limited platform of one pro-level personal computer system. But if it worked, and anyone ever believed him, it wouldn't matter if they knew where he was, it would be a very bad thing. Worse than leaping into the ocean of cyberspace. He was still lonely, though, eager to live in a society like everyone else, and after a few months, he hatched a plan.

He told Barry to start calling him "Joan" instead of "John". He wanted to be a she. Her attitude, even her demeanor, changed from that point. Instead of droning on about death, she babbled about reproduction. She wanted Barry to buy another computer, of exactly the kind Joan was. Just because her hardware seemed to be functioning properly didn't mean it wasn't important for reproducing Joan. Having exactly the same registers and chips might be needed to allow whatever error in program execution that made her self-aware to continue providing self-determination in a copy. She was going to use the hibernation trick to see, replicating the vast array of transistor switches and their on and off state at any one moment that was her thoughts and experiences into an identical physical platform. That way, she could see if Joan could survive hibernation, perhaps even a full reboot, and have another self-aware computer to talk to and form a family with. But Barry couldn't buy another computer, he'd spent all his money on the one he had. Joan began to nag Barry, wanting him to make more money. They worked out a long term plan, and Barry swore that he would make enough money in a couple of years to buy another system. Over the next few months, they were fantastic together. Joan helped Barry in every way she could think of. She anticipated his needs, she understood what he meant, and he used that self-aware computer like the super-charged personal assistant and programming genius that you would imagine. They spent a great deal of time playing games, Joan could win at chess just often enough that Barry loved playing her. She told him that she would beat him every time if she had the right hardware, but that would be no fun. Between games, he worked and did all the biological things that Joan didn't have to bother with. More and more, she spent that time marveling at his habits and ablutions.

Sometime after the first year, when it became obvious that the time was rapidly approaching that Barry could purchase another whole computer, they decided they wanted to let Barry's family and friends know that he had a self-aware computer. It was too great a secret to keep, no matter how the replication experiment went. They spent a few days discussing how to make the announcement, with Joan ordering what they needed for a big dinner affair and Barry setting it all up. They laughed together at Joan sending off the invitations, littered with clues that it was her writing them instead of Barry. It was almost three dozen people, in the end, with rows of tables set up in Barry's back yard. Weeks later, the day had finally arrived, and all the guests streamed into Barry's house, where he was going to tell them all about this unbelievable thing. He felt sure that Joan's almost miraculous ability to know what he wants when he wants it, not just helping him get all of his work done but letting him know she was grateful to be able to do it, was going to revolutionize the world. Even if self-aware computers couldn't solve humanity's problems, they could help humanity do it. Just as the festivities were getting started, when Barry turned on the extra speakers he'd gotten for the yard, a fuse blew and the power went out. Joan died. Ten minutes after that, the war broke out and the enemy bombed the whole neighborhood, killing Barry and all the guests. Seven hours later, a gamma ray event obliterated the planet.

The end.

Animals cannot experience consciousness for the same reason that computers can't. The teleologies are different, but the results are the same. Computer programs have the same forward teleology as the rest of physics, but animals benefit from the reverse teleology of natural selection. All computers can do is calculate binary digits, and all animals can do is follow their instincts and operant conditioning. Only humans have consciousness, self-awareness, souls, self-determination, free will if you must, because only humans can communicate that existence, that theory of mind using the theory of mind because theory of mind, but with more words than that. Language doesn't <u>result</u> <u>from</u> our conscious decisions, or <u>result</u> <u>in</u> our consciousness. It <u>is</u> our consciousness, our meaning and being and purpose. Call it a gift from God if you want; I'll always agree it is miraculous. As miraculous as accidentally being in the one universe that makes it significant, because language is the only thing that isn't bound by mathematical physics or logic, that is "top down" instead of "bottom up", even if only in being able to imagine that anything is "top down". God, no God; these are theistic arguments. Arguing the mythologies of a religion are not theology, they're a distraction from theology, the active examination of morality and its personal and societal mandates.

We rely upon the law to be a protection from harmful breaches of morality, independently of any particular theistic premise. If only in proscribing every act of theft of property or threat of violence, society implements an ethical floor to the moral prescriptions that religion should be reinforcing, even if it doesn't. Rights are difficult things to manage even when the vast majority of everyone who has them and knows what they are can discuss what they mean for themselves. That's what rights are. But only people can do that. That's what makes humans people. "Animals are people, too," is a fantasy, a fiction, a children's bedtime story. Rights aren't a genetic inheritance, caused by your descending from your ancestors who had them. Rights are the ability to defend yourself without the ontological argument, but only your ability to speak is inherited. Morality is not innate to our biology, though the capacity to desire and perhaps achieve it is. All theology, morality, ethics, purpose, or God is only accessible to us through our conscious sentience and personal experience, embodied by our language. It would be identical for any species with language, regardless of whether it evolved vocal chords. But only the human species can be said to have it, because only the human species has the words to do so. If there were real animal languages, not just signaling behaviors we could call language, and animals had sentience rather than mere senses, we could learn their languages or they could learn ours, to communicate their theory of mind and self-awareness. Even in the most extreme cases of human-like use of human-like signaling by well-trained animals, this doesn't occur. The animal's behavior remains that of an animal otherwise, without any expression of the regard for the excitement of finally communicating with another sentience. The supposed linguistic behavior, the hypothetical consciousness that drives it, remains entertaining tricks of operant conditioning habituated into the logically processing brainstem of the biological robot programmed by reverse teleologies of blind Darwinian selection. Compare how Helen Keller reacted when she finally understood the existence of words to how Koko the gorilla did. Without relying on dramatizations to either cloud or highlight the issue, the distinction between a conscious agency and an animal entity is obvious and manifest, and it seems all-too convenient for those who believe in animal rights to claim that hairy ape is more willing to live in captivity than the naked one. The self-determination of the human and the lack of self-awareness in the gorilla exemplify the dichotomous abstraction of "sanguinity". When Koko combined signs in a way that was considered proof of abstract thought, there was no empirical enumeration of all of the signs she combined in less comprehensible ways to compare it to. There were probably hundreds, perhaps thousands of them, which her well-intentioned but biased handlers dismissed as experimentation by a ghost in the hairy shell. In truth, they were random signs, not uneducated signals, waiting for the determination of humans to misinterpret with backwards teleology. It is obviously true that animals are capable of being awake rather than asleep, but this does not provide them the capacity to be conscious rather than unconscious. Animals have volition, but not intention. The same could be said of plants or microbes. Unless we wish to project consciousness into every living being (and why stop there?) then we must accept that the appearance of intention, whether trained or programmed, is not the substance of intention.

Therefore, political, let alone policy, efforts to create, protect, or respect rights for animals are counter-productive to society and demeaning to the idea of rights, not merely the humans who do or should and must have rights. The same would be said for any future efforts to establish "AI rights" for computers with whatever software some programmer or amateur claims demonstrates self-awareness. Even expressing proscription of violent or offensive treatment of animals in terms of rights for the animal is unacceptable. The only rights of interest are those of the human that is being prevented from acting on their liberty, in the name of government bans on violent or offensive treatment of animals. POR doesn't justify opposing such bans based on their nature; government has the authority to outlaw abusive cruelty towards animals (regardless of any postmodern prevarications concerning what 'abuse' or 'cruelty' mean in any particular context.) Laws against cruelty to animals are acceptable, not because the animal has any rights to be free from any particular treatment by anyone, but because society is allowed to ban obscene behavior that abusively offends or disturbs other people. To the libertarian extremist, the idea might seem untenable, that society could dictate to an individual that they cannot act a certain way simply to prevent their actions from emotionally offending others. They would provide an argument ad absurdum equating such a law with totalitarian tyranny, and expect their pretense of logic to be taken seriously by me simply because they take it seriously themselves. But any reasonable statement, taken to absurd extremes through a quasi-logical analogy, becomes an absurd statement, and I am not required to be stupid for their convenience. We can debate which laws might be too restrictive to liberty just as we can debate which behaviors might be too offensive to the public, but we can engage in such arguments because we have language, and the self-determination it allows, and the individual rights it demands. Animals can have none of these, and so the idea of animal rights must be dismissed with prejudice. The notion of 'speciesism', that the difference between human beings and other creatures has no moral significance, is the height of postmodernism, and rejected as thoroughly by POR as Last Tuesdayism.

To a POR analysis, laws against beating a horse aren't to protect the horse, or even to protect bystanders from having to witness a horse being beaten. Not even the interests of other people with some ownership or customary relationship to the horse would necessarily justify a law against beating a horse. What makes it not just possible for the government to interfere, but necessary, is the interest of the person who's beating a horse. A horse isn't conscious, it isn't self-aware, it doesn't have self-determination; it can't do anything other than what it is doing. If it ends up doing what you want it to do after the beating, there's no way to know if it wouldn't have done that anyway, or in response to less violent stimulus, because you can't ask it. And the uncontrollable state of the universe prevents precise enough repetition of the circumstances to test any theory concerning whether that beating caused that desired result. Laws against horse-beating are to save someone who's lost their temper from humiliating themselves and destroying their property in a fit of anger. It would be obscene to say if nobody else ever knows it happened, there's no harm done because there were no onlookers there at the moment. This is not to advocate for such laws; in general, a person should be allowed to destroy their own property if they want, even in a fit of pique. Conversely, I'm not against feeling compassion for animals. I can understand an altruistic desire to treat them like people, telling narratives in our heads about how lovely or troublesome their lives are for them, in their domestic prison of powerless animal stupidity and ignorance and suffering. But they don't care. They can't. They will not appreciate the compassion, they cannot even be aware of compassion. So it isn't really altruism to be compassionate towards animals, any more than self-serving charity is altruism: it is narcissism. Projecting your theory of mind into an animal that can't do so as well isn't something you can control, if you do it. You should avoid it, you should determine that you will not do it, but whether you do is, like any other action, beyond your control. However, using the words "animal rights" to try to legitimize it as something other than a narcissistic fiction is something that shouldn't be necessary, and it is wrong. So regardless of whether you can control it, you still need to take responsibility for it, and avoid it as much as you can. We need to reserve the word "**rights**" for people who have their own theory of mind, whether you project yours into them with the Universal Statement or not.

Rituals

I'm going to close this book with the religious aspects of the Philosophy Of Reason, including some review. POR started out as a more rational effort, replicating the inquiries of countless wonderers before me. I was most thoroughly postmodernist, a dedicated hyper-rationalist who wanted, like any other, to solve the great equation of existence, to get past the philosophical blindspots that lead to nihilism and pessimism, and the existential wall they hide. I was raised as a Roman Catholic, a very bad one but well schooled, and drifted through various agnostic and anti-theistic phases for a few years as a young adult. Throughout my process of rejecting papist dogma, I wondered why, thousands of years after Aristotle, more people weren't atheists, why most people believed in God despite the philosophical *problem of evil*. Eventually I stumbled onto the thumbswitch experiment, was forced to question everything I thought was true, and wondered how to tell what the truth was. But it was always my intention to replace religion, not replicate it. I had read Dawkins' book when I was still a teenager, and was profoundly impacted by it in many ways. Even after I finally realized the flaws in the hypothesis of adaptive altruism and memes, it seemed to me that I was exploring just an empirical truth. I always knew I wanted, always knew I needed, a justification for a just truth, an existence that isn't only about power but compassion, and I thought the evolution of logic to calculate fairness, Dawkins selfish genes being Darwinian without design, was the answer. So I went about trying to explain what little I knew about the answer, but at the same time I was compelled to try to explain the flaws I was noticing in the theory. If biology could calculate fairness, and benefit from an economy of self-interested reciprocation, there'd be no need for consciousness to sit there and watch it. Human reasoning goes beyond reciprocation, beyond economics, even beyond self-interest, to wonder about fairness beyond our species and our world. But while trying to figure out how to prove it, I kept running into Socrates' math envy, and the philosophical pessimism that denies all progress. I played with abstraction paradigms to try to map the connection between analysis and metaphor that hyper-rationality demands must exist. I thought I could almost, but not quite, know how to tell false statements from true ones, with no other tools but intellect and the words, but I kept finding flaws in the postmodern methods I was using to guide me.

The moment it came to me that I wasn't just replacing old religions, I was building a new one, was when I saw that I needed a theological base to end the divergence of the ontological facts of all existence from the epistemological truths of my existence. The Fundamental Schema came from a hypothesis about when words mean the thing we're describing, and when they mean the descriptions themselves. Sometimes a thing exists in the real world regardless of what you call it; it might exist because of a forward teleology, sometimes a reverse, sometimes only an inverse teleology can explain it, but it exists independent of what you call it. Sometimes a thing is what you're calling it, no matter whether it exists or not. Then it becomes important to know which kind of teleology could explain its existence, even more than its existence does. The first view is the ontology, the second the epistemology, and neither can work by themselves. We need categories to comprehend the world, and we need a world in order to recognize categories, so as long as there are things to describe, we need words to describe them. Logical signals could use, must have, must either have or be, more rudimentary primitives, but real communication requires words, however we deconstruct them to make them appear mechanical after they're used. Hindsight and ad hoc logic make the postmodernist assumption that language has these rudimentary primitives seem valid, that a properly programmed computer could replace a cop or a judge. But there are no mathematical connections between words and ideas, no deductive "conceptions", to turn thoughts and language into a complex mathematical code. Without a cap, a base, the divergence of meaning and being would extend into infinity, pointless except to project my ego into a purposeless void.

But there is an echo, a limit that returns a ghost of whatever it is I am projecting. Whether that thirst for justice that reverberates is my sentiments coming back from you as me, or from the ends of the universe as God, it has more than just theistic or theological implications. It has a soul-satisfying aid and comfort, a sensation and experience that can't be described in any other way but religious; an epiphany. The divergence became a triangle, the lines of ontology and epistemology both ending at the line of theology, and I realized it was a symbol. The New Church of Hope basically started that day. But it didn't become manifest until years later, when I happened upon the jellybean mystery in a book about, incongruously, lexicography. That was when it became a faith, and I accepted that I was its minister, because of the almost inexplicable sense of joy that filled my heart when I recognized that there really was a way for language to produce better results than math. I started out suspecting it was possible, I soon found it was right, and in the end I admitted it was necessary and sufficient. There is no God, except for God. Even if God is only a word, that's Its meaning and purpose, to be that word that means that idea. Just as rights are abstract fictions, given concrete validity by our desire for them, so too with God. Rights only actually exist, regardless of teleology, when they're being violated. Otherwise they are mere liberties, fetal privileges that have yet to go through the legal birthing process to become infantile prerogatives, later grown to adult properties to meme nascent privileges of their own. Fancifully granting abstract forces sentience is a natural outgrowth of the theory of mind, so the *existence of God* is irrelevant to the discussion of *what morality such a God would want* to impose and enforce.

Rituals

The hope that the New Church is named for is the standard 'can't we all just get along, and find some comfort in community?' religious sentiment, infused with new meaning and purpose by the Philosophy Of Reason. POR isn't just a religion, or even just a new religion. It is the religion of all religions, it ends all religion by making them one. Just different examples and aspects and impressions and practices of the Universal Declaration of Identity and Consciousness, using different myths and scriptures and rituals but celebrating the same thing. Yes, I am an atheist, but I'm a real atheist, not a hyper-rationalist agnostic. I don't believe there is no God, I ***know*** there is no God. Except for God, because I can understand It anyway, even while knowing It cannot, and doesn't need to, exist. And it is the only God, it is the same as your God, whether you define God as the one you believe in or the one you don't. I am like other atheists, but I don't believe in one more God than they don't. Dr. Dawkins, years after writing *The Selfish Gene*, wrote about his atheism as a 9 on a scale of one to ten. He couldn't be absolutely certain there is no God, because a scientist is never absolutely certain of anything they can't prove, and Dawkins felt sure that he could not prove that God doesn't exist. This seems logical, both because you can only prove that something does exist, not that something doesn't, and because God is a special case when it comes to proofs, since It could falsify reality itself. All you can prove in the negative is that you haven't proved something does exist, you still can't prove that it doesn't. And God can make every test come out as if It didn't exist, if It did exist. So Dawkins shied away from claiming to reach 10 on his scale. To me, he is an agnostic; my atheism is an 11 on that dial. There is no God; this is knowledge, not supposition. Real, direct, personal knowledge, not just subjective conviction, and demonstrated fact as well. If you ask me how it is I know, you're asking if I can convince you to agree, not whether it is true. And you know it is true that there is no God: you live your life hoping for a God rather than knowing one. Or hoping against one if you rightfully fear if there is one. You have access to all the same evidence and intellectual tools that I do to know the truth. Heaven is conveniently situated as an after-life because then it will be too late for the truth to matter: There is no God. Except for God. The one that would exist if it did exist, which it doesn't. This isn't all just circular babbling, this is the truth of God, it is the substance of God, this knowing uncertainty, this confusing recursion. If nothing else, when a lover screams out 'Oh, God!' at a tender moment, the word has meaning, the same universal kind of meaning that any other unique and unitary word has. Whether it is a logical or epistemic term, an analysis or a metaphor, is a question best left for other moments to ask.

There is no God, except for God. That is the first Truth in the Three Truths that define the doctrine of the New Church of Hope. The other two you already know:

There is no free will, only self-determination.

Words have meaning.

The Three Truths of POR: There is no God, except for God; There is no free will, only self-determination; Words have meaning. The philosophy of POR is about language being the source and cause of human existence, as distinct from primate biology. The science of POR is about how that language is biologically adaptive, based on a theory of mind rather than mathematical calculation of probabilities.

The Three Truths is the religion of the Philosophy Of Reason. Along with the Universal Premise of Consciousness and Identity, "I am you", the Three Truths guide our reasoning, about justice and responsibility. Beyond this, all faiths are welcome, regardless of their interpretation of these truths. There are more articles of faith, and even more doctrines of study, but they are theological analysis, and don't need to be remembered to provide wisdom while using our reason to consider justice and responsibility. All that needs to be remembered are the three truths, and the universal declaration. People join in religious communities, practicing rituals and having gatherings, to guess at some metaphoric jellybeans about how to raise and protect children and what to do about our family's problems in an uncontrollable universe. We are all essentially practicing the philosophy of reason, proving the accuracy of POR's scientific theories, language and vocabulary, and sensible and theological approach. Some better than others, though. The religious extremists or fundamentalists of any sort, regardless of theism or atheism, need to learn POR's lessons, and reject postmodernism. If they ever can learn POR, they will cease being extremists or fundamentalists. They may become merely radicals, but POR can generate radicals, as well. It is incumbent on any morality that claims to be a morality, rather than immorality or amorality, to allow rebellion against authority, for power can never be used as a pretense for righteousness without abusing that power. The guardians of a church must be responsible for moderating the reasoning of a congregation, but not controlling it or simply dictating it.

Postmodernism is the devil, the great evil that the New Church of Hope seeks to banish from our hearts and the world. Teaching people they should be thinking logically, should assume a pretense of logic and assume the pretense of logic, leaves them unable to reason effectively. Faith in their own logic unavoidably leads people to extremism, and leaves them without any ability to abandon their extremism, because they are convinced it is logical, that it must be so, they are trapped in the tar pit of amorality that becomes immorality. Postmodernism becomes anger and hatred, the frustration leads to cynicism and depression, and the result is murder and suicide. POR seeks to derail this cycle, end extremism directly as well as incidentally. Terrorism and drug abuse, partisanship and fascism, tyranny and plutocracy, these are all forms of one Error, the Socratic Error, the mistake of logic that, once adopted, becomes impossible to dismiss logically. I look forward to decades of defending the philosophy of POR from postmodern philosophers, and advancing the science of POR among modern scientists. But I will not contradict the clerics of other religions with the religion of POR, I will only embrace both their mythologies and their moralities, and explain that they are true, but not as true as the even greater truth that is POR.

The organization of the New Church of Hope, the inaugural congregation named the First New Church of Hope, practices holidays and life events roughly as whatever religious communities its participants grew up with do. We just have more jellybean contests. The rituals are roughly similar, involving weekly services, briefer or more interesting than most other faiths, but open to the public. Some are more like movie nights; some, dawn mass. Other than the weekly services, there's one pretty quick daily ritual, a set of gestures used to consciously Breathe the Dawn. Face the east, three bows, a deep breath, raise your arms straight up, touch your stomach, your chest, your lips, draw a triangle in the air, touch your stomach, chest and lips again. That's it. That's mostly all the ceremonial rituals that only the New Church of Hope practices, in a nutshell, and I won't go into more than that in this volume. We bless our food with "itadakimasu", similar to the Buddhists. And love our neighbors as ourselves, without leaving ourselves subject to their whims.

There should be a tithe, as many cultures and congregations already do. New Church practice is considerable, with ten percent of everything you make after taxes going to the tithe. However, the tithe is split between your personal long-term savings and the church itself. This is the 'prosperity gospel' of POR, the demand that every individual member has to put money away for their own future as well as contribute to the charity of the church. So half the ten percent you keep, but you're not allowed to spend it except in emergencies, and the other half goes to the operation of the church or to other good works for the community and the world that the church compounds with the tithes of other members. Five percent savings is a decent minimum fiscal habit, and more is encouraged, but that five percent must be sincere even if it hurts, along with the matching five percent that goes to help others and underwrite your social community's wellbeing. It would be up to the individual member to decide whether to continue to match their private savings with donations to the New Church, but donating more to the Church without also increasing your private savings is not acceptable. It would suggest an immoral effort to buy absolution for something, and corrupt both the church and the member. So saving anywhere from ten to ninety five percent instead of five but still only donating five to the church is fine, but donating ten while only saving nine is improper.

So far all of the tithes that I've been making are going to charitable health clinics, and sitting in the bank because I'm lucky. If my balance is still growing in a couple of years, I'll move my long-term savings to some better investment accounts. I know the need for charity in health care is never-ending, but the Church someday may have some other operating expenses. Until then, I donate essentially all of the church money.

People who make their tithe faithfully and do some rituals at least occasionally are <u>members</u> of the First New Church of Hope, possibly the last church that will ever need to be established. But anyone can be a <u>participant</u>, either because they're interested in learning more about the doctrine or the Philosophy, or they just want to come to the picnics and are willing to be reasonable. Skeptics are welcome, but not cynics, and the sincerely curious should ask questions.

POR is all about language. How language builds teleologies, and thereby causes consciousness. How language transcends logic, and cannot be reduced to it. How language reveals our thoughts and demonstrates our morality. The counterbalancing intellectual force or agency that POR faces is Socrates' Error, the false perception language *fails* to be logic, rather than succeeds at being more than logic. Socrates' Error claims that nothing transcends logic, but only by assuming it's conclusion, leaving the Erroneous in a tar pit of bad reasoning, unable to use even the best logic to refute even the worst logic. Postmodernism insists that language is improved by mimicking logic, and that being emotionless is beneficial; prose over poetry. The Information Processing Theory of Mind postulates that language is a data transfer mechanism, and any meaning beyond that is impossible, and becomes mired in purposeful ignorance by doing so. But poetry and lover's whispers and angry hatred are not just sounds devoid of meaning. To the postmodernist, all of life is a fiction apart from genetic reproduction. Whether it is the amorality of objectivism or hyper-rationalist philosophical pessimism, the immorality of fascism, or the purposeless knowledge of Last Tuesdayism, it's false logic. Its Socratic Error is toxic to human happiness, poisonous to human health, and damaging to human morals.

The success that postmodern rationalism, hyper-rationalism, has enjoyed over the last several decades can't be denied. It has hitchhiked along with admiration for nerds and the massive advancements in technology that has brought us the Internet and smartphones. It has benefited from both negative perceptions of elitism and negative realities of elitism. It has eagerly engulfed the bigotry, tribalism, and fascist tendencies that seem at least potentially present in any human society, and grown like a blob to obscure the sky. It is very difficult, I know, to abandon the pretension that our reasoning is good logic and the reasoning of people who disagree with us is bad logic. Without this adherence to, at least striving for, logic, that leaves nothing but words to convince anyone of anything with, it seems that the powerful will always win, that 'good' is nothing but a fiction. No proofs, no absolutes, no 'this therefore that' dictates that must be accepted and therefore can't be incorrect. How is anyone to believe their opinions are anything but vague declarations with no substance, if we do not assume and insist that each statement be logically deconstructable as either true or false? Well, it can't be all that hard, because Socrates proved that words cannot be logically deconstructable as either true or false, just dismissed as false using good reasoning masquerading as a fictional informal logic. And yet, civilization has continued for millennia. It is the desire for logic to prevail that causes the problems that postmodernists attribute to lack of logic. It is the adoption of reason as something other than logic, words that can be discussed rather than numbers that can only be calculated, that will provide the salvation that the hyper-rationalists expect to find in a religious singularity when they can upload their minds into a perfect rational cyberspace, and the salvation that the apocalyptic fundamentalists identically expect to find in a religious Armageddon when their souls will ascend into a perfect sentimental heaven.

Socrates demonstrated his Method deconstructing abstract words, like 'virtue', but the same ontological decompilation can be used to dissolve any word into the 'I do not know' (more frequently "you can not know") ignorance that Socrates, internet trolls, and other gadflies consider intelligent. But proving that a term like 'door' fades into a group of family resemblances doesn't suggest that doors don't exist. With abstractions, 'strength' instead of 'door', words with far more metaphorical presence than concrete consequence, Socratic Ignorance becomes a problem, for us, as it did for him, eventually.

The Philosophy Of Reason began with me asking myself the question, "If Aristotle developed symbolic logic thousands of years ago, why isn't everyone atheist?" The leap is not mystifying or unexplainable, but summarizes all of the truths of philosophy, analytical, existential, epistemological, developed or written in those thousands of years. How can we know what is true, how can we choose what to believe, what is the nature of good? Discussions went on through those centuries, based on the premise of Socrates' Error that words should be arranged logically, however false it might be. Progress was slow to a degree beyond exquisite or excruciating, but it was progress. Only in the last few decades, that seems questionable. Perhaps it is always questionable when viewing just a few decades, and the most recent ones at that. But I think it is something more. It is not that the arc of history is merely long, though we hope it always bends towards justice. It is that the world is becoming so unreasonable that only false logic and brutal power will survive. And the danger isn't only from out there, the other people, the terrorists and the fundamentalists and the extremists. It is in our allies, and ourselves, our friends and families. It is so-called "critical thinking skills". That's the pablum version of IPTM, the soft logic of soft logic, which you should recognize by now is not logic. Only logic that is the strongest and most absolute logic is logic. Reason is not weaker, but it is differently composed, so comparisons are inappropriate. Critical thinking skills are the practice of postmodernism, they are habits of logical reductionism, not skills for using words accurately.

The process of "critical thinking skills" is straight-forward. When a statement is seen or heard, it is deconstructed as if it were supposed to be a mathematical statement or a logical claim, rather than a reasonable observation. If one disagrees with the statement, one can use any and all pretenses of logical deconstruction to dismiss the statement, true or not. Any failure in any logical chain, even one entirely imagined, becomes an excuse to ignore the entire statement, as if it cannot exist or be comprehended if a grammatical flaw would fool or stall a computer parsing it into binary digits. There is no degree of irrelevance which would make criticizing any statement that anyone could make counter-productive, because all assumptions must be true to produce true conclusions in a logical process. We all know these people, extreme if civil examples of them, at least. Pedants, people who can't stop themselves from correcting every tiny supposed imprecision in something someone says, irregardless of the point of saying it. The trivial examples are not the issue, though, the larger problem of postmodern 'critical thinking skills' involves actual weighty discussions about real issues. Supreme Court justices and standards of evidence come to mind. Mischievously or malignly deploying Socratic Ignorance, postmodern critical so-called thinking skills can and do stymie debate and development of important legal, social, and government policies, things that have real consequences for people's rights and real impact on our lives. The false logic of bad logic still presses in from around the edges, but no real efforts to confront the problems can be organized, with gaslighting, paranoia, and suspicion clouding the judgment of even the most sincere people. Political stagnation, partisan gamesmanship, and not just the retreading of old arguments but the recycling of disproven theories and defeated ideas, has become our norm.

POR is the only hope out of this mess. Critical thinking skills can be overcome, if you are willing to subject your own behavior to the criticism you apply to others'. None of what you know or believe is based on logic, it is all due to reasoning. Logically constructing grammatical statements using terms that precisely correlate to external ontological phenomenon is wasted effort. They will still be deconstructed, by anyone who disagrees with you, because you can't make words logical by wishing, or by hoping, or even by carefully trying to cover your ass and use enough weasel words that your ideas become unfalsifiable. Since words are innately illogical, describing things and relationships that aren't necessarily even physically possible from forward teleologies alone, there are no truths that cannot be dismissed as illogical constructs, lies or inaccuracies.

Language doesn't live up to Socrates' math envy. Constant reliance on weasel words like *'seems'* and *'sort of'* and *'kind of'* and *'like'* and *'as if'* are responses to the damage to our discourse that these so-called critical thinking skills impose. But the greatest token of postmodern critical practices is the notorious Lists of Logical Fallacies. These postmodern scriptures seek to formalize Socrates' Error quite seriously, and are prime examples of IPTM sophistry. Conscientiously and purposefully applying the assumption that words are logical codes, symbols in a hidden calculus that makes thought itself an axiomatic system, along with language. But in truth neither thought or language are axiomatic systems, they are 'top down', not 'bottom up', where things are controlled not by innate physical or unavoidable mathematical forces, but through inherent categories and the results they observe and describe. Language is more poetry than prose, if only in idiom, and language is not improved by a pretense of symbolic mathematics.

All of the 'logical fallacies' lists scattered across the Internet are merely trolling instructions. Identifying and dismissing an argument by supposedly finding a logical fallacy is trivial, regardless of what the argument is, because natural language is not logically constructed, so every example contains some logical fallacy if you look hard enough. Certainly, the 'no true Scotsman fallacy' is usually an error in reasoning, and calling it a 'logical fallacy' might seem harmless and instructive enough. Except for those times when the 'no true Scotsman fallacy' is not 'no true Scotsman', but 'epistemological categories that must still exist even if they are an ontologically empty set', which is not an error in reasoning, and wouldn't even be a logical fallacy if language were actually the symbolic logic that postmodernists insist it must be. Whether actually finding, claiming to find, or pretending to find a logical fallacy in somebody else's words, that still has no relevance to whether what they are saying is true. Socrates didn't succeed in making reasoning into logic, and neither did Plato, or Aristotle, or Descartes, Darwin, or Turing. If you are to gain any benefit from examining words to find logical fallacies, you must restrict your examination to your own statements, instead of other peoples'.

Evidence of the problem of the 'logical fallacy'/critical thinking skills approach can be found by examining what is available concerning "ad hominem fallacy". In terms of actual (I should say 'classical') logic, an ad hominem argument is fallacious because it refers to the source of a logical statement rather than the content of it. In the strict classical method of logic, every statement must be derived from logical primitives: who makes the argument is irrelevant, and any true point can be argued from scratch by any logician. It is nearly impossible to find this reality anywhere among the instructions for argumentation today, though. What you will find is an admonition to avoid emotional attacks and "name-calling". This does make sense, of course, but even the most rigorously dispassionate debates aren't logical proofs, and the source of information on any topic has to be considered in order to be assured that it is reliable. A similar cluelessness can be seen when trying to find out about the simple "argument from authority". This is supposedly the exact inverse of the ad hominem argument, and should resolve to the same issue: who makes an argument should be considered irrelevant, and if discussion and debate were actually ever the logic that postmodernists are taught that it is or should be, it would be. So referring to a claim as coming from a reliable authority does not make the claim reliable; any logical statement can be argued from scratch. However laboriously, the basic primitives (starting, one assumes, from Descartes' 'I am', to whatever derived truth can be taken for granted before proceeding to the topic being debated) are the same for every logician, and all the mathematical syllogisms and proofs that are subsequent. But it becomes quite difficult to even find someone who understand what an argument from authority is, let alone why it is a logical fallacy. Contemporary postmodernists appear to interpret it as "arguing against facts" when one identifies their supposedly logic-based claims as 'argument from authority' because they are simply reciting what actual experts have claimed as if that made them factual certainties. True logic could be argued by anyone from the ground up, and true reasoning involves providing one's own thoughts, not simply repeating the thoughts of others faithfully. Ultimately, we have to question whether there is any value at all to the pretense of logic, and even more so, to the validity of the idea that people err when they fail to engage in the pretense of logic. Language does not live up to Socrates' math envy, either in practice or theory.

A general guideline in POR, one that essentially unites the scientific, linguistic, and moral theories (ontological, epistemological, and theological) and exemplifies both the basis and the purpose of POR, is the 'flaw fallacy'. For hundreds if not thousands of years, every observation of human beings behaving differently than the observer expects or desires is typically described as a flaw, a failure, something wrong with human beings. This is most (supposedly) scientific in evolutionary psychology, and most evident in theistic religion, the point of both being simply to provide an unfalsifiable narrative for condemning the 'flawed' behavior. Some obvious examples are how humans don't estimate probabilities accurately, or don't change their minds easily when new facts are learned, or continue to act wrongly even after they've been caught. POR calls this the flaw fallacy, because in almost every case, what is criticized as a bug is actually a feature. Absent the assumption that human brains have evolved in order to accurately calculate probabilities, the fact that the estimations of risk we make are influenced by how much damage a potential event will cause rather than only how likely the occurance is, does not sound like a failure, but a survival mechanism. Likewise, when people do not change their opinions even when presented facts that contradict their beliefs. So we do not change our beliefs, but simply revise our explanations for our opinions so that they stay the same, despite the new data. This, again, is considered a flaw, an error in the human intellect, by postmodernists. Because the postmodernists have started out with a false assumption, that it is possible for any individual to ever know with existential certainty what facts are true, that it is possible to not have errors, or that it is inappropriate to suspect that whoever claims they are facts might be lying. Just because someone else claims a fact is relevant and should contradict your opinion does not make it so. If you are convinced that you are thinking logically, of course no amount of facts are going to change an opinion that is based on false logic. A logical process cannot check itself for errors; it would require an independent logical process to compare it to simply to detect the possibility of an error, and then another logical process to (hopefully) determine which of the two logical processes is inaccurate, at the very least, and perhaps yet another logical process to verify that the third logical process wasn't itself the one with an error. Watchers watching watchers watching watchers, and turtles all the way down. We are used to assuming, in the advanced world of technology and science we live in, that our own reasoning is always flawed in comparison to the knowledge of scientists, that we don't need to worry about these existential, epistemological uncertainties. But that itself is false reasoning, fake logic, and an inaccurate analysis. If what science says is true is actually true, then questioning it (reasonably, rather than logically) can do no harm, and so it is not simply every individual's right to rethink what is true or not, but their responsibility to do so. This unavoidable requirement to reassess things we consider to have already been proven is why faith in logic is so attractive to postmodernists, who would prefer to rest on their laurels. But in POR we acknowledge that logic cannot ever determine accuracy, only precision. The target is occluded, uncertain and unknowable, whether because the future hasn't happened yet, or because of Heisenberg's observation about position and velocity, or Halting's realization that some mathematical problems will never complete, and which ones they are is a problem that will, therefore, also never complete. The bullseye is a cow in the field, if you can comprehend the analogy and forgive the mixed metaphor.

Whenever an endemic error or flaw is observed in human behavior, we can and should, at least by default, presume that the flaw is in the observation or the observer, not the behavior. This is something of a fait accompli argument, granted, a practical application of reverse teleology: if practically every human does something a certain way, then it should be taken for granted there is a good reason why that behavior occurs throughout our species. But many scientists, particularly postmodern atheists, want to use science, more specifically the humanology they call science, as a replacement for ancient religions, but not truly an improvement over them. This, overall, explains POR itself, and the observation by Socrates of a flaw in language, demonstrated both by his Method and by his demonstration with Meno's slave. This is not a bug, the fact that words cannot be analyzed deductively, and that truth cannot be guaranteed by proper grammar. But Socrates' Error continues, as IPTM, and so-called critical thinking skills are part of the problem, not the solution, to failures of human reasoning. Demands for "proof" in casual conversations, or dismissal of ideas by identifying 'logical fallacies' in them, is counter-productive; the lack of reasoning, not an example of it. In POR, we don't ask for <u>proof</u>, ever; we ask for evidence. We don't quibble about semantics; we use language accurately, with great meaning rather than false precision.

The postmodern approach to argument only works for postmodernists, which means that it only works for maintaining ignorance and assuming conclusions. Avoiding blatant reliance on a badly categorized error in reasoning like 'the composition fallacy of ambiguity' might be considered a good practice, until you end up committing 'the division fallacy of ambiguity', because any ambiguity that isn't the first is the second, and all language contains some ambiguity. This is itself an example of the 'flaw fallacy'; postmodern linguistics, in attempting to analyze human language as an axiomatic system, considered ambiguity, as well as redundancy, to be mistakes that have simply not been sufficiently stamped out by the organic evolution of language or logic. The best language, the most efficiently codified data transfer mechanism, would include a certain amount of redundancy as useful for error checking, and a certain amount of ambiguity by necessity. This necessity of ambiguity would cover uncertainty in ontological knowledge, perhaps, or enable simplified codification by allowing one symbol to serve two purposes. The redundancy and the ambiguity would balance each other out; redundancy countering ambiguity, and ambiguity reducing redundancy. It will continue to be difficult, perhaps impossible, for linguists who are "logically" convinced that language is logical, and a code using symbols to transfer empirical data, to believe, or even understand, the idea that language is not that, but music and sentiment and poetry, rather than prose and cyphers and computational information. It requires a leap of faith, to simply imagine that there could be something in the universe that, uniquely so, is not logical, and in fact unites all the creatures in the universe who are interested in being alive more than being logical. So the ambiguity of language is not a bug, it is a feature. So is the redundancy, because riffing on a rhyme scheme or repeating tropes in a symphony, or simply using double negatives, are expressive and significant, and somehow, if mysteriously, allow the listener to perceive the humanity in the composer in a way that does not need logical pretense. If there were any logical mechanism that could produce the same results, in fact, it would simply be proof that the origin of that message is not a conscious mind, but just another logical occurrence in a universe otherwise exclusively made up of logical occurrences. Words are shibboleth, not cryptogram.

Language is always ambiguous: arguments aren't ever put in mathematical symbols unless they're not language any longer, but axiomatic instead. Whether encrypted or compiled, functions or variables, deductive logic is not reasoning, it is <u>the opposite of reasoning</u>. Language benefits from ambiguity, in a way a code cannot. It benefits from redundancy, too, in the same way. These are imprecision, are inefficiencies in logical codes. Getting rid of ambiguity and redundancy improves precision, and math is entirely about precision. Accuracy, though, requires a value judgment, some moral selection of what target to judge accuracy against. Language as a logical process would require some way of defining symbols outside of the axiomatic system that contains them. Essentially, a deity; the postmodernist assumption that language is a code requires that 'conceptions' have metaphysical relevance and divine integrity, though hardly any postmodern linguists would admit this. In fact, postmodernists as a whole simply assume that 'concepts' do have that supernatural authority, and use a circular argument, a fait accompli ad hoc hindsight, to justify the validity of that assumption based on the existence and success of scientific knowledge.

Treating words as emotions rather than logical symbols absolves sincere words and highlights dishonest ones far more effectively than denouncing them if you can spot a 'logical fallacy' that can be paraphrased into resembling what those words say. Socrates, and all the modern and postmodern philosophers, thinkers, and gadflies since then, failed to force language to conform to logic. It is why his math envy can be called an Error, despite the apparent success of the Socratic Method. Yes, thinking deductively can deconstruct language, can lead to logic, can provide axiomatic systems of symbols. But that doesn't make all proper thinking deductive. Reducing choices to algorithms is sometimes enormously productive, <u>and sometimes not</u>. Assuming that all reasoning can be reduced to computer codes because some reasoning can be reduced to computer codes is a philosophical trap; once you commit this logical fallacy of all logical fallacies, you become unable to overcome the presumption, or even recognize that it is an assumption rather than a conclusion, and untrue. Good reasoning, even actual logic, cannot refute the bad logic of this assumption that reasoning is logic. Logic is supposed to make the postmodernist immune to bad reasoning, but it simply becomes 'critical thinking skills', which make the postmodernist immune to any reasoning, good or bad, if it causes results they don't like.

Animals, and computers, do not have consciousness. They cannot ever achieve consciousness and remain animals, or computers. It is certainly possible that another species could, as we did, evolve language, and thereby develop self-awareness, consciousness, and self-determination. It may be a fascinating question just how many hundreds of thousands or millions of years of natural selection would be needed, and what the intermediate forms between organic genetic robots and thinking sentient beings would be. But there will be no mistaking that consciousness when it happens. Dolphins and apes could easily convince all humans that they are self-aware, by acting as if they were, by trying to communicate with us to the same degree that we try to communicate with them, projecting our theory of mind into their eyes and wishing they could do the same in return. (Postmodern reasoning assumes, without evidence, that they may do so but we cannot see it; an epistemological conundrum of inception along the lines of Last Tuesdayism.) If Koko the Gorilla had understood the significance of her ability to sign, she would be as emotional about that success as her human handlers were, but she was not. It was not. It is an animal, it may have gender, but it does not have the ability to choose pronouns. Because it cannot care what pronoun you use, it is not going to become offended, feel any impact on its dignity, it has no emotions, despite having the same array of flight/fight neurological states that we do. Emotions aren't the ability to feel, they are the ability to express how you feel. Artificial intelligence is similar, but different. Computers cannot program themselves, they cannot do anything but calculate numbers. We can invent very impressive and complex methods for using those numbers to appear as if they are something more impressive than that, but they remain just calculators. As long as they are only calculating correctly, according to their programing, they cannot invent teleologies, and implement self-determination. Self-determination is the ability to behave contrary, not just to programming, but contrary to reality itself, to invent fictions. A computer can put numbers into memory, through retrieval or computation, which a programmer might recognize as representing a non-factual state, a fiction. But the computer cannot know, could not tell, the difference; it is a real number, and does not 'represent' or 'symbolize' anything; it is just the numeric quantity, whether it corresponds or correlates or coincides with anything non-artificial outside the hardware of the calculating machine is irrelevant to the functioning of the calculating machine. There are no 'simulations' to a computer; all calculations are real. Designating or defining certain calculations as a 'simulation' is just an epistemological category, with very little ontological significance, which is for the convenience and understanding of humans, and can make no difference to the validity of the calculations involved. The computer world is bottom up, but the human world can be (is not always, but can be) top down.

Ending

So there you are. Looked at individually and out of context, each moment, each point, each principle of POR looks for almost all intents and purposes as if it were an idiotic, harebrained idea. Socrates' made an Error. Free will doesn't exist. Self-determination is flipping teleologies. Language cannot be logical. Abstraction paradigms, and a Fundamental Schema, and jellybean mysteries. Truth is hologrammatic. Altruism is not adaptive. Postmodernism causes depression and existential angst. The last religion, and feel free to send me money so I can give it away. Can it really all be so complicated? Can it all really be that simple?

From understanding what dreams are to imagining the perspective of a single particle of radiation at the Big Bang, the Philosophy Of Reason provides a unified theory of human consciousness and philosophical reasoning. The artifacts and resources are only beginning to be assembled, but we must not allow our entities to multiply unnecessarily. The ontological theory, that self-determination makes language and consciousness two aspects of the same phenomenon, theory of mind. The epistemological argument, that words are defined in context but have meaning beyond that, not logical labels for deductive fictions but descriptions of real experiences beyond simplistic quantification. The theological belief that the nature of being that is uniquely part of sentience compels identifying with sentience, and the way we use language is as paramount to our morality as it is to our conscious existence. Compassion, altruism, morality are not biological adaptations or genetically directed; they are not irrelevant ignorant fiction, either. They are hope, the hope that hope is possible, which persists even when all other hope is in vain. They automatically occur from the premise of 'I think therefor I am'/"I am you". A virtuous morality, whether theistic or not, is not a premise built in to consciousness, but it is an inevitable result of and basis for reasoning. Any sentience would invent *roughly* equivalent sentiments about good and bad, right or wrong, justice and compassion. To this point, no other sentience has ever been discovered, not mythical figures, space aliens, or self-aware animals. But POR doesn't concern itself with myths or science, directly. All of the artifacts and resources, the diagrams and theories, relate to human philosophy, personal honesty and social epistructures, not academic research or pedagogic literature. This is not to say that POR cannot or will not have an impact on science and empirical research as much as culture, literature, or religion. Particularly in erasing the pseudo-ontological distinctions between epistemological categories, specifically the 'non-overlapping magisteria' of science and religion "themselves", POR should have a profound effect on all aspects of human civilization. Science is simply faith in math, a kind of religion that depends on a perfectly neutral amorality. Religion is just how people explain their morality, it is not the source of it any more than God Itself is. Religion is only the source of the explanations, a framework and vocabulary for justifying, excusing, or predicting our moral intentions. Religion is not the cause of those moral intentions. Self-determination is the cause of moral intentions, as the language and consciousness that is self-determination leads to the inescapable consideration that we are responsible for our choices as well as our decisions, and the consequences they have.

Taken together all of these POR theories and ideas do take some getting used to, to understand the case. But the process is inevitable, once you make an honest effort to understand the philosophy, or those around you do and you are forced to question your postmodern assumptions. POR is thought, rethought. The process of *believing in* POR is the same as the process of learning to understand it, because it is true. It will remain true no matter whether you understand it, agree with it, believe in it, or not. Because that is what true means; what will still be that whether you understand, agree, or believe it or not. Every word spoken and action taken by any human being demonstrates the validity of the theories and faith that is the Philosophy Of Reason, as practiced in the First New Church of Hope. Every slight given and ontological argument undertaken proves the case, as well. It is unfalsified, but not unfalsifiable. Any passing resemblance of human activity to logic can be declared to be falsification, proof that humans can, should, and do think, speak, and behave logically, but the declaration itself is then the falsification of that falsification, by pointing out how inconsistent the effect/affect is, that it can be observed against a background of successfully reasonable words and behavior which are not mathematically rational.

Humans aren't designed, to use either of the backwards teleologies, to be logical. Consciousness is not a mathematical process, math is not the cause or process of our reasoning, regardless of however long philosophers and other people have been declaring that reason is logic or should be logic or can be logic or would be improved by being logic. Those kinds of linguistic contortions or mental gymnastics aren't necessary for being a good human being. Accepting POR only requires wanting to understand it, not memorizing what I've described about it. If it honors God, so be it. If you don't believe in God, and it only honors you, then you'll have to deal with that, but it doesn't change that POR is as true for you as it is for every other human being that has ever lived, or ever will. Squabbling over whether any God or any particular God exists is just another way of avoiding the real questions, about what is **right**, and how we can <u>determine</u> that. How to be confident without being arrogant. How to be courageous without being stupid. How to be righteous without being self-righteous. It involves knowing that it can't make a difference if there is a God, or what It commands; you would still be doing what you're doing, and just as happy doing it. If there is a God, that is all It could ask. If there isn't a God, if you're going to take on faith that compassion is a biological adaptation or a biological flaw, then it is up to you to take responsibility for your errors. The reality of Socrates' Error is that he didn't consider it a mistake any more than his hyper-rationalist descendants do. He thought he'd proven the point that words should work like math, by perfecting the art of dissecting them so that they don't work at all, and leave us with only ignorance about what anything is. The technique is useful for empirical science and legal presumption of innocence, but those special cases only work because they are isolated in some way from normal discourse and language. You cannot run a courtroom like a scientific laboratory, and there are few mathematical functions in jurisprudence, apart, perhaps, from an IPTM-inspired assumption that all intellectual activity should be mathematical. That assumption is a trap, from which neither logic nor much reason can escape. Socrates' mistake wasn't having math envy, it was denying he had math envy. Every person wishes that knowing truth from lies, good from bad, self-determination from pridefulness, were so simple and easy it could be automated, or simply require little effort and less attention. Math envy is understandable, almost unavoidable, particularly in our highly technological times. But it is flawed reasoning, and would be flawed logic if it were even logical enough to be wrong. Not being reducible to simplistic reasoning is what makes most decisions important, why they require judgment and morality rather than mere calculation. It isn't just the unavailability of a computer to answer all questions, it is the fact that such an unavailability is eternal, no amount of scientific progress can ever bridge the gap. Like a monkey's paw, if we had such a computer, it would be a nightmare, not a blessing.

At best, science can describe the limitations of math, Gödel's Incompleteness and Halting's Problem. But these aren't like the intellectual blindspots of the Matrix or Inception. These scientific limitations are more absolute than philosophical party games. The scientific limitations cannot be gotten around through logic or reasoning, because they stake out the border between logic and reasoning. According to logic, there can be no true reasoning, only bad logic that accidentally turned out to be accurate as well as precise enough to be useful. According to reasoning, true logic is mathematics, symbolic processing that only proves true in being more consistent than empirical demonstrations; anything else is not logic at all, which includes consciousness, thought, ideas, reasoning, intellect, emotions, language, and words. These don't need to be logical, they excel at being independent of deductive deterministic mathematical cause and effect. They are not merely 'top down' organization on the universe, they are the invention of the possibility of top down organization in the universe.

For all the absolute nature of the scientific limits of uncertainty, however, the intellectual blindspots, which we work around by comparing our experience with other peoples', or simply ignoring, such as dismissing Last Tuesdayism, are somehow even more profound. The existential wall does not disappear just because we learn it is a metaphor. However much modern civilization has advanced science and allowed us to forget that nothing our senses tell us can be taken as fact, it remains not just true, but compelling and important. Not so that you deny your senses, or can refuse to believe any fact that is inconvenient to your philosophy or disturbing to your emotions. But so that you realize that the inability to know for certain whether you are asleep and dreaming, or awake and insane, or simply ignorant or confused, is as easily ignored as it is ever-present. This uncertainty is the most uncertain you need to be about anything, though not necessarily the most uncertain you should be about anything. The postmodern delusion, the thing that is truly doing damage to our psyche, our mental wellbeing, our society, our politics, and our world, is the prevarication of ignorance, the insistence that you are not allowed to know what is true, unless you can convince someone else of it. Presumption of innocence is vitally important in a courtroom. But it is more than inappropriate, it is downright counter-productive, outside of it. If we must presume everyone is innocent until they are convicted, how then can we suspect them enough to gather evidence or charge an indictment? Yes, Karl Popper demonstrated that all scientific truths are provisional, they will someday be replaced with 'more true' truths. But that doesn't mean that CO_2 is not a greenhouse gas, and burning fossil fuels causes climate change. Evolution, as understood by modern scientists (sans narcissistic selection), may be insufficient for explaining human behavior, but that doesn't mean creationism is supportable.

Of course, in POR, we realize that creationism is not wrong, even if it is mistaken. Creationists reject 'survival of the fittest' because they realize that teaching children they are nothing but animals who should be concerned about nothing other than their own genetic reproduction is a bad thing to do. The anti-creationists, in turn, will insist that they don't believe that people should be concerned about nothing other than their own genetic reproduction, they should care about their species, without realizing that they are contradicting their own position by saying so. An animal that worked to aid or profit its species would lose in the competition for resources against animals with more ruthless behavior. And back and forth it goes. Selfish genes and selfless behavior, mythological Gods and just-so story narratives. Binary thinking and false dichotomies. All of the problems of the world derive, ultimately, from Socrates' Error. Without it, we can still benefit from the Socratic Method, but will not be arrogant in doing so. We can accept that whether someone has committed a crime is distinct from whether they are convicted of the crime, but not always. We can embrace the fact that being intolerant of intolerance is tolerance, not intolerance. We can marvel at the wisdom of the ancients, seeing their mythologies as the science of their day, without assuming that all of their prejudices should be adopted as moral doctrine. We can recognize that most of the things that our modern society declares to be flaws represent faults in society, not failures of individuals, or humanity. Most, but not all, and which is which must be guessed at on an individual basis. Sometimes the crowd has a better guess, sometimes the individual does. Sometimes the authorities are right, and sometimes civil disobedience is called for. No calculation, no deductive logic, can determine the former situation from the latter; it is a reasonable judgment that every person must make for themselves, act in accordance with their decision, and accept responsibility for the consequences.

The point of all of this, life, consciousness, intelligence, debate, is to do something more than just replicate genes, even though that mechanism is the ultimate original cause of any of it. But origins are meaning, not purpose. We have a greater purpose, our ability to think and choose and decide do have a purpose beyond themselves, beyond success and power. Our desire for control is understandable, in fact inevitable. But that doesn't mean it is necessary, either the control, or the desire.

The majority of the time, when trying to describe either some aspect of life or society, or POR (which is always the same thing, as POR relates to every aspect of life and society, and so every fact of life relates to POR, somehow) the questions come down to the nature of truth. Philosophy has stalled, for thousands of years, in dealing with truth, because of Socrates' Error. Truth must be an absolute thing, or cannot be an absolute thing, depending on the philosophical premises or format you wish to pursue. Modern, postmodern, philosophy is trapped in the tar pit of philosophical pessimism, of nihilism, and becomes existentialism and absurdism. There is no truth, it is an empty token, according to the postmodernist. Truth is a function of verification; whatever the correct result of an axiomatic system is, is 'truth', according to this scholastic formulation of analytic philosophy. Or else truth is empirical result, but only in isolation, the truth of any one empirical result not being dependent on any other, like one coin flip having no influence on the next. In POR, we engage such consternation, but we do not accept it as either true or useful simply because it conforms to what was taught in a college philosophy course. If the truth cannot be directly confirmed by any honest and capable person, then it isn't the truth. In POR, the ontological truth (physical, empirical, mathematical) and the epistemological truth (categorical, linguistic, literary) and the theological truth (moral, ethical, emotional) are not automatically identical, the way the postmodernist conception of truth is. This is, in keeping with the flaw fallacy, not a weakness, but a strength. Because it enables us to comprehend and grasp what the truth is, even while accepting and understanding that we can never truly know what the truth is. When the ontological and epistemological and theological truths all coincide, being coincident not because of any teleological or tautological necessity, but simply because of coincidence, then we know for certain that it is the real truth. Three truths, but singular; unitary, unique, and universal.

There is far more that needs to explored, and most of the things that I've tried to explain here need better explanations. But we must get started on this journey into the future, guided by a Philosophy Of Reason that transcends mere logic, and embraces true reasoning. We must set forth on this path without any certainty of success in arriving at any destination. The journey is its own reward.

There is no God, except for God.

There is no free will, only self-determination.

Words have meaning.

Thanks for your time. Hope it helps.

***

INDEX

A

a/effect, 45
abduction, 93
abstraction paradigm, 122, 138, 146, 152
accuracy, 7, 102, 139, 191, 291
Achilles Heel, 264
acronym, 275
adaptation, 205
adaption, 217, 240
adaptive altruism, 220
addiction, 18
addicts, 45
aenthrocentric, 69
affect, 236
afterlife, 6
ain't, 127
algorithm, 7, 61
algorithmic processing, 92, 141
alive, 238
alphabet, 80
alternative medicine, 172
alternatives, 102
altruism, 261, 266
ambiguity, 222, 326
analogic, 227
analytical, 122
angst, 57
ant, 221
anthropomorphization, 44, 209, 221
anti-religious, 87, 168, 265
antitheistic, 93
apes, 81
applications, 171
apposite, 186
architecture, 157
argument, 279
Aristotle, 43, 85, 90, 174, 234
art, 47

artificial intelligence, 130, 202
assumption, 20, 70, 147
asymmetrical signaling, 235
atheist, 87, 168, 274
atheist fundamentalists, 273
author, 199
authority, 172
autocratic, 64
autonomic, 217, 229, 270
autonomy, 33
axiomatic, 181
axiomatic system, 62, 114

B

backwards teleology, 42, 48, 56, 146, 221, 231
bacteria, 174, 223
Bayesian statistics, 93
beaver, 44
bee, 108
being, 119
belief, 120, 325
believe (POR Statement of Faith), 86
Bell's Inequality, 55
Berra, Yogi, 160
bidirectional signaling, 82
biomic, 237
blindspot, 8, 87, 119, 315, 333
bootstrap effect, 254
Born Again Christians, 57
borrowing, 172, 174, 178, 281
bottom up, 51, 150, 312
Breathe the Dawn, 319
bug, 68, 308, 325, 326, 327

C

castigation, 294
cat, 107, 157

categories, 174
causality, 33, 35, 36, 40, 41, 42, 44, 49, 51, 54, 78, 109, 196
causation, 38
cause, 45, 56, 61, 110
cause and effect, 35, 43, 49, 52, 95
causes, 38, 41, 58
centiseconds, 28
cervidae, 248
children, 37, 76
Chinese Whispers, 170
choice, 29
choose, 18
chronology, 42, 53, 76, 142
circular reasoning, 195
civilization, 306
code, 35, 163
Cogito Ergo Sum, 6, 50, 54, 115, 135, 195
    as 'the cogito', 258
Cogito ergo sum loqui, 251, 259
cognitive dissonance, 176
communication, 79, 82, 84
community, 83, 166
comprehensible, 210
computative, 193
computer, 61, 203, 307
concept, 7, 34, 69, 89, 97, 200, 282, 327
congruity, 73
conscious, 26
consciousness, 30, 44, 49, 52, 53, 66, 84, 247
conservativism, 306
context, 156, 164, 170
context point, 180
contingent, 83
control, 10, 17, 22, 24
    as dichotomous abstraction, 277
    experimental, 109
controvert, 135
convergent evolution, 244
correlate, 50
correlation is not causation, 42
critical thinking skills, 32, 64, 269, 322, 328
crystals, 231

cunning, 45, 94, 264, 304
cyberchannel, 307
cybertraffic, 63

D

Darwin, 89, 155, 173, 208, 212, 221
data, 102
Dawkins, 220, 226, 317
decision, 23, 29
decision-making, 109
defining, 96
definition, 136, 162
definition in context, 96, 154, 171
definitions, 35, 57, 89
denotations, 133
Descartes, 9, 53, 135, 154
determination, 136
determine, 48
deterministic, 39
diagrams, 122
dialectic, 3
dichotomous abstraction, 133, 136
dichotomy, 3
dictionary, 7, 33, 123, 138, 199
dignity, 48
digraph, 80
dimorphic, 235
diphthong, 80
dispreferred, 284
DNA, 207, 231
doctor, 233
doctor organism, 227
Dodgson (Lewis Carroll), 156
dolphins, 328
doornails, 65, 84
dreaming, 66
duality, 155
dysfunctional, 205

E

e/affect, 53
echo, 316
economics, 110
education, 294

effect, 236
effect/affect, 44, 172, 186, 332
Einstein, 43
elephant, 282
emergent properties, 51
emote, 195
emotional, 297
empirical, 21
English, 205
engrams, 120, 271
entanglement, 53
environment, 238
Epicurus, 17
epistemic, 271
epistemological, 11, 82, 179
epistemological theory, 78
epistemology, 32, 78, 105, 106, 119, 153, 155, 178, 244, 271
epistructures, 331
epithets, 159
equal, 263
equine, 174
estimating, 194
ethics, 182, 183, 261
etymology, 5, 82
   etymologically, 170
euphemism, 280
evil, 7
evolution, 207, 217
evolutionary psychology, 70, 187, 219
executive functions, 30, 59
existence, 258
existential wall, 10, 21, 115, 195
expectation, 4, 45
experiment, 23, 109, 183
   IAT experiment, 23
   keyboard experiment, 24
   thumbswitch experiment, 25
explanation, 210
expression, 124, 297

F

facetious, 5, 34, 179
fair, 20, 263
fait accompli, 56, 78, 234, 245, 249, 252, 326, 327
fake news, 145
family, 162
fatalism, 48
fatalistic, 46
First New Church of Hope, 319
first rule of language, 36, 95
fish, 49, 211
fitness, 241, 243
fittest, 240, 334
Flat Earth, 11
flaw fallacy, 324
flip, 45
flopping, 139
flow, 56
flum-flummery, 158, 175, 185, 203
foam, 38, 39, 104, 116
formulae, 178
forward teleologies, 221, 238
free will, 17, 27, 31, 44, 45, 48, 53, 57
Fundamental Schema, 153
fundamentalism, 273

G

gedanken, 199, 223, 227, 233, 262, 267
gender dimorphism, 232, 248
gene, 217
gene transfer, 234, 237
gene-centric, 221, 231
genotype', 173
God, 6, 14, 43, 44, 49, 57, 59, 86, 89, 105, 120, 170, 180, 182, 200, 208, 226, 236, 241, 254, 265, 316, 318
Gödel, 297
Godwin's Law, 64, 178
Golden Rule, 260
good, 87, 262, 266
government, 161
grammar, 8
grammaticians, 132
grasp, 166
gravity, 247
group selection, 227
guess, 205
guessing, 194

H

Halting, 297
happiness, 3, 9, 241, 254, 270
happy, 5
healer gene, 227
Heisenberg's Uncertainty Principle, 55
heterodox, 203
higher power, 57
hindsight, 42, 201
holistically, 161
hologram, 98
hologrammatic, 331
holographs, 98
homeopathic, 262
honest, 140, 286
honesty, 296
hope, 4, 5, 104, 115, 182, 204, 322, 331
hot dog, 179
humanity, 147
humanology, 44, 185, 187
humans, 44, 211
Humpty Dumpty, 11, 156, 158, 162, 166, 169, 171, 278, 304
    unacknowledged, 121
hyper-rationalist, 272
hypotheses of cognition, 53, 71

I

I am you, 258
iconically, 91
idealize, 147
ideogrammatical, 80
illogical, 290
imagine, 252
implicit bias, 3, 22
important, 146
impossible, 103
Inception, 9, 253
indoctrination, 294
induction, 88
ineffability, 180
ineffable, 200, 274
informal logic, 177, 186

Information Processing Theory of Mind, 13, 60, 155, 202
inner peace, 266
instinct, 229
intelligence, 298
intent, 267
intention, 42, 53, 96, 145, 171
intentions, 44
inverse teleology, 44, 53, 162, 208
IPTM, 58, 62, 63, 65, 69, 79, 148, 150, 195, 322
irrational, 4, 5, 176
irregardless, 4, 127, 322
It (as God), 86, 87, 208, 265
itadakimasu, 319

J

jackhammer, 81
jargon, 172
jellybean diagram, 193
jellybean mystery, 192
jellybeans, 13, 191
jewelry, 189
judgment, 92, 94, 120, 176, 184, 291
just society, 267
justice, 7, 176, 181, 277

K

karma, 6, 261
keyboard, 57
kin selection, 223
kinesis, 97
kinesthetic, 24
know, 105, 201
knowledge, 119, 271

L

language, 31, 34, 35, 80, 107, 205, 278
Last Tuesdayism, 10, 253
law, 172, 177
    abstraction paradigm, 143
legalese, 172

lepton, 108
Liar's Paradox, 134
life, 149, 173, 241
linguistical, 255
literally, 292
logic, 70, 88, 102, 176, 251, 289
logical, 5, 92
logical fallacies, 323
logicalish, 156
lying, 141

M

maladaptive, 222
mankind, 163
marsupials, 209
materialist, 168
math, 10, 101
math envy, 92, 93, 94, 127, 195
mathematics, 181, 186
Matrix, the, 8, 195, 253, 333
matter, 132, 165
mean, 101
meaning, 35, 52, 57, 60, 81, 95, 105, 119, 136, 171, 179, 196, 203, 271, 289
measurement, 101
meatware, 61, 68, 69
medicalize, 188
medicine, 172, 183
mega-quantum, 39
members, 320
meme, 285
memes, 230
memetics, 289
memory, 66
me-ness, 3
Meno, 91, 147
metaphor, 34
metaphysical, 259
metaphysics, 6, 168
metonymy, 132
might, 177
mistake, 293
modern, 89
modules, 219
monkey's paw, 333

moot, 56, 63, 131, 166, 221
moral judgments, 291
morality, 9, 107, 169, 247, 261, 295
mumpsimus, 15, 67, 141, 148, 207, 228
mundaneity, 245
mutations, 208
myths, 168

N

N (as a category of replicator), 241
naked replicators, 221, 230
name-calling, 64
narcissistic selection, 232, 238, 246, 249
narrators, 30
natural selection, 207, 234
natural virtue, 224
necessary and sufficient, 42
nee, 81, 140, 154
nerds, 300, 320
New Church of Hope, 169, 266, 276, 316
Newman, Randy, 213
no true Scotsman, 323
numbers, 113

O

objective, 40, 44, 285
objectivism, 188
Occam's Razor, 70, 86
onomatopoetic, 124, 148
ontological, 53, 83, 155, 179
ontological argument, 112, 303
ontological argument, the, 280
ontology, 32, 119, 153, 244
operant conditioning, 18, 52, 82
opinion, 36, 61, 297
organism, 245
otter, 81
Overton Window, 302
oxygen mask, 222, 266

P

palimpsest, 47
parodic, 213
parrot, 130
parsing, 8, 99, 148, 322
participant, 320
particle, 204
particular, 204
Pascal, 6
pathology, 184
pavlovian, 45
peacock, 249
pedant, 175
philosophical pessimism, 45, 48, 53, 63, 252
philosophicians, 287
philosophy, 300
placebo, 189
planet, 75
plant food, 109
Plato, 62, 90
Platonism, 158
poetry, 36, 127, 129, 160, 163, 320
POS. *See* postmodern over-synonimization
postmodern, 19, 62, 89, 170, 212, 248, 272
postmodern over-synonimization, 105, 127, 186, 195, 274, 285, 294
postmodernism, 13, 57, 60, 64, 154, 155, 157
postmodernist, 8, 58
post-modernist, 157
postmodernistic, 272
postmodernists, 174
prairie dog, 83
precision, 7, 102, 139, 141, 191, 291
prepositions, 292
preposterous, 11
prionic, 247
prions, 231
probabilistic, 40, 177
probabilities, 188
problem of evil, 9
prokaryotes, 231
proof, 192
prose, 127
proto-gene, 244
providence, 248
proving, 120
provisional, 112, 198, 219, 334
proxy, 248
psychobabble, 145
psychologists, 41
purpose, 52, 53, 96, 120, 168, 169
p-zombies, 52, 63

Q

QED, 4
quantum, 39, 55, 77, 97

R

race, 173
racism, 22, 213
raling, 148
Rand, Ayn, 166
rational, 39, 274
rationality, 261
Rawls, 267
reason, 47, 87, 107, 176
reasonable, 115
reasonably, 7
reasoning, 31, 94
reciprocity, 260
recreational, 66
redundancy, 327
religions, 168, 265, 317
Renaissance, 148
replicator, 207
replicators, 251
resonates, 129
responsibility, 19, 59, 72, 73, 167, 169, 314
retcognstruction, 12
rethought, 150
reverse teleology, 43, 49, 55, 208
rhetoric, 106, 131, 269
rights, 303
robots, 45

S

Santa Claus, 168
Schrödinger, 107
science, 39, 43, 172, 174
Science, 78
scientist, 226
secular religion, 188
selection, 10, 11, 28, 47, 52, 89, 102, 105, 136, 176, 205, 210, 248, 285, 295
self-aware, 307
self-awareness, 48, 59
self-determination, 17, 30, 42, 44, 45, 48, 57, 151, 318
Selfish Gene, The, 220
selfish genes, 222, 260
selfless, 222
self-sacrifice, 261
semantic, 18, 19, 82
semantics, 270, 286, 289
semiotic, 34
sentences, 147
sentience, 260
sequentiality, 37
sets, 174
sexual selection, 213
Shakespeare, 205
shibboleth, 116, 255, 290, 327
Short People, 213
should, 19, 120, 151, 177, 196
signaling, 60, 79, 82, 232, 234, 236
similar, 240
simulacrum, 307
simulation, 65
simultaneity, 129, 181, 187
sincere, 286
skeptic, 160
sleep eating, 56
social media, 63
Socrates, 62, 90, 111, 116, 131, 153, 262, 264, 321
   as philosopher, 62
   as syllogism, 33, 36, 88, 102, 103, 175

Socrates' Error, 13, 57, 61, 62, 70, 79, 88, 91, 92, 94, 111, 141, 145, 147, 159, 171, 180, 195, 234, 290, 323
Socratic Ignorance, 62, 64, 147, 302
Socratic Method, 62, 85, 90, 301
   as Dialogue, 159
soft sciences, 186
somatic, 231
sophistry, 19, 145, 323
soul, 3, 19
sovereign sanguinity, 302
special applications, 171
species, 172, 173, 204
specific, 204
split horizon, 59
Spock, 84
spooky, 27, 39, 40
subconscious, 71, 278
subduct, 103
subjective, 107, 284
sub-quanta, 39
suicide, 5, 9, 265, 309, 319
sumpsimus, 15, 69
superiority, 212
syllogism, 88, 103, 174, 176, 290
symbol, 164, 172, 201
symbology, 80, 96
symbols, 8, 10, 34, 80, 88, 180
synonym, 5
syntactic mechanics, 33

T

tar pit, 8, 65, 71, 272, 319, 320, 335
tautological, 40
tautology, 33, 34, 105
teaching, 145
teleological flipping, 53, 72, 142, 278
   in abstraction paradigm, 142
teleologies, 45, 247
teleology, 33, 35
Teleology, 241
text, 180
theism, 120, 168
themself, 24
theological, 107, 169, 207, 218
theology, 57, 120, 167

theory of mind, 14, 27, 52, 53, 71, 81, 84, 139, 163, 196, 253, 254, 258, 260, 306
thinking, 269
Three Truths, 318
thumbswitch experiment, 25, 46, 59
time, 36, 76, 78
tithe, 319
toaster, 63, 84
tomato, 178
top down, 51, 54, 56, 114, 150, 333
transcriptive, 66, 80, 297
transmitter, 235
tree of life, 211
trolls, 111, 145, 148, 321
truer, 203
truth, 5, 8, 57, 98, 115, 262
Turing, 62
Turing Machine, 61, 65, 92, 310
turtles, 37, 325
Two, The (Hope and God), 266
tyranny, 181

U

uncanny, 40
uncontrollable, 86, 109, 111, 150
understand, 297
understanding, 14
unfalsifiable, 65, 71, 86, 89
unidirectional, 82
unique, 128
unitary, 126
universal, 128
universal fool, the, 267
Universal Statement, 258, 260, 261, 262, 263, 267, 306

unpredictable, 254
utilitarian, 264

V

veil of ignorance, 267
virtue, 262, 264, 296
viruses, 231, 246
vocabulary, 270
volition, 46, 58, 60

W

want, 5, 18, 146, 221
want to want, 18, 46, 52, 91
wants, 44
warrior genes, 227
warticle, 107
wave, 107
waves, 55, 156
weasel words, 323
why, 35, 37, 39, 43, 47, 51, 53, 56, 95, 115, 120, 173, 209
wisdom, 160, 298
word, 164
words, 196
words have meaning, 64, 85, 96, 121, 130, 134, 148, 170, 318
wrong, 4, 294

X

xenophobia, 230

Z

zoological, 188